OKLAHOMA CITY

ALSO BY ANDREW GUMBEL

Steal This Vote: Dirty Elections and the Rotten
History of Democracy in America

London

Berlin

OKLAHOMA CITY

What the Investigation Missed—and
Why It Still Matters

{ ANDREW GUMBEL
AND ROGER G. CHARLES }

WM
WILLIAM MORROW
An Imprint of HarperCollins*Publishers*

FIRST EDITION

Library of Congress Cataloging-in-Publication Data

Gumbel, Andrew.
  Oklahoma City / Andrew Gumbel and Roger G. Charles .— 1st ed.
    p. cm.
  ISBN 978-0-06-198644-4
1. Oklahoma City Federal Building Bombing, Oklahoma City, Okla., 1995.
2. Bombings—Oklahoma—Oklahoma City. 3. Bombing Investigation—Oklahoma—Oklahoma City. I. Charles, Roger G. II. Title.
  HV6432.6.G86 2012
  363.32509766'38—dc23

                                                                2011044673

12 13 14 15 16 OV/RRD 10 9 8 7 6 5 4 3 2 1

*To those whose lives were shattered or lost on April 19, 1995,
and to the admirable men and women who wanted it
told as it was*

CONTENTS

PROLOGUE

There are, as a result of the investigation and the presentation of the evidence in this case, a number of questions unanswered. . . . It would be disappointing to me if the law enforcement agencies of the United States government have quit looking for answers in this Oklahoma bombing tragedy.
—RICHARD P. MATSCH, PRESIDING JUDGE IN THE
McVEIGH AND NICHOLS TRIALS

I'm thoroughly convinced we're going to have another domestic terrorist act in this country that is going to be beyond our imagination, beyond Oklahoma City.
—KERRY NOBLE, REFORMED MILITANT FROM
THE RADICAL FAR RIGHT

Why read about the Oklahoma City bombing, after so long? Many Americans think of the events of April 19, 1995, as a jarring interruption to an otherwise peaceful decade, a disturbing story whose shockwaves, mercifully, did not resonate for long. They remember it as the work of two disaffected army veterans from the heartland, who pulled together their deadly payload from ordinary farm fertilizer and delivered it in a Ryder truck to a city unprepared for such destruction.

But that is only part of what happened. While the guilt of the two principal defendants, Timothy McVeigh and Terry Nichols, was established beyond doubt at trial, many other things were side-stepped: the dysfunction within the country's law enforcement agencies, which missed opportunities to penetrate the radical right and prevent the bombing; the question of who inspired the bombing and who else might have been involved; and evidence contradicting the government's repeated insistence that investigators had everything under control and that, ultimately, the system worked.

This litany may sound familiar from the controversies following the September 11 attacks, and it should. Many of the same institutional problems and misplaced political priorities that blinded the country to the threat from al-Qaeda in 2001 were responsible, six years earlier, for a refusal to take the threat of paramilitary violence from the radical right with the requisite seriousness. Attorney General John Ashcroft was more interested in public decency and outlawing medical marijuana than in reports of suspicious foreigners enrolling in flight schools; likewise, his predecessor, Janet Reno, pushed her Justice Department to crack down on deadbeat dads while playing down reports of radicals advocating bombings, assassinations, and shootings.

One problem, as in 2001, was a failure by law enforcement agencies to see past their own rivalries. Another was an assumption that the threats were just empty rhetoric from the mouths of social outcasts incapable of holding down a regular job, much less doing real damage.

The lessons of Oklahoma City have never been properly articulated. Yet they are important, because the conditions that led to the deaths of 168 people at the Murrah Building in downtown Oklahoma City, and the shattering of thousands of other lives through grief or injury, could easily be replicated. McVeigh was a traumatized veteran of the first Gulf War, who felt validated by his experience of warfare but returned home to disillusion, recession, and a bleak future of dead-end jobs. He found solace in his fascination with firearms and survivalism, bounced around the country on the gun-show circuit, and shared the company of angry young men like himself. Sometimes they blamed blacks and Jews; other times they directed their anger at the federal authorities. When a government siege at the Branch Davidian religious compound in Waco, Texas, went horribly awry in early 1993, McVeigh and his cohorts decided it was time to stop complaining and take action, because a government capable of deploying tanks against civilians and watching children burn to death could not be counted on to leave anyone in peace.

No two moments in history are exactly alike, of course, but it is not difficult to see how new McVeighs could emerge from the wars in Iraq and Afghanistan, the lingering devastation of the 2008 economic meltdown, and the anti-establishment rage embodied by everyone from the Tea Party and Occupy Wall Street to the violent racists threatening to put a bullet in the brain of America's first black president. The government is no better at tracking political extremism or mental instability in the armed forces than it was in the early 1990s. Too many dangerous people have a measure of military training, as a much-discussed Department of Homeland Security report found in 2009; too many have access to a fearsome array of firearms and explosives.

The choices made by McVeigh and his fellow conspirators were abhorrent, but their story is still quintessentially American, a story of hopes raised and dashed against a backdrop of violence, political agitation, and individual restlessness. "The personality susceptible to the dream of limitless freedom," Jonathan Franzen wrote in his novel *Freedom,* "is a personality also prone, should the dream ever sour, to misanthropy and rage." McVeigh and his friends were just such personalities, with an added layer of idealistic fervor to spur them beyond their resentments to deadly action. They saw themselves in the same mold as the eighteenth-century revolutionaries who fought off British rule. They called themselves patriots, seeing little or no contradiction between the violence they advocated and the many wars waged by their government in the name of honor, freedom, and country.

"America has always had a war culture," the social historian Billy Gibson wrote in *Warrior Dreams,* a remarkable study of America's paramilitary frenzy in the wake of Vietnam. "This culture has two fundamental stories, one celebrating the individual gunman who acts on his own (or in loose concert with other men); the other portraying the good soldier who belongs to an official military or police unit and serves as a representative defender of national honor." Intriguingly, McVeigh fit both categories—first as the exemplary infantryman who won medals in the Gulf, then as the underground warrior convincing himself that a bold statement in Oklahoma City could trigger a general uprising. In both incarnations, he was indeed the good soldier, confident of his mission and clear about his cause.

Many people were shocked when McVeigh dismissed the children who died in the Murrah Building's day-care center as "collateral damage," the necessary price of warfare. But these words were military terminology he had learned in the army. McVeigh was extraordinarily callous in his choice of target, and he made a crucial strategic error in killing so many innocent people, because his act provoked only revulsion and snuffed out the revolution he hoped it would start. Still, he defended the military integrity of his actions to the end.

In many ways, this is a story of failure. The radical far right wanted to wage a war of "leaderless resistance," in which hardened fighters would form paramilitary cells and make command decisions that would be shared on a need-to-know basis. But these were not people temperamentally disposed to waging a subtle war of attrition, and they lapsed easily into indiscipline and poor judgment. Everything about the Oklahoma plot screamed overkill, where a more carefully targeted attack might have been more effective. Several people in the far-right believed McVeigh would hit the federal courthouse next to the Murrah Building as part of a nationwide assault on the judiciary. Others thought he would detonate the bomb at night. But McVeigh had his own ideas.

The government's law enforcement agencies also failed—by taking their eye off the radical right at a time when advocacy groups were sounding the alarm, and by shying away when presented with evidence of actual criminal behavior. The FBI and the ATF spent a lot of energy after the bombing blaming each other for the warning signs they missed, and for information they failed to share about known radicals congregating to plot a revolutionary war. But both agencies were at fault.

The overwhelming pressure to hunt down the bombers gave rise to a sledgehammer approach to questioning and apprehending McVeigh's closest associates, offering them and others a chance to destroy evidence and rehearse stories. The government stopped investigating certain suspects—Michael and Lori Fortier, Steve Colbern, and Roger Moore—because it was more interested in securing their testimony against McVeigh and Nichols than in exploring their deeper involvement. That, too, constituted a profound failure.

Once the shape of the case was set, the search for other suspects, or a larger conspiracy, came to be viewed as a risky fishing expedition. Evidence that might have established links between McVeigh and other criminal cells was ignored. In some cases, it was destroyed.

CHALLENGING THE OFFICIAL ACCOUNT OF A MAJOR HISTORICAL event can seem presumptuous, even foolhardy. Journalists and authors, after all, do not have subpoena power, forensics laboratories, or polygraph kits. We cannot interview 18,000 witnesses or run down 43,000 leads, as the Oklahoma City investigators did.

What we do have, in this case, is the opportunity to review the government's work from start to finish. This book is based on records that have been unearthed for the first time, including the complete archive of documents shared with the defense teams in the two federal trials and in Terry Nichols's state trial in Oklahoma. We also have a voluminous body of writings from Nichols, who did not utter a word for ten years after his arrest but agreed to discuss the case with us in great detail.

Much of the freshness of our perspective comes from the people at the heart of the effort to bring the bombing perpetrators to justice: law enforcement managers and street agents, federal prosecutors, even—as the quote at the beginning of this preface demonstrates—the trial judge. Many continue to harbor strong feelings about what they experienced, the pressures they faced, the screw-ups, manipulations, and lost opportunities, and the shocking number of talented senior investigators—the ones best placed to penetrate the bombing's enduring mysteries—who were prevented from contributing to a case that should have been the crowning pinnacle of their careers.

Institutionally, the narrative was kept simple and straightforward. A sign on the prosecutors' office door read: DON'T BURY THE STORY IN THE EVIDENCE. But many of those quoted in these pages remain skeptical that all the perpetrators were caught, that the FBI and the other investigative agencies tracked down every lead, that the case really was, as Oklahoma's then-governor Frank Keating put it, "the FBI's finest hour."

Oklahoma City was by far the largest criminal investigation in the United States before 9/11. In hindsight, it looks less like a detective story than an anti–detective story, in which government investigators chose *not* to follow the evidence wherever it led. Instead, they closed down critical lines of inquiry, for fear of what they might find and what it might reveal about their own failings.

The official narrative of two sad misfits acting alone underwent some corrections at trial. Nichols was cleared of first-degree murder and spared the death penalty, following a series of prosecutorial setbacks and "gotcha" moments on the witness stand. Still, the trials were principally about the government's evidence, as trials almost always are; attempts by the defense teams to extend the case to possible coconspirators, or to the involvement of other countries, fell largely flat.

Michael Tigar, who was brilliantly effective as Nichols's lead defense attorney, has written how the full story never quite seems to be told at trial but is reduced to "shadows on the courthouse wall"— shards of witness narrative here and forensic evidence there, all of which needs to be ascribed meaning and fashioned into shape for the jury. Some of that epistemological uncertainty applies to this book, too. The FBI did not record its interviews, so its witness reports are fraught with problems of interpretation. Did the agents ask the right questions? Did they write down the answers accurately? Were they, too, interested in telling their bosses what they wanted to hear? Were there deliberate attempts, motivated by internal politics, to keep things out of the written record? Some of the FBI's missteps were exposed at trial, particularly under cross-examination of witnesses who did not like the way their statements were misinterpreted. But the witness testimony itself was problematic. Federal law does not preclude FBI agents and prosecuting attorneys from taking witnesses through their statements before trial—an exercise which, if done honestly, can conceivably enhance precision but, in practice, can look a lot like coaching or coercion.

Without the full story, it can be tempting to look at those shadows on the wall and construct phantoms—shapes and patterns that are seductive for one reason or another but do not have the solidity of documentable truth. Government agencies responding to criticism of the Oklahoma City case have frequently sought to tar their detractors as conspiracy theorists, dishonest information-brokers pulling together random pieces of information to serve a self-interested agenda. Some of that tarring has been richly deserved. Just as there was nothing simple about the people who perpetrated the bombing, there was nothing inherently crude or sinister or conniving about the investigators and prosecutors who brought them to justice. If they were incompetent or dishonest, it was not by default.

That said, the "conspiracy theory" label has also been misused and manipulated by government officials who have preferred not to engage with their critics or address their mistakes. Daring to criticize the ATF for inconsistencies in its agents' accounts of April 19 is *not* the same as accusing the agency of collusion in the bombing. To draw that inference, as the ATF has sometimes done, is lazy, dishonest, and a deliberate attempt to confuse the real issues.

This book makes no apologies for humanizing its characters, whether they are lawyers, prosecutors, law enforcement officers, rescue workers, bereaved victims, white supremacist agitators, or hardened criminals. They are all human beings, which makes them complex, flawed, idiosyncratic, inconsistent, and prone to disagreements with their friends and associates. Humanizing them is not the same as indulging or excusing them; nobody reading this book will come away feeling that its subjects have been given a free pass for their transgressions. But it is important not to caricature or demonize even the worst of them, because understanding can come only with an appreciation of the messiness, complexity, and ambiguity of their motives and interactions.

The Oklahoma City bombing *was* a conspiracy, and McVeigh and Nichols were charged accordingly. The real question is: how far did the conspiracy go? In preparing for trial, the FBI and prosecution wanted to keep things simple, so the jury would see a clear path to conviction. In the process, they mangled evidence, withheld documents, distorted testimony, gave deals to potential suspects, and lost sight of crucial chunks of the real story. The government was fortunate that its desire to pin the crime on McVeigh coincided with McVeigh's own desire to take full credit and become a martyr-hero to his cause. Both sides, in the end, colluded to cover up the truth.

An author has an important advantage over law enforcement or even the most adept trial lawyer: he can weigh the available information without worrying where it might lead, or who it might compromise, or whether it will meet some high burden of proof. The following pages are an attempt to reconstitute events as they happened, to understand what went right and wrong, to separate what we know from what we don't know, and to identify the appropriate lessons. Those who are still living can speak for themselves and are entitled to be heard. The dead deserve as much truth as we can offer.

One

The Road to Oklahoma

Sometime in mid-April 1995, Cliff Mogg and Dan Humphries, two bomb disposal experts from Kirtland Air Force Base in New Mexico, were ordered at short notice to drive more than five hundred miles across the Great Plains to Oklahoma City. The men do not appear to have been told much about their mission. When they arrived, they were put up in a nondescript chain hotel on the north side of town and ordered to stay put until told otherwise.

One day passed, then two, then three. Still they were told to keep to themselves.

Military explosives and ordinance disposal teams are often deployed to help protect high-level dignitaries, but Oklahoma City was expecting no such official visits in the latter half of April 1995. Mogg's written orders from the 377th Air Base Wing designated him an explosive technical escort, and his brief included "emergency response to incidents involving DoD [Department of Defense] munitions/explosives/weapons systems." Had the men been summoned to defuse a bomb?

If so, they were not given the chance. Just after 9:00 A.M. on April

19, a huge explosion ripped the heart out of the Alfred P. Murrah Federal Building in downtown Oklahoma City, killing 168 people and injuring hundreds of others. Mogg and Humphries never came close to the truck carrying the bomb. They were not asked to help determine the cause of the explosion or to join the incipient criminal investigation.

Instead, with the city in chaos, they left Oklahoma City as mysteriously as they had arrived.

Years later, when he was no longer with the military, Cliff Mogg acknowledged the strange episode. "Yes," he told the investigative reporter Don Devereux, demonstrating considerable surprise to have been tracked down, "I was there."

Had there been a tip-off about the bombing, prompting the mission? Did the government try, and fail, to stop the explosion at the last minute? Mogg answered that it was not for him to say, and rushed to get off the phone.

EARLY ON APRIL 18, A LITTLE MORE THAN TWENTY-FOUR HOURS before the bombing, the Ryder truck that would later wreak such devastation was backed up against a storage locker on the edge of Herington, Kansas, more than 250 miles from Oklahoma City. A tall, wiry army veteran named Timothy McVeigh was loading fifty-pound bags of ammonium nitrate into the rear and quietly fuming. Terry Nichols, McVeigh's best friend from the army, lived just a few minutes away. Nichols was almost never late, but he had not shown up at 6:00 A.M. as agreed.

The two men had once enjoyed a deep friendship, but lately it had degenerated into sour recrimination and mutual suspicion. Two days earlier, McVeigh had used explicit threats to strong-arm Nichols into driving to Oklahoma City to help him drop off a getaway car a few blocks from the Murrah Building. Should McVeigh drive over to Nichols's house, brandish his Glock, and threaten his wife and infant daughter? They had acquired all the bomb components together and had committed at least two major robberies. They had more than enough guilty knowledge of each other's activities to pose a real threat if one of them bailed.

McVeigh was determined not to back down. Months earlier, during the first of many bitter arguments, McVeigh had warned Nichols that he knew where his brother, ex-wife, and twelve-year-old son lived and would not hesitate to eliminate them. "No one," he said, "is going to stop me from carrying out my plans."

Nichols awoke at 5:30 A.M., with plenty of time to make the appointment, but he wanted to mull it over one more time. Later, he would remember wanting nothing to do with a bombing, certainly not one that would take dozens of innocent lives. He would say he didn't know McVeigh's target, or when he intended to strike. Nichols wanted to assume that McVeigh would bring down a federal government building only at night, when it was largely empty.

Nichols's misgivings did not prompt him to do anything to stop the bomb plot. But he certainly had doubts about McVeigh. His friend, who came across to many people as jovial and easy to like, had been behaving erratically for months, partly under the influence of the crystal meth he used to fuel himself on his frequent cross-country car journeys. His temper had grown more volatile, the threats of violence more sinister. For a few weeks the previous summer, he even had a furtive sexual affair with Nichols's Filipina wife, Marife—a dirty secret that spilled out only later. McVeigh was also showing signs of undisciplined thinking and impulsive decision-making. If he had a properly elaborated plan for building and delivering the bomb, Nichols did not know it. And did not want to know.

Still, Nichols calculated he was better off confronting McVeigh than risking the safety of his family at home. So he drove over to a Pizza Hut about a quarter of a mile from the storage locker, parked his GMC truck, and cut through two or three vacant lots. It was now 6:30 A.M., and, as he approached, he could see the rage in McVeigh's face.

"You're late," McVeigh said coldly. "I've already got the truck half-loaded."

"Hey," Nichols responded, "why don't we take a few minutes and discuss things?"

"There's nothing to discuss," McVeigh snapped. "It's time for action."

Nichols chose not to engage him further and helped load the rest of the fertilizer sacks.

Over the next hour, they moved most of the contents of the storage locker: three fifty-five-gallon barrels of nitromethane, about three hundred blasting caps, Tovex high explosive arranged in long skinny "sausages," packets of a binary explosive called Kinestik, spools of shock tube and black-powder cannon fuse, some five-gallon measuring buckets, and a dozen empty fifty-five-gallon drums, half-metal and half-plastic, that would hold the components once they had all been assembled.

Nichols believed this was all he would have to do. But McVeigh asked him to follow behind the heavily laden Ryder truck for a few miles to make sure it was handling the road correctly. They rode north on Highway 77, back toward Junction City, where McVeigh had been staying. After about eight miles, McVeigh turned off unexpectedly at the entrance to Geary Lake State Park. Nichols followed McVeigh up a hill, and both men got out of their vehicles.

"What's wrong?" Nichols asked. "Why are you up here?"

"We're going to make the bomb here," McVeigh announced, "and you're going to help me."

Nichols blanched. "You're crazy! You've got a big bright yellow Ryder truck parked on top of a hill sticking out like a sore thumb for everyone to see. You may as well stick up a sign advertising what you are doing. Anyone on the highway can easily see you here as well."

McVeigh responded: "Then we'll move down near the lake and do it where we're more concealed."

Nichols made no further protest. He had a history of submitting to domineering figures in his life, of whom McVeigh was the latest and most dangerous. He had nothing to offer but quiet acquiescence. And so, the two men drove back down the hill and began the laborious business of building a five-thousand-pound weapon of mass destruction.

On Arkansas's death row unit an hour outside Little Rock, a white supremacist double murderer named Richard Wayne Snell was counting down his final hours and scaring the daylights out of his guards. "Within the next ten days there will be hell to pay," he predicted. Repeatedly, Snell talked about a bombing and told his guards that his execution date, April 19, would be a bad day for everyone.

Snell was a seasoned criminal, condemned for gunning down the only black state trooper in southwestern Arkansas during a routine traffic stop. He had joined the radical far-right in the early 1980s and thrown himself into a ragtag campaign to bring down the government with a wave of bombings, acts of sabotage, and assassinations. Most of these plots came to nothing, because of bad planning, poor weaponry, or wavering on the part of the plotters. He was regarded as the most dangerous of them; a week before, at a clemency hearing, he made approving reference to Hitler's deputy, Rudolf Hess, and said he'd probably shoot the trooper all over again.

April 19 was an iconic day for the right. Not only was it Patriots' Day, the anniversary of the "shot heard 'round the world" at the battle of Lexington and Concord in 1775; It also marked the two-year anniversary of the calamitous end to the Waco siege. The incident had triggered congressional hearings, official investigations, and political fallout for the Clinton administration. For the radical right, Waco was the moment when the much-detested federal government showed its true satanic colors. Putting Snell to death on the anniversary was a blatant provocation, if not also a call to arms.

Twelve years earlier, Snell and his associates had themselves planned to destroy the federal building in Oklahoma City. Their plan was to use missiles rather than a bomb; they gave up only after one of their homemade rockets blew up in the hands of their munitions expert. This was spelled out at the time by Snell's closest associate, an egomaniac racist preacher and cult leader named Jim Ellison. "We need something with a large body count to make the government sit up and take notice," Ellison told his followers. "I want the government to know that the right wing has spoken, that the Second American Revolution has begun."

His words were later echoed almost exactly by a disenchanted army veteran seen by many in the movement as a younger Wayne Snell, someone with the same revolutionary fervor and fearless commitment. His name was Timothy James McVeigh.

ON APRIL 17 OR 18, CAPTAIN KARYN ARMSTRONG, A VETERINARIAN conducting research into respiratory illnesses at the Walter Reed army Institute of Research outside Washington, D.C., received an unusual phone call. The man said he was from the Pentagon but never properly identified himself. He wanted information on treating lung injuries caused by pressure waves from large explosions. Captain Armstrong said she was not qualified to reply, because she treated animals, not humans. When the man insisted, she suggested that he get in touch with her boss, Dr. Adolph Januszkiewicz.

Dr. Januszkiewicz, also a respiratory specialist, later spoke to someone claiming to be from either the Aberdeen Proving Ground in Maryland or from his own command at Fort Detrick—the doctor could not recall which. This person was also asking about blast injuries.

"They identified themselves as being the liaison at the Pentagon to the governor's office of Oklahoma," Captain Armstrong recalled. "They never left a name, they never left a phone number. They always called us, and neither of us were medical doctors. I'm a veterinarian and he's a Ph.D."

Armstrong and Januszkiewicz thought little of the incident until after the Oklahoma City bombing. Then, whenever the subject came up, someone would invariably start humming the *Twilight Zone* theme.

A NIGHT OR TWO BEFORE THOSE CALLS, A GOVERNMENT-CONTRACTED steam-generating plant in downtown Oklahoma City experienced a loud, but minor, blowout. Within minutes, the city police were pounding on the control room window and pummeling the duty manager with questions about a "major explosion and possible terrorist takeover of the building." The manager had to talk them out of calling the bomb squad.

"I explained [that the] situation was under control and back to normal," the manager later wrote in his duty log. "They said in the future to please pick a slower night for them for this to happen. He [unnamed police officer] said, y'all scared the SHIT out of the people in the hotel. . . . We blamed it on the full moon, laughed, and on their way they went."

The hotel was, presumably, the one in the Convention Center right next to the Trigen plant. But the record does not explain why this night was so busy for the Oklahoma City Police Department. Explosions and terrorist attacks were not exactly commonplace in the heartland. At least one noteworthy alert, though, reached Oklahoma City over that Easter weekend. On Good Friday, someone from the FBI called the fire department and told them to watch out for suspicious people coming into town over the next few days.

After the bombing, the OCFD's chief of operations, Charles Gaines, publicly denied he had received any alert, but he was contradicted by his head dispatcher. "That's right," the dispatcher, Harvey Weathers, said. "On Friday the 14th, Chief Gaines received a call from the FBI, and we were told to be on the alert for terrorist activity in the near future. I passed that information down the line." There were no more specifics.

When Weathers's account appeared in the media, the fire department brass changed their story and said an FBI agent had called with a generalized warning about a possible attack on an American city by Aum Shinrikyo, the Japanese group that had staged a sarin gas attack on the Tokyo subway three weeks earlier. But Weathers told the FBI that this version was not correct, either. "That call did come," Weathers insisted. "A lot of people don't want to get involved in this deal."

TERRY NICHOLS WAS HAVING AN OUT-OF-BODY EXPERIENCE. HE AND McVeigh had spent several hours assembling the bomb when he felt himself floating in midair inside the cargo area of the Ryder truck, tilting forward and looking down at himself drawing nitromethane out of a barrel into a bucket. "How can I be a part of this?" he remembered thinking. Still, he kept working. When McVeigh and Nichols first pulled up to the edge of Geary Lake, McVeigh drew him into the back of the truck and rolled down the door completely. Nichols thought they needed more light and fresh air, and persuaded McVeigh to prop the back door open about a foot and open the passenger-side door.

Still, the quarters were maddeningly cramped. In Nichols's account, McVeigh began to fill the fifty-five-gallon drums with ammonium nitrate. This should have been pretty straightforward, but the AN prills had absorbed moisture and stuck to each other in large, unwieldy clumps. They had to be pulled apart until they were small enough to shove into the barrels.

Nichols's main job was to measure out twenty-pound quantities of nitromethane using a siphon pump, and add them to the ammonium nitrate in each barrel. He had to take care to spill as little as possible and minimize the liquid's exposure to the air, because nitromethane evaporates very quickly. "Absolutely no mixing was done," Nichols said. "The fertilizer went in a barrel first, then the fuel—that was it. No stirring, nothing."

Occasionally, one of the men peered out of the truck to see if anybody was watching. At about 9:00 A.M., a car with a boat and trailer pulled into the park and stopped at the boat ramp about three hundred yards ahead of them. An off-duty soldier and his son got out and launched their boat to go fishing.

McVeigh closed the side door facing the lake, but kept opening it a crack to see what was happening. Once or twice he asked Nichols to look for him. A sharp wind was churning the lake, and after an hour the man and his son steered the boat back in and left. The fisherman, an army sergeant named Rick Wahl, was almost as alarmed by the seemingly abandoned Ryder truck as McVeigh and Nichols were by him. Wahl noted both the Ryder and Nichols's GMC pickup and decided to keep a good distance. He even looked for a place to turn around quickly in case of trouble.

As McVeigh and Nichols were filling the eleventh barrel—the last one they would have space for, in Nichols's version of events—their nitromethane supply ran out. Each one's first impulse was to blame the other.

"Either your calculations are wrong, or this cheap scale is off," Nichols said.

McVeigh asked if Nichols had any diesel fuel in his pickup.

"Only what I have in my tank," Nichols said. The GMC held about twenty gallons, and it was nearly full.

"Go siphon out about ten gallons."

"With what?" Nichols protested. The siphon he had been using for the nitromethane was too fat to fit in his fuel tank.

McVeigh produced a length of quarter-inch plastic tubing from Walmart, which Nichols eyed skeptically. "It's going to take a long time with that small hose, and I don't think it's even long enough to work," he said.

McVeigh had no time for grumbling. "Just do it."

The tubing was crucially too short to reach the bottom of the bucket, and with the wind whipping erratically, some of the diesel spilled onto the ground, leaving a fuel mark later discovered by the FBI.

Once Nichols finished siphoning and filling the last barrel, McVeigh cut a slit into the side of the remaining ten or twelve bags of fertilizer, poured some of the diesel in, closed up the slits with duct tape, and then shook the bags around. He lined them along the driver's side of the cargo hold to add to the bomb's explosive punch.

There was little risk that the first eleven barrels of ammonium nitrate and nitromethane would not do the job by themselves. They added up to almost five thousand pounds of high explosive; as long as one of the barrels ignited successfully, it would set off a chain reaction and detonate the rest. But McVeigh preferred to err on the side of overkill. He, like Nichols, had received only rudimentary explosives training in the army and did not necessarily know better. Indeed, their lack of expertise raises the question of whether anybody, at Geary Lake or elsewhere, helped them put the device together. Both men later insisted they worked unaided. But the accounts that each of them gave are also riddled with puzzling inconsistencies.

On the technical details, McVeigh's version is far skimpier than Nichols's. One explosives expert suggested that by the time McVeigh agreed to discuss how he built the bomb, close to five years after the fact, he might simply have forgotten what he did, or perhaps never entirely knew. Nichols, though, remembered everything. That raises a broader issue of veracity, because it was supposedly McVeigh, according to both men, who did the brain work of wiring the bomb and constructing its boosters and detonators. What are the chances the master bomb-maker would turn out to be so clueless, or oddly forgetful?

There are two other possibilities. Either Nichols was the real bomb-maker but never wanted to embrace that dubious historical distinction—especially after McVeigh willingly claimed sole responsibility—or both men took their direction from someone else.

THE RADICAL FAR RIGHT NEVER FORGOT WAYNE SNELL'S 1983 PLOT to destroy the Murrah Building. "Blowing up a federal building . . .

was not a novel idea," said Jack Knox, an FBI agent who helped run down Snell and Ellison in the 1980s and was once on their assassination list. "It was floating around out there."

One of Snell's closest friends, Louis Beam, discussed bombing the Murrah Building as early as the mid-1980s. Beam was a veteran of the Texas Ku Klux Klan and a fearsomely talented public speaker, who repeatedly pressed his friends in the Aryan supremacy movement to wage an all-out war against the federal government. Two of Beam's friends confirmed that, in the 1980s, he had talked with a Klan leader from Oklahoma about attacking the Murrah Building, although they were unsure who first proposed the idea. They were also certain that Beam and Snell both knew about the 1995 Oklahoma City bombing before it happened.

"Snell knew about the bombing," Bruce Campbell, Beam's confidant and fellow propagandist for the antigovernment cause, said in a 2009 interview. "Louis was very close to Snell."

Cheri Seymour, who at one time worked as a secretary to the Aryan Nations and hosted Beam several times at her home, said Beam went to see Mary Snell three weeks before April 19 and gave her a message to pass on to her husband that "Armageddon was coming on the day of his death." This meeting was later corroborated by an unconnected government informant.

Mary Snell gave plentiful indication that she knew—or hoped—something was up. "April 19," she wrote in a letter to the Militia of Montana intended to whip up outrage in the run-up to her husband's execution, "is the first day of a weeklong sacrificial preparation for the GRAND CLIMAX ceremony celebrated by those who follow the Luciferian religion."

Was it possible that she or her husband were in on the bomb plot, or at least knew it was in the works? "I have no solid information," said Bill Buford, the ATF's top agent in Arkansas at the time of the bombing, "but the pieces fit together too neatly for him not to have known."

The FBI never talked to Beam after the bombing, and conducted only one relatively perfunctory interview with Mary Snell. But they had plenty of information indicating that Beam knew about the bombing before it happened. A career criminal named Roy Byrd told the bureau from an Arizona prison about a phone conversation he had with Beam in the summer of 1994, in which Beam said that "something big" would happen in Oklahoma City, Denver, or Dallas on the anniversary of Waco. When Byrd asked what it was, Beam replied that it would be similar to the plot of a notorious underground novel, in which a band of white supremacists drives a truck loaded with ammonium nitrate and fuel oil into the basement of FBI headquarters in Washington, D.C., and blows up the building. Byrd did not mention the novel by name, but he was clearly referring to *The Turner Diaries,* a cult book on the fringe of the gun-show circuit, written by one of America's leading neo-Nazis, William Pierce. *The Turner Diaries* was Tim McVeigh's favorite book.

According to Byrd, Beam did not mention anybody by name. He said only: "They've got some kid who's going to do something."

McVEIGH WAS PROUD OF HIS BOMB DESIGN WHEN HE DESCRIBED IT to Lou Michel and Dan Herbeck of the *Buffalo News,* who interviewed him extensively on death row for their book *American Terrorist.* The main trigger for the blast, McVeigh said, was a bucketful of Tovex sausages he placed at the center of the barrels of fertilizer soaked in nitromethane. He ran two lengths of fuse cord from the truck's cab into the cargo hold, via separate holes that Nichols drilled for him. He inserted the fuse ends into nonelectric blasting caps. He used duct tape to attach the blasting caps to lengths of shock tube, which snaked their way to the Tovex. McVeigh only needed to light the ends of the fuse cord inside the truck's cabin and the bomb would ignite. The black-powder fuse burned at a rate of about thirty seconds per foot—he measured off a two-minute length and a second, five-minute length. The burning fuse would trigger the blasting caps, which would then ignite the shock tube, set off the Tovex, and—boom—the ammonium nitrate barrels would detonate in a split-second chain reaction.

This scheme was basically workable, according to experts who reviewed it, which helps explain why it has gone largely unchallenged since *American Terrorist* was first published in 2001. But it does raise some basic questions. McVeigh took particular pride in the two independent fuse lines, describing them as the "perfect redundancy." He even described a third redundancy—a pile of explosives, which, he said, he kept at his feet. If all else failed, he intended to ignite them by firing his pistol.

This all sounds very meticulous, but to a seasoned bomb expert it comes across as faintly ridiculous. Pharis Williams, a veteran explosives expert and government consultant, said a professional bomb-maker would never rely on one central ignition point. "It would seem," he said, "that someone who is proud of his redundancy would also boost every barrel."

Indeed, Nichols's version suggests this is exactly what they did. In his scheme, the two lines of fuse cord were connected to a single, central point where they were attached to a booster (the binary explosive Kinestik) as well as twelve separate lengths of Primadet shock tube. These Primadet tubes were then connected to each barrel, where they were attached to another Kinestik and a Tovex sausage via a prefitted nonelectric blasting cap. Nichols thus describes the bomb as having not one but a dozen ignition points, creating a dozen redundancies.

Nichols's account is more convincing throughout. McVeigh made no mention of securing the barrels in the back of the truck, while Nichols describes how, at McVeigh's direction, he cut and hammered down lengths of four-by-four wood beams so there would be no danger of the barrels shifting during transport. McVeigh neither describes nor names the Primadet, which he and Nichols had stolen in a quarry robbery months earlier. Instead McVeigh focuses on self-aggrandizing details that seem dubious at best—for example, how he considered closing the ends of the blasting caps with his bare teeth. McVeigh was a fanatical reader of *The Turner Diaries* and another novel by William Pierce, *Hunter,* and was no doubt familiar with a scene in the second book in which the warrior hero blows up a Mossad office in Virginia. The book describes him arranging barrels of ammonium nitrate and fuel oil around a single fifty-pound box of Tovex. Was this what McVeigh was thinking of when he gave his description of events at Geary Lake that April morning?

By midday, McVeigh and Nichols had finished. McVeigh suggested throwing the empty fertilizer bags into the back of the truck, but Nichols was concerned that some could survive the bombing and leave fingerprint traces. So he took the time to roll them into bundles, attach them with duct tape, and toss them in the back of his pickup truck. He also took his Makita drill, which he had used to bore holes for the cannon fuse, the siphon pump, and the bathroom scales. Everything else—the dolly they used to load the nitromethane; the empty nitromethane barrels; the last, unused white plastic barrel; their two five-gallon buckets; and a bunch of tools, including a hacksaw, hammer, left-over tubing, and pliers—was left in the back of the Ryder.

McVeigh closed the side and back doors and padlocked them. Then he sauntered to the lakeside to splash water on his face and hands, and slipped into a change of clothes.

The two men stared at each other one last time. McVeigh climbed into the truck, Nichols into his pickup. When they reached Highway 77, Nichols headed north toward the U.S. Army base at Fort Riley, where he would drop in on a military surplus auction. In his rearview mirror, he saw the Ryder truck retreat and vanish on its trip south.

IN THE REMOTE HILLS OF EASTERN OKLAHOMA, MANY OF THE MOST prominent members of a fringe religious community known as

Elohim City spent April 18 on the move. The community's figure-head, Robert "Grandpa" Millar, was getting ready to lead a group to Little Rock to protest Wayne Snell's execution and to take his body back for burial. Millar was Snell's spiritual adviser, a role he later insisted was not an endorsement of his criminal career but rather an expression of compassion. Millar liked to say that everybody came to him through Jesus, and he accepted them all.

In April 1995, Jesus had sent Millar quite the collection of odd-balls, dropouts, silver-tongued charlatans, and out-and-out crimi-nals. They attended services in the igloo-like Elohim City church (Millar had an aversion to straight lines and right angles in build-ings), camped out in an assortment of caravans, squat houses, and makeshift structures made of ammunition crates and bright orange polyurethane, showed off their collections of assault weapons, pistols, and black-powder explosives, and shared in the fear that the federal government would one day descend to kill them all.

Among the visitors was Mark Thomas, a neo-Nazi preacher who lived most of the year in abject squalor in rural Pennsylvania, where he sired a stream of children and plotted attacks on gas and electricity plants, railroads, and communications facilities. Thomas came to visit his sixteen-year-old son Nathan, who had been living at Elohim City on and off for two years and participated in perim-eter security patrols. According to a government informant, Nathan bragged about converting his AK-47 assault rifle to full automatic and making homemade napalm. Two of Mark Thomas's skinhead protégés from Pennsylvania, Scott Stedeford and Kevin McCarthy, visited for about a week; they were both members of a neo-Nazi punk band named Cyanide, along with a more permanent Elohim City resident, Michael Brescia, who had fallen into the same White Power scene in Philadelphia in the early 1990s.

Since the previous fall, Stedeford, McCarthy, and Thomas had been members of a white supremacist bank robbery gang that vari-ously called itself the Company or the Aryan Republican Army. Stedeford had taken part in five robberies in Ohio, Iowa, and Missouri, netting more than $80,000; McCarthy had been in on four. Mark Thomas was not a direct participant, but he was heavily involved in planning and expanding the gang's activities. The idea was to steal enough to finance a full-frontal assault on the federal government. Less than a month earlier, on March 29, the gang had hauled in $29,000 from a bank in Des Moines. Two days later, they elected to disband for four months—an unprecedented period of inactivity suggesting some side project involving one or more of them, or a compelling need to lay low for an extended time.

One might expect these men to stay around to pay homage to Wayne Snell, whom they regarded as a hero, but instead they rushed far away. Mark and Nathan Thomas left on Monday, April 17, for Allentown. That same day, Stedeford and McCarthy drove to Fort Smith, Arkansas, to buy a twelve-year-old Chevy Suburban, and did not return.

Most Elohim City residents lived simply and were mostly unaware of the criminal connections these people had in the wider world. The women concentrated on child-rearing and housework and were kept away from the business of the elders. The children, some the product of polygamous or even incestuous relationships, were home-schooled according to the community's bizarre interpretation of Christianity, which held that white Americans were the true children of Israel, while Jews were the spawn of Satan and blacks even worse. Millar and his immediate family knew much more about their visitors' revolutionary ambitions. And so did one of the more peculiar residents in the community, a gangly German named Andreas Strassmeir.

Strassmeir shared a small stone house with Mike Brescia, and hosted Stedeford and McCarthy over Easter. He had been in the army back in Germany, drifting into radical right-wing circles in the United States through his friendship with a white supremacist lawyer named Kirk Lyons. Lyons, in turn, was friendly with Millar, and entrusted Strassmeir to his care after the young German exhausted all other offers of hospitality. Strassmeir's grandfather was said to have been one of the Nazi Party's earliest members, with a membership card number lower than Hitler's, while his father had been a prominent aide to Helmut Kohl, the German chancellor who oversaw reunification after the fall of the Berlin Wall. At Elohim City, Strassmeir ran the security detail, a platoon of teenagers and young men who marched around the four-hundred-acre compound with old SKS assault rifles loaded with cheap Chinese ammunition and low-budget Remington sniper rifles. Occasionally they sported bayonets, especially to scare outsiders.

Grandpa Millar liked Strassmeir and allowed him to live, as one of his friends put it, "in his fantasy world being field marshal of Elohim City." Strassmeir's relations with the other residents were significantly more strained. With his gawky manner, rigid Prussian upbringing, and foreign accent, he was never fully accepted. His abrasive intelligence rubbed people the wrong way, and he was a shambles of a human being—forever forgetting or breaking things, swearing and cursing.

One of Strassmeir's best friends was Pete Ward, one of three brothers living at Elohim City, who had been brought up by Christian missionaries in Africa. Pete was not blessed with much initiative, and was known for following Strassmeir around like a puppy. His brothers, Tony and Sonny, got into trouble for stealing firewood and hitting up young women for money.

Just before the bombing, they and their parents and kid sister all disappeared from Elohim City without warning. Sonny was later reported to have spent several more days somewhere in Oklahoma before heading to Georgia. Most of the others took off for New Mexico. A Sunday-school teacher who taught the Wards' little sister, Priscilla, later told the FBI that the girl had come to her, very upset, and indicated that something had happened but would not say what. "Everyone was shocked that they would leave so suddenly," Kennilee Mooney, the teacher, told the FBI.

Years later, Strassmeir would deny there was anything strange about these multiple departures on the eve of the bombing. He felt protective toward his former friends and concocted a strange argument that their comings and goings meant nothing, because they were not living in the community at the time. "How can they leave if they were not there?" he asked.

This was, of course, a linguistic absurdity. The bank robbers, and the rest of them, *were* there, and they did leave.

Again, he insisted: "They did not leave, because they were not there."

DAYS BEFORE MCVEIGH AND NICHOLS BUILT THEIR BOMB, KEN Stern of the American Jewish Committee issued a remarkably prescient report on the dangers of the country's burgeoning militia movement. "Do not be surprised if there is militia activity next week in your area," he wrote to AJC supporters on April 10. Stern had no special inside knowledge, but he and a group of other academics and professional hate-group watchers had been monitoring extremist newsletters and Internet chat rooms for months.

Stern's warning was imprecise in that McVeigh and Nichols did not belong to a militia; they were too extreme for that. But he was absolutely correct when it came to gauging the degree of public anger and alienation from the federal government, and the risk that someone on the extremist fringe could resort to radical measures. The militia movement had been growing with a vengeance, a symptom of the rapidly changing times. On the heels of the dramatic collapse of family farming across the heartland in the 1980s had come recession and the rapid loss of defense-sector jobs at the end of the Cold War. Cheap immigrant labor was eroding the stability of many semiskilled and unskilled jobs. And under Bill Clinton, the first U.S. president in half a century not to have served in uniform, there was an unprecedented push toward gun control, first with the passage of the Brady

Bill, which instituted the country's first system of background checks on firearms purchases, and then with the 1994 assault weapons ban.

The majority of the disaffected people were not criminals; they wanted only to stand up for themselves and their gun rights. Two specific instances of catastrophic overreaching by federal law enforcement pushed the political temperature toward the boiling point, however. The first was the 1992 Ruby Ridge incident, in which a seemingly routine attempt to pressure a survivalist in Idaho into becoming a government informant degenerated into a ghastly mountainside shootout. And the second was the disastrously mishandled siege at Waco.

The militias started talking about federal law enforcement agents as the "shock troops" of a New World Order intent on stripping Americans of their rights. Wayne LaPierre, the head of the National Rifle Association, wrote a notorious fund-raising letter in which he denounced the feds as "jack-booted government thugs . . . wearing Nazi bucket helmets and black storm trooper uniforms to attack law-abiding citizens." G. Gordon Liddy, the Watergate-era presidential "plumber" turned radio host, encouraged listeners to open fire on agents of the Bureau of Alcohol, Tobacco and Firearms, whose actions had initiated both the Ruby Ridge and the Waco disasters. "Don't shoot at [their chests], because they got a vest on underneath that," Liddy said. "Head shots. Head shots . . . Kill the sons of bitches!"

The militias, Stern wrote in his report, "constitute a new manifestation of violent hate-group activity" whose targets now included government employees. Some people, he said, were advocating killing, and he feared the threat was serious. He was right.

EARLY IN THE AFTERNOON OF APRIL 18, THE WHITE SUPREMACIST CAUSE Foundation received a baffling phone call at its North Carolina headquarters. CAUSE was a legal advocacy organization, and its name was an acronym for the five places in the world most heavily populated by white people—Canada, Australasia, the United States, South Africa, and Europe. Kirk Lyons, the man behind it, was a former personal litigation lawyer from Houston, who saw himself as the right wing's answer to the ACLU; he defended the Ku Klux Klan's free speech rights and made sure skinheads and neo-Nazis were prosecuted only for their criminal behavior, not their political beliefs.

Lyons, an amateur historian of the old Confederacy, was on his way to a Civil War reenactment when the call came in, so his friend and partner Dave Hollaway took it instead. The young man on the line didn't give his name, and launched into a diatribe about a Waco lawsuit that CAUSE was pursuing at the time. The suit had not gone far enough, he said, and it was time to send the government a clear message.

"Usually people are ranting when they call," Hollaway recalled, "but this guy was young and very clear in his message and tone. That set off a master warning light in my head. I said, 'Let me give you some unsolicited legal advice. If I was your lawyer, I'd say you need to be careful about calling people up and making statements like that. You're perilously close to the edge of your First Amendment rights.'"

Hollaway was a talker; CAUSE's phone records show the call lasted eighteen minutes. He said there were three kinds of freedom in America—the ones guaranteed by the jury box, the ballot box, and the cartridge box. "Really," Hollaway said, "you want to exhaust the first two before resorting to the last."

Hollaway later told the FBI he was sure the caller was Tim McVeigh, taking time out from his final bomb preparations to sound off to someone he thought might be sympathetic.

BETWEEN HIS PARTING WITH TERRY NICHOLS AND THE EARLY MORNING of April 19, Timothy McVeigh was like a ghost, flitting from place to place across southern Kansas and northern Oklahoma. The phone call to the CAUSE Foundation was just one of many puzzles. After the bombing, people reported sightings of him at gas stations, in diners and restaurants; in company and alone; in the Ryder truck and in other vehicles entirely. He couldn't possibly have been in all these places, nor could he have stomached the impressive diet of burritos, steaks, and hamburgers he was witnessed downing.

McVeigh gave a rudimentary account of his movements in one of his first interviews with his defense team. He avoided the main highway, I-35, he said, driving instead a few miles farther east, down Highway 77. Sometime in the afternoon of April 18, he stopped for gas. Later, he pulled over at a rest stop to check that the bomb barrels had not moved. He tossed his truck rental agreement and a fake ID into the back of the truck before closing it up again.

Once across the Oklahoma state line, he found a McDonald's for dinner, then walked into a cheap chain hotel to rent a room but decided to spend the night in the truck instead. He said he was alone at all times.

Later, the FBI found witnesses who not only contradicted that, but said he might have been traveling in a convoy. It was often the same vehicles the witnesses cited: the Ryder truck, of course; McVeigh's beat-up old yellow Mercury Marquis, which, in his account, he had stashed days earlier in downtown Oklahoma City; a white sedan; and a brown Chevy pickup.

An Oklahoma gas station attendant who said she served McVeigh remembered a companion with slicked-back black wavy hair. At a steakhouse in the small town of Perry that night, several customers spotted someone resembling McVeigh, and one of the owners also described a friend of his, standing six feet tall and weighing 260 pounds, with curly brown hair. On the morning of the bombing, the postmaster of the tiny town of Mulhall, not far from Perry, reported standing next to McVeigh and another man as they ordered coffee at Jackie's Farmers Store.

Taken one by one, these stories are of dubious investigative value, and likely to be tainted by imperfect recall and the power of suggestion. Taken together, though, they make at least the beginnings of a case that Timothy McVeigh was not alone as he commandeered his weapon of mass destruction toward its target.

THE MORNING ROUTINE IN THE WILBURN HOUSEHOLD IN OKLA-homa City was always chaotic. The three adults—Glenn, his wife Kathy, and Kathy's daughter Edye—had jobs to run to, and it was a scramble to dress and feed Edye's two boys, Chase, age three, and Colton, age two.

On April 19, Glenn was getting ready to leave with Kathy, when he noticed that Chase didn't have his shoes on. He picked up the boy, plonked him on the wet bar, and fit first one shoe and then the other.

"You're a good boy," Glenn said as he kissed him on the forehead. "Paw-paw loves you."

Chase was a big presence and a natural-born joker. Glenn stopped to notice how much he had grown over the previous couple of months. Kathy suggested playfully that they should trade Chase in for a girl named Shirley.

"I'm not Shirley!" Chase replied indignantly. The adults laughed.

Glenn and Kathy headed to the garage—it was up to Edye that morning to drive the boys to their day care on the second floor of the Alfred P. Murrah Federal Building.

"Bye, Shirley," Kathy said.

"Don't call me Shirley," Chase said. He was half enjoying the joke and half bristling at it.

"Bye, Shirley. I won't call you that," Glenn said.

Those were the last words he ever said to his grandson.

"He was so funny," Kathy later remembered. "He was such a funny little boy."

● ● ●

APRIL 19 WAS A DESIGNATED TRAINING DAY FOR THE OKLAHOMA County Sheriff's bomb squad, but they had no plans to come downtown. It was up to a deputy named Bill Grimsley to collect their truck at the county jail and drive it to their training area in the northeastern part of the city. He was not supposed to stop along the way; the truck had large lettering on the side that read BOMB SQUAD, and was apt to scare people.

But Grimsley made several stops, first at the county courthouse, where his day job was to supervise the security staff, and then at a Mc-Donald's, where he bought himself an Egg McMuffin. Naturally, he was seen. After the bombing many people became convinced that they had stumbled on some dark secret involving an attempt to stop the bombing at the eleventh hour. Some, like Norma Joslin, a clerk with the county court, worried they might be targeted for assassination if they revealed what they had witnessed; when Joslin was called before a grand jury in 1998, she insisted on being driven directly into an underground garage and escorted into the courtroom. The FBI was also curious, and grilled every bomb squad member over a period of months.

It didn't help that the sheriff's department put out a series of confusing, even contradictory, statements. First, officials denied the bomb truck had been downtown at all. Then they told at least one media outlet that the entire bomb squad had been training near the Murrah Building, wearing blue jeans instead of their uniforms. By the time they got around to the truth, few were inclined to believe it.

It was Grimsley himself who created much of the confusion. Worried he might get into trouble for disobeying the rules, he told his superiors he had driven the truck straight to the training facility. At first they chose to believe him. Then they tried to cover for him. "Bill was notorious for getting into little kinks like that," said Kyle Kilgore, the bomb squad's dog handler. "The only thing that saved us was that our bomb squad schedules are put in yearly, one year in advance." Those schedules showed that April 19 was indeed a training day—just a bizarre coincidence.

• • •

THERE WERE OTHER, LESS FARCICAL STORIES OF UNUSUAL LAW ENforcement activity. Renee Cooper, a deputy clerk at the county courthouse, said she saw several men in dark jackets with bomb squad markings outside the federal courthouse at 8:00 A.M. Claude Criss, a private investigator, said he saw them, too, and they were rooting through the bushes. Debbie Nakanashi, a window clerk at the Center City Post Office across the street from the Murrah Building, indicated to a congressional investigator that she had seen sniffer dogs but was ordered by her superiors not to talk about them. According to Randy Yount, a state park ranger who helped with the rescue effort, explosives experts spent all night looking for a bomb in response to a warning that one had been planted inside the federal courthouse.

It is tempting to give credence to these reports, because they all center on the same location and suggest, however vaguely, that there was a tip-off. Throw in the mysterious air force EOD team and the FBI warning to the fire department, and we have multiple indications that some part of the government—perhaps more than one part— heard about a coming attack. Still, the accounts add up to a fractured picture at best. Nobody in authority has ever acknowledged having advance warning of a major explosion, and many agencies, particularly the FBI and ATF, have vehemently denied it.

If a bomb squad was out looking for a device, who could they have been? On the morning of April 19, the head of the Oklahoma Highway Patrol's tactical team, John Haynie, was in Oklahoma City with a bomb truck, even though he was stationed in Ardmore, near the Texas border. Ostensibly, he was in town to run another training session—quite a coincidence. In 1998, Haynie told a grand jury that his session was called to hone his team's surveillance skills. OHP time records, however, show that at least three of the team members who might have been expected to attend were off work or on vacation.

Could Haynie have been involved in a different operation, with the training session acting as a cover story? Haynie, exactly the sort of sure-footed senior officer people would turn to in a crisis, who had spent almost a decade tracking intelligence on Elohim City, refused to comment. "There's no benefit that I can see to talking about anything to do with anything I've ever done," he said.

A question also hangs over the Oklahoma State Bureau of Investigation, which brought three out-of-town agents into Oklahoma City on the evening before the bombing, for reasons it has never adequately explained. Rick Stephens, who came in from the Tulsa area, would not say if he or other OSBI agents had been forewarned of a bomb attack. "That's been rumored for years," he said. Invited to issue a categorical denial that the OSBI was responding to a threat, he said: "I won't confirm or deny anything."

THE RYDER TRUCK WAS FIRST SPOTTED IN DOWNTOWN OKLAHOMA City at around 8:00 A.M. At least two dozen eyewitnesses saw the truck over the next hour, many of them reporting that it was accompanied by a brown Chevy pickup, a white sedan, and an aging Mercury. These vehicles made themselves conspicuous in and around the Murrah Building, sometimes parked, sometimes driving, other times roaring into the building's underground garage. McVeigh was seen in more than one of them, and always with at least one other person.

Years later, McVeigh told Michel and Herbeck, his prison interviewers, that he did not drive into Oklahoma City until 8:50 A.M. But an African-American commuter named Leonard Long spotted someone fitting his description—a "tall, slim, white man" with a dark ball cap worn backward—about fifty minutes earlier. McVeigh, Long said, was inside a brown pickup switching lanes at high speed near the Murrah Building. Long remembered the encounter because he narrowly avoided a collision and because the man next to McVeigh, a stocky, dark-complexioned man in a camouflage jacket, spewed racial insults at him.

Shortly after 8:00 A.M., an employee of the Kerr-McGee Oil Company saw two men walking away from the YMCA building, also on Fifth Street, toward a yellow Mercury parked in the oil company's lot two blocks farther south. The men matched the description of McVeigh and his companion given by Leonard Long.

About half an hour later, Kyle Hunt, a banker, spotted a Ryder truck another block or so south of the Kerr-McGee building. Close behind was a four-door sedan with three men inside. "One of the men was looking up, straining his neck. The group looked lost," Hunt later said. "As I pulled closer, the driver of the sedan warned me off. I got an icy-cold, go-to-hell look from the young man that I now know to be Timothy McVeigh. It was unnerving."

Two more sightings seemed to confirm the bombing crew as lost, or at least *at a loss*. The first was at Johnny's Tire Company, on a hill a few blocks northwest of the Murrah Building. Mike Moroz, a mechanic, told the FBI that two men in a Ryder truck pulled into the store and almost hit the flag banners hanging from a covered part of the forecourt. The driver, whom Moroz later identified as McVeigh, asked for directions to Northwest Fifth Street, the address of the Murrah Building. The man seemed confused, so Moroz invited him to step out of the truck and take a look down the hill at the one-way system. He was wearing a dark ball cap back to front with no hair showing.

Oddly, after the McVeigh figure told Moroz he knew where to go, he and his companion sat on the forecourt for several more minutes. Moroz and his manager wondered aloud what they were up to and joked that they should put up a sign outside, saying DIRECTIONS: $5. Finally, the truck moved on, taking a hard right and moving back downhill.

The second sighting was at a warehouse loading dock southeast of the Murrah Building in an industrial zone named Bricktown. David Snider, the warehouse foreman, was expecting a delivery and waved expectantly when he saw a Ryder truck rolling slowly toward him. The driver, he noticed, had a dark complexion, dark hair and mustache, and was wearing sunglasses. His passenger, who could have been McVeigh, had short, blond, military-style hair. "They were both looking in the side-view mirrors, and they looked like they were looking for an address," Snider said. He quickly determined that they were not friendly, and he started yelling obscenities at them. The truck driver sped on.

Minutes later, James Linehan, a lawyer, encountered the yellow Mercury on the corner of Fourth and Robinson. He described the back of the car as "caked in Oklahoma dirt" and the license plate either obscured or missing. The time was exactly 8:38 A.M.; he was on his way to court and kept time on the clock of his black Jeep Cherokee. The Mercury was slowing to a crawl, so Linehan pulled out to overtake. But the yellow car abruptly edged over and almost pushed him into the oncoming lane. "I am thinking, basically, hey idiot, what are you doing?" Linehan recalled. "I don't want your crappy yellow paint on my car."

He got a good look at the driver, who was scrunched up over the steering wheel and looking up at the Murrah Building. He thought at the time it was a woman in a hooded top but wondered later if it was McVeigh in disguise. Then the Mercury made a sharp turn into the Murrah Building's underground parking lot. Linehan saw it disappear and remembered thinking: "That car doesn't belong in there."

Danny Wilkerson, who ran the convenience store at the Regency Towers apartment building on Fifth Street, said a man strongly resembling Tim McVeigh walked in at around 8:40 A.M. and bought two Cokes and a pack of Marlboro cigarettes. (McVeigh was not a smoker.) Wilkerson noticed a Ryder truck parked outside and asked McVeigh if he was moving in. McVeigh said he was not. As he walked out, Wilkerson watched him and noticed a second man in the cab. Moments later, Wilkerson saw the Ryder truck again, this time on the far side of the street, pointing in the direction of the Murrah Building, a moment captured on one of the few pieces of video surveillance tape shown at McVeigh's trial.

What did all these sightings mean? Officially, the FBI concluded they were the result of witness confusion, compounded by wall-to-wall news coverage. Not one of the eyewitnesses who saw McVeigh that morning was called to testify at trial, because the government determined that every one of them was wrong to say he was not alone. But as Danny Coulson, one of the FBI's most experienced investigators, put it: "If only one person had seen it, or two or three . . . but twenty-four? Twenty-four people say, yes I saw him with someone else? That's pretty powerful."

Newly available information from law enforcement and from sources inside the radical right suggests Coulson was right to be skeptical of his bureau colleagues. Not only do these sources say that McVeigh had company on April 19. They also say that McVeigh and his coconspirators intended to drive the Ryder truck into the basement of the Murrah Building or the federal courthouse next door, but had to change plans in a hurry because the truck exceeded the height limit for the garage.

Dave Hollaway, of the CAUSE Foundation, was flabbergasted by what he saw as a lack of foresight. "They couldn't get the truck into the parking garage, and that's why there was all that turning and stopping," he said. "The guys weren't exactly the brightest bulbs on the tree. . . . If they had had any kind of guidance—if I'd been doing it—there would have been nothing left of the building."

Several pieces of evidence fit the scenario. Five days before the bombing, Jane Graham, a union official with the Housing and Urban Development agency, spotted three men acting suspiciously in the underground garage and later came to believe they were sizing it up as part of the plot. James Linehan's account of the morning of April 19 points to suspicious activity involving one or more vehicles tearing in or out of the garage. And there is no doubt: the height clearance on the garage was too low for McVeigh's twenty-foot truck.

After the Ryder made a first pass at the Murrah Building, a number of people saw it trying to squeeze into an alley between the federal courthouse and the Old Post Office Building, which houses the bankruptcy court. The alley, however, was blocked by a large U.S. Marshals Service truck, and the Ryder truck backed out again. This was first reported in the late 1990s by a member of the Oklahoma Highway Patrol. But it has since been confirmed by two very well placed officials. The first of these was Tom Hunt, who in 1995 was the local head of the Federal Protective Service, with responsibility for the security of the courthouse complex and the Murrah Building. He personally knew the marshal's deputy blocking the alley. "The Ryder could have gotten only partway through," Hunt said. "I'm glad. I would have hated to see those judges get it that day."

The second official was John Magaw, the director of the Bureau of Alcohol, Tobacco and Firearms, who was privy to just about everything in the bomb investigation. Magaw acknowledged that McVeigh's initial plans turned out to be "too difficult, or . . . would have drawn too much attention." Magaw could not confirm the specifics, either on the garage or the alley, but he thought both scenarios were plausible. "[McVeigh] drove around and couldn't find a place," Magaw added. "Wherever he meant to put it was too tight—the truck wouldn't fit. There was a piece of information about that. . . . If you have heard he intended to drive it into the garage, I wouldn't argue with that."

Thereafter, the truck and its occupants would have had to find a place to mark time while a new plan was formulated. Running into David Snider put the kibosh on dawdling in Bricktown. One reason for driving toward Johnny's Tire Company could have been to take advantage of the higher ground to send or receive radio messages.

One can imagine the frenzy among the members of the bombing crew, as the clock ticked toward 9:00 A.M. The truck and its deadly load had been driving around Oklahoma City for close to half an hour, glaringly visible to dozens of witnesses, and they still had no firm idea what to do with it.

• • •

At 9:32 A.M. Eastern Time, James Howard Miller picked up the phone at the Department of Justice's Executive Secretariat, where he worked as a secretary, and heard a man say a federal building had just blown up. "He's saying he's standing across the street, watching it," he told two coworkers.

None of them believed it; Miller's main job was to screen calls, and his phone extension was commonly referred to as the "nut line."

Only later, once the news broke, did it dawn on him that 9:32 A.M. in Washington was 8:32 A.M. in Oklahoma. Nothing at that point had blown up yet; it seemed someone with a lot of inside knowledge had prank-called the federal government.

Just across the National Mall, another teaser arrived at the offices of Republican congressman Steve Stockman of Texas. It was an unsigned, handwritten note, sent by fax, and written so obscurely that the staffer who first read it tossed it away. Later it was retrieved, and Stockman gave it to the FBI.

The one-page message came from the offices of Mark Koernke, a prominent Michigan Militia leader acquainted with McVeigh and Nichols. It read: "First update. Bldg 7 to 10 floors only military people on scene—BATF/FBI. Bomb threat received last week. Perpetrator unknown at this time. Oklahoma." The word "Oklahoma" was underlined.

The most interesting thing about the message was the 8:59 A.M. time stamp. In both Michigan and Washington, that was more than an hour before the bomb went off. A staffer later said the fax machine had not been reset since daylight savings time began, so it really arrived at 9:59, or 8:59 in Oklahoma. That was still three minutes before the bomb went off. And even if *that* was inaccurate, and the fax came in just after the explosion, as the FBI later determined, it is still a mystery how Koernke's people received the news so fast.

● ● ●

A FEW MINUTES BEFORE 9:00 A.M., McVEIGH'S BACKUP PLAN WAS IN place. The bomb would be detonated in the handicapped parking spot on the Murrah Building's north side. The configuration of the barrels—most likely designed with the intention of driving the force of the explosion into the underground garage's key support pillars— would now concentrate the blast toward the building itself, rather than the street.

A few minutes before the explosion, according to several witnesses, somebody moved the yellow Mercury to within eighty feet of the detonation site, probably along the same side of Fifth Street as the Ryder truck. The brown Chevy pickup was on the other side of Fifth Street, in front of the Journal Record Building. Shortly after, someone with long blond hair—perhaps the same person seen by James Linehan at the wheel of the Mercury twenty minutes earlier—waved the Ryder truck into position. This time, it seems more certain that McVeigh was inside, with the swarthy John Doe seen repeatedly over the previous hour. They had already lit both fuses. They exited, each walking calmly toward one of the getaway vehicles.

Glenn Grossman, an employee of the Oklahoma Department of Securities, watched this scene unfold from his fourth-floor office inside the Journal Record Building. In the few minutes before 9:00 A.M., he looked out twice. The first time, he saw the Mercury parked in front of the Ryder truck. It caught his attention, because he used to own a 1978 Mercury Marquis and was familiar with the vehicle. The second time, the Ryder had pulled in front. Someone was standing by the driver's side of the Mercury. On the sidewalk, a skinny woman with long blond hair was yelling and gesturing wildly at him. "They were together," Grossman told the FBI, "and she was frantic about something."

A different perspective on the same events was provided by Daina Bradley, a young African-American woman who was inside the Murrah Building visiting the first-floor Social Security office with her mother, sister, and two children. She and her sister saw the Ryder truck through the building's plate-glass windows as it pulled up. She did not see who was driving, but she got a good view of the passenger as he climbed out, walked to the back of the truck, and then started walking forward again at high speed. "It was a olive-complexion man with short hair, curly, clean-cut," she said at McVeigh's trial. She said he was wearing a blue jacket, jeans, tennis shoes, and a white baseball cap with purple flames on the sides.

A third view was offered by a catering truck driver named Rodney Johnson, who had to swerve out of the way of two people stepping in front of him on Fifth Street. To his right, Johnson noticed the Ryder truck parked against the building. To his left, he saw the brown Chevy pickup. He later identified one of the people in front of him as McVeigh. The other man, he said, was stocky, with black hair, and wearing a jacket. "I expected them to make some kind of move once they saw the truck barreling down at them," Johnson said. "They didn't flinch one bit."

At least two other witnesses claimed to be present as the cannon fuse cord burned down to detonation point. Leah Moore, a pedestrian who was walking on the north side of Fifth Street saw the Ryder truck in the handicapped zone and decided she would complain about it. Not far away from Moore, outside the YMCA building, seventy-year-old Levoid Jack Gage was waiting for a bus and noticed the Ryder truck and the brown pickup as he lit a cigarette. Both witnesses were lucky to survive.

This narrative of the final minutes could not be more different from the version presented in court. The government asserted, simply, that McVeigh lit one or both fuses while he was still driving the Ryder truck, and hopped out as soon as he parked in front of the Murrah Building. He was on his way to the Mercury, parked in an alley a few blocks away, when the bomb exploded. Nobody was with him. McVeigh offered a similar version in his prison interviews with Michel and Herbeck, describing how he popped in a pair of earplugs as he pulled the Ryder truck into position and walked purposefully behind the YMCA building at Fifth and Robinson to shield himself from the explosion.

The witnesses aren't alone, though, in insisting that they saw what they saw. They are backed up by the government's own contemporaneous documentation and by an account of the investigators' assessment of events, which appeared in the *Los Angeles Times* six months after the bombing.

A minute-by-minute timeline of the first few weeks of the investigation compiled by the Secret Service makes clear that extensive efforts were made to match the testimony from Glenn Grossman and Daina Bradley with time-lapse calculations based on video surveillance footage recovered from the Regency Towers, half a block away. At this stage, the witness accounts were treated with the utmost seriousness. Both the Secret Service timeline and the *Los Angeles Times* report, published in October 1995, allude to the lapse between the last time the Ryder truck was captured on tape and the explosion, a period of just over three minutes. In the scenario described to *Times* reporters Rick Serrano and Ronald Ostrow, the fuses were lit before the Ryder truck came to a halt—just as McVeigh later told it— leaving about a minute between the time the truck was parked and the explosion.

McVeigh was soon at the wheel of the Mercury, driving north out of Oklahoma City and back toward Kansas. The brown Chevy pickup was seen leaving in the same direction, along with a white sedan similar to the one spotted close to the Ryder truck the day before. The bombers probably did not see the explosion, but they must have heard it and perhaps surveyed the damage it caused. A deafening rumble shook the entire city, a spasm of destructive violence like no other across the Great Plains.

{ Two }

9:02 A.M.

Just after 9:00 A.M. on April 19, Stanley Brown was standing at his office window at the Oklahoma Military Academy, admiring his view of the city. The air was cool, the sky a pristine blue, and it promised to be a beautiful spring day.

That was when the detonation hit him. "You could feel the blast," he said. "It nearly blew my hat off." Some of the ceiling tiles in his office smashed to the floor, and he looked out and saw a large plume of smoke rising from the high-rise buildings three miles to the south. Major Brown was a Vietnam War veteran, a major in the Oklahoma National Guard, and a senior member of the Oklahoma County Sheriff's Office bomb squad. "You see that plume of smoke," he said, "and you know damn well, everybody needs to get their balls wrapped up and go."

He and another National Guard major ran for his pickup to head downtown. As he later wrote in a meticulous chronology, he felt a pair of explosions, which made him think there had been not one but two bombs.

• • •

AT THE FEDERAL COURTHOUSE, GARY KNIGHT OF THE OKLAHOMA City police thought he was experiencing an earthquake. He was in a soundproof, windowless courtroom on the first floor, watching his pregnant wife at work as she called a defense witness in a civil suit against four of Knight's OCPD colleagues. He couldn't hear a lot at first, but he certainly felt the initial jolt, which was like being rear-ended in a car.

The shaking grew ever stronger, the fluorescent lights swung dangerously, and ceiling tiles tumbled down. Gary Purcell, the trial judge, brought down his gavel. "Gentlemen," he said, "I believe that was a bomb."

The corridors outside were thick with smoke. People yelped and stumbled from the jury rooms on the outer side of the courthouse, where the plate glass had imploded. On his way out, Knight saw a U.S. marshal shepherding people out even though he was covered in blood and glass fragments. "At first I thought it was our building," Knight said. "The federal courthouse handled big interstate drug cases, and I thought someone had put a bomb in the courthouse." Only when he stepped outside and saw that the back of the Murrah Building was shattered did he understand which building had been hit.

BERTHA NICHOLS BARELY MADE IT THROUGH THE DOOR OF THE Regency Towers apartments when the force of the detonation spun her around and knocked her more or less into the arms of her husband, Richard. He was a maintenance man, and his first reaction was to think the Regency's boilers had blown. Then he remembered that their eight-year-old nephew Chad was still strapped into the backseat of their bright red Ford Festiva. They both dashed outside to retrieve him.

The Nicholses walked into a gust of flying glass and debris. Bertha ducked into the backseat and started tugging on the seat belt to pry

Chad free. Richard might have joined her in the effort, but he heard an extraordinary whirring sound coming from the direction of the Murrah Building and turned to look. "I seen this humongous object coming to us out the air. And it was spinning like a boomerang. And you could hear this 'woo-woo-woo-woo' noise," he later testified.

Nichols was looking at the 250-pound rear axle from the Ryder truck, and it was hurtling directly toward him. "Get down!" he screamed.

He reached into the car and pushed his wife down onto the floorboard. The axle hit the windshield on the passenger side, throwing the vehicle back several feet. Nichols lost his grip on his wife, and on the car itself, which jerked violently past his outstretched hands. He ran back to where it came to a halt on the sidewalk. "I grabbed my wife," he said, "and I grabbed Chad, and I kind of hovered over them like an old mother hen." Somehow, they all escaped serious injury.

MAJOR BROWN ARRIVED AT THE MURRAH BUILDING ELEVEN MINutes after the explosion and found a scene he described as "pure hell." Bodies and body parts were visible everywhere, along with office furniture and reams of paper spilling out over the wreckage. Screams punctured the dust-choked air, and many of the cars along Fifth Street and in the Journal Record parking lot were on fire. The sidewalks were buckled and the parking meters either twisted or plucked out of the ground. Brown smelled the distinctive odor of ammonium nitrate, mingled with the dust and smoke.

Brown immediately worried that another bomb might be ready to explode once the rescue workers, news reporters, and political leaders arrived on the scene. It was what his training had taught him to expect. Some of the firefighters and doctors and nurses gathered around and asked him what he thought, and he told them he didn't have a good feeling at all. For the next several hours, Brown halfexpected to be blown to smithereens.

• • •

GLENN WILBURN, WHO HAD BEEN PLAYING WITH HIS GRANDCHIL-dren less than two hours earlier, raced to the Murrah Building as soon as he realized it had been hit. He felt the low rumble of the blast from his office building, eighteen blocks away, and was on his way up to the roof for a better view when he learned that the explosion was right next to Chase and Colton's day-care center.

"It was kinda eerie going downtown," he later recalled. "It's a heavy business district, and there was no traffic. It was like every-thing had frozen in the city." There was no way of getting close to the Murrah Building, so he parked four blocks away and started run-ning. He came to the crest of a hill, and the full horror of the explo-sion came into view.

"I knew then that our boys were dead," he said. "There was no way they could have survived, just from looking at the scene. Where our boys were was nothing but a big pancake of rubble."

TWENTY-ONE INFANTS, TODDLERS, AND PRESCHOOLERS HAD BEEN dropped off at the America's Kids day care that morning. Three teachers were also on duty; a fourth had called in sick. The numbers might have been much higher, but three weeks earlier there had been a controversial change of management. Danielle Hunt, the popular, outgoing day-care operator and director, had been pushed out before the end of her contract to make way for a rival who was friends with an assistant building manager. Many parents were uncomfortable; they didn't know anything about the new operator, and they weren't happy that the young woman she appointed to run the center, Dana Cooper, was still a year from finishing her early childhood education degree.

Many parents had pulled their children out in protest and sent them elsewhere—an extraordinary stroke of good fortune. When the bomb exploded, one teacher was putting the infants down for a nap right next to the windows overlooking Fifth Street. Another was leading the older children in a round of "I Love You, You Love Me," from *Barney*, which was everyone's favorite television program.

Nobody near the windows stood a chance. The infants were killed instantly, and most of the others, including Dana Cooper and the two other teachers, perished as soon as the building collapsed. The six children who survived were all on the south side of the facility. Two of them, a sparky pair of red-headed toddler siblings named Rebecca and Brandon Denny, had gone to the front door to wait for a muffin delivery man, who arrived every day at 9:00 A.M. The muffin man saved their lives—although Brandon, then three years old, suffered severe head injuries and went on to have four brain surgeries.

Three more children under the age of five died in the building, all of them accompanying parents or grandparents to the ground-floor Social Security Administration office, where the worst of the death and destruction was concentrated. The visitors and government workers who crowded into the SSA's marble-floored office space on the building's north side had nowhere to escape. Those who were not skewered by flying glass, or flung against the workstations or the walls, were buried under nine floors of rubble when the side of the building came down. Forty people died in this place alone, almost a quarter of the total, and many others suffered horrific injuries. Daina Bradley, the young African-American mother who saw Timothy McVeigh's companion through the plate-glass windows moments before the detonation, heard her two small children screaming as the floor gave way and large slabs of concrete pounded down around her. She ended up trapped in the basement for hours in a pool of frigid water, her left arm pinned behind her head and her right leg wedged beneath a giant concrete boulder. Another large lump of concrete was perched directly above her face and might have killed her if it had fallen just a few more inches. Her sister, Falesha, lay nearby, her head badly injured. For a while, they could hear each other moaning. Bradley's mother and both her children perished.

The injuries and trauma suffered throughout the building were

almost beyond description. In some cases, bodies were literally shredded, or crushed under falling concrete, or impaled on filing cabinets
or pieces of flying structural steel rebar. According to the Oklahoma
City Fire Department rescue operations chief, who witnessed the
horrors firsthand, some people were blown fifty feet through six ma-
sonry block walls. Limbs were severed and blown off. One of the
dead toddlers was decapitated; another was found with the top of his
skull sheared off. A Hyundai car emblem was embedded in someone's brain.

In the fifth-floor customs office, a forty-four-year-old secretary
named Priscilla Salyers tumbled more than five floors until her body
was pressed between slabs of broken concrete. Her head and face were
clamped so tight she could not separate her teeth wide enough to spit
out her gum. In the gloom she scrabbled around with the one part of
her body she could move, her left hand, until she felt something. It
was a hand. She squeezed and tugged it closer, only to realize that it
was stone-cold and attached only to a forearm severed at the elbow.
Still, she did not let go. She was too shocked to feel the horror of the
moment. As the hours passed and she waited in growing desperation
for the rescue she fervently hoped would come, that disembodied
hand made her feel oddly comforted and less alone.

Salyers and the others most directly impacted by the bombing
bore no responsibility for the government operations at Waco or Ruby
Ridge, or any other paramilitary offensive that might have spurred
McVeigh and his coconspirators into action. The employees in the
Social Security office, and the Federal Employees Credit Union,
and the Housing and Urban Development offices, were poorly paid
bureaucrats trying to make ends meet, as were many of the people
they were servicing. They posed no threat to the Patriot Movement's
gun rights, or to their civil liberties, or to their freedom to establish
churches preaching the supremacy of the white race. More than 80
percent of the deaths—138 out of 168—were entirely unrelated to
law enforcement, the military, or even tax collecting. The Bureau of
Alcohol, Tobacco and Firearms, which was most likely at the top of

the bombers' target list, did not suffer a single fatality. Neither the IRS nor the FBI had any presence in the building. Even on McVeigh's terms, the bombing was notable only for its gratuitous carnage or, to use the chilling military term he preferred, "collateral damage."

THE ALFRED P. MURRAH BUILDING WAS NOT A PARTICULARLY strong structure, nor was it as well-protected as it should have been. At the time of its opening, in 1977, the otherwise unimaginative nine-story block of steel-reinforced concrete and glass gained attention and praise for its energy efficiency, particularly during air-conditioning season. Nothing was especially wrong with its construction—all follow-up studies agreed it had been built to specification—but neither was anything especially right.

The columns were reinforced by relatively fragile single-lengths of steel rebar. After the bombing, a study sponsored by the Federal Emergency Management Agency concluded that reinforcing the columns with hoop steel instead would have probably prevented the catastrophic pancaking effect on the building's north side. Had the Murrah been built to the specifications standard in earthquake zones, it probably would not have collapsed at all, mitigating about 80 percent of the damage and saving 80–90 percent of the lives lost. The cost of such additional reinforcement would have been negligible, about one-eighth of 1 percent of the overall construction budget.

One-eighth of 1 percent of $14 million, the price tag for the whole building, comes to about $18,000. That was less than the planners spent on drawing up their budget, an amount so small it would have caused barely a hiccough in the approval process. For $18,000, the federal government could have spared the country its worst single trauma since Pearl Harbor. The bombing would have still been a tremendous shock, and some of the injuries just as horrific. The property damage would have been almost as extensive. But the death toll would have been limited to just fifteen or twenty people.

The Ryder truck, of course, should never have been able to get so close to the building. In the years since, especially after 9/11, it has become standard for federal buildings and law enforcement agencies to be scrupulously well-guarded, with concrete barriers and other obstacles keeping vehicles at a safe distance. But even in the 1990s, federal building management agencies were well aware of the dangers, and how to address them.

In 1988, the National Research Council, part of the National Academy of Sciences, outlined the basics in a widely distributed but little-read report on improving structural integrity, establishing secure site perimeters, and deploying appropriately trained security staff to ward off risks and identify suspect characters. The NRC's report highlighted the risk of an explosive-laden vehicle, and even suggested that one of the first things to do after receiving a threat was to close any on-site day-care centers.

The Murrah Building was targeted, in part, because it complied with none of these recommendations, unlike federal buildings in Dallas or Omaha, which McVeigh and his friends also cased. It never had more than one guard on duty, a subcontractor who worked for a private security outfit rather than the government. And the Murrah Building, along with the federal courthouse and the Old Post Office court building immediately to the south, went unguarded altogether for five hours out of every twenty-four.

In hindsight, one can appreciate how nonsensical it was to assume, as some people clearly did, that because the Murrah Building received no specific threats it was not in danger. For two years before the bombing, the ATF had received agency-wide threats over Ruby Ridge and Waco, suggesting—as one of the lead authors of the National Research Council study argued—that the day care should have been moved to a different building. "I was disappointed they couldn't adopt some of the things we recommended," John Pignato, author of the NRC study, told the *Kansas City Star* a week after the bombing. "I'm not saying we could have saved everybody, but I certainly think we could have contributed to some (lives) saved."

Some people, however, were keenly aware of the potential threat. Early in 1995, Magistrate Judge Ronald Howland of the Oklahoma City federal bench met with Tom Hunt, the head of Federal Protective Service, to discuss vulnerabilities at all three downtown federal buildings. "I've always been a security guy," Howland explained. "I just felt we needed better security." His two specific concerns were the five-hour gap in security coverage on weekdays, and the alley between the federal courthouse and Old Post Office Building, where judges drove in on their way to a dedicated underground parking area. What would happen, Judge Howland asked, if some unauthorized person drove into that alley? What would happen if someone tried to blow up the place?

"Judge," Hunt replied, "I have asked everybody. I've asked my agency, I've asked the Marshals and the GSA [General Services Administration]. I've asked agencies with offices in the Murrah Building to pay for additional security." No one, he said, was willing to put up the funds. "Even my own bosses said, don't ask again."

In February 1995, Hunt was asked for a risk assessment on the Oklahoma City buildings under his jurisdiction. This resulted in a document cataloguing the security holes, along with a list of suggested remedies. But his bosses didn't want to hear this. "They told me, you have to realize the United States has not had that many terrorist attacks," Hunt said. "Everybody wanted a federal building that was really open to the public, because of the Social Security office and army recruiting and HUD in there. They wanted an atmosphere that said, come on in and do business with us."

Hunt was told to rewrite his assessment to say everything was fine as it was. To his enduring chagrin, he did as he was told—not explicitly endorsing anything other than the alarm system, but not openly criticizing anything, either. "I changed it and signed it," he said. "I should have put a page in there saying I was signing it under duress, or something to that effect . . . When that bomb went off I thought, oh man, they're going to put me in a cell." He might not have achieved anything by protesting more than he did, but he has never stopped asking what he might have done differently.

Hunt was never called to account for the bombing, no doubt because his bosses knew the efforts he'd made to beef up security. But those same bosses seemed worried about what he might reveal to the media. For weeks, they sent him on out-of-town work trips, to Brownsville to help investigate a murder, to Houston to do a risk assessment on the Johnson Space Center, to the Virgin Islands and New Mexico. "I said, why are you sending me to all these places? I've got a bombing," Hunt recalled. "My agency wanted me out of the way."

The mistrust did not end after Hunt retired in 1999. The day after he left, he said, GSA employees came to his office with bolt cutters to cut the locks off his filing cabinets. He was sure they were looking for his Murrah Building files. He had taken everything home for safekeeping. He knew private lawsuits would try to pin blame on one branch of government or another. "I was not going to leave it to others to say I had nothing to do with this," he said.

FEW ISSUES ABOUT THE BOMBING GENERATED AS MUCH INTEREST, OR misunderstanding, as the question of whether there was more than one explosion. Major Brown of the National Guard felt a double thump from three miles away, as did some survivors inside the Murrah Building. Most persuasive were seismographic readings done by the earthquake monitoring systems administered by the Oklahoma Geological Survey at the University of Oklahoma in Norman, fifteen miles south of the bomb site, which showed an initial jolt, or cluster of jolts, right around 9:02 A.M.; then a second set between seven and eleven seconds later.

For several weeks after the bombing, Raymon L. Brown of the OGS maintained that based strictly on geological data, there were probably "two events"—in other words, two bombs. Other experts, including Thomas Holzer of the U.S. Geological Survey, disagreed. Dr. Brown eventually changed his mind, stating that there were other plausible explanations for the data he had collected. By that time, though, all sorts of wild theories were running loose.

By the end of July, retired air force general Benton K. Partin sent a report to Congress, asserting that the Ryder truck bomb alone could not have caused all the damage, and that additional explosive charges must have been strapped to the pillars inside the building. General Partin made some elementary mistakes, including an over-estimation of the strength of the concrete pillars and a failure to appreciate the power of gravity to pull down part of the building once key support columns had been weakened. But these flaws in Partin's findings did not stop a number of paranoid antigovernment activists from accepting this and further alleging that the government itself had brought down the building—for political reasons too far removed from reality to be worth dissecting here.

What really happened was this: when the ammonium nitrate barrels ignited, a vast initial shock wave expanded outward in all directions, shattering windows, smashing into cars parked on the street, and ripping into the guts of the Murrah Building. Brute force is the signature of this kind of explosive; ammonium nitrate won't set fire to a building necessarily, but it will generate a destructive blast that can rip off facades and roofs, shatter walls and internal supports, and create conditions for a partial or total structural collapse.

The first wave was followed by a second one, known as the negative blast-pressure wave, so called because it is caused by air rushing to fill the vacuum created by the initial explosion. Rick Sherrow, who spent three decades as an explosives expert with the ATF, gave an authoritative explanation of the phenomenon when he wrote up his independent inquiries for *Soldier of Fortune* magazine. "During an explosive detonation," he wrote, "large quantities of expanding gases are forced outward in the form of a positive-pressure wave. This creates a vacuum behind them. As the pressure of this wave dissipates, a negative-pressure wave is formed by gases (and debris) being sucked into this vacuum. This negative wave often is powerful enough to cause additional damage, in some cases finishing off what had just been weakened by the positive wave."

In other words, if the initial blast had not already sheared or shattered the three main support columns of the building on its own, the negative blast-pressure wave might have done so. Add to that a likely reverberation or tamping effect from the surrounding buildings, and it's easy to understand why those columns on the north side gave way. The second series of jolts recorded by Dr. Brown could have been the negative blast wave, or the collapse of the building, or some combination of the two.

McVeigh and his coconspirators probably knew nothing about negative blast-pressure waves, or the other likely effects of detonating a truck bomb. And it is unlikely that they studied the structural defects of the Murrah Building, or knew about the relative fragility of the reinforced concrete. Dave Hollaway, the curiously well-informed deputy director of the CAUSE Foundation, did not hesitate to acknowledge that the bombers blundered their way to notoriety. "They got lucky because the bomb knocked the face of the building off," said Hollaway, who had some explosives knowledge from his army days. "Often, it's the collapsing of the air back in that does most of the damage. When it blew off . . . it set up a fanning wave, which shattered the pillars on one side of the building. . . . That's what resulted in the multiple damage. That was just lucky."

THE BOMBERS' LUCK WAS A NIGHTMARE FOR RESCUE WORKERS DIGging their way into the bowels of the building. Lumps of concrete were still tumbling from the wreckage, and large slabs hung precariously by what looked like thin threads of rebar, causing minute-by-minute concern about the safety of the firemen, police, nurses, and doctors. The largest slab, a 32,000-pound monster, became known as the "Mother Slab," or the "Slab from Hell." The basement area where most of the victims were trapped was dank and slowly filled with frigid water from the ruptured pipes. The rescuers named it "the Pit."

A kind of frenzy gripped everyone involved. The rescuers became as uncertain as the survivors that they would get out alive, and their nerves worked on them in strange and unpredictable ways. At one point, a group of workers digging through the rubble of mangled cabinets and desks began to find large quantities of money which they gave to FBI special agent Franklin Alexander for safekeeping. At first, Alexander shoved these bills into the cargo pockets of his fatigue pants, for lack of a better place, before he woke up to reality and told his fellow rescuers: "Forget about the money, it doesn't matter right now. Look for people!"

John Avera, an Oklahoma City police sergeant, broke down several times when the FBI interviewed him about his experiences in the building. He was asked about the friends and colleagues he had encountered, and about the people he had helped, but he was unable to visualize any of them clearly. "There were a lot of bodies. I remember seeing lots of torsos," he said, in a daze. "But I just can't remember their faces."

One victim he saw had literally been scalped—the rolls of skin and blood hanging down from his bare skull. As Avera pushed deeper into the Pit, he was hit on the shoulder by a piece of falling debris and had trouble moving his neck. His T-shirt and jeans were covered in blood; the dust penetrated his lungs and made his breathing labored. Every few minutes, he had to wipe his glasses clean from the dust and spray from broken water pipes. He tried removing his glasses, but that didn't work, either.

Then he came across Baylee Almon, a baby from the day-care center, who had celebrated her first birthday just the day before. He did not know if she was alive or dead. Her clothes and shoes had been shredded; she was wearing only her white ankle socks. He picked her up and thought her neck was broken. He cradled her so he would not inflict any further head or neck damage, and listened for any sign of breathing. There was none.

Soon, a photograph of a lifeless Baylee being carried out of the Murrah Building by a gentle giant of a firefighter would become *the* iconic image of the bombing, a moment captured by two amateur photographers whose work would be published on the front pages of newspapers and magazines around the world. But finding that firefighter was no easy task.

Avera ran outside with the baby and tried to hand her off to a nurse or doctor. Everyone he approached told him to find someone else. Nobody, it seems, could bear to hold the dead child, much less face the prospect of handing her over to her devastated parents. Avera couldn't understand it. Finally, Chris Fields of the Oklahoma City Fire Department came up to him, rather than waiting to be asked, and scooped up Baylee's remains as though it was the most natural thing in the world.

THE FIRST ASSUMPTION ABOUT THE BOMBING WAS THAT IT WAS THE work of Middle Eastern extremists. In some cases, the assumption prompted hysterical reactions directed at Muslims generally. "Shoot them now, before they get us," wrote Jeff Kamen of *New York Newsday*. But spring 1995 was also a period of heightened "chatter" from Middle Eastern groups threatening the United States, not least because Ramzi Yousef, the mastermind behind the 1993 attack on the World Trade Center in New York, had recently been arrested in Pakistan and extradited to the United States.

A few weeks earlier, the federal judiciary had received a stark security warning, not about the radical far right, or the anniversary of Waco, but a fatwa issued by Iranian extremists against the U.S. Marshals Service and the buildings it was charged with protecting. (This was perhaps one reason Judge Purcell so quickly believed the rumbling in his soundproof courtroom was a bomb.) The grievance resulted from an episode during the World Trade Center bombing trial, when a deputy marshal accidentally stepped on a copy of the Koran in a courtroom scuffle. There was no indication that Oklahoma City was likely to be singled out for attack, and one of Purcell's colleagues said the briefing was mostly about preventing intruders from bursting into the building to create a hostage-type situation.

The Middle Eastern theme dominated cable news coverage for the first several hours. One of the earliest eyewitness reports spoke of three Arabs driving away from the bomb site. A local Jordanian-American, Abraham Ahmad, shot to the top of the suspect list because he fit an eyewitness description and was booked on a flight to Italy directly after the explosion. Ahmad was grilled by customs officials in Chicago, then intercepted when he reached London and sent back to Washington for questioning by the FBI. His luggage traveled on to Rome, where local police pulled it apart on arrival.

The government took no chances with anyone else, checking and double-checking passports at Will Rogers International Airport in Oklahoma City and assigning a dozen Arabic-language translators to decipher surveillance traffic. The translators were kept on even after it became clear this was a domestic attack, to the irritation of the Pentagon, which had loaned them to the FBI.

The real experts, those federal and local law enforcement agents with direct experience of the radical right, were never in doubt about the true nature of what had happened. About an hour after the bombing, Oklahoma's police and fire chiefs were standing on the north side of Fifth Street with the assistant city manager and Bob Ricks, the special agent in charge of the FBI's Oklahoma City office. They were contemplating the ghastly scene when Ricks, unprompted, looked at the others and said, "This is the anniversary of Waco."

As the FBI's public face throughout the fifty-one-day Branch Davidian siege two years earlier, Ricks well knew the fury it unleashed. Militia groups had attacked him in their newsletters, and he was already wondering if the bomb had been meant for him.

A similar gut feeling gripped one of Ricks's longest-standing FBI colleagues, Danny Coulson, just recently appointed as special agent in charge of the Dallas office. Coulson knew the legacy of Jim Ellison and Wayne Snell from his time in charge of the bureau's Hostage Rescue Team. Exactly ten years earlier, on April 19, 1985, Coulson ordered the HRT to move in on a heavily armed religious compound in rural Arkansas run by Ellison under the name of the Covenant, the Sword, and the Arm of the Lord. The four-day siege ended without a shot being fired, largely thanks to Coulson's patience and the intervention of Robert Millar, the patriarch of Elohim City, who acted as a go-between and induced Ellison to surrender peacefully.

Coulson later wrote that when he heard about the bombing, he grabbed his weapons and drove as fast as he could through a driving rainstorm up I-35 to Oklahoma City. On his way, he received a phone call from Rita Braver, a correspondent with CBS.

"Everybody in Washington is saying it's Middle Eastern," she said. "Do you think that's right?"

"No it's not. It's a Bubba job."

"It looks like all the other truck bombings coming out of the Middle East," Braver persisted.

"It's Bubbas," Coulson said. "It's April 19."

TIM MCVEIGH MADE A REMARKABLY CLEAN GETAWAY, THOUGH ANY number of things could have gone wrong for him. The Mercury was leaking oil. It had a lousy transmission, a questionable battery, and a broken fuel gauge. On its rear was a large primer stain, making it easy to spot if anyone decided it was suspicious. McVeigh's task was to navigate his way out of the city without being spotted by the police officers, firefighters, and volunteer rescue workers rushing in the opposite direction. He could have broken down or been stopped at any moment.

McVeigh's only mistake was not having a license plate for the back of the Mercury Marquis. After months of planning, it was extraordinary that McVeigh could have slipped up over something so elementary. It is a wrinkle in the story that has generated endless theories but almost no cogent explanations. The FBI scoured the streets looking for the license plate; and at least two witnesses reported seeing it hanging by a single bolt in the days leading up to the bombing. But the feds found nothing. Later, McVeigh said he removed the plate when he stashed the car in an alley on April 16, presumably because he did not want an overcurious cop or traffic warden to trace the car back to him. But he never explained why he didn't reattach it.

The government ascribed the oversight to recklessness or simple incompetence. But when McVeigh bought the Mercury five days earlier in Junction City—to replace a Pontiac station wagon with a blown head gasket—he had taken care to switch his Arizona plates to the new car, even though they were the wrong plates. "Nice and solid, two screws right on top," he told one of his defense lawyers shortly after his arrest. At least on April 14, it was very important to him not to drive around without plates.

The best way to understand the scenario is if McVeigh was not alone. Everything he did up to the moment he drove away from the Murrah Building suggests the Mercury was intended not as a getaway vehicle but rather as a "drop car"—a vehicle to carry him a short distance away before being ditched. That, in turn, implies that he was expecting a ride the rest of the way.

On the front passenger seat he left a sealed envelope stuffed with documents describing the motivation for the bombing, a collection that acted both as a manifesto and as a signature taking responsibility for the carnage. They included a historical article on the battle of Lexington and Concord, provocative quotes from Samuel Adams, Patrick Henry, Thomas Jefferson, and Winston Churchill; a copy of the Declaration of Independence, on the back of which McVeigh had scrawled: "Obey the Constitution of the United States, and we won't shoot you"; a chunky paragraph from John Locke arguing for the legitimacy of war against those who would take away our liberty; and a long passage from *The Turner Diaries,* in which the narrator justifies the car bomb attack on FBI headquarters as a message to the "politicians and the bureaucrats" that they can run but not hide.

Had these documents been discovered in an empty car, they would have generated endless speculation and analysis in the media, as McVeigh later said he hoped they would. If he was planning to drive the Mercury just a short distance, it becomes more understandable that he would not want to spend more than a few hundred dollars on it. He needed to transfer the Pontiac's license plates for the trip down from Junction City so nobody would stop him en route. Equally, it made sense to remove the license plates when he stashed the car, so nobody could easily link him to the Mercury while it sat unattended for three days. McVeigh left a note under the windshield: "Not abandoned. Please do not tow. Will move by April 23. (Needs battery & cable.)" And he put a piece of tissue paper over the gas cap to alert him if someone had tried to siphon off any fuel. According to Terry Nichols, who accompanied McVeigh to Oklahoma City on Easter Sunday, he had the Arizona license plate in his hand when they rode back to Kansas. When Nichols asked why he had unscrewed it from the Mercury, McVeigh said he didn't want it stolen.

After the bombing, the car's ownership was bound to be traced through the VIN number, which was clearly visible through the windshield. Since McVeigh could easily have bought a drop car under an assumed name, at a dealership where he would not be recognized (unlike the one in Junction City, where he knew the owner), we must assume he wanted this to happen. One suspects his real desire was to enjoy the public notoriety associated with the bombing while living the life of a full-time outlaw and, perhaps, planning and carrying out other attacks. That's what Earl Turner did in *The Turner Diaries.* And it was something he more or less announced in a letter to his sister Jennifer, eighteen months or so before the bombing. "If someone does start looking for me," he wrote, "(I have 'ears' all over the country), that's when I disappear. . . . Believe me, if that necessity ever comes to pass, it will be very difficult for anyone to find me."

Another reason to believe the Mercury was meant as a drop car was that McVeigh had another vehicle. This was not discussed at trial, or disclosed to the news media at the time. But on January 4, 1995, McVeigh bought a ten-year-old Ford Ranger pickup truck in Michigan. The FBI's records say nothing more about it—where it was kept, what kind of condition it was in, whether it was ever recovered—but this could have been the vehicle McVeigh intended to use after he made his getaway from Oklahoma City.

SOMETHING CLEARLY WENT WRONG WITH THE "DROP CAR" PLAN, BE-cause McVeigh ended up driving the Mercury out of Oklahoma City and another sixty miles to the north. Perhaps he panicked and felt there was no time to stop and switch cars. Or a fight broke out between McVeigh and his companions. The FBI came to believe McVeigh wanted to kill the kids in the day-care center as revenge for the children who perished at Waco. Did the others, believing they were targeting the federal courthouse, try to stop him? Or did they abandon him once they saw the scale of the slaughter they had perpetrated?

In McVeigh's account, he walked alone from the Ryder truck through a maze of back alleys as the fuse wire burned toward detonation point. He was just past the YMCA, kitty-corner from the north entrance to the Murrah Building, when the explosion rocked everything around him. He dodged a severed power line whipping dangerously in his direction, hopped out of the way of a tumbling pile of bricks, shrugged at a woman coming out of a shop, swapped glances with a couple standing forlornly in front of a shattered storefront, and exchanged a line of conversation with a private mail deliveryman on his rounds.

"Man," McVeigh reported the man saying, "for a second I thought that was us that blew up."

"Yeah, so did I," McVeigh said he replied.

McVeigh walked to his car in an alley off Eighth Street, checked his gas tank, and tried several times to start the Mercury. It coughed and sputtered but would not engage. Just as he was about to give up, it kicked into gear. He navigated the one-way system on to Broadway, which runs parallel to I-235, paused as a fleet of police cars and fire engines hared toward downtown, and turned north onto the freeway back to Kansas.

None of the bystanders McVeigh described has ever been traced—one of many problems with his account. The Mercury was probably parked much closer to the Ryder truck, as discussed in the last chapter. In the minutes after the explosion, two more eyewitnesses saw McVeigh and the muscular, olive-skinned character in an alley a block and a half southeast of the Murrah Building—a different direction from the one in McVeigh's version. Germaine Johnston, a Housing and Urban Development worker who was hit in the head by flying glass and debris, staggered out on her own and thought immediately of walking to her husband's office to tell him she was all right. On her way, she saw a man she later identified as McVeigh, as well as a second, shorter, darker man. She said they were standing next to a yellow Mercury just like one she and her husband had once owned.

"What happened?" the McVeigh figure asked.

Johnston told him.

"A lot of people killed?"

"I don't know," she responded weakly. Johnston was thrown by the question, because he seemed entirely indifferent to the fact that she was bleeding from the head, caked in concrete dust, and wet from the ruptured pipes that had sprayed her on her way out of the office. "I thought he was going to ask me if he could help me, or if I was okay, or something," Johnston recounted. "Several people had already done that."

Later, Johnston realized something else noteworthy. At the spot where she talked to the McVeigh figure, the alley had a clear view of the Murrah Building. A few yards farther back or forward, the building would have been obscured.

AT A DINGY MOTEL OUTSIDE SPOKANE, WASHINGTON, A TWENTY-two-year-old skinhead named Chevie Kehoe banged on the door of the manager's living quarters and insisted he turn on the television.

Kehoe was then at the dawn of a criminal career that would send him on a vicious cross-country robbing, bombing, and killing spree. Lately he had been living on and off at the Shadows Motel and RV Park, which he used as a gathering point for fellow neo-Nazis and skinheads who wanted to build an Aryan paradise in the Pacific Northwest. The manager, Jeff Brown, was more or less a friend who chose to turn a blind eye to gunshots or loud pops coming from Kehoe's quarters. "Bud," as Brown called Kehoe, would experiment with small explosives and blasting caps in his room, setting them off inside the pages of motel phone books. In addition to a library of do-it-yourself guerrilla warfare manuals, Kehoe kept an arsenal of shoulder weapons and explosives, including a supply of fertilizer, mothballs, and black powder, which he would cook up into home-made bombs.

Brown was asleep when he heard the banging at his door. Kehoe was yelling for him to turn the TV on to CNN. "Ten minutes later," Brown told a newspaper reporter, "the news is breaking there was a bomb going off in Oklahoma City."

Kehoe looked thrilled. "It's about time," he said.

Several days earlier, Kehoe told Brown that something would happen on April 19 to "wake people up." "I look back on it," Brown said, "and he obviously knew about it beforehand."

Kehoe moved in the same circles as Tim McVeigh. Both traveled the gun-show circuit and dropped in on radical communities around the country. In the months before the bombing, Chevie and his younger brother Cheyne spent extended periods at Elohim City, taking shooting lessons from Andreas Strassmeir and participating in discussions on how to bring down the government. A former associate of Chevie's, who accompanied him twice to Elohim City, later told the feds he remembered a conversation in late 1994 about a "delivery" that needed to be made very soon. Despite repeated inquiries, Kehoe refused to explain what this delivery was.

WAYNE SNELL HAD A RESTLESS NIGHT. HE ROSE AT 1:45 A.M., PUTting on his day clothes and monitoring the television outside his death row cell, which was kept on at his request. Between news bulletins, he sat at his desk and wrote. At 4:00 A.M., he ordered a hearty breakfast of eggs, chicken sausage, grits, biscuits, and gravy, which put him to sleep for an hour or so. He woke in time to watch the 6:00 A.M. news, before dozing off again. Much of the local coverage was about Snell's execution scheduled for 9:00 P.M. that night. He seemed pleased that the tone was not unduly negative. At this stage, he still had his final appeals pending and was hoping for a last-minute reprieve.

Once news from Oklahoma City broke, Snell's guards noticed an immediate change in demeanor. He chuckled, nodded in approval, and seemed to find a renewed inner calm. He spent much of his last day writing and munching on sunflower seeds. In the afternoon, for his final meal, he downed six pieces of fried crappie, hushpuppies with buttermilk, a salad with blue-cheese dressing, and three-quarters of a large white onion.

According to his lawyer, Jeffrey Rosenzweig, Snell had misgivings about the way the bombing was carried out. He reportedly told his attorney that a professional bombing crew, the sort he associated with during his criminal heyday, would never have targeted children. It is impossible to know if this was a genuine reservation, or a way of distancing himself a little. The bombing certainly did not dampen

Snell's revolutionary spirit—quite the contrary. As he was strapped down and wheeled into the death chamber, he issued a final statement that spooked everyone who heard it.

"Governor Tucker," he said, "look over your shoulder. Justice is on the way. I wouldn't trade places with you or any of your political cronies. Hell has victory. I am at peace."

OTHER MEMBERS OF THE RADICAL FAR RIGHT WERE UNHAPPY WITH the bombing, understanding that it would not be a catalyst to additional antigovernment action so much as a huge screeching brake. Some of McVeigh's fellow revolutionaries were disgusted by the deaths of blameless civilians. Even those who did not fault the bombing's morality still attacked its operational stupidity. Kale Kelly, an Aryan Nations adherent and antigovernment revolutionary, said bluntly that McVeigh should have killed more federal agents and fewer innocents. Andreas Strassmeir, who acknowledged knowing and liking McVeigh, thought a bomb was the wrong weapon and a public office building the wrong target. "The whole militia movement basically died that night," Strassmeir said many years later. "Whatever he did achieve worked against anything he believed in."

Some of the statements coming out of the Patriot Movement were, of course, self-serving. Nobody wanted to catch heat from the vast government investigation—least of all Strassmeir, who later came under close scrutiny as a possible suspect. But the reactions were also unmistakably tinged with contempt, if not anger, toward McVeigh. "Didn't he case the place?" Strassmeir asked incredulously. "You're talking about a public building. Even Tim knew not everyone in there was a murderous BATF agent. You can't be that dumb."

Some people dropped hints that McVeigh had unilaterally changed the intended plan, or that the attack was much more vicious than they had been led to believe ahead of time. One was Jack Oliphant, a one-armed World War II veteran who led the Arizona

Patriot Movement and almost certainly knew McVeigh from his time in the dusty desert town of Kingman. A couple of weeks before the bombing, one of Oliphant's neighbors overheard him saying that "something big" would happen before the end of the month. In one of many newspaper interviews after the bombing, Oliphant said: "The bastard has put the Patriot movement back 30 years. . . . If he'd blown up a federal building at night, he'd be a hero." Another hint came from a white supremacist prison gang leader named Bobby Joe Farrington, who told the FBI that McVeigh's job had been to blow up the federal courthouse as part of a national campaign against judges who displeased the movement. Farrington said he had met McVeigh, whom he knew as "Sergeant Mac," and could only conclude he was an idiot who had "fucked it up."

ABOUT AN HOUR AFTER THE EXPLOSION, A TALL, ATHLETIC MAN WITH a goatee, wearing blue jeans, a ball cap, and a blue windbreaker, made a dramatic appearance at a shattered window on the Murrah Building's ninth floor. To his left was a makeshift sign on which he had scrawled ATF - TRAPPED - NINTH FLOOR. In his right hand was a small lockbox.

Special Agent Luke Franey said he had been on the phone with an ATF colleague when he felt the walls and ceiling falling in. He could hear screams from the Drug Enforcement Administration next door. A gust of air pressure flung him out of his chair and into a hallway, where he landed, covered in rubble. He may or may not have lost consciousness, but after checking himself for injuries—and finding nothing but "minor scrapes and cuts"—he kicked and chopped his way through a wall, only to realize with horror that the DEA's part of the building was gone. Then he went to his fellow agents' desks, scooped up as many documents and keepsakes as he could find and put them in the lockbox he held up in the window. He also picked up his own children's savings bonds and some family photographs.

Franey told this story for years afterward, but something about it did not add up. On his way out of the building, he said, he broke through three Sheetrock walls with his bare hands and climbed down an outside ledge at a perilous forty-five-degree angle before descending a blood-smeared staircase. His hands were banged up, and he said he had them bandaged as soon as he could. He also had a cut on his head.

Yet in a video shot later that morning, Franey's hands are not bandaged, and he can be seen vigorously shaking hands with Bob Heady, the commander of the sheriff's office bomb squad, with no obvious discomfort. There are no cuts on his head, or any other indication of bodily injury. While other survivors were caked in dust and grime, his face and clothes remained clean.

Danny Coulson of the FBI, who helped gather the physical evidence during the first week of the investigation, said he had no problem climbing up the southeastern staircase and walking into the remains of the ATF office without jumping onto ledges or clambering across broken Sheetrock. Franey's ATF colleague Harry Eberhardt concurred, saying the route "was used many times by searchers and other agents." Even John Magaw, the ATF director, made little attempt to defend Franey when asked about him in 2009. "He sometimes overstates things," Magaw said. "I think people who have worked with him have learned to take these things with a grain of salt."

What really happened? Did Franey enter the building after the bombing on a sensitive mission to retrieve documents, or weapons? Magaw said he did not know but did not rule it out. If Franey was in radio contact with his colleagues, as he said, why make such a spectacle of his presence?

Franey was not the only ATF agent with a questionable story that morning. His boss, Alex McCauley, the ATF's resident agent in charge in Oklahoma City, claimed he was in an elevator when the explosion occurred. He said that he and DEA agent Dave Schickedanz went into free fall, plunging from the eighth floor to the third. Three times, with smoke wafting in, they tried and failed to open the elevator doors. On the fourth try, they squeezed themselves out to the third floor and made their way to a stairwell, bringing ten or fifteen other survivors with them. When they realized the stairwell had crumbled, they used a bedsheet as a rope to shimmy down toward a "chain of rescuers," who brought them all to safety.

This story was circulated in an ATF news release and repeated in court by Joe Hartzler, McVeigh's chief government prosecutor. But two technicians working for the Midwest Elevator Company—Duane James and Oscar Johnson—challenged it. They were on the scene within minutes to see if anyone had been trapped. Nobody was, and the technicians said there was no way any of the elevators could have free-fallen. Each elevator had a mechanical brake at the top that would freeze the hoist ropes, and there was another brake beneath each elevator car in case the ropes got cut. None of these backup systems was even activated; the ropes were all intact.

The technicians said McCauley and Schickedanz probably slid no more than four or five feet as the emergency brake came on. "If you fell six floors and it was a free fall," James said, "it would be like jumping out of a six-story building. I'd ask 'em how long they were in the hospital and how lucky they were to survive."

The elevator story became a public relations nightmare for the ATF, and almost certainly factored in the decision to transfer McCauley quietly out of Oklahoma City in the summer of 1995. He left the ATF shortly after.

At the time of the bombing, the ATF was fighting for its survival because of the Waco disaster, and one of John Magaw's main goals was to restore its public image. He saw the bombing as an opportunity to paint the agency in heroic colors, and his staff was irresistibly drawn to Franey and McCauley's gritty survival stories. But the holes in those stories did the ATF real damage, because they eroded the agency's credibility within the bombing task force and spawned all sorts of wild theories on the media fringes and on the Internet. To the extent that the ATF jumped on the stories as publicity material, they backfired. When Magaw was asked in a 2010 interview about the photograph of Franey in the ninth-floor window, he responded: "I wonder if that was one of the pictures that was staged." The picture was, in fact, taken by a local news photographer unstaged. But Magaw's response might have given away more than he meant to.

TIM MCVEIGH WAS CRUISING SMOOTHLY TOWARD THE KANSAS border. A few miles past the tiny town of Perry, he saw a highway patrol trooper's vehicle roaring up behind him at more than ninety miles per hour. The trooper, Charlie Hanger, was on his way to help a distressed motorist. He had been called to Oklahoma City earlier that morning, only to be turned around and told to return to regular patrolling duties. The Mercury was sticking to the speed limit, and Hanger might not have noticed it at all, if the large patch of primer on the left rear panel had not guided his eye to the missing license plate. He was a gruff, no-nonsense trooper who had cruised up and down Oklahoma's highways for nineteen years, and he rarely missed a driver committing an obvious infraction. He slowed as he fell in behind the Mercury, took a second look at the back bumper, and turned on his siren.

McVeigh had to think fast. He had a loaded Glock pistol in his pocket, as well as a backup ammunition clip on his belt, so he could easily take care of Hanger if he wanted. But what was worse for him: a dead cop and a race to stay ahead of a multistate manhunt, or the inconvenience of a traffic ticket or two?

In McVeigh's own account, he decided to spare Hanger because he was a state trooper, not a federal officer. But the decision cannot have been made calmly. A calm man would have stayed put, using the time Hanger took to lean into his window to decide whether to hand over his license or put a bullet in the trooper's brain. McVeigh, oddly, decided to step out of the car right away.

Hanger wasn't taking any chances. Two weeks earlier, on this same stretch of road, a driver had fired at one of Hanger's highway patrol colleagues. So he crouched behind his open door for cover, waiting until he could see McVeigh's hands, before moving forward.

Hanger told McVeigh why he'd been stopped and asked for a bill of sale to prove the Mercury was his; McVeigh said the dealer was still filling out the paperwork. Hanger expressed some skepticism. When McVeigh was asked for his driver's license, he reached into his back pocket, revealing a suspicious bulge under the armpit of his windbreaker. Hanger took the license, ordered McVeigh to lift up both hands, and told him to unzip his jacket very slowly.

"I have a gun," McVeigh conceded.

Hanger pressed his left hand against the bulge in McVeigh's jacket and used his right hand to push the barrel of his own pistol directly against McVeigh's head.

"Get your hands up and turn around," he said. He frog-marched McVeigh to the back of the Mercury and spread-eagled him across the trunk.

McVeigh complied, and told him: "My weapon is loaded."

Hanger responded: "So is mine."

Hanger lifted the Glock out of McVeigh's pocket and threw it onto the shoulder. McVeigh told the trooper about the ammunition clip and a knife in his jacket. Hanger took both and threw them on the shoulder also. Then he handcuffed McVeigh, pushed his gun against McVeigh's back, and walked him back to his vehicle.

"You know that one wrong move on your part could have gotten you shot," Hanger told him.

McVeigh shrugged. "It's possible."

Hanger wanted to establish just how tough a customer he was dealing with. McVeigh sought to minimize the concealed weapon, saying he had a permit for one in New York. But Hanger was hardly reassured by a Black Talon "cop killer" bullet he found inside the Glock. Was the gun or car stolen? McVeigh had no registration papers or proof of insurance.

The trooper radioed in the Mercury's VIN number and the

Glock's registration number; both were clean. He also asked the dispatcher to run a check on McVeigh, to see if he had prior arrests or outstanding warrants. He did not.

McVeigh seemed resigned to spending a day or two in jail. If he was lucky, he could arrange bail and still vanish underground before anyone associated him with the bombing. It certainly helped that Hanger had not touched the sealed white envelope on the passenger seat. When they left for the Noble County lockup, it stayed where it was.

They talked briefly on the twenty-minute ride into Perry. McVeigh was anxious to get his Glock back; Hanger said he'd have to sort that out with the court. McVeigh asked Hanger what kind of service pistol he was carrying—it was a SIG 228—and even dared him to drive his car faster. Hanger didn't take the bait, but took comfort in the jocular tone. McVeigh felt calmer, too: although his wrists were cuffed and he was heading into custody, nobody was yet associating him with the bloodshed in Oklahoma City.

Shortly after 10:30 a.m., as McVeigh was being booked, the Oklahoma City Fire Department announced the discovery of another bomb at the Murrah Building. Word spread that it might be bigger than the first—exactly what Stanley Brown had dreaded all morning. On Fifth Street, where Brown was stationed, the reaction was pure panic. People sprinted as fast as they could across the Robinson intersection and over a small hill. Firefighters stopped some of them and asked where the secondary device might be, but nobody could say.

Brown was amazed to see Bob Heady, the commander of his own bomb squad unit, running away with the crowd. Before Brown had time to think, he was running after him. "I had to tackle his ass," Brown said. Heady came crashing to the ground.

"Bob," Brown cried, "you're the goddamn bomb squad!"

Heady was not pleased, but Brown talked him out of jumping

back up and making another run for it. "I couldn't understand it," Brown recounted. "I mean, he's a Vietnam veteran. Maybe I was dumb as dirt but my attitude was, we needed to be there."

Inside the building, and especially in the Pit, where collapsed floors had ensnared the largest number of victims, the rescue workers did not know how to break the news that they were being ordered out. A suburban fire crew had been sitting with Daina Bradley while she was pinned down in six inches of freezing water. She begged them not to go. They did not know what to say, and neither did Mike Shannon, head of the fire department's rescue operations. "If she were my wife, I would not have wanted her to be left alone," Shannon later wrote. He crawled into the hole where Bradley lay, removed his helmet, and offered up a prayer. When a deputy came to retrieve him, he told Bradley the team would be back with better tools and equipment, a white lie designed to make her feel a little better.

It has never been proven that there was a valid reason for the bomb scare. Shannon was told a device was found on a staircase, but none was ever identified. Danny Defenbaugh, a senior FBI agent who was not in Oklahoma City on April 19 but later headed up the investigation, heard that the scare was triggered by a gas leak. To complicate matters, the FBI received calls that two possible bombers were running away from the scene. The "bombers," Defenbaugh said, turned out to be technicians from the Oklahoma Gas & Electric Company, who were there to cut off the building's gas supply.

A more sinister explanation, which federal and local authorities have tried to deny over the years, was that the evacuation was ordered to recover ordinance and weaponry that government agencies were storing illegally in the building.

When Don Browning, a dog handler with the Oklahoma City police, was ordered out, he met a woman wearing a red jacket from either the ATF or the FBI, who told him the building had been secured so the feds could recover some crucial "files." Browning immediately suspected the "files" were ordinance and weaponry. When he entered the building the first time, he recognized boxes of small arms ammunition and blocks of C-4 plastic explosive. "I'm real familiar with C-4," Browning explained. He would not be the last person to tell a similar story.

Randy Yount, the state park ranger, was part of a group of rescue workers led down to the basement by an ATF agent. They pried open a door and had to remove large chunks of concrete before going further. He thought they were on a straightforward rescue mission until he and the others were led into a concrete-walled room packed with rifles, pistols, hand grenades, plastic explosives, and "thousands and thousands" of ammunition rounds. The ATF supervisor, whom Yount did not know, referred to this material as "evidence." Yount remembered him saying: "There are some things here that we need to get out of the building. . . . If anybody has a problem with not talking about what you are fixing to do, you are welcome to leave. Nobody will hold it against you or reprimand you." They all stayed, carrying the crates to the plaza area on the south side of the building and loading them into white vans so they could be taken to a secure storage facility.

Nobody in authority has ever fully confirmed this account. Oklahoma Highway Patrol officer Shane Slovacek later told the FBI he knew of an ATF vault full of confiscated weapons and small-arms ammunition, some of which turned up in the debris. The sheriff's department video—the one capturing Luke Franey's unbandaged hands—included footage of rescue workers lifting semiautomatic weapons out of the rubble. Yet another witness, an elevator company inspector named Virgil Steele, said in a sworn statement that he had helped the ATF carry out a vast assortment of weapons and materiel, including AR-15 and M-16 assault rifles, handguns, thousands of rounds of ammunition, hand grenades, C-4, and at least three "antitank missiles or shoulder/hip–type rocket launchers."

John Magaw, the ATF director, confirmed that the 10:30 A.M. alert was really about weapons and explosive materials that belonged to government agencies. He remembered that agents recovered two black cases containing high-powered weapons that morning; they had been stored either in the ATF office or the Secret Service office, both on the ninth floor.

The interruption lasted forty-five minutes. In his handwritten journal, Stanley Brown noted that the fire department made great efforts to figure out what triggered the bomb scare, without success. John Haynie, the head of the Oklahoma Highway Patrol's tactical team, reported much the same. He had made repeated efforts to find out who raised the alarm, but he never found anybody—"or, at least, no one who would admit it."

AT AROUND 11:00 A.M., CHARLIE HANGER ESCORTED TIM MCVEIGH up to the fourth-floor booking area inside the Noble County court-house. A television set was on, with uninterrupted coverage of the bombing. Hanger exchanged expressions of dismay with Marsha Moritz, the employee processing the jail admissions. McVeigh said nothing, and did not react. He glanced at the television a few times, but mostly he looked away.

Hanger cited McVeigh on four charges: transporting a loaded firearm in a motor vehicle, unlawfully carrying a weapon, failure to display a current number plate, and failure to maintain proof of liability insurance. Moritz asked McVeigh to take off his jacket and empty his pockets. He was carrying two commemorative Revolution-ary War coins, a spare pair of earplugs, some aspirin, four .45-caliber bullets, and $255 in cash. Most striking to her was his T-shirt. The front had a picture of Abraham Lincoln and the words SIC SEMPER TYRANNIS, which John Wilkes Booth shouted after delivering the fatal gunshot. "Thus ever to tyrants." The back showed a tree and the Thomas Jefferson quote: THE TREE OF LIBERTY MUST BE REFRESHED FROM TIME TO TIME WITH THE BLOOD OF PATRIOTS AND TYRANTS.

Moritz took mug shots and asked McVeigh some routine questions, which he answered willingly until she requested the name of his closest family member. McVeigh acted as if he hadn't heard. So she asked again. Hanger walked over to the booking counter as a precaution. Moritz explained that she wanted a name only for emergencies; she was not going to contact McVeigh's family to tell them he had been arrested.

Hanger remembered McVeigh's Michigan driver's license and asked about the address listed on it: 3616 N. Van Dyke Road, in the tiny farming town of Decker. "Who lives there?" he asked.

McVeigh said it was a place where he had stayed a number of times, and that it belonged to the brother of a friend he met in the military.

"Well," Moritz suggested, "do you want to use that?"

McVeigh agreed, and offered up the name James Nichols. He had been using the address for several days, ensuring that any law enforcement interest would lead to one, if not both Nichols brothers. The Nicholses themselves later saw this as one of a number of signs that he had set them up as fall guys. Many in the Patriot Movement later credited McVeigh with a certain nobility for keeping his mouth shut and denying the existence of a broader conspiracy, but on the day of his arrest he didn't hesitate to lead law enforcement straight to two of his best friends.

Moritz and Hanger had no way of grasping this and saw no reason to suspect that this calm, well-spoken young man had anything to do with the ghastly images on TV. At most, they were aware of something a little off. After McVeigh was escorted to his jail cell, Moritz said to Hanger: "Wasn't that a strange T-shirt that he had on?"

"What do you mean?" Hanger asked.

"Well, it had a strange saying on it," she said.

"Well," he responded, "I didn't read it."

● ● ●

BACK IN OKLAHOMA CITY, CHARLIE HANGER'S BOSSES IN THE HIGH-way patrol picked up on McVeigh's arrest within a couple of hours, because they were interested in anyone who had been stopped in the immediate aftermath of the bombing. OHP passed on the information to the governor's office, and Dennis Dutsch, the governor's security chief, tried to alert the FBI.

The FBI agent Dutsch spoke to, though, told him flatly he was not interested. "We don't have anybody in custody," he insisted. Dutsch never got the agent's name, but he understood his message. "What he was saying was, we're doing our job. Stay out of it," Dutsch said.

And so McVeigh went undiscovered by the feds for another forty-eight hours.

SHORTLY AFTER THE EVACUATION ORDER WAS RESCINDED, DR. ANDY Sullivan received a call at the Oklahoma City Children's Hospital. The rescuers needed an orthopedic surgeon to help extricate a woman trapped under a pile of rubble and Sullivan, the orthopedics chair at the University of Oklahoma medical school, was the man for the job. Sullivan knew he was risking his life, so he took off his wedding ring and removed the wallet from his trouser pocket. If he died, he wanted his wife and sons to have these as keepsakes.

Sullivan arrived with a rudimentary amputation kit including scalpels, a saw, various tourniquets, anesthetics, and tranquilizers. A fire crew led him and his fellow surgeon David Tuggle to the Pit, where Daina Bradley was lying. She was breathing only with great difficulty and her skin was dust-gray. Just getting close was a challenge. Tuggle was too large to climb into the space where she was trapped; Sullivan, who was shorter, could do so only after a firefighter hacked off a jutting piece of metal. Even then he had to crawl in, military combat–style, and lie on top of her with his feet pointing up toward her face.

Sullivan began experimenting with a nylon rope he planned to use as a tourniquet only to be interrupted by another evacuation order. The firefighters told the doctors they had to leave immediately.

"Don't leave me, don't leave me!" Bradley screamed. "I'm going to die!"

"It was gut-wrenching," Sullivan said. "You don't leave somebody that's going to die." But they had to anyway.

THE NEW EVACUATION WAS PROMPTED BY THE DISCOVERY OF A BOX, eighteen inches square and three feet deep, which was marked "Class A Explosives." Rescue workers discovered it in the rubble of the day-care center. The sheriff's department bomb technicians thought it was a rocket-propelled grenade launcher, but actually it was an antitank TOW missile, which had tumbled out of a fifth-floor vault belonging to U.S. Customs.

The missile's warhead was empty, but it still qualified as a destructive device under the National Firearms Act, because it contained rocket fuel. "It's an extremely dangerous weapon [even] without the warhead," said Bob Sanders, a former assistant director of the ATF. "Possession of a TOW missile is perfectly lawful for a law enforcement agency . . . but storage in a public building is against public safety and against the law."

As the FBI later established, customs had no paperwork on it. The agency had obtained three inert TOW missiles from the Anniston Army Depot in Alabama in the late 1980s for use in a sting operation, but the official documentation showed that all three had been returned. So there was no ready explanation of what this missile was doing in the Murrah Building at all.

The sheriff's department and highway patrol transported it safely down a fire truck ladder and into the secure trailer tank of the sheriff's office bomb squad truck. Oddly, when Bob Heady, the bomb squad chief, filed his report, he wrote that the missile arrived at the sheriff's department safe storage facility at 11:00 A.M., more than three hours earlier than the actual time.

This could have been a mistake, but it also suggested, erroneously, that the TOW missile was the cause of the *first* evacuation order—the one for which nobody would take responsibility. By the time the federal trials were over in the late 1990s, this revised order of events had become received wisdom, stated as fact by the FBI and the media.

But we know from Stanley Brown's contemporaneous notes, from an exhaustive account written by Mike Shannon of the Oklahoma City Fire Department, from John Haynie's statements to the FBI, and from other witnesses, that the TOW missile was discovered between 1:30 P.M. and 1:45 P.M. and removed about twenty minutes later.

Heady did another odd thing: As soon as he learned that Stanley Brown was taking notes for a journal, he ordered him to put them in a safe and never take them out again. When Brown was asked why he thought Heady would issue such an order, he said: "I don't know. Bob's a squirrelly man."

But Brown did as he was told and did not show the notes to anyone for fifteen years.

WHILE DR. SULLIVAN AND DR. TUGGLE WERE WAITING FOR THE all-clear, they created a plan to extricate Daina Bradley. They knew they had to be quick, and they also knew they could not risk administering an anesthetic given her weakened state. The most they could offer was a tranquilizer to help her forget the ordeal once it was over. It was a grim prospect. They needed her to remain fully conscious while they hacked off her leg under the worst of circumstances.

When they first shared their plan with her, she cried and shook her head in disbelief, saying she couldn't tolerate the pain. They told her that if they couldn't cut off her leg, they would have to leave, because the building was in danger of collapsing at any moment. Slowly, she changed her mind. Sullivan had almost no room to maneuver in the confined space and realized he could not cut through her calf bones, as he would have preferred. He would have to cut through the ligaments in her knee, greatly increasing the risk that she would bleed to death. He had to do this with his left hand, even though he was right-handed. The only light would be from the lamp on his fire-rescue helmet.

"I don't know if I can do this," he told his colleague.

"You've got to," Tuggle replied.

Tuggle crawled next to Bradley and administered the tranquilizer to her neck. Sullivan thought about his wife and children, as well as Bradley, and offered up a prayer for all of them. Then he set to work. A fireman was perched above him, his hands checking for tremors in the concrete crushing Bradley's leg. If he felt anything, he was to get Sullivan and Tuggle out immediately, regardless of the condition of the patient. The fireman also had a harness attached to Bradley so he could pull her out as soon as the operation was over.

Sullivan plunged the first of his scalpels into Bradley's flesh, the single hardest act of his medical career. "She started kicking and screaming, so I had to more or less pin her free left leg against the wall while using my left hand," Sullivan said. He desperately wanted the operation to go quickly, but he broke his first blade, then a second, then a third, and a fourth. He could not properly see what he was doing, and Bradley did not stop yowling.

At one point, he cut into a large vein and thought he had severed an artery. Eventually, the flow of blood ceased, and he continued. Twice, he thought he had finished when he hadn't. "We'd pull her out, and she was still attached, and she would scream," Sullivan said.

By then he was out of surgical blades, and had to use his pocket knife to sever the last pieces of flesh from Bradley's thigh stump. As soon as Sullivan was done, he rolled out of the hole and let the others take over. A dozen men pulled Bradley onto a spine board to transport her to the hospital. An ambulance arrived, later than expected, and the two doctors made frantic efforts to keep the patient alive as they drove to the University Hospital. "She kept lapsing into unconsciousness," Sullivan said. "And so we'd scream at her and shout at her and slap her and try to do anything we could to keep her breathing."

They succeeded. Bradley survived.

{ Three }

WE GOT HIM

Within an hour of the explosion, FBI director Louis Freeh made a mercurial decision: asking Weldon Kennedy, the special agent in charge in Arizona, to lead the investigation, instead of following customary practice and selecting the richly experienced head of the local field office, Bob Ricks.

The most common explanation was that Ricks had been the bureau's press spokesman at Waco and was too closely associated with the disastrous end to the siege, even though he was involved in few, if any, key command decisions. At the time of the bombing, Freeh was facing congressional hearings on Waco and was no doubt concerned not to hand extra ammunition to his House and Senate interrogators.

But Freeh was also in the process of replacing every field division supervisor with people his detractors referred to as FOLs, or Friends of Louie. He wasn't just building a hierarchy of grateful loyalists; he was also attacking the FBI's ingrained culture. Many times, Freeh expressed contempt for the bureau's top-down management culture, preferring to sit down with field agents, who, he said, "do the real work for the FBI."

Freeh clearly saw Ricks as part of that culture, and two years earlier, the two men had been rivals for the director's job. Freeh, who had only a six-year career as an FBI agent in New York before climbing the ladder to a federal judgeship, was very much the outsider candidate. He had connections in the Clinton White House, which is why he was chosen, but he also had good reason to fear the criticism and resentment of the bureau veterans. The man he picked to supplant Ricks was inescapably a veteran, too, but one just months from retirement. Kennedy had won his spurs negotiating a peaceful end to a prison riot in Atlanta in the 1980s and was a popular and reliably safe pair of hands. He could also compensate for Freeh's lack of exposure to the American heartland. As Freeh, the inveterate New Yorker, once put it: "I never learned to do good ol' boy."

Kennedy could not have been more surprised when he was pulled out of a drug trafficking conference in El Paso and ordered onto the first plane to Oklahoma City. "I was not a Friend of Louie," he said. "He didn't know me, and he didn't trust me."

Kennedy faced troubles from the start. Even though Ricks was not the official on-scene commander, his staff still treated him that way. And that led to an atmosphere of mistrust, political scheming, and reluctance to share information. "The one [team] is not necessarily helping the others," Ricks explained. "It just creates an additional layer of bureaucracy."

RECOVERY OF THE RYDER TRUCK'S REAR AXLE FROM RICHARD NICHols's Ford Festiva at the Regency Towers, the first significant piece of evidence, should have been a breakthrough moment for law enforcement, but instead it turned into a feud over bragging rights.

Mike McPherson, an Oklahoma police sergeant who passed the Towers every day on his way to work, was the first to claim that he'd found the axle piece, wiped it clean of grease and grime, and located the vehicle identification number. Almost immediately, two city traffic cops insisted they were the ones who brought both the rear and the front axle to the feds' attention.

The FBI dismissed both stories, saying it was Melvin Sumter, the videographer for the sheriff's office, who found the rear axle and called in Jim Norman, one of the bureau's most experienced agents, to take it to the FBI's temporary command post three blocks away. Another agent then called the partial VIN number into the National Insurance Crime Bureau and learned it belonged to a 1993 Ford truck registered to the Ryder Rental Truck company of Miami.

From an investigative standpoint, it didn't much matter which version was correct, because the upshot was the same. Several people found parts of the truck within a three-block radius of the bomb site, and every bit helped. McPherson's story about finding the partial VIN number does not square with FBI interview records or with two separate published accounts, but it is also possible he made the discovery before the FBI, and the work was simply replicated.

The problem with this episode was the tone it set. A number of rival investigators wanted to be written into the historical record, even if doing so meant contradicting each other for bragging rights. It would not be long before law enforcement agencies supposedly united in a common purpose would be accusing each other of withholding information, obstructing the investigation, and lying.

INVESTIGATORS MADE ANOTHER EARLY BLUNDER BY FAILING TO secure the Murrah Building as a crime scene. This was understandable in the first few hours, when firefighters, doctors, and citizen volunteers tended to the injured and dying and did not think twice about trampling over the wreckage to reach them. But the problem persisted, even after the FBI and the city fire department began to impose some order. They established a perimeter shortly after 10:30 A.M., but it was barely more than a block in each direction. Later in the day, once the FBI had taken full control, the perimeter was expanded to about a quarter of a mile—three or four blocks each way. That was almost certainly not large enough to safeguard important evidence, either. James Powell, a bomb squad officer for the ATF, later told Justice Department investigators that the usual protocol was to block off the entire debris field plus an extra 25 percent. Even the smaller perimeter was ineffective; Powell observed soldiers and Red Cross volunteers roaming at will to offer refreshments to the rescue workers.

Many basic tasks that could have yielded valuable results were overlooked. Nobody, for example, thought to cover and protect the bomb crater before a light cloudburst hit at about 3:00 P.M., or before a much bigger storm rolled in that evening. Evidence collectors were directed to sift through the debris with rakes. "If you can't see it at rake's length, it's not worth picking up," Dave Williams, the FBI's on-site forensic supervisor, was heard saying. Ed Kelso, the head of the FBI crime lab's evidence response team, later told a Justice Department inquiry this was wrong, because smaller pieces—for example, any fragment with a hole drilled through to run detonating cord or shock tube—could indeed prove valuable. Two on-site technicians walked away in disgust. LaTonya Gadson, an evidence processor at FBI headquarters, said the materials sent back to her were a "mess," showing no signs of sorting or sequencing.

Williams took much of the blame for the fiasco. But ATF director John Magaw thought the Federal Emergency Management Agency also bore responsibility. "It was [FEMA's] first time on a major crime scene," he said, "and their gut instinct was to save lives. But you can save lives and protect the scene a little bit if you at least think about it." The ATF was not without blemish, either. Someone in the organization made a wildly inaccurate guess that the Murrah Building was destroyed by a 1,000–1,200-pound car bomb, roughly the same size as the device planted at the World Trade Center in 1993. Magaw provided this estimate to CNN audiences four hours after the bombing, and it made its way into a number of the army's early internal reports. Episodes like this did not endear Magaw to leaders of the investigation's task force.

THE SHOCKWAVES FROM THE BOMBING DID NOT JUST STIR LAW EN-forcement to action; they were keenly felt at a nondescript two-bedroom home in Pittsburg, Kansas, 250 miles northeast of Oklahoma City. This was a safe house used by the Aryan Republican Army, the bank robbery gang motivated not just by money but by a determination to start a white supremacist revolution. The house was crammed with much the same paraphernalia McVeigh and his associates had been gathering: wigs, disguises, fake IDs, phone cards, and police scanners; pistols and semiautomatic weapons; timers, switches, live grenades, pipe bombs, blasting caps, shock tube, and gallon jugs of nitromethane.

The ARA had grown increasingly explicit about its desire to wage war on the government, and real questions would soon arise about the possibility that members of the group were in on the bomb plot. The previous fall, its members discussed setting up revolution-ary cells, each one specializing in derailing trains, or attacking power plants, or infiltrating and ransacking military installations. In Janu-ary 1995, the ARA's core members got drunk, donned masks, and shot an eccentric recruitment video—a bewildering, almost campy mix of race hate, gun fetishization, and old-fashioned revolution-ary fist-thumping. The main speaker calls himself Commander Pedro and plays a hammy version of a Latin-American *guerrillero* in olive drab fatigues. He refers to "federal courthouses that need to be demolished"—possibly McVeigh's original brief—and justifies killing in the name of the revolution. "We have endeavored to keep collateral damage and civilian casualties to a minimum in all our operations," he intones. "So far we have been successful, but as in all war some innocents shall suffer. So be it."

When he wasn't dressing up as the warrior-buffoon, Commander

Pedro was a wayward Irish-American child of the sixties named Pete Langan, a high-school dropout whose father had worked for the CIA in Saigon during the Vietnam War. When the family relocated to the Washington suburbs, Langan turned to drugs and petty crime, drifted down to Florida, and ended up in prison for holding up a department store. He was short and slight, even a little effeminate, which made him easy prey for his larger cell mates. He was determined to survive, arming himself with knives and small petrol bombs, dreaming up escape plans—one briefly successful—and turning to white supremacism. "I was," he later said, "a small person you didn't wanna fuck with."

After years of odd jobs, a failed marriage, intermittent problems with alcoholism, and increasing involvement in Aryan Nations and the Christian Identity movement, Langan went to prison again for robbing a Pizza Hut in Georgia. This time, he got lucky and was recruited as an informant by the Secret Service, which had become alarmed after overhearing one of his oldest friends from Maryland, Richard Guthrie, talk about blowing up the White House and killing President George H. W. Bush. Langan was an odd and—quickly— disastrous choice of informant, but he gratefully accepted the early release from prison and the free ride back to his home in Cincinnati. Within weeks he ditched his Secret Service handlers, hooked up with Guthrie, and disappeared. The pair of them decided, with gleeful abandon, to become full-time warriors against the system.

Guthrie was a volcanic sidekick, a scam artist and arsonist who once dreamed of becoming a Navy SEAL but did not have the temperament for military life. During his time in the navy—including a stint in explosives and ordnance-disposal training—he regularly went AWOL or made up bogus illnesses. He was court-martialed after painting a swastika on his ship and left the service with a less-than-honorable discharge. Out of uniform, Guthrie traveled the country, building up contacts in the white supremacist movement. He bragged about torching abortion clinics and shooting interracial couples, and came to see war against the government as his life's sole purpose. To earn a living, he scammed department stores and staged car accidents to collect on the insurance.

By April 1995, Langan and Guthrie had carried out a dozen bank heists, first as a twosome and then adding recruits, including Kevin McCarthy and Scott Stedeford, Mark Thomas's punk musician protégés from Philadelphia. They scoped out targets, parking spots, and getaway routes, and adopted a military-inspired checklist Guthrie called Basic Armed Resistance Tactics. Once the job was under way, they donned cheap Halloween masks of ex-presidents (an idea from the surfer-heist movie *Point Break*). After they had cleaned out the cashiers' drawers, they left a fake explosive device, often decorated to match the season. At their most recent job in Des Moines, it had been an Easter basket containing a fake pipe bomb and a smoke grenade. They always used drop cars, cheap junkers they would acquire under a false name—often, the name of a prominent FBI agent— and dump close to the crime scene.

Later, there would be plentiful reasons to suppose that McVeigh was acquainted with the ARA or even involved in some of the robberies. He and they traveled the same gun-show circuit, and their movements often overlapped, including a long stretch in early 1995 when they were all in Arizona. McVeigh told his sister Jennifer he had been involved in a bank robbery, as the FBI would learn a little later. Both Terry Nichols and Nichols's ex-wife, Lana, came to suspect the same thing. None of the ARA principals, meanwhile, had a viable alibi for April 19.

According to Langan and Guthrie, they were at the safe house for most of the day. In the morning, Langan drove a van into Joplin, Missouri, for repairs—a trip he later described as an "ironclad alibi," though nobody claimed to have seen him there. Guthrie said he sat down on the living room couch with a cup of coffee at about 9:45 A.M. and saw news of the bombing on television. If the event shocked him, or filled him with human sympathy, he never mentioned it. Langan later described Guthrie as "a raving psychopath, a cross between Ted Kaczynski and Ted Bundy"—an exaggeration, perhaps, but also a hint at his propensity for unbridled violence. Guthrie saw the bombing as the start of a long and violent struggle against the federal government. "Simply put," he later wrote in a prison memoir, "within ten years, it's my opinion that this country will resemble Sarajevo."

Guthrie's memoir records almost no events for the month of April; this was the period when the ARA had supposedly elected to disband for several months. Guthrie does say that Langan traveled to Kansas City early in the month to visit his lover. Guthrie wittily refers to the woman—he has no reason to think it is not a woman—as Langan's "mysterious." But Langan was a secret cross-dresser, and when he wasn't fomenting revolution with neo-Nazis, he was seriously considering a sex-change operation. Recently he had been wearing dresses, high heels, lipstick, and nail polish, and attended gender-bending parties under the name Donna McClure. His "mysterious" was a fellow transsexual, known as Cheryl, whom he met at a New Year's Eve church mixer.

Was Langan wedded to the revolutionary cause or committed to a path of self-discovery that his white supremacist cohorts would not only find repugnant but might see as grounds to kill him? (McCarthy, following an unbending interpretation of Leviticus and Deuteronomy, believed that homosexuals and cross-dressers should be put to death.) Langan's secret life as Donna does raise the possibility that he was the woman spotted on April 19 in Oklahoma City—first at the wheel of McVeigh's Mercury and later waving the Ryder truck in toward the Murrah Building. An artist's sketch of one of the eyewitness sightings in Oklahoma City bore some resemblance.

KEVIN MCCARTHY AND SCOTT STEDEFORD ALSO HAD NO ALIBI FOR April 19. McCarthy was a deeply disturbed kid, just shy of his eighteenth birthday, a stringy, hard-core skinhead with a history of drugs, alcohol, and mental illness. Stedeford was, in theory, more stable, twenty-seven years old, and dedicated to his music. He fell into the right wing revolutionary movement via the underground neo-Nazi punk scene in Philadelphia. When he discovered a talent for bank robbery, he imbibed deeply from the radical philosophy that went with it and came to feel it was his right and his religious duty to kill enemies of the white race. "Unfortunately," a chastened Stedeford later reflected, "I was exposed to some poor role models and incorrect information at the wrong time in my life."

The first time the FBI asked McCarthy where he and Stedeford were on April 19, he said they were at the safe house in Pittsburg with Langan and Guthrie; they had arrived back from Elohim City three days earlier and saw news coverage of the bombing on television. But Langan said McCarthy and Stedeford did not return until early April 20. Guthrie concurred. So the FBI talked again to McCarthy, who now said he heard about the bombing on the car radio as he and Stedeford were returning from a trip to Iowa to register a newly purchased Chevy Suburban. The FBI accepted this alibi even though it, too, was contradicted by other evidence. Paperwork tracked down by the bureau shows that the Chevy was registered in Iowa on April 21, not on April 18 or 19. No motel records or other documents have ever surfaced to show that McCarthy and Stedeford were in Iowa on April 19.

When McCarthy showed up at the house, more than twelve hours after the bombing, Langan asked if he had been involved and was not inclined to believe his denial. A few months later, according to Langan, McCarthy confided that he had legal "liabilities" concerning the bombing and he might need to go underground. Langan was not interested in helping, in case he was later accused of collusion in the bombing plot himself.

Guthrie had his own suspicions—or perhaps more concrete knowledge—about McCarthy. In July 1995 he visited Mark Thomas, McCarthy's neo-Nazi mentor in Pennsylvania, and told him: "Your young Mr. Wizard took out the Murrah Building." A month later, Guthrie, McCarthy, and Stedeford robbed a bank in the St. Louis suburbs and left a newspaper article about McVeigh and the Oklahoma City bombing on the drop car's front seat. Guthrie told the FBI this had been his idea, although he was also drunk on tequila and nearly sabotaged the robbery by showing up late. The newspaper article could have been a signature, or an expression of support for the bombing, or a dangerous way—typical of Guthrie's reckless irreverence—of taunting the government with the revelation that one or more of the bombers was now in the bank robbery business.

The FBI learned all this well before McVeigh's trial. They also had a revealing conversation with Mark Thomas's ex-girlfriend Donna Marazoff, the embittered mother of two of his children. Marazoff said Thomas vowed revenge against the government after Ruby Ridge and Waco. "We are going to get them," she quoted him saying. "We are going to hit one of their buildings during the middle of the day. It's going to be a federal building. We will get sympathy if we bomb the building."

Thomas never said anything so explicit in public, but he did offer a robust defense of the bombing when a *Washington Post* reporter interviewed him in January 1997. "Government rules people by fear, which is terrorism," he said. "Therefore, if you're gonna have people who are going to construct a government of, by, and for the people, they're gonna have to use force to exert their will over their public servants. . . . For example, the bombing of Oklahoma City. There have been no Ruby Ridges or Wacos since that time."

Thomas was the only active ARA member who could properly account for his whereabouts on April 19. He was at his rambling, filthy farmhouse outside Allentown, Pennsylvania, with his latest girlfriend and brood of children.

In Oklahoma City, FBI agents immediately began hunting for video surveillance footage of the crime scene in the hope that it would lead them directly to the perpetrators. The search was a little slapdash, because no proper chain of command had been established in the hours after the explosion and nobody had a clear idea of where to look.

Most promising were two security cameras perched on the northwest and northeast corners of the Murrah Building. Both were trained on the Fifth Street entrance and the parking slots outside; if they had been working, they could have captured the final moments before the bombing. The equipment was badly damaged in the explosion, but investigators thought there was a good chance the footage was recorded remotely and still intact at another location.

Frustratingly, the cameras were not hooked up to any video system, and had not been for a long time. "The wires were cut ten years before I got here. There were no monitors, nothing," said Tom Hunt, the head of Federal Protective Service, responsible for security at the Murrah Building. It was a cost-cutting measure, which Hunt said he had "screamed about" since taking the job.

The FBI was furious, particularly since the eyewitness testimony suggested that McVeigh, and whoever was with him, had not worn masks or other obvious disguises. "It would have been perfect evidence," said Danny Defenbaugh, who would succeed Weldon Kennedy as head of the investigation. "But the morons didn't have it fixed."

The lack of footage seemed so incredible that for years some people believed the FBI was withholding it to maintain its position that McVeigh acted alone. Oklahoma City's Channel 4, the most sensationalist of the local news outlets, produced a report to this effect in late 1995. And, in 2004, the raw, entirely unredacted Secret Service timeline of the first few weeks of the investigation was made public and appeared to show the same thing. The timeline contained two separate references to such videotape evidence and described more than one suspect getting out of the Ryder truck. For years after, the FBI was bombarded with complaints and lawsuits demanding release of the footage.

But the Secret Service had not seen any video footage itself and later acknowledged in court that some of the material in its timeline was based on speculation only. Some of the things in the timeline ascribed to the tapes were very similar to eyewitness testimony of Glenn Grossman, Daina Bradley, and others. FBI agents directly involved in collecting and analyzing the videotape data later said the Secret Service had confused these things and made a mistake. It was also possible the confusion arose elsewhere in the heat of a fast-moving, high-pressure investigation.

The FBI certainly furthered suspicions that videotape evidence had been suppressed, because it responded evasively to Freedom of Information Act requests. But caginess by the FBI's records department is not proof of concealment. The most unequivocal evidence comes from a Physical Security Survey Tom Hunt conducted two months before the bombing, which states: "There are no surveillance systems on the exterior of this building." Since Hunt never forwarded his document to the FBI, it is not clear the bureau ever realized it existed.

The absence of working cameras is arguably a *greater* scandal than suppressed footage, because it points to the federal authorities' fundamental failure to protect its own employees and the public. After Waco, the FBI and ATF were picking up endless chatter that they and the federal judiciary were targets for revenge attacks. A few months before the bombing, a vandal smashed a window at the Oklahoma City federal courthouse and did more damage inside. Don Rogers, the General Services Administration's on-site manager at the Murrah Building, received a personal threat and set up a video surveillance camera, with recording capacity, outside his first-floor office door. He also hired a private security guard. When other agencies in the building asked for video surveillance equipment, Rogers gave inconsistent responses. The HUD office on the sixth floor was told yes; the day-care center no.

Rogers and his GSA bosses always cited budget constraints in refusing to consider video protection for the building as a whole. When Hunt started his job, two years before the bombing, he was alarmed by the nonfunctioning exterior cameras for several reasons— including cases where the federal government had been sued for lulling people into a false sense of security. "I said, we need to get those cameras fixed," he recalled. "But nobody would do it. 'In that case,' I said, 'we need to take them down.' But nobody would do it."

The camera outside Rogers's office—which was not authorized by Federal Protective Service, as protocol dictated—could have been useful, because it looked directly on the place where the Ryder truck pulled up. There is no evidence the FBI recovered the camera or even knew about it. When Rogers was asked in 2011 about his private security setup, he denied knowing anything about it. When shown evidence of its existence in the Physical Security Survey report, he wavered and said: "If there was a security camera, fine. But it was all so darn long ago."

And so, the investigation had to look elsewhere. On the morning of April 19, John Hippard made a first, unsuccessful pass at collecting footage from the Regency Towers apartment complex, the last big building the Ryder truck would have passed as it approached the Murrah Building along Fifth Street. He and his colleagues were seen playing with one of the exterior cameras, which had become detached from the wall. But it was not until the afternoon that an Oklahoma City policeman recovered that day's footage (which was still recording in the first-floor security office), and it took another week for the building manager to dig older footage out of the files he kept at home. Hippard had more luck at the Journal Record Building, where the head of security handed over everything right away. But with the electricity out, the tapes could not be ejected from the video machines. Danny Payne, the security chief, simply handed over the players themselves.

Over the first twenty-four hours, the FBI built up an inventory from six separate sites: the Regency Towers, the Journal Record

Building, the Bank of Oklahoma at Fourth and Robinson, the Oklahoma Public Library, the Southwestern Bell Building, and Anthonys department store. Later, they also received footage from the post office. They tried to recover material from a number of businesses on Sixth Street, only to discover that the cameras were dummies, like the ones at the Murrah Building, or captured images in real time without recording them.

A number of on-scene FBI agents, especially those who had worked bank-robbery cases, wanted to examine the tapes right away, but they were sent instead to the Bureau's crime lab in Washington. Walt Lamar, the Oklahoma City agent most disappointed by this decision, called the lab technicians a few days later to ask what they had seen on the tapes. He was told: "Nothing of evidentiary value."

Lamar didn't believe it. As soon as the tapes were returned, he examined the Regency Tower batch, working his way back from 9:02 A.M. on April 19. It wasn't long before he stumbled on grainy footage of a Ryder truck driving past. "Son of a bitch, there's the truck!" Lamar exclaimed. The lab technicians had missed it.

The Regency Towers footage provided the most vivid exhibits presented at trial: the truck heading toward the Murrah Building a few minutes before the explosion, and also a snapshot of Terry Nichols's blue GMC pickup passing on Easter Sunday, proving that he had come to Oklahoma City to help McVeigh drop off the Mercury. The Journal Record Building footage was useless, because the lone external camera was pointing into bright sunlight. The FBI expended considerable effort trying to enhance it, appealing to NASA and other government agencies, to no avail. Much of the rest of the available footage was of the time-lapse variety and distressingly incomplete. The post office footage stopped on April 17, two days before the bombing, and did not resume again until May 25.

DAVE HOLLAWAY, THE RAZOR-SHARP, INCAUTIOUS DEPUTY DIRECTOR of the CAUSE legal foundation, cannot account for his whereabouts on April 19. Like Kevin McCarthy, he has provided a number of versions of his movements, none of which have stood up to scrutiny. There has been no suggestion from any quarter that Hollaway was involved in criminal activity, but it seems extraordinary that a man with a steel trap of a memory should suddenly forget where he was—on this, of all days. Hollaway claims to have spoken to McVeigh the day before the bombing and attempted to talk him out of doing anything stupid, but immediately following that call, Hollaway went to the airport and vanished from sight. Did he try to stop the attack? Was he checking on one or more of CAUSE's clients to make sure they were not involved?

For years Hollaway told people that he flew to Texas for the second anniversary of the Waco disaster. He said he drove to Waco in a rental car with a gaggle of high-powered Houston lawyers who, like him, were involved in suing the federal government over its handling of the siege. He spent the night in a motel, attended the ceremony, then walked into a media tent, where he first learned about the bombing. He told the flamboyant litigator Dick DeGuerin he thought the bomber had called him the day before. DeGuerin told him it would be smart to call the FBI, which Hollaway subsequently did.

Almost none of this story is true. A number of people who knew Hollaway well said they were sure he was not at the Waco ceremony. Confronted with this, Hollaway acknowledged that he did not, in fact, attend. He said he learned about the bombing as he was about to go to the ceremony and decided at the last minute to duck out to avoid the media scrutiny. Still, he drove up from Houston with DeGuerin and two other lawyers.

The lawyers did not concur. DeGuerin was on a ranch in west Texas, not in Waco, and said he neither saw nor spoke to Hollaway that day. One of the other lawyers, a friend of Hollaway's named Joe Phillips, said he didn't remember seeing him, either.

When Kirk Lyons, Hollaway's boss at CAUSE, learned many years later that Hollaway had not attended the memorial, he sounded genuinely surprised. His best recollection, he said, was that Hollaway called him late that morning and asked permission to extend his car rental so he could travel to Oklahoma City. But two of Hollaway's friends who traveled to the bomb scene, Jim Pate and Rick Sherrow of *Soldier of Fortune* magazine, never saw him there. Hollaway said he might have briefly considered the trip but never went. "In those circumstances," he said, "I want to be as far away from Oklahoma City as I can get." Asked for a third time where he was that day, he said, irritably: "It's sixteen years ago. I mean, who cares?"

ONE PERSON WITH A SURPRISINGLY SOLID EXPLANATION OF HIS whereabouts on April 19 was Andreas Strassmeir, the former German army officer living at Elohim City. Strassmeir faced all sorts of trouble after the bombing, because he had met Tim McVeigh at a gun show and formed a bond with him. He had also thrown considerable energy into arming and training the residents of Elohim City for a possible showdown with the FBI, violating several federal laws. If anyone in Hollaway's circle needed help that day, he was it.

Hollaway acknowledged he didn't know what his friend was capable of. "Andi," he said in 2010, "would be a dangerous guy if you let him loose. He knows the difference between right and wrong, but if the gloves were off, he'd be killing as many of them as he could. The only reason he doesn't is because he's intelligent enough to know that the costs outweigh the benefits. . . . If there were some kind of revolt in the country, you could count him in."

Did Hollaway try to contact Strassmeir that morning to make sure he could account for his whereabouts? Hollaway later insisted he did no such thing. But Strassmeir, a strikingly disorganized and unworldly person, somehow came up with a watertight alibi. Even Kirk Lyons, his lawyer, agreed that Strassmeir wasn't likely to have come up with this on his own. "Andi had no authorship in any part of his life here," Lyons said. "It was all done by other people."

The authorities were told that Strassmeir and another Elohim City resident spent the morning of April 19 repairing a fence for an elderly farming couple a few miles away. Not only did the wife mark the hours the two men worked; at least one other neighbor remembered that one was called Andi. Aside from his military career and his flights into the United States, it was perhaps the most rigorously documented moment of Andreas Strassmeir's life.

THERE WERE THINGS ABOUT ANDREAS STRASSMEIR THAT HIS FRIENDS in the revolutionary Patriot Movement did not know and would have been intrigued, or appalled, to find out. Despite his pedigree as the grandson of a Nazi, he was fascinated by Israel and spent three summers on a kibbutz in the Jezreel Valley, near the Golan Heights. He had enrolled in Hebrew classes as a teenager in Berlin, and spoke the language fluently. During his second stint at the kibbutz, he was given an Uzi and put on security detail; during his third, he was sent on patrol on the Green Line between Israel and the West Bank, a job usually reserved for the military. When he was asked in an interview if he had worn an Israeli Defense Force uniform, Strassmeir's expression changed noticeably and he broke into an embarrassed smile before insisting he had gone out in jeans.

Strassmeir acknowledged that he "bumped into" General Rafael Eitan, the architect of the 1982 Israeli invasion of Lebanon—an encounter captured in a photograph of them at Golan Beach, near Lake Galilee. And he did not explicitly deny that he had contact with Mossad, the Israeli security service. Strassmeir agreed that Mossad was in the habit of meeting its foreign contacts at kibbutzim. When asked if Mossad ever visited the Tel Yosef kibbutz when he was there, he answered: "How would I know? If Mossad had been on the kibbutz, nobody would know—those boys know their business."

Strassmeir was a German army officer by then, and his career took an interesting turn when he returned home: he was seconded to intelligence work. Up to that point, his experience with the Bundeswehr had been unremarkable, even undistinguished. He washed out of the military academy in Hamburg without graduating and drifted from assignment to assignment, ending up as a mortar fire control officer. But his infantry battalion now used him to sniff out East German informants and spies. At some stage, Strassmeir was asked to fill in as the head of the battalion's intelligence unit, which gave him access to the entire army's internal reports. Asked if his superiors thought he did a good job, Strassmeir suddenly became coy. "What superiors?" he said. "I wasn't doing this."

When Strassmeir first came to the United States in 1988, to take part in a 125th anniversary reenactment of the Battle of Gettysburg, he arrived not on a simple tourist visa but on an open-ended multiple-entry visa, which he obtained, he said, by "pretending to be a traveling businessman."

One of the first people he contacted in America was Vince Petruskie, a retired air force colonel who had spent time in Berlin and appeared to have a long-standing friendship with Strassmeir's father, Günter, an influential political operative in the conservative Christian Democratic Party. Petruskie was also widely suspected of using the air force as a cover for a CIA career in counterespionage and counterinsurgency. Strassmeir did not deny that the reason Petruskie had been in Berlin during the Cold War was to assassinate Soviet agents; Kirk Lyons said the family loved to tell him the story of Petruskie killing a Soviet spy in the 1950s and leaving him hanging in the Reichstag ruins. Petruskie was also believed to have been part of the Phoenix Program, a covert CIA operation in the late 1960s and early 1970s to "neutralize" civilian supporters of the South Vietnamese National Liberation Front.

Strassmeir came to the United States hoping to get hired by Petruskie to conduct off-the-books drug interdiction operations on the U.S.-Mexico border. He was told Petruskie was in line for a high-level job with the Drug Enforcement Administration if George H.

W. Bush won the 1988 presidential election, and that Petruskie was interested in hiring Strassmeir as part of a rejuvenated black-ops crew, similar to the one he operated during his CIA career. In the end, though, Bush never invited Petruskie to join his administration and Strassmeir had to make other plans.

This history strongly suggests that Strassmeir was not the radical right-winger he appeared to be, and might even have been a government agent of some sort, spying on extremists in the United States. It is an allegation that first surfaced soon after the bombing and has prompted much speculation since. Strassmeir himself acknowledged that it was "not too far-fetched" for people to think this. "Actually at some point I was recruited, but it didn't come through," he said, clearly referring to his dealings with Petruskie. "Bush wanted him, but Congress had an objection to Operation Phoenix."

Who might he have worked for? The Germans were certainly interested in intelligence on American radicals, because they worried that money and propaganda materials from the United States were fueling neo-Nazi violence at home. The Israelis were interested, too. But there are also reasons to doubt Strassmeir was willing to do this kind of work—or indeed that he worked much at all.

Strassmeir seemed a different person from the moment his plans with Petruskie fell through. He struck many of his American hosts as listless and lazy, wore out several welcomes, and wound up relying on the kindness of Kirk Lyons, who knew him only indirectly through Civil War reenactment circles, and Dave Hollaway, whom he met through Lyons.

"We called him Sofa-meir," Lyons said, "because if you came around at 4:00 P.M., that's what you saw on my couch—Andi, sacked out." Strassmeir stayed up all night painting toy soldiers but showed little interest in anything else. Hollaway thought he was a "shameless hobo" who couldn't observe social niceties or take a hint when he was not welcome. "Remember, Dave, what happened the last time they frustrated a German artist," Strassmeir would say.

When Strassmeir's residual pay from the German army ran out, Hollaway found a way to employ him as a gopher for his computer company. He signed a bogus consultancy contract with Strassmeir's brother, who ran a computer firm in Munich, and reimbursed him for the $2,000 deposited in Andi's German bank account each month. When that arrangement broke down—because Hollaway's company could no longer afford it—Lyons decided to hand Strassmeir off to Grandpa Millar. The living in Elohim City was cheap, and Strassmeir stood some chance of finding a wife there and qualifying for a work permit.

Instead, Strassmeir preached revolution. Lyons and Hollaway strongly disapproved of his efforts to arm the Elohimites for Armageddon, and acknowledged they essentially lost control of him. They suspected he had become a true believer after all, and eventually went to great lengths to bail him out of trouble. Vince Petruskie was unhappy, too; according to Lyons, he would "go nuclear" at the very mention of Strassmeir.

If there was a moment when Strassmeir definitively turned his back on government intelligence work, it might have been June 1990, when Houston played host to the G-7 summit of world leaders and Lyons somehow rustled up an invitation for Strassmeir to meet one-on-one with Helmut Kohl, the German chancellor. "I set it up through the embassy," Lyons said. "I knew they were coming, so I asked what would be a good time and set up a meeting." Clearly, at that moment, Strassmeir still enjoyed considerable cachet in international political circles. But he refused to go.

FEMA, THE FEDERAL EMERGENCY MANAGEMENT AGENCY, PLAYED a valuable role in bringing heavy equipment and medical supplies to the disaster site, including breathing apparatus for the rescuers, but it also threw its weight in ways that caused deep resentment. The agency deployed more than five hundred staff members—roughly half of its entire Urban Search and Rescue force—and instantly rubbed locals the wrong way by treating them as subordinates. Firefighting and police teams felt they were being shunted aside, as though their efforts counted for nothing. "I don't want to sound overly critical," the assistant city manager, Joe Van Bullard, said, "but . . . they were assholes."

FEMA was in high favor in Washington at the time. James Lee Witt, the director, was a friend of President Clinton and had run the Arkansas Office of Emergency Services when Clinton was governor. Witt mistakenly thought he was acting at the direct behest of the president and could boss everyone around. Even the army was not immune. FEMA made extravagant demands for military airlifts to transport men and material, and if its requests were not met, "went whining through the back door of the White House," in the words of one military memo writer. In his memoir, written a few years later, Witt described himself as "the administration's voice on the scene" and claimed the authority to take charge of every other agency. His job, he said, was "keeping these people moving in the same direction." Nobody else believed he carried this authority, and his high-handed manner made him a butt of jokes. The task force nicknamed him Mr. Nit—for Nit Witt. "That's what everyone felt about the guy," one senior task force member said.

Even the unflappable Weldon Kennedy was taken aback when one of Witt's deputies tried to pull rank over the FBI at a conference meeting. Kennedy recounted: "He starts in, 'Leon said this, and Leon said that, and Leon said something else.' My agent said, 'Who the fuck is Leon and what does he have to do with this?' Turns out, he was talking about Leon Panetta, the White House chief of staff. We had nothing to do but laugh. I told him, 'Mr. Panetta is not directing this investigation.'"

On the second day, FEMA tried to tell the fire department to stop digging, so its search-and-rescue specialists could insert high-tech cameras and hearing devices in the rubble. The fire department said the odds of finding anyone else alive were steepening fast, and they couldn't afford the time it would take to plant the devices. FEMA countered that any remaining survivors might be accidentally bulldozed if rescuers did not locate them first.

Kennedy had to remind FEMA this wasn't their decision to make, but they still would not listen. Kennedy called Louis Freeh, who called Janet Reno, who called the White House. According to Kennedy: "Someone in the president's office, I assume Leon, called Mr. Witt and told him to cease and desist. That didn't make FEMA very happy."

According to many people, it made FEMA vindictive. Instead of providing equipment to anyone who needed it, free of paperwork, they started charging item by item, even for shovels. FEMA told Don Browning, the Oklahoma City police canine unit officer, that he and his dog were no longer performing rescue work and would now provide security for the FEMA rescue teams instead. One FEMA manager threatened to have Browning arrested for handing out FEMA rain suits to city firefighters. "He was screaming that it was FEMA's gear and it was not to be touched," Browning said.

Kennedy became increasingly exasperated that Witt would not turn over the Murrah Building to his criminal investigators, even after it became clear no more survivors could be found. "We submit," Kennedy told Witt a week after the bombing, "that you're dragging this out as a training exercise for your people." The FBI did not gain full control for eleven days.

FEMA even took credit for the rescue effort of others. One news release put out by a FEMA offshoot from northern California claimed it was FEMA, not the Oklahoma City Fire Department, that carried the dead bodies out of the Murrah Building. On FEMA's main Web site, a summary of events still posted after more than fifteen years gives the impression that no rescuer entered the Murrah Building on April 19 until FEMA arrived at 6:00 P.M. "One of the first assignments," the site explained, "was to search the second-floor nursery for victims." The city fire department was in the building nine hours earlier and recovered the children's bodies well before FEMA showed up.

A similar blindness to the fire department's contribution can be found in Witt's book, *Stronger in the Broken Places*. "In those first hours before the search-and-rescue teams arrived," Witt writes, "firemen managed to clear the site for hazardous materials, create a floor-by-floor manifest of who might've been in the building . . . and begin the excruciating task of contacting relatives, friends, and business associates of the Murrah workers." There is no mention of the extraordinary effort to rescue Daina Bradley, nothing about the personal hell first responders went through to bring out the survivors and tend to their injuries. Many in Oklahoma City never forgave Witt—for any of it.

It didn't take the FBI long to determine that the Ryder truck had been rented from a body shop in Junction City, Kansas. The owner, Eldon Elliott, had a flourishing side business moving soldiers in and out of Fort Riley, the home of the army's 1st Infantry Division, and owned a fleet of trucks. He was called by Ryder headquarters in the mid-afternoon and told not to talk to anybody until the FBI showed up. Special Agent Scott Crabtree appeared on his doorstep shortly afterward.

Elliott told Crabtree that a man calling himself Robert Kling had picked up a twenty-foot van on Monday, April 17. Elliott had prepared a damage assessment report, which he gave to his office manager, Vicki Beemer. The man was about five foot ten, medium build, with light brown hair cut short. Beemer, who was interviewed next, said Kling had provided a social security number and a South Dakota driver's license number, which he read out but did not hand over. When he gave his date of birth as April 19, 1972, she commented on his upcoming birthday and joked that she had been married longer than he had been alive. Kling provided no phone number. His purported new address in Omaha, Nebraska, 428 Maple Drive, was almost identical to his purported address in Redfield, South Dakota, 428 Malt Drive, but Beemer didn't think anything of it. He was, after all, a cash-paying customer. She had a fuzzier recall of his physical appearance than Elliott, saying only that he had short light brown hair. She remembered a second person being in the shop with Kling, but couldn't describe him.

The employee with the most vivid recall was Tom Kessinger, a mechanic who was in the office on his break when Kling and Beemer started talking. Kessinger described Kling as talkative and nervous. He agreed with the others about the hair, and also noticed his chin was pushed up and out and had a wrinkle. Kessinger remembered that the second man wore a black T-shirt, with a tattoo sticking out below the sleeve on his left arm. He appeared younger than Kling, and was wearing a ball cap with a blue-and-white zigzag pattern.

Crabtree returned to his office and ran a check on Kling's official data. Everything—the driver's license, the addresses, the social security number—was bogus. He contacted Elliott's body shop again, and said all three witnesses had to come to Fort Riley for fingerprinting and more interviews. In the meantime, they should not discuss their memories, in case it compromised their testimony.

This sequence is important, because federal prosecutors would later dissect it to the tiniest detail to argue that Robert Kling must have been Timothy McVeigh, and that no second person was with him when he rented the truck. Both contentions would prove problematic.

The follow-up interviews revealed a clearer picture. Kling called the shop on Friday, April 14, and booked a vehicle through Beemer. He said he was driving to Omaha, then into Iowa and back to Omaha again. Beemer got the impression he was an active-duty soldier, and she offered him the standard military discount. When she asked how big a truck he needed, Kling asked for one that could carry at least five thousand pounds. This was odd, as customers usually specified the number of rooms they were moving, not the weight; Beemer had to consult a chart twice before deciding he needed a twenty-footer. She asked if Kling wanted some extra miles at no further charge, but he asked for two extra days instead. She didn't see why he would need more than the two days he had already booked if his moving story was genuine, but she said nothing.

Early the next morning, on April 15, Kling came in and paid Elliott the full $280 on the rental—in cash. That was a little un-usual—he was asked only for the $80 deposit—but Kling said he wanted to make sure he didn't fritter away the money over the week-end. And he wanted no insurance. He said he was used to driving heavy-duty M35 cargo vehicles, "deuce-and-a-halfs," as part of his duties at Fort Riley, and felt confident he could handle a similar-size moving truck. Elliott accepted that.

In this second interview, Elliott said he, too, had seen a second person when Kling came in to pick up the truck. Like Kessinger, he remembered the cap with blue stripes and agreed that this second man was shorter than Kling, about five foot seven or eight. He had no memory of the man's face. Prosecutors later asserted that Elliott had spoken to his coworkers overnight and allowed Kessinger's mem-ories to contaminate his. Elliott never accepted this explanation and maintained that his story was consistent. "I told 'em there was two gentlemen in here," he said four years later, after the trials were over. "I never remembered what the second guy looked like, but there were two guys here together." Nothing in the FBI documentation suggests he gave a *different* account in the second interview, only that it was *fuller.* That account included details Kessinger did not mention, such as Elliott's memory of a light-blue sedan parked outside. When Vicki Beemer was reinterviewed, she also recalled a detail Kessinger had not offered—that the second man had crossed behind Kling to get an ashtray, suggesting he was a smoker.

The federal prosecutors were right that these weren't the world's most observant or reliable witnesses. Elliott said he saw a car parked outside; Beemer said there was none. Elliott first described Kling wearing military-type clothing on the Monday. Then he said he was wearing it on the Saturday; he couldn't remember what he was wearing on the Monday.

Still, all three agreed there were two men, and agreed on their basic physical characteristics. After the interviews, a sketch artist named Ray Rozycki asked them to match facial features in a book with what they remembered. Kessinger was by far the most forthcoming witness, but he was not entirely satisfied with the composite sketches Rozycki produced. The Kling portrait was close enough, he said, but the second man was hazier. Rozycki had done his second sketch head-on, even though Kessinger had seen him only from the side, and omitted the ball cap. But Kessinger did not feel comfortable saying anything at the time. "Hell, you know," he said, "when the FBI tells you to point, you point."

Two hours after he was booked into the Noble County jail on the gun and license plate charges, Tim McVeigh tucked into a bologna sandwich and lay down for a nap. He stayed asleep, or pretended to be, for the rest of the afternoon, rising for just a few hours before retiring again at about 10:00 P.M.

McVeigh later told his cell mate Herbert Ferguson he was catching up on sleep he lost in the army. More likely, he was avoiding conversation with the assorted drunks and petty criminals who were all transfixed by the bombing and talked of nothing else. Some of McVeigh's cell mates later expressed skepticism that McVeigh was sleeping, remembering big bags under his eyes. But extreme sleepiness is also a symptom associated with withdrawal from crystal methamphetamine, which McVeigh had been taking regularly.

McVeigh expected to be granted bail and sent on his way within twenty-four hours. But on Thursday morning, April 20, he learned his bail hearing was delayed because the judge was tied up in a divorce case. This was a break for the FBI, which had not begun to figure out McVeigh's connection to the bombing. Had his hearing gone ahead as scheduled, he could have upped and vanished.

McVeigh called Brent Goad, a local bail bondsman, so everything could be set ahead of time. "Man," he told him, "I've gotta get out of here."

Goad said he could do nothing until a judge heard his case and set bond. Even then, someone would need to cosign the paperwork. An unnerved McVeigh talked about getting out another five or six times in the course of the two-and-a-half-minute conversation. "He said 'please,' he was calm," Goad said. "But he was persistent."

McVeigh recovered his composure and made sure to appear cool before his cell mates. "He was not nervous," said Mark Gibson, an assistant district attorney for Noble County given the job of prosecuting him on the traffic charges. "He was not upset about being arrested or about being charged. He said he had never been arrested for anything before. But very militaristic. Everything was, 'Yes, sir,' 'No, sir,' speak when spoken to, and standing erect, very polite, very . . . soft-spoken."

As soon as the FBI had the composite sketches, detectives from multiple agencies fanned out from Fort Riley to see who might recognize them. If the bombers rented the Ryder truck in Junction City, there was a good chance they either lived or had stayed nearby and someone would know them. If they were out-of-towners, they might have registered at a motel and left traces there.

Mark Bouton, a burly FBI agent based in Topeka, was paired with a local sheriff's deputy, Garry Berges, and together they began what they thought would be a tedious tour of motels along I-40 on the eastern end of town. One, the Dreamland, was cut off from the others because of construction work on a bridge, so they decided they should go there first.

The owner, Lea McGown, was a fastidious German woman

who kept a close watch on her guests. When Bouton and Berges showed her the sketches, she thought the first one looked like Timothy McVeigh, a guest who had stayed for four nights over the Easter weekend. But it wasn't an exact match; she remembered McVeigh having smaller lips, lighter eyes, and a longer, slimmer neck. She also remembered him—correctly—as standing about six foot one, not the five foot ten described by the body shop witnesses.

But McGown had other reasons to be suspicious of McVeigh. He hadn't wanted to show her his driver's license. His car, an old Mercury, looked alarmingly shabby, and had an Arizona license tag, hanging by a single screw, which did not match the tag number he wrote on his registration card. There was a further mismatch between the Arizona plate and the Michigan address he gave. McVeigh said he traveled a lot on the gun-show circuit and didn't really live anywhere; the Michigan address belonged to a friend who let him use it on official forms. McGown deliberately put McVeigh in room 25, next to the office, where she could keep an eye on him.

News of the bombing gave McGown another big reason to be suspicious; she had seen McVeigh on several occasions with a Ryder truck. McVeigh said he was moving into the area and needed a few days to get straight. McGown hadn't questioned that at the time, but now she wondered about the truck and a six-foot trailer McVeigh had parked on the grass in front of her office. The trailer was loaded with something that jutted up about four feet. She couldn't tell what it was, because it was covered with a tarp and tied down with thick coils of rope.

It is not clear how quickly the FBI realized the significance of what McGown had to tell them. Bouton and Berges, by their own accounts, had McVeigh's name as early as 1:30 P.M., and certainly no later than 3:00 P.M. on April 20. Yet several hours went by before this information was relayed to their superiors back at Fort Riley, and hours more before it was transmitted to Oklahoma City and Washington, D.C. The Ryder truck sighting, the most important detail linking McVeigh to the bombing, was not even mentioned in the criminal complaint supporting McVeigh's arrest on bombing charges, which was written around noon the following day. How did it get missed?

According to Bouton, he and Berges spent a few minutes chatting with McGown about the bombing, then asked if she'd seen anyone over the previous week with a Ryder truck. "Yes," she replied, "and he was acting kind of funny with it."

McGown told Bouton that McVeigh had trouble closing the rear latch on the truck and motioned as if he didn't want her to see what was inside. When Bouton saw McVeigh's handwritten registration form, his heart leaped with excitement, because the writing slanted to the left, just like Robert Kling's signature on the Ryder rental form. Bouton said he knew that only 4 or 5 percent of the population writes with a backward slant.

Bouton interviewed four people that afternoon—McGown, her seventeen-year-old son Eric, and two construction workers staying at the motel—who recognized the John Doe One sketch as McVeigh. Bouton said he didn't have time to phone in his findings, because the county sheriff sent him and Berges to another motel to look into a possible John Doe Two. At the second motel, he phoned an FBI supervisor at Fort Riley, Michael Pulice; according to Bouton, Pulice refused to get too excited and said to bring his information to a debriefing session at the army base that evening.

McGown's version of the encounter was much briefer, and less cordial. When Bouton and Berges arrived, she said, they barged past an older couple, who were checking in, and placed some papers in front of her. McGown told the law enforcement officers to wait until she finished with her guests. When she looked at the papers and saw the composite sketches, she recognized the John Doe One as McVeigh, and mentioned his name. But Bouton said they were looking for someone named Kling, not McVeigh. This upset McGown, who didn't like to be second-guessed. She pulled out McVeigh's registration card, but when Berges reached out to grab it, she naturally pulled it back. She wanted a copy for her files before handing it over. Bouton and Berges had no other questions.

"They took the card, turned around, and left," McGown said. "And I thought, 'That's it, I'm never gonna see that card again.'"

McGown did not remember Bouton and Berges asking anything about the Ryder truck, but she must have said something because a teletype to FBI headquarters based on that day's investigations described McVeigh leaving the Dreamland Motel in the early hours of April 18 "in a Ryder rental truck." That teletype, however, was not written until 4:15 A.M. the following morning, a seemingly extraordinary timelag. According to Joseph Bross, who was running the Fort Riley end of the bombing investigation at the time, supervisors like Michael Pulice were rapidly growing inured to reports of Ryder rental trucks because they were receiving so many of them. At the time Bouton called in, the number one lead the FBI was chasing in Kansas was a military explosives and ordnance expert named Michael Fleenor, who was suspected—mistakenly—of going AWOL from the base and was reported—also mistakenly—being seen filling a Ryder truck with gas shortly before the bombing and asking for directions to Oklahoma City. (He was quickly cleared of suspicion.)

Even when Bouton presented his findings to an evening meeting of more than a hundred agents at Fort Riley, the Ryder truck angle—which Bross remembered him specifically mentioning—did not resonate. The teletype sent to Washington and Oklahoma City in the middle of the night hardly played it up, mentioning the truck only in passing several hundred words into the document. And the emergency response team in Washington was unimpressed. Joseph Bross said the duty supervisor he spoke to dismissed the entire McVeigh connection, saying the bureau's focus at that point was on a Middle Eastern plot. (In fact, the John Doe sketches had already been made public, and while Abraham Ahmad, the Jordanian American from Oklahoma City, was still being questioned, the Middle Eastern angle was fading fast. Ahmad himself was quickly cleared.)

What is curious is that while investigators failed to recognize the significance of the Ryder truck, they had no difficulty recognizing the importance of the registration card. McVeigh did everyone the favor of checking in under his real name and listing James Nichols's farm address in Michigan, when he could have used the Robert Kling alias and the same bogus address in South Dakota. That information quickly generated leads in Michigan and brought the Nichols brothers into the picture for the first time. But the truck was somehow overlooked, and because of that establishing McVeigh as the lead suspect became much more difficult. Without the link to the truck, McVeigh was just another guy with a passing resemblance to a police sketch.

Most likely, the Ryder truck lead failed to generate the attention it warranted at several different points along the way. It is difficult to judge from Bouton's paperwork how much he and Berges learned from Lea McGown on their first visit to the Dreamland, and how much they picked up when they returned the next day—he combined both visits into a single witness interview report. Bross said that, from where he was sitting: "We just had so many Ryder trucks." Washington, meanwhile, was overwhelmed, especially on the night shift, and would soon bring in reinforcements to shore up a struggling Criminal Division. Oklahoma City was also copied in on Bross's teletype and should have seen the Ryder truck reference, but did not.

Once Bouton got the full story from Lea McGown, his findings raised two significant problems that would later dog the federal authorities as they prepared for trial. First, McGown and others heard voices coming from McVeigh's room on Sunday evening, April 16. Asked about this repeatedly over the next two years, McGown remained adamant that she heard live voices, not the television. Her testimony implied that at least one other person had access to the room, because McVeigh had yet to return from Oklahoma City, where he and Terry Nichols had gone to stash the Mercury. He got back around 1:00 A.M. McGown remembered a "velvety" male voice she had heard in earlier phone calls she put through to room 25.

She was not alone in associating other people with McVeigh at the Dreamland. Bouton also interviewed a Chinese restaurant delivery boy called Jeff Davis, who brought food to room 25 on Saturday, April 15, and later insisted that someone other than McVeigh opened the door. The FBI tried repeatedly to get him to change his testimony, both in their initial interviews and on the eve of McVeigh's trial. They felt the man who took the single serving of moo goo gai pan must have been McVeigh, but Davis never wavered.

Second, McGown told Bouton she had seen McVeigh bring a Ryder truck to the motel on Easter Sunday, a day before Robert Kling picked up his vehicle from Eldon Elliott's. The FBI would insist she was mistaken. But she and her son remembered their first sighting of the Ryder in some detail, and their story was corroborated by at least two other motel guests who testified in court. Shortly after the McGowns returned from a family Easter lunch, they saw McVeigh backing up the truck near the swimming pool. They told him he had to park on the other side of the property, and McVeigh complied without question. They noticed that this Ryder was different from the one they saw later. It looked older; its yellow paint was bleached by exposure to the elements, and it had no writing on the back. The second truck was brighter and newer.

This was the first and, arguably, the strongest of many clues that more than one Ryder truck was involved. Investigators would grapple with that later. For now, the priority was establishing Robert Kling's real identity and running him to ground. Standard accounts of the bombing suggest Bouton's visit to the Dreamland provided the first, and most important, link to McVeigh. But there was also a second line of investigation, beginning the same day, which yielded not only McVeigh's name but also his physical characteristics and contact details.

SHORTLY AFTER THE JOHN DOE SKETCHES WERE COMPLETED AND distributed, two young military policemen walked into a well-known firearms and pawn shop near Fort Riley. They showed the sketches to the owner, Pat Livingston, who recognized them right away. He told them: "This is a customer of mine, I've sold him several guns. I don't know his name offhand. I'll have to get back to you." Livingston was also pretty sure he'd seen John Doe One and John Doe Two together.

Livingston was popular on the base with commanders and the rank and file, and he also had multiple contacts in law enforcement. He remembered that John Doe One had something to do with a bounced check, and after looking through his financial records, came across the name Timothy James McVeigh and all his details: a bad check McVeigh had written in September 1993 for a TEC-9 semi-automatic, and an ATF background check form known as a 4473, which gave McVeigh's full name, height, weight, date and place of birth, and driver's license number. McVeigh had purchased three guns from Livingston, starting in 1991, when he was still in uniform. The first was the Glock he was carrying when Charlie Hanger pulled him over.

"My impression of McVeigh was that he was a gung-ho young G.I.," Livingston said. "He was real nice. He didn't cuss. He was a respectful young man." Slowly, he recalled more about McVeigh's darker-skinned companion, the one who looked like the John Doe Two sketch. "He was short and stocky," he said, "but the thing that was impressive about him was that he had a real thick neck, an unusual stocky neck. He had pockmarks on his face, and he had that hat. It looked like a foreign soccer hat, all chartreuse and blue and pink. I remember that stupid hat, because it was unusual."

Tom Kessinger had remembered a brightly colored hat, and now Livingston was noting one as well. And the hat didn't come from the composite sketch, because Ray Rozycki, the sketch artist, had left it off. The one thing Livingston didn't have was a name for John Doe Two. It wasn't that he couldn't remember. He was pretty sure he never knew it.

Livingston called his best friend in law enforcement, county police detective Al Riniker. "I told him I knew who the Oklahoma City bomber was," he said. "I was excited because I figured I had identified the first terrorist." Livingston also called the Criminal Investigation Division at Fort Riley, triggering an initial discussion of who McVeigh was, where he had served, and how long he had been out of the army. A check of McVeigh's records revealed a single bar fight that ended with him breaking his nose; otherwise, his army disciplinary record was clean.

The events of the next few hours are something of a blur. It is not clear the FBI was given the information from Livingston in a timely fashion; Joseph Bross, who was in charge of the FBI operation at Fort Riley that day, said he never received it. Communication between Fort Riley and the task force in Oklahoma City was intermittent, mostly due to the command post being inundated with tips and potential leads. The FBI in Oklahoma City burned through two fax machines in the first twenty-four hours. But there were other organizational issues. "Literally, people in Oklahoma City had no idea what was going on in Junction City," said Steve Chancellor, the army CID commander at Fort Sill, Oklahoma, who drove up to the bomb scene within hours and stayed for close to three weeks. "I was talking to Mr. Ricks, and he would give me a list of questions. I would call the army CID at Fort Riley. They would give me the answers, and I would tell them to Mr. Ricks, who would give me more questions."

Chancellor said it took more than twenty-four hours for the commanders at Fort Riley to pick up the phone and talk directly to Oklahoma City. They did not fax over Ray Rozycki's composite sketches until Chancellor asked them to. When the task force made those sketches public, at about 3:00 P.M. on April 20, the phones and fax lines went even crazier. Half of Middle America, it seemed, had seen one John Doe or the other.

Still, the puzzle pieces came together. Pat Livingston provided the name McVeigh and a reason to find him suspicious. In the early evening, when Mark Bouton came up with the Dreamland Motel registration card, it not only confirmed McVeigh as a suspect but gave investigators a vital new clue, the Nichols farm address, which tallied with the information on McVeigh's Michigan driver's license.

In Decker, about a hundred miles north of Detroit, James and Terry Nichols were known for their connections among the radical fringe of the militia and "common law" movements, which rejected all personal ties to the government. The local sheriff told the FBI he regarded both Nichols brothers as "crazies" and had a thick file on them, including a five-month-old statement from James's ex-wife, Kelli Langenburg. She said they had been setting off small homemade bombs and rockets, and she believed James kept large quantities of fertilizer and fuel oil on the farm. The FBI contacted Langenburg, who confirmed that McVeigh was a friend of the Nicholses and had stayed at the farm many times. She also said her sister Lana used to be married to Terry Nichols and was in regular touch. By late evening, investigators at the Oklahoma City command post had half a dozen names, deemed to be "of extreme interest," pinned up on a bulletin board. Robert Kling was one. McVeigh was another. Terry and James Nichols were there, too.

When Pat Livingston heard the investigation was zeroing in on a couple of guys named Nichols, he looked into his records again and realized he had sold Terry two Glocks just a few months earlier—the same sort of pistol he had sold McVeigh in 1991. Terry Nichols, he recalled, was a furtive man who was a regular at army surplus auctions at Fort Riley. "Nichols was a slimy, conniving guy who wouldn't look you in the eye," Livingston said. "I wouldn't trust him as far as I can throw him." When Nichols came in to purchase his second Glock, he asked if Livingston sold blasting caps. Later, Nichols asked the same thing at a nearby store that Livingston also owned. Even in the deeply entrenched gun culture in and around Fort Riley, people interested in explosive components tended to trigger alarm bells. "I told him we didn't deal in anything like that," Livingston said. "Knowing me, I probably called the feds."

Livingston heard from a friend in the surplus business that just a month or two earlier, Nichols had been shipping military supplies—mostly uniforms and boots—to the Philippines. He appeared to have come into some money, because he was spending more lavishly at auctions, and overspending on basic items like shovels. A few days before the bombing, Livingston sent out a recall notice on the Glocks, but Nichols was not responding. "He wouldn't sign for a registered letter. Nothing," Livingston said.

Livingston was not entirely surprised at the bombing of the Murrah Building, because he'd been hearing noises about just such an attack for months. He heard a lot of things from behind the counter at Pat's Pawn & Gun Shop. Two years before, he had tipped off the army CID that the Michigan Militia was actively recruiting at Fort Riley and spreading inflammatory rhetoric about avenging Waco. The CID brass didn't want to believe him at first. Much more recently, he had heard that someone was going to blow up a federal building, probably in Kansas City because the FBI and the ATF shared offices there.

At the end of March, the chatter intensified, but the target changed—instead of Kansas City, it was Omaha, Dallas, or Oklahoma City. Livingston put in a call to the Joint Terrorism Task Force in Kansas City and made sure he took down the name of the officer he spoke to. (His name was Reid, badge number 4857, and the date was March 30.) "I'd heard so much of this crap, and it sounded kind of foolish that somebody would do this," Livingston said. "I didn't have no name, or how, or when. I was just hearing rumors. But I called them and warned them. That's all a guy can do."

ANOTHER CLUE POINTING TO BROADER KNOWLEDGE OF THE BOMB plot arrived on the afternoon of April 20 at the offices of the Liberty Lobby, a radical right-wing group based in Washington, D.C., whose publication, *The Spotlight,* was required reading for much of the Patriot Movement. The clue was a handwritten envelope, postmarked

"Oklahoma City" and dated April 17. The writing was not an obvious match for either McVeigh or Nichols. It contained a Depression-era photograph of rural Oklahoma with the caption: "Dust Storm Approaching at 60 Miles Per Hour" and a newspaper clipping about Gordon Kahl, an iconic gun-toting tax rebel who died in a shootout with the feds in 1983 and went on to inspire revolutionaries like Wayne Snell and Bob Matthews.

Mark Lane, the Liberty Lobby's top lawyer, understood immediately that the postcard might be evidence and told his colleagues not to touch it. (Too late—they already had.) He made copies of everything, and mailed the original envelope and its contents to Janet Reno's office.

Almost a year later, Lane received a phone call from Larry Mackey, one of the federal prosecutors, saying he'd heard a rumor about an interesting postcard but could not locate it.

"Well, you had it," Lane told him. "And now you don't have it. Is that correct?" Lane said he would be glad to send Mackey another copy, but without the opportunity to conduct chemical tests on the originals it was unlikely to be of much value. Lane never heard anything about this again.

TERRY NICHOLS WAS AT LAST SHOWING SIGNS OF NERVOUSNESS. By his account, he had known nothing about the bombing until the morning of April 20, twenty-four hours later, when he visited a cable television shop and was shocked by the news on the screens. He bought three newspapers to try to determine if this was the bomb he and McVeigh had built. Again, one senses a wall of denial. Could he really doubt the origin of the explosion that gutted the Murrah Building? Still, he took no action until 5:00 P.M., when he drove to the Herington storage unit and cleared out McVeigh's belongings.

Even at this point, he appeared to be following McVeigh's instructions as much as looking out for himself. One item was a box of three hundred electric blasting caps, wrapped in Christmas paper, that he and McVeigh considered using but chose not to. "Tim," he recounted, "said he'd pick those up later but if they were still there by Thursday night that I was to pick them up." Nichols seemed almost robotic, programmed to go to the storage locker when he was told. But some self-preservation kicked in, because he also removed McVeigh's Ruger mini-30, his rucksack and duffel bag, and the license plate McVeigh had taken off the back of the Mercury. Nichols also swept up some white ammonium nitrate pellets he noticed on the floor. "I figured I didn't want anything left in there that could be incriminating to me if it was McVeigh who actually did the OKC bombing," he later explained. He was still saying "if"—allowing room in his mind for doubt, or hope.

Nichols drove home and tossed the gear into his garage. Arguably, it was more of a liability there than in storage, but Nichols seemed oblivious to the danger. He continued to act as though nothing could happen to him.

At FBI HEADQUARTERS, LOUIS FREEH WAS RIVETED BY THE GROW-ing evidence on the Nichols brothers. He wanted a team to surround Terry's house in Kansas, and another to raid James's farm in Michigan. He pestered the local special agents in charge to make these things happen as fast as possible and was not happy when they needed more time. Freeh "continued to call and interrogate the SACs almost continuously," according to Buck Revell, a veteran G-man who had retired shortly before the bombing and objected strongly to Freeh's handling of it.

Pressure from the top continued through the night. Freeh's own performance was being scrutinized hour by hour by the attorney general and the White House. His two top commanders in the bureau's Strategic Information and Operations Center, the equivalent of the White House Situation Room, monitored the investigation constantly. Larry Potts, the FBI's acting deputy director, and Bob "Bear" Bryant, the assistant director in charge of national security, refused to leave their desks, even to catch a few hours' rest. Instead, they downed one coffee after another and chain-smoked. They were, in the words of their SIOC colleague I. C. Smith, "out on their feet." Smith told Potts: "For God's sakes, Larry, go home." But he wouldn't do it. "They were caught up in this paranoia that the investigation would go down the tubes if something happened that was not on their watch," Smith recalled. "These people were zombies."

At about 5:00 A.M., April 20, the Secret Service was told the FBI was sending its elite Hostage Rescue Team to Junction City to smoke out Terry Nichols. At the same time, the ATF and FBI were en route to the Decker farm for a joint operation. But the feds still needed more evidence, and some very basic information, such as an address for Terry Nichols.

Time was of the essence, because nobody at this stage knew if the Oklahoma bombing was a one-off. The prospect of follow-up bombings was a major preoccupation in the regular conference calls between the field commanders and headquarters. "Maybe this wasn't one person. Maybe it was ten people hitting a federal building in every city," one senior FBI manager on the calls said. "There was intense pressure to get the thing solved."

Yet the case against the three leading suspects was still painfully thin. Pat Livingston and Lea McGown had connected the John Doe One sketch to Timothy McVeigh, who had connections to the Nichols brothers. The brothers' radical ideas, which McVeigh probably shared, indicated hostility toward the federal government. James Nichols's ex-wife talked about ammonium nitrate bomb experiments on the farm. But that was all. These shards of information hardly constituted a conclusive case; a little countervailing evidence could eliminate them as suspects.

The case against McVeigh looked especially problematic at this stage. His exemplary military record included the Bronze Star for his "flawless devotion to duty" during the 1991 Gulf War. He had undergone explosives training, but not enough to teach him to build a large bomb. McVeigh had left the army with an honorable discharge at the end of 1991, and whatever he had been doing since did not involve any discernible criminal activity.

In the evening of April 20, Walt Lamar, the FBI agent who had monitored the video surveillance tapes, suggested an offline search on McVeigh from the bureau's National Crime Information Center. Everyone in law enforcement knew what an *online* search was—agents could access the NCIC's computer database and check a suspect's criminal record. An *offline* search involved calling NCIC's offices in Clarksburg, West Virginia, and asking a technician to search reel upon reel of magnetic tape for vehicle or criminal record checks. If McVeigh had ever been pulled over or asked for his ID, the NCIC might have picked up a trace of it. Lamar put in the call, saying it was top priority. It was several hours before the NCIC came back with an answer.

AT FIRST, LANA PADILLA, TERRY NICHOLS'S EX-WIFE, SEEMED TOO normal to have any association with participants in a bomb plot. She was a real estate agent in Las Vegas, a homeowner and divorcée with three children, two by a previous marriage and one, twelve-year-old Josh, by Nichols. When agents Alan Gough and Dan Walters dropped in on her office at about 8:30 A.M. on April 21, she was stunned to learn it was about the bombing and even more stunned to see pencil sketches of McVeigh and her ex-husband. (They probably came from Kelli Langenburg.) She knew about Nichols's radical politics, of course. She mistrusted his friendship with McVeigh, whom she regarded as dangerous and a bad influence. But she never thought Nichols would involve himself in blowing up a federal building, if only for the sake of their son, Josh, whom he adored.

Padilla said the sketches were accurate, though she'd never met

McVeigh and recognized him only from photographs. She volunteered Nichols's address, and said she had spoken to him that morning. Had he sounded normal? Yes. A bit rushed but normal. Padilla said they had argued about their son, as they often did. She did not initially describe the substance of the argument, because it concerned a troublingly large amount of money she did not know how to explain. But she went to her safe and copied some documents Nichols had given her five months earlier. They told the whole extraordinary story all by themselves.

The previous November, Nichols abruptly left the country for the Philippines. He had a young Filipina wife, Marife Torres, a mail-order bride he married when she was still a teenager, and had made several trips to visit her family. But this time he seemed scared for his life. Padilla had ample opportunity to size him up, because he stayed with her and her new husband for almost two weeks before his departure. She wondered if he was suicidal. He insisted on sleeping with a loaded revolver in his waistband.

At this point, Nichols and McVeigh were in the gun-show business, but their relationship had deteriorated. McVeigh kept calling, so she did not think the rift was serious. She assumed Nichols was having money problems and was depressed about his marriage. Marife had left for the Philippines in September, right around the time Nichols quit his previous job as a farmhand, and did not say when she might return. Nichols, meanwhile, had no home; he had been living in cheap motels and communicating with calling cards.

When Padilla asked how long Nichols planned to be in Asia, he responded by giving her a crudely taped-up brown paper grocery bag and told her to open it if he did not return within sixty days. Padilla and young Josh both found this deeply disturbing. "Josh started to cry on the way back from the airport. He said, 'I'm not going to see my dad again,'" Padilla recounted. The very next day, she tore open the package despite Nichols's strict instructions. She found a recent amendment to his life insurance policy, replacing her with Marife as his beneficiary. There were two power-of-attorney forms, giving her the authority to sell a handful of stocks Nichols owned, and some precious metals sitting loose in the bag. In an envelope addressed to her, she found a list of things "to read and do immediately." Two items jumped out. The first was about a recently rented storage unit in Las Vegas, whose contents he wanted her to sell for Josh. The second described a package he had hidden behind one of her kitchen drawers, which he said was intended to provide for Marife and his infant daughter, Nicole.

Finally, Padilla found a sealed envelope addressed to McVeigh's sister Jennifer. Inside was a second envelope, addressed to McVeigh. It was a brief note, all in upper case, with more references to storage units. Two more lines leaped off the page. Both were cryptic, but had the unambiguous ring of bad news. The first was an exhortation to McVeigh: "YOUR ON YOUR OWN. GO FOR IT!!" The second left Padilla thunderstruck: "As far as heat, none that I know of, this would be for the purpose of my death." Her eyes locked on that last word. "It was a suicide note," she remembered thinking. "A damn suicide note. Terry was going to kill himself!"

The FBI focused instead on the word "heat" and what appeared to be a criminal plot tying him to McVeigh. The "GO FOR IT!!" line suggested Nichols was an enthusiastic participant in whatever it was. It was not long before Padilla was whisked to the FBI office for more detailed questioning. The special agent in charge, Randy Prillaman, told her right away that Nichols and McVeigh "were both going to fry."

Padilla kept talking. She said she waited until Josh flew to Michigan for Christmas in mid-December 1994 before daring to look behind her kitchen drawer. She and her older son, Barry, dismantled the unit and found a Ziploc bag stuffed with $20 and $100 bills—$20,000 in all. Padilla was confused, because she thought Nichols had been on the verge of destitution. "What is he doing?" she wondered. "Robbing banks?"

Next she visited the storage locker, where she and Barry found gold coins, gold bars, and silver bullion stacked neatly in boxes, along with some small green stones that looked like jade. It was all worth many tens of thousands of dollars. She was not surprised to find Nichols's tent and fishing gear, along with supplies of freeze-dried food, but she was baffled by the wigs, masks, makeup, and panty-hose.

Nichols returned from the Philippines in mid-January, and flew into a fury with Padilla for opening the brown paper package. When she confessed to taking $5,000 from the kitchen drawer, he replied: "You can't do that, Lana. I need that money." He was angry; the veins in his neck were bulging. At that moment, the phone rang, and McVeigh asked for Nichols. When they finished speaking, Nichols said he needed to lend the money to McVeigh. Padilla was unimpressed, but in the end she and Nichols compromised. He would take back $2,000, leaving $3,000 for her and Josh. This was the money the two of them were still arguing about on the morning of April 21, just before the FBI arrived.

As Padilla kept implicating Nichols further, the agents realized they needed to keep her and the rest of her family secluded. So they moved into Circus Circus, one of the less glamorous hotels on the Las Vegas Strip. They were checked in under assumed names and shuttled from there to the FBI office for the next six days.

First, the FBI needed Padilla to tell them about Nichols's psychological makeup to help them arrest him without anyone getting hurt. They knew he was now living in a house he had purchased after his return from the Philippines and feared he might barricade himself in and initiate a long siege. Marife was back now, too, along with Nicole, so innocent lives were at stake.

THE CASE AGAINST MCVEIGH RECEIVED ANOTHER BOOST EARLY ON April 21, when a man who had worked with him as a security guard in upstate New York walked into the FBI's Buffalo office. Carl LeBron said he had befriended McVeigh, only to become so alarmed by his talk of radical action he started recording their conversations. He was afraid McVeigh's threats had come to fruition in Oklahoma City, not least because McVeigh looked like the John Doe One sketch on the front of that morning's newspaper.

LeBron and McVeigh had teamed up for about eight months in 1992, after McVeigh left the army, to guard an aerospace research company not far from the Buffalo airport. McVeigh distributed radical literature and encouraged LeBron to read *The Turner Diaries*. The siege at Ruby Ridge was a big topic of conversation, as was Waco; LeBron said McVeigh had made a pilgrimage to Texas during the fifty-one-day standoff and came back furious at the ATF and FBI. In their more recent exchanges, McVeigh talked about "doing something he had wanted to do" but was unclear about specifics.

LeBron's tip gave the FBI two things it badly needed to establish probable cause to arrest McVeigh: a psychological profile suggesting he was capable of mass murder, and a motive for the bombing. The bureau eventually lost interest in LeBron because he lacked credibility; he spouted off about UFOs and mini-submarines the government was using to smuggle hard drugs. In the moment, though, he was downright providential.

When Terry Nichols awoke on April 21, he finally started doing something about the incriminating items around his house. McVeigh still had not shown up and he understood, somewhere behind the walls of denial he had erected, that this was ominous.

First he went through McVeigh's rucksack, telling himself he was doing it to look for a set of "rabbit ears," a portable indoor antenna for his television. McVeigh was supposed to have driven the antenna out from Las Vegas along with the TV, but Nichols hadn't found it in the storage locker or anywhere else. His search became near-obsessive, a pretext perhaps not to think too hard about events 250 miles to the south. On the morning of the bombing, he went into town to ask about the price of a basic roof antenna, and balked when he heard it would be $200 or $300. On April 20, he reluctantly ordered cable service, rationalizing to himself that Marife would appreciate the choice of channels. Still he kept looking for his antenna. "Silly as it may sound," he later wrote, "I did want those rabbit ears."

He found no rabbit ears in the rucksack, but he did pull out a hand grenade. That sobered him in a hurry. As soon as he could get away—after the cable guy had come and gone—Nichols drove to a river north of town and tossed both the grenade and the license plate from the Mercury into the rushing spring water. He also buried an incriminating 50-caliber rifle. On his return, he remembered he had two half-empty bags of ammonium nitrate in his garage. He emptied them into a plastic bucket and hastily sprinkled the contents on his front lawn. The fertilizer was so thick, a seventy-five-year-old farmer across the street later said it looked like wet snow. The bags had nothing to do with the bombing: Nichols had bought them a month earlier, thinking he could make money by grinding up the contents and scooping them into small containers. Several people later testified they had seen him selling them at gun shows. "He was," one surplus dealer said, "the only dumbass I ever did see do it."

Two more items in the garage worried Nichols: the box of blasting caps wrapped in Christmas paper, which he had retrieved from the storage locker, and another box, containing sixty-eight nitromethane tubes, part of a binary explosive kit called Kinestik. Nichols didn't want to ditch the boxes, but he didn't regard the storage locker as safe, because there was no telling what McVeigh might reveal if he was in custody. So he dug a hole under the crawl space in his basement and buried them, along with some Primadet shock tube, smoke grenades, hand flares, and two bomb-making handbooks.

It wasn't much of a hiding place, but it was effective.

● ● ●

THE NCIC OFFLINE SEARCH PAID OFF, SHOWING THAT A HIGHWAY patrol trooper in Noble County had run a criminal record check on Timothy McVeigh about an hour and a half after the bombing. Mark Michalic, an ATF agent on the task force, looked at a map and saw that Noble County was directly on the road from Oklahoma City to Kansas. With mounting excitement, he started making phone calls.

"Holy fuck! He's sittin' in jail!" Michalic announced after talking to Charlie Hanger. That got everyone's attention.

Michalic called Jerry Cook, the Noble County sheriff. "Have you still got this guy?" he asked. He hardly believed the good news. "Hold on to him," Michalic implored. "Don't let him go!"

He couldn't have cut it any finer. The arraignment hearing postponed from the day before was at last going ahead, and McVeigh was already downstairs, waiting to enter court. The judge was running late, again, or McVeigh might have been gone already.

"Spin that boy around and put him back in your hotel," Michalic said as calmly as he could manage.

Michalic put his hand over the receiver and told his colleagues: "We got him."

The room erupted in cheers.

{ Four }

TIM AND TERRY AND JAMES
AND . . . THAT'S IT

Shortly after noon on April 21, Tim McVeigh found himself in an overcrowded room in the Noble County courthouse under a barrage of questions.

"Do you have any idea why the FBI wants to talk to you?" Agent Floyd Zimms asked.

"Yes," McVeigh responded. His eyes were expressionless.

"What do you mean by yes?" asked Zimms's colleague Jim Norman.

"That thing in Oklahoma City, I guess."

It was a lame, uncharacteristically incriminating response, but McVeigh was exhausted and demoralized. Barely two hours earlier, he had still been hopeful as he waited in an empty courtroom to be called in to the judge. But then Sheriff Cook, whom he had not previously encountered, told him the judge was running late, and McVeigh began to suspect something was up.

McVeigh couldn't help noticing people looking at him strangely. His cell mates were being taken outside one by one, and he figured, rightly, that they were being questioned about him.

Meanwhile, Sheriff Cook and McVeigh's prosecutor, Mark Gibson, had to decide what protocol to follow before the feds arrived. Gibson didn't want to keep McVeigh waiting indefinitely, because he had already been in custody for forty-eight hours without a hearing, so he pushed to proceed with a bond hearing. Gibson even got on the phone with the FBI and told them they needed to hurry. "Until you've got something," he said, "we've got to treat this guy like we treat anybody else. If bond is set, and you're not ready and he can make bond, he's going to make bond."

Gibson asked McVeigh where he was from and what his financial circumstances were. He needed to consider how likely it was that his defendant might flee, or commit other crimes while out on bond. Even without the bombing, McVeigh fit into a number of high-risk categories. He had been arrested with a semiautomatic and a cop-killer bullet, and he had no fixed address. (He told Gibson he was traveling from Arizona to Michigan and lived "here and there.")

Bail was set at $5,000, far beyond his means. McVeigh tried to charm the judge, pointing out that he had no criminal record and meant no harm. The judge appreciated his input, but it made no difference. He was sent back to the fourth floor, where he made three separate calls to a local public defender, Royce Hobbs. He could only leave a message and, shortly after, the lines went dead. A passing jail employee told him they must be out of order, and McVeigh slammed the receiver in frustration.

It was Sheriff Cook who cut the phone lines, on the recommendation of Walt Lamar, the first FBI agent to arrive in Perry. Lamar told Cook he should lock down the courthouse, surround it with crime tape, and set up a press area in anticipation of the coming media scrum. "You really think all that is necessary?" Cook asked. Lamar knew it was. The first thing he had encountered after arriving via helicopter was a television news crew from Tulsa. Shortly after, the phones started ringing with inquiries from other reporters. "If they are calling," Lamar told Cook, "they are coming."

Moments after McVeigh realized the phones were dead, he heard the whirring of a second FBI helicopter. This one contained a whole team of investigators, who had first stopped at the site of McVeigh's abandoned car on I-35 and discovered its trove of antigovernment literature. That, along with the timing and location of the arrest, made them feel sure they had their man. Unfortunately, it also put them in a gung-ho mood that did little to induce McVeigh to open up. Rather than questioning him in an intimate setting, they found the biggest room available, the county elections office across the hall from Sheriff Cook's cramped workspace, and invited every law officer on the scene to pile in.

McVeigh answered the agents' perfunctory questions about his name and weight and height, but stopped when asked for his birthplace. He was back in soldier mode, determined to give nothing away to the enemy. He would not even sign a form advising him of his rights.

"There should have been two people max in the room with McVeigh," a seasoned bureau agent on the scene lamented. "I'm in no doubt he wanted to shout to the heavens that he did this."

Instead, McVeigh merely listened as the FBI told him how he had been identified, and showed him the John Doe One sketch. His main concern was that someone might shoot him as FBI agents escorted him from the building. A crowd of several hundred was already massing noisily outside.

THE ENTIRE DETROIT DIVISION OFFICE OF THE FBI WAS MAKING preparations to descend on James Nichols's farm. They took their time, because they wanted to be sure their raid didn't turn into an armed standoff, and because they still needed to establish whether Nichols was a suspect, a material witness, or just a guy who kept spectacularly bad company.

Joe Martinolich, the Detroit special agent in charge and one of the bureau's most widely respected senior managers, knew Nichols was a person of interest by midnight on April 20 and had his assault team assembled by dawn. Martinolich asked the Sanilac County sheriff, Virgil Strickler, to keep the growing law enforcement presence hidden until they were ready to pounce. Strickler knew the layout of the Nichols farm, and also had a good idea who had been coming and going over the past several months.

Most important, Sheriff Strickler provided access to his informants. One was Daniel Stomber, Nichols's neighbor who said he had seen James and Terry make bombs out of fertilizer, peroxide, and bleach, and detonate them in plastic soda bottles. He recalled how James Nichols boasted about his bomb-making skills. He also remembered the brothers' vitriolic comments about Waco, including James saying he wouldn't be sorry to see someone pop off a federal judge or even assassinate the president. Stomber further remembered a camouflage-clad friend named Tim—he did not know his last name—who had lived on the farm for a while but moved away in early 1994.

Another witness said that in December 1993 he saw two white men enter a hobby shop in Marlette, about ten miles south of Decker, and ask for 100 percent liquid nitro model airplane fuel. One of the men gave his name as Terry Tuttle and left a bogus phone number that was one digit off James Nichols's real number. The store assistant said he stocked only 10–15 percent liquid nitro but would order the stronger stuff. Two weeks later, the men returned, but the store would not or could not fulfill the order—probably because pure liquid nitro airplane fuel can be used as an explosive. The surname Tuttle was later established as a frequent alias of McVeigh's.

This was now more than enough to seek a search warrant on the Decker farm. And, in the early afternoon, the feds were given the perfect opportunity to move in, as James Nichols got in his car and started driving south. He later said he was simply going about his business, stopping at the bank and at an auto parts store to pay for repairs on a tractor engine. But he also mentioned that, just before he left his house, a neighbor tipped him off that some farmhouse in Decker was about to be raided. So he could have left for his own protection.

As Nichols drove south, he saw helicopters, news trucks, and an ambulance heading in the opposite direction. As soon as he arrived at the bank, he asked the staff to turn on a radio so he could find out what was going on. He later claimed he still had no idea this had anything to do with him. His account adopts an almost ridiculous tone of aw-shucks innocence: "I tried to imagine who in this area could be involved in anything nasty enough to interest federal law enforcement agencies," he wrote. "I couldn't think of anyone. . . . Who could it possibly be?"

Soon, the feds were crawling over every inch of his property. When he returned from Marlette, the crush of police vehicles and satellite trucks surrounding his house was so great he had to ask a state trooper for help getting through. The trooper asked him who he was, then called over an FBI agent, who conducted a thorough body search and went through the contents of Nichols's car.

AGENT STEPHEN SMITH HAD A PROBLEM: HE COULDN'T FIND TERRY Nichols's house in Herington. He was the advance man for an entire FBI search team, but nobody had checked the address provided by Lana Padilla before he took off from Fort Riley. By the time he learned from local police that Nichols lived at 109 South Second Street, not 901, the rest of the team was already closing in.

Smith did a quick drive-by, noticing Nichols's blue GMC pickup outside the modest wood-framed house, before he ditched his rental car and returned with a colleague in a more weather-beaten Cutlass Supreme. With luck, nobody would notice them. They sat, and watched, and waited.

BACK IN LAS VEGAS, THE FBI HAD BEGUN QUESTIONING TWELVE-year-old Josh Nichols. Agents wanted to know everything—about the week he had just spent in Herington with his father, about his father's movements, about any contact he had had with Tim McVeigh.

The boy was initially leery but opened up a little to a female agent named Debbie Calhoun. She asked Josh about his family and the time he spent on the Nichols farm in Michigan. She also asked Josh if he had any contact with explosives. "My dad has a lot of guns," the boy replied. "We shoot and we make some little bombs sometimes."

Both Calhoun and Lana Padilla, who was in the room at the time, were stunned. Neither said anything, preferring to let Josh keep talking. "I know how to build a bomb," he went on. "It really isn't hard. My dad and I used to build them all the time."

Calhoun was soon convinced Josh knew more about the bombing than he was letting on—as was his mother. During a break in questioning, shortly after the family learned that McVeigh had been found, Josh whispered to Padilla: "Mom, there were going to be other bombs. There were supposed to be three bombings. Don't tell anybody." Josh went on to say: "The plan was to do one, followed by two others. Three altogether."

If Padilla had been able to think straight, she would not have allowed the FBI to ask another question without calling a lawyer. But she clung to the belief that Nichols had nothing to do with the bombing. Maybe Josh and Terry had some information to point the FBI in the right direction, she rationalized. Let them tell what they know, then the family's lives could return to normal.

As his brother was being apprehended in Michigan, Terry Nichols was driving home from a lumberyard and heard on the radio that McVeigh had been taken into federal custody. Even more shocking, he learned that he and his brother were wanted in connection with the bombing and should be considered "armed and dangerous."

He could not drive home fast enough, and immediately asked Marife if she had been watching the television coverage. She had not. She was fuming about the conversation he had had earlier that morning with his ex-wife, and was threatening—not for the first time—to go back to the Philippines. She didn't like his relationship with Lana, or with Josh, or with Tim McVeigh, and was sick of dealing with all of them. Nichols was too frazzled to fight back, so he turned on the television. When he saw the two composite sketches, he felt momentary relief—he did not think John Doe One looked like McVeigh, and neither did Marife. But when he heard Janet Reno, the attorney general, calling for the death penalty, and President Clinton vowing to deliver justice that was "certain, swift, and severe," Nichols had visions of heavily armed agents barreling down on the house. "I panicked," he recounted, "and I said to myself, this is a case where they will definitely shoot first and ask questions later."

Nichols phoned his brother James, and Lana, but reached neither. When CNN started calling from Los Angeles, he barked at Marife to pick up their infant daughter, Nicole, and get in the car. The safest place for them, he decided, was the Herington police station. In the garage, he gave everything a once-over. He noticed a fuel meter he had bought a few weeks earlier to resell at a gun show, only to realize it was broken. "I have to do something about that," he said quickly. Interestingly, he disregarded a siphon pump sitting on a shelf directly above the fuel meter, which he had used three days earlier to mix the bomb components. The only thing he picked up was a crate McVeigh had dropped off the previous week. He was concerned about a single item in the box, a mercury switch, and decided he should get rid of it before going to the police.

Nichols made an otherwise curious stop at a warehouse store on the southern edge of Herington, where he used the anonymity of the parking lot to smash the mercury switch on the asphalt. Later, he told the feds he intended to go shopping, but changed his mind once he sensed he was being followed. That, though, was largely untrue: Stephen Smith and his colleague Jack Foley had overshot the Surplus City store and turned around only once they realized Nichols was not heading out of town after all.

Marife was in a daze of her own. She could tell her husband was extraordinarily agitated, but she had no clear idea why. She blurted out the question uppermost in her mind: "Are you involved in this?" And Nichols answered no. He fretted that he did not know the way to the police station; Marife told him to calm down. He confessed he had not told the truth the previous Sunday when he said he had gone to Omaha to pick up McVeigh. He had, in fact, met McVeigh in Oklahoma City, and lied about it at McVeigh's direction. That, he said, was the reason he thought the feds might be after him.

Around 3:00 P.M., the Nichols family walked into the police station like three strays begging for shelter. Nichols told Barry Thacker, the deputy chief, that he wanted to talk to someone about the radio reports and assured him he was neither armed nor dangerous. At that very moment, Dale Kuhn, Thacker's boss, was on the line with an FBI supervisor, who told him that a hotly sought-after bombing suspect had just entered the building. Smith, Foley, and two other agents hovered outside, too afraid to enter as they entertained the notion that Nichols and his wife and infant daughter might somehow take the police department hostage. Kuhn assured the supervisor that, no, Nichols was not threatening anyone. But the police chief certainly understood the significance of the situation. He raced to the front desk and suggested that everyone move out of public view. All three Nichols family members were searched for weapons, even eighteen-month-old Nicole, who was held by her mother as an officer ran a finger around the top of her diaper.

Then the FBI agents ventured in and ordered everyone into a training room in the basement. Nichols asked why he was being mentioned in the news reports about the bombing. The agents said they did not know but wanted to ask him some questions.

"Good," Nichols countered, "because I have some questions for you."

• • •

MORE THAN ELEVEN HUNDRED MILES AWAY, IN KINGMAN, ARIZONA, the news reports on McVeigh hit his old army buddy Michael Fortier like a punch in the gut. Not only had Fortier known about the bomb plot; he had come perilously close to taking part himself. Since the start of wall-to-wall coverage of the bombing, he had not stopped fretting.

As soon as McVeigh's name aired on the news that Friday lunchtime, he went over to his neighbor Jim Rosencrans's house and announced: "Tim's the one that did it." Rosencrans's girlfriend later remembered how nervous he was. Rosencrans, who was close to Fortier and regularly did drugs with him, never had any doubts that their friend Tim was involved. "Damn, our boy has been busy," he thought.

Fortier shook his head in amazement. "Wow," he said, "that shit's intense." Then he and his wife, Lori, went around the house, ditching all the incriminating material they could find.

The FBI came calling that same afternoon.

McVEIGH WAS STILL WORRIED ABOUT HIS SAFETY. HE REMEMBERED how Jack Ruby gunned down Lee Harvey Oswald in the Dallas police headquarters in 1963, and told his captors he wanted a helicopter airlift from the courthouse roof rather than having to face the restive crowd outside. The FBI took his request seriously; if someone took a potshot, an agent could get hit just as easily as McVeigh. But the roof was deemed unsuitable for a helicopter landing. So they opted instead to drive him in a sheriff's department van to a secured helicopter staging area a short distance away.

First, though, they had to overcome a legal hurdle, as Royce Hobbs, the public defender McVeigh had sought to reach, made an unexpected appearance and demanded a hearing with Judge Allen. The judge agreed—over the objections of Mark Gibson, who refused to attend. All Hobbs could do, though, was advise McVeigh to find himself a federal public defender.

Finally, around 5:00 P.M., it was time to move. This was the public's first chance to see McVeigh, and the timing was perfect for the evening newscasts. The prisoner emerged from the courthouse in his orange jailhouse jumpsuit, his hands cuffed and his legs in irons, and the crowd exploded. People were shouting "baby killer," and worse. Several agents clustered around him, scanning the crowd for signs of trouble. McVeigh looked up at the surrounding buildings, worried that someone with a rifle might be on the rooftops. His gaze was vacant, emotionless, a snapshot image the media would feast on and designate as the face of a ruthless killer.

In a moment, he was gone—into the sheriff's van and, shortly after, onto a helicopter to Tinker Air Force Base outside Oklahoma City. Taking him to the federal courthouse next to the Murrah Building was out of the question; there was no telling what an incensed crowd would do if it got near him and, besides, the courthouse was too badly damaged to be functional. Tinker would work fine as a venue for the arraignment. A federal magistrate judge, Ronald Howland, was ready and waiting. After that, McVeigh would be taken to a specially prepared wing of El Reno federal prison outside Oklahoma City, his home while he awaited trial.

The lasting impression that Danny Coulson, the senior FBI agent in Perry, retained of McVeigh from that afternoon was his utter surprise at finding himself in the feds' clutches. "McVeigh," he said, "regarded his arrest by Charlie Hanger as a minor inconvenience—he thought he'd be out of jail and on his way in short order. He was shocked we got to him as fast as we did." Coulson sat next to him on the helicopter, putting his hand on McVeigh's shoulder and telling him sternly that he needed to behave himself.

"Act like a gentleman, and you will be treated like a gentleman," Coulson said. "If not, you will be very sorry. Do you understand me?"

"Yes sir," McVeigh replied. "I understand."

●   ●   ●

WHEN DANIELLE HUNT, THE FORMER OPERATOR AND DIRECTOR OF the America's Kids day-care center, saw McVeigh's face flash across her television screen, she knew at once he was involved. He was the same tall, lanky young man with a military buzz cut who had visited the day-care center in December, claiming he had two young children and asking her a lot of strange questions. He wasn't interested in the kids' daily routines, or in the teachers and their qualifications. He was interested only in the layout of the place and the security arrangements—whether there were cameras, and how many entrances and exits the day care had. He was transfixed, too, by the plate-glass windows next to the infants' nap area. "There's so much glass," he said, over and over. Hunt told him how the children liked to paint pictures on the glass, and look out at the changing seasons. "Now, thinking back," she recalled, "he must have been imagining how easy it would be to blow up the children."

McVeigh showed up at the tail end of the business day in battle-dress uniform and said he was a military recruiter transferring from Wichita within a few months. He was looking for a place for his three-year-old and an infant. He had no name tag on his uniform, and no badge or other form of identification. He would not give his name, or his children's names.

When Danielle's soon-to-be husband, Tom, the head of the Federal Protective Service, came to pick her up, McVeigh became visibly nervous. "How did he get in?" he asked. Danielle Hunt replied: "He's my husband and he's also a federal agent, so he has keys to the whole building." McVeigh insisted on moving around a corner where they could not be seen. Shortly after, he left by a secondary door so he would not have to cross paths with Tom Hunt again.

As the Hunts drove home, Danielle told Tom her visitor didn't have a name tag. Tom immediately sniffed trouble. "If he's a recruiter," he said, "he has to have his name and his grade and the words 'U.S. Army.'" But at that point there was nothing he could do.

Danielle told her story to the FBI but nothing ever came of it—

most likely because when she gave her account in the immediate aftershock of the bombing, she confused the timing of McVeigh's December visit with another incident at the Murrah Building in early March, involving two suspicious men who went from office to office telling people they wanted to apply for a job. Her testimony could have been devastating to McVeigh, forever erasing any doubt that he knew about the day-care center in advance and strongly suggesting that he targeted the kids deliberately. If the FBI had reinterviewed her, they could have connected her story with the known movements of McVeigh and Michael Fortier, who were in Oklahoma City on December 15 (but in Arizona in early March).

They did not. "I was really shocked they did not call me as a witness," Hunt said. "I can't imagine why they didn't."

THE FEDS HAD McVEIGH, BUT THEY ALSO HAD A PROBLEM. HE WAS not a close fit to the composite sketch of John Doe One. Once he was in custody, they could have shown either his picture or the man himself to the employees at Eldon Elliott's body shop. But the FBI chose not to, not even when they arranged a lineup for the Oklahoma City witnesses on the first weekend after the bombing. Eldon Elliott was not shown a photograph of McVeigh, or formally asked if he was a match for Robert Kling, until June 8, forty-eight days after McVeigh was tracked down and arrested on federal charges. If he had an opinion about the face being flashed all over the news, he didn't volunteer it.

The feds never properly explained their thinking. They weren't overly impressed with the body shop witnesses and might not have wanted to rely on them too heavily at this early stage. They were even beginning to conclude that the sketches were unreliable. Though they were growing more certain that McVeigh was responsible for driving the truck into Oklahoma City and detonating the bomb, there was the possibility that someone else rented the truck from Eldon Elliott's.

Plenty of things did not fit right. McVeigh's fingerprints were never found at the body shop—not on the counter, which the FBI took the trouble to dismantle and haul off to their lab in Washington, and not on the Robert Kling rental agreement. John Doe One was five foot ten (Vicki Beemer said he was about the same height as her husband), while McVeigh was six foot one. The body type and the facial features were not quite the same, either. Each witness who had linked McVeigh to the composite sketch—Lea McGown, Pat Livingston, Carl LeBron—had other reasons to be suspicious of him. None made the identification on physical resemblance alone.

MEANWHILE, SOME STARTLING EVIDENCE SURFACED THAT JOHN Doe One might be someone else entirely. Once the composite sketches were released, Angie Finley, an ATF agent in Tulsa, received a phone call from a confidential informant, a slightly built former debutante on the Tulsa social circuit with killer looks, blond hair, and a black swastika tattooed on her left shoulder. The informant, who was later revealed as Carol Howe, had spent much of the previous half-year in Elohim City, providing evidence of illegal weapons handling and numerous threats by the residents to wage war against the government.

Howe had come to the ATF as a result of romantic as well as political entanglements. Following a short marriage to a White Power activist, she became involved with Dennis Mahon, a bombastic neo-Nazi leader whose checkered résumé included cross-burnings in Germany and a bizarre appearance on Oprah Winfrey's television chat show. Mahon ran a Dial-A-Racist hotline in Tulsa, which Howe called after she was confronted by some African-Americans at an outdoor party, fell off a platform, and broke both her heels.

Mahon became Howe's protector, then her suitor, flattering her into posing in eccentric military uniforms and draping her in nothing but a Nazi flag. Soon, though, she was accusing Mahon of molesting her. When she took out a restraining order, it attracted the attention of the ATF, which had been looking into Mahon for years. Howe thought working as an informant was an ideal way to get even, and was soon reporting on Mahon's fondness for detonating homemade grenades and outlining plans he had to blow up a Mexican-owned video store.

The ATF asked Howe to conduct a drug buy on behalf of the Tulsa Police Department, which they said was to test her loyalty. They also polygraphed her, and tapped her phone and wired up her apartment for both audio and video. Amazingly, Mahon was willing to forgive the court order as soon as she renewed contact with him. And she proved very effective at delivering incriminating material, both on Mahon and on his friends at Elohim City. Weekends in the community gradually extended into longer stays, during which Howe eavesdropped—and reported on—many conversations about fomenting revolution, including specific threats to blow up government buildings.

Howe said she could provide a match for the composite sketches—to people other than Tim McVeigh. To her, John Doe One looked like Pete Ward and John Doe Two resembled his brother Tony. Finley passed the information to her superiors, who shared it with the FBI. And the FBI, in turn, decided it needed to talk to Howe. While McVeigh was still being plucked out of jail, Finley and an FBI agent from Tulsa drove Howe to Oklahoma City to be extensively debriefed.

The encounter did not show the FBI in its best colors. The bureau's notes, typed up in an official insert, are marred by every conceivable error, including grotesque misspellings, inaccurate dates, and a general lack of understanding of the subject. Still the gist of Howe's reporting was clear. The two men she fingered most damningly were Mahon and Andreas Strassmeir. Mahon had not only expressed a desire to blow up a federal building, he named Tulsa and Oklahoma City as possible targets. He also had a plan to initiate mass race riots by destroying power lines at the height of summer and creating panic.

Howe described Strassmeir as contemplating "assassinations, bombings, and mass shootings," and characterized Elohim City as an armed encampment whose armory included more than three hundred rifles, MAC 90s and Ruger mini-14 semiautomatics and "various fully automatic weapons," possession of which is flagrantly illegal.

One would think this information constituted a major new lead. But Carol Howe was a touchy subject for federal law enforcement. The ATF had abruptly discontinued her services a month before the bombing, claiming that she had become mentally unstable. Now that decision looked distinctly unwise, particularly since the information she provided before her dismissal had been viewed as both credible and alarming by her immediate handlers. So the FBI and ATF decided, together, to recall her and send her back into Elohim City to see what connections she could pick up to McVeigh or any possible coconspirators.

It was never more than a halfhearted initiative, and the onus of further investigation was placed almost entirely on her. The feds sent neither uniformed agents nor covert operatives into the community to help. No effort was made to interview Andreas Strassmeir, or Pete or Tony Ward, or any member of the Millar family except one inconsequential son-in-law who offered nothing useful.

Bob Ricks, the head of the FBI's Oklahoma City office, who had been aware of Elohim City for years, maintained that, contrary to appearances, investigators took a strong interest in links between the community and the bombing. But, he said, they saw little benefit in conducting aggressive interviews without acquiring some baseline knowledge first. Elohim City was difficult to penetrate or monitor— because of its remoteness, because it had no useful phones to tap (its one main line was too public for sensitive conversation), and because of its hostility to outsiders. "Generally we don't want to ask questions until we know the answers," Ricks said, "and we had a vast unknown in Elohim City. . . . We had no leverage, no evidence of criminal conduct. Without something to use as a hammer, conducting interviews would have done us no good."

That defense holds only to a point. The feds did have considerable leverage over Dennis Mahon, because of Howe's evidence that he'd made and detonated grenades. And they could have had more leverage still over Strassmeir, who was arming Elohim City even though, as a foreigner, he had no legal right to purchase weapons.

In these early days of the investigation, though, Elohim City was mostly the subject of a turf war between the FBI and the ATF. The FBI wanted to know what the ATF knew, but the ATF—as its director, John Magaw, has subsequently acknowledged—was reluctant to share. Even after the ATF gave the FBI its Carol Howe file, the feds continued to suspect that more information was being suppressed; that the ATF was sitting on potentially explosive information and running "hip-pocket informants," in Ricks's phrase, who were kept out of the official record for reasons of internal bureaucratic convenience. Danny Defenbaugh, who would take over leadership of the investigation from Weldon Kennedy, struggled with the problem for months on end. "When you get agencies working together in a joint Task Force, they should be holding hands, not keeping their fingers crossed behind their backs," he said. "[The ATF] didn't handle it well, nor did we know in a timely manner what we should have known."

The FBI carries its own share of the blame. It seems inexcusable, given the bureau's usual practice of chasing down every lead, that Carol Howe's allegations were not pursued more aggressively. At least one senior FBI agent, Danny Coulson, came to believe the investigation into Elohim City was deliberately shut down for reasons of bureaucratic cowardice or incompetence. When Bob Ricks was asked in an interview why Dennis Mahon was never questioned about his threats to blow up a federal building in Oklahoma, he answered, simply: "I don't know."

Nobody was more delighted or relieved by the feds' inaction than the Elohimites themselves. Once the bomb went off, Robert Millar and his followers feared the FBI and ATF would descend with a full array of paramilitary hardware. Some of that was fed by paranoia and exaggerated notions of how much the government was spoiling for a fight. Some of it, though, was entirely rational, given the community's ties to right-wing radicals, and its links, both direct and indirect, to McVeigh.

"The feds were looking for excuses to come after us," Andi Strassmeir said. "We slept in our fatigues and boots, with rifles by our side."

IN THE HERINGTON POLICE STATION, TERRY NICHOLS TOLD THE FBI he was willing to answer any questions, even without a lawyer present. The agents said repeatedly that he was not under arrest and could leave any time. He stayed put, partly to support his contention that he had nothing to hide and partly to figure out how much the FBI had on him. But if he thought he could outsmart the feds, he was wrong.

The agents found him weird and suspicious, and the impression only deepened as the hours passed. They were struck when Nichols said he no longer used his social security number and when he refused to sign a form advising him of his rights because he objected to the word "interrogation," which reminded him of the Nazis.

A short time later, as he authorized the FBI to search his house and his pickup, he expressed concern that they might mistake some items for bomb-making equipment. The subject of bombs had not yet come up, and Agent Scott Crabtree wrote in a search warrant affidavit the following day that Nichols gave no reason why the FBI might make such a mistake. Rightly or wrongly, the line struck the agents as a tacit admission. Over the next nine hours, Nichols would tip his hand further, ducking and evading questions and telling so many demonstrable lies his credibility never recovered.

Nichols described how he and McVeigh became friends during basic training at Fort Benning, Georgia, in 1988. They were close for a while, and McVeigh stayed at the Nichols family farm for several weeks in early 1993. But Nichols claimed he'd had only minimal contact for several months, and then only to ask McVeigh to transport his television set from Las Vegas, as he had promised. This was not true, as phone records and other evidence would later demonstrate.

Nichols continued to use the television to explain away his movements on Easter Sunday, when he helped McVeigh stash the Mercury in Oklahoma City. He said he drove to Oklahoma City alone—in fact, he and McVeigh convoyed down—and picked up both McVeigh and the TV on a street corner. (The television, which Nichols genuinely wanted, was in a storage locker in Kansas all along.)

Years later, Nichols acknowledged that he agreed to drive to Oklahoma City not because of the TV but because he was afraid of what McVeigh would do to his family if he said no. He could not tell the FBI that, because it would open him up to other questions about his involvement, which he was not ready to answer. "I lied to them and said I had picked up my TV . . . to make my story sound more plausible," he said. "I was in denial at that time and was trying to distance myself from McVeigh and his evil act as much as possible."

Still, Nichols dropped hints that McVeigh was up to no good—in ways that did not involve him. In his account of their return journey to Kansas, Nichols told the FBI that McVeigh had pointed out the upcoming Waco anniversary and announced, cryptically: "You will see something big in the future."

"What are you going to do," Nichols recalled asking, "rob a bank?"

"Oh, no," McVeigh responded. "I got something in the works."

McVeigh later complained to Michel and Herbeck that Nichols had "hosed" him with lines like these, and the judge presiding over the two men's trials certainly believed Nichols had incriminated his partner. Nichols described McVeigh as "nervous" and "hyper," and when asked about the bombing told the FBI his friend "could be capable of doing it." But Nichols later insisted: "I did not rat him out. I did not admit McVeigh actually did the bombing. I really didn't give the FBI much useful information."

That much appears to be true. Nichols's interview did far more immediate damage to his own cause than it did to McVeigh's. Time and again, his responses made him look like he was hiding something. He claimed he couldn't remember much about the rest of the journey back to Kansas, because he became "sleepy-tired" and kept losing the thread of the conversation. He said that several times during the drive McVeigh asked him what they had just talked about, and he couldn't remember. Nichols's interrogators thought that was a lame excuse to drop an uncomfortable subject. Their sense was that McVeigh and Nichols were in the final stages of planning the bombing and had plenty more to talk about that Sunday night.

Some of Nichols's lies were more sophisticated. He realized that someone—the fisherman and his son, for example—might have seen his pickup at the lake. He said McVeigh had called early that morning to borrow his truck, saying he wanted to drive around and shop for a new car. Nichols collected him at a McDonald's and asked to be dropped off at Fort Riley so he could attend a surplus auction. McVeigh was supposed to pick him up at noon but did not arrive until after 1:00 P.M. When McVeigh was late, Nichols went to a different auction in another building, the one he really attended and signed in for, and hung around for the extra hour.

By this stage, however, Nichols couldn't put any story past his interrogators. They had already decided to take him into custody as a material witness and were mostly stringing him along until the warrant arrived. In fact, their bosses in Kansas City had the warrant ready as early as 4:45 P.M. but sat on it while they waited to see what Nichols would spill on his own. Nichols's defense team would later argue that denying him knowledge of the warrant was deliberately misleading. A federal public defender who heard about the interrogation on the radio made several attempts to let Nichols know he was volunteering his services, but the message never got through. Nichols chose to believe he would soon be back in his car, heading home with Marife and the baby.

WHEN JENNIFER MCVEIGH HEARD HER OLDER BROTHER'S NAME ON the radio, her first concern was to avoid being sucked into the bombing conspiracy herself. She was in Florida, visiting friends and family on an extended spring break. But many people knew she was close to Tim, despite their six-year age difference, and knew she shared many of his political ideas. She was not surprised that he had involved himself in a big, revolutionary act, because he had all but told her already.

A month or two earlier, Tim had written to warn her that something big would happen "in the month of the Bull" and that she should stay in Florida for as long as possible. He wanted to protect her and told her to burn the letter, which she did the same day. Jennifer was living in her father's house in Pendleton, New York, and working (much to the FBI's amusement) at a Jell-O wrestling bar while attending community college; so she had some flexibility in her schedule. He wrote a follow-up at the end of March, making sure she had done as he asked. "Send no more [mail] after the first of April," he said, "and then even if it's an emergency, watch what you say because I may not get it in time and the G-men might get it out of my box, incriminating you."

Jennifer understood the need to take precautions. The night before she took the long drive down to Pensacola, she separated everything she had from her brother into two boxes. She kept the first one, containing his high school yearbooks, military records, medal citations, and other personal documents, in her closet. McVeigh had sent most of this material at the beginning of the year for safekeeping; he hadn't told her why, but she must have guessed he was preparing for a new life underground. The second box, containing McVeigh's letters, photographs, political literature, and a videotape accusing the government of mass murder at Waco, was more sensitive. She asked her best friend, Rose Woods, to keep it at her house while she was away.

When she heard about the bombing, she was staying with an old friend, Dennis Sadler, and his family in the Florida Panhandle. She kept her reactions quiet until she heard about her brother's arrest. She was out on a driving errand with Sadler at the time, and immediately asked him to take the wheel. She smoked a lot of cigarettes on the way back to the house. When she called her family, she learned the FBI was already at her father's house, asking about her relationship with her brother. She did not have much time. She took a handful of clippings from *The Turner Diaries* she had with her and burned them in Sadler's laundry room. When the FBI appeared, a short time later, they searched the house and Jennifer's pickup, finding a collection of right-wing literature.

The FBI wanted to bombard her with questions, but she would not cooperate. Like her brother, she saw the feds as the enemy. They came back to question her again and again over the course of the weekend, and she became only more resistant. "Defiant" was the word the feds used to characterize her. But she soon learned how persuasive the FBI can be.

SINCE MCVEIGH HAD BEEN IN THE MILITARY, THE ARMY WAS GIVEN the job of rounding up look-alikes to participate in a lineup for eyewitnesses who had seen him with the Ryder truck on the morning of the bombing. Twenty-four men were dispatched to Oklahoma City from Fort Sill, and five were selected. At first, the task force leadership worried the similarity was just too great and told Steve Chancellor, the army's point man: "You got McVeigh's brother, cousin, and uncles." They were, Chancellor said, "scared shitless."

But the witnesses did fine. Mike Moroz, the mechanic at Johnny's tire shop who had reported McVeigh asking for directions around 8:30 A.M., was the only one who hesitated a little. He chose two people, including the man in custody. McVeigh was clearly fingered as a guilty man—by people who also swore they had seen him with others.

AT 9:00 P.M. THAT NIGHT, A GAGGLE OF FBI AGENTS DESCENDED ON Okemah, a tiny speck of a town about seventy miles east of Oklahoma City, convinced they were about to make another major arrest. The name of their hot lead was Ray Jimboy, a Native American who had served in McVeigh's unit during the Gulf War. He was a ringer for John Doe Two—short, stocky, muscular, with dark hair and deep brown eyes. His fellow soldiers reported he had a temper and was covered with scars from knife fights. He also had a history of political activism.

Louis Freeh was so gung-ho for Jimboy that he sent Bob Ricks and a handful of his best men to supervise the operation. But it didn't work out as planned. Jimboy not only had an alibi, he was falling-down drunk, and had clearly been on the bottle for years, in no state to participate in a major criminal conspiracy. Ricks broke the bad news to Freeh, only to have the director tell him to put Jimboy under twenty-four-hour surveillance—personally.

Ricks couldn't believe it. "I got to watch this drunk myself," he said, "and I was a special agent in charge." It took another full day before the FBI brass finally cleared Jimboy, by which time the humiliation of Bob Ricks had descended to a whole new level.

TERRY NICHOLS WAS DIGGING HIMSELF IN EVER DEEPER. HE SAID HE had some knowledge of bomb-making, but insisted he'd never put it to use. Eight hours in, close to midnight, he acknowledged that he had bags of ammonium nitrate in his house, the ones he stored to sell off at gun shows. He said he hadn't mentioned this earlier because he was worried it would "make me look guilty to a jury."

By this time, the interviewing agents knew about the material witness warrant and felt they could throw tougher questions at him. Agent Crabtree asked about the package of materials Nichols had left for Lana Padilla when he flew to the Philippines the previous November. Nichols described it as a sort of will, drawn up in case he did not return. Nichols was flummoxed when Crabtree asked him about the two most incriminating phrases—the "go for it!!" line and the sign-off, "As far as heat, none that I know of."

Agent Smith later testified: "He sat there and looked at us for approximately a minute, and did not respond to the question." The warrant was served shortly afterward.

Even at this stage, the FBI lacked concrete evidence to tie Nichols to the bombing. Mostly, they had leads to check out—the ammonium nitrate bags, McVeigh's possessions in his garage, the Herington storage locker. Two FBI agents sent to guard his house pending a formal search spotted some blue-rimmed barrels in the garage, reminiscent of a large number of blue plastic shards found at the bombing scene. (The government would later argue that these were incriminating, but they were most likely from recycling bins on the Murrah Building's first floor.) The agents also saw a large number of ammunition and fuel cans, and picked up a strong odor of ammonium nitrate. None of this looked good, but it didn't prove anything, either.

When investigators went to U.S. District Judge David Russell for the warrant to hold Nichols as a material witness, they chose not to tell him that their suspect was, of his own free will, sitting in the Herington police station and talking up a storm—a symptom, perhaps, of their nervousness about the solidity of their case. A first version of the warrant stated, erroneously, that Nichols had attempted to leave the country and would be a flight risk if he was not taken immediately into custody. The Justice Department later explained this away as an innocent blunder by Jim Reynolds, the department's top anti-terrorism lawyer.

A new warrant was subsequently drawn up, this one stating that if Nichols were "left to his own devices, it would be impracticable to secure his presence"—a tortured form of wording that, again, ducked the fact that he was very much present and cooperating.

AS THE INITIAL FLURRY OF BREAKTHROUGHS BEGAN TO SLOW, THE FBI resorted to its hallmark taste for extreme thoroughness to hunt down additional suspects. The mania for detail started with Louis Freeh, who made it his personal business to pick out the lineup photographs that witnesses would be shown alongside McVeigh's. This was normally a low-level job for a field agent. "I was micromanaging," Freeh acknowledged in his autobiography, "which nobody likes the boss to do."

The bureau was prepared to track every last person McVeigh had encountered in the military, if that was what it took to find coconspirators. Steve Chancellor, the army's point man on the task force, was asked early on how many people trained with McVeigh at Fort Benning, and he said about a hundred. Then he was asked how many were in his infantry company, and Chancellor said just a few more. But, he cautioned, they should take a baseline number—120, say— and double it to account for a large turnover during the three years McVeigh served. The agents soon returned to ask how many people were in McVeigh's battalion. Chancellor said between 500 and 600, maybe 1,200 over three years. Soon they were asking about the entire brigade.

Chancellor looked skeptical. "Now you're talking in the thousands. Five, ten thousand people over three years," he said. And how many people were stationed at Fort Riley? "I looked at this guy," Chancellor recounted, "and thought, you got to be shittin' me. We're looking at 32,000 people. And the agent said, 'Okay, I think we'll stop.'"

● ● ●

CHARLIE HANGER RETURNED TO PATROL DUTY ON SATURDAY MORNing after two days off and instinctively checked the inside of his police cruiser to make sure nothing connected to McVeigh was left behind. On the rear floor behind the passenger seat, he spotted something: a crumpled business card for Paulsen's Military Supply in Antigo, Wisconsin. The front had an ink drawing of a tank and a military helicopter. The name DAVE, all in upper case, and a Chicago-area phone number were on the back, along with these words, in McVeigh's unmistakably spindly handwriting: "TNT. $5 a stick. Need more." And, beneath the phone number: "Call after 01 May, see if I can get some more."

Dave was Dave Paulsen, the son of the owner of Paulsen Military Supply, who had been in frequent contact with McVeigh in late 1994 and early 1995. When the FBI first saw the card, they immediately suspected Paulsen of providing McVeigh with bomb-making materials. TNT could have been used as a detonator in Oklahoma City; the feds did not yet know any different.

When the FBI tracked him down, the following evening, Paulsen acknowledged meeting McVeigh at a gun show in Kalamazoo in December 1994 and said he purchased some AR-15 assault weapon parts that McVeigh had on his display table. In exchange, McVeigh said he wanted dynamite. Paulsen told him repeatedly over the next few weeks that he could obtain some, but he had no intention of following through. They arranged a meeting to make the swap, but Paulsen was a no-show.

Paulsen was on the lookout for "interesting" gun parts and figured McVeigh was a good source. McVeigh also offered him blasting caps, at $500 a pop, and Paulsen said at the gun show that he was interested in those, too. McVeigh subsequently called him more than thirty times, both at work and at home—more calls than Paulsen was prepared to admit to initially.

Paulsen told the FBI he never intended to purchase blasting caps from McVeigh and only told him he would to maintain their connection. The FBI became suspicious enough to put him through a long grind of interviews, and these intensified after Paulsen failed a polygraph test. Paulsen was asked if he sold explosives to McVeigh; if he had discussed blowing anything up with McVeigh; and if he had more than one face-to-face meeting with McVeigh. On all three questions, Paulsen answered no; on all three, the polygraph showed his responses were "indicative of deception."

Paulsen remained under investigation for weeks until the FBI was satisfied he was not involved in the bombing. At one point, he broke down in tears in front of an agent, clenched his fists and exclaimed: "That son-of-a-bitch McVeigh, that cocksucker skinny son-of-a-bitch, I could kill him!"

His frustration and anger were understandable: McVeigh had dropped his business card in Trooper Hanger's cruiser as a deliberate act of revenge, exacted because Paulsen had let McVeigh down. McVeigh acknowledged as much to Michel and Herbeck. He let Terry Nichols know, before the bombing, that he not only planned to make trouble for Paulsen but would do the same to anyone who got in his way. McVeigh even showed Nichols the business card with his incriminating scrawl on the back.

"The impression I got was Tim was telling me this as a warning to me not to betray him," Nichols recounted. "McVeigh said that whenever someone screws him, his act of retribution in return would be multiplied by a factor of ten, at the minimum."

THE SEARCH OF TERRY NICHOLS'S HOUSE IN HERINGTON WAS NOT exactly the FBI's finest moment. Early on, they decided to seek court warrants for the search and not use the consent forms signed by Nichols and Marife. The agents wanted to take the time to assemble a full evidence recovery team and make sure the place was not booby-trapped. While the Nicholses were being questioned, however, the perimeter was breached at least once.

According to the Nicholses' home phone records, a call was placed from the house to James Nichols's farm in Michigan at about 8:40

P.M. on April 21 and lasted close to twenty minutes. Terry Nichols was in the police station basement, so he could not have made that call. Marife Nichols was not allowed home that night, not even to pick up a few toiletries and a change of clothes for herself and the baby. And James Nichols could not have received the call, because he was in federal custody. One possible explanation is that an FBI agent in Herington entered and got on the line to a colleague in Decker in violation of all the safeguards. An FBI report detailing the activities of the on-scene agents stated that "no law enforcement officers had entered the Nichols residence or the detached garage," but failed to offer any alternate explanation for the phone call.

The evidence recovery team came in from Omaha the following morning, supplemented by local agents and forensics and fingerprint experts flown in from Washington—fifteen people in all. It wasn't until 4:30 P.M. that they received the all-clear to move in, by which time they could have been amply briefed on information provided by Nichols. He had drawn a map of the property showing the location of all his firearms and ammunition, and had gone through the inventory of his gun-show supplies, including the ammonium nitrate sprinkled on his lawn and the broken fuel meter. He said the duffel bag and rucksack in the garage were McVeigh's, as well as the Ruger. For some reason, none of this was passed on, making the search seem much more hazardous.

The initial search lasted close to twelve hours, and yielded some valuable evidence, including five sixty-foot lengths of Primadet shock tube with nonelectric blasting caps attached, and a pink customer receipt for forty large bags of ammonium nitrate fertilizer purchased at the Mid-Kansas Co-op on September 30, 1994, by Mike Havens, later established as a Terry Nichols alias. The receipt would be pivotal at trial, because it had McVeigh's fingerprints on it. Its discovery, though, was a little odd: it was found in a kitchen drawer, behind some dish towels, wrapped around two gold coins Marife intended to use to pay for her passage home. Why would Nichols keep such an incriminating piece of evidence? Why would he keep it *there*?

Nichols himself insisted he gave the receipt to McVeigh at the time of the purchase and never saw it again. "Why would I wrap that receipt around two one-ounce coins and put it with my other coins? It makes no sense," he wrote years later, long after he had admitted purchasing the ammonium nitrate and using it to mix the bomb.

It might be easier to accept the good faith of the FBI recovery effort were it not for the breach in security the night before, and the lack of a fully rigorous sequence of photographs—showing the unopened drawer, the drawer with the exact placement of the contents, and the contents separated one by one. Nichols believed the FBI might have planted the receipt, but had no corroborating evidence. McVeigh might also have planted it to incriminate the Nichols brothers. He was never formally invited into the Herington house, but he could have gone there on the night of April 17, while Terry and Marife were driving Josh to the Kansas City airport.

The first search ended at about 4:00 A.M., but soon the team was sent back to retrieve a number of items they overlooked the first time. They had missed the fuel meter, which was sitting in pieces on a crate in the garage. They also had to collect Nichols's old Michigan license plate and sift through the garbage cans. In their first search of Nichols's books, they managed to pull out works on health food and cancer but missed Nichols's copy of *Hunter,* William Pierce's follow-up to *The Turner Diaries,* which features sniper killings of interracial couples and the destruction of a Mossad office by an ANFO bomb. On Sunday afternoon, more than twenty-four hours after the search began, Marife Nichols wondered why there was still no sign of the $5,000 in cash and a bag of gold coins she knew were hidden beneath her mattress.

FBI managers and street agents who heard about the botched search could only shake their heads. When agents came back a third and fourth time for additional search warrants, a U.S. attorney dealing with the paperwork was overheard saying: "You gotta be kidding me." Back at headquarters, assistant director Bear Bryant was about to ream out the Omaha special agent in charge for sending such a lousy evidence response team when he learned that the operation was being directed by the Kansas City SAC, a protégé of his named Dave Tubbs. He went quiet again.

Two weeks later, on May 8, Marife was given permission to collect clothes and toys from her house. When the FBI agents accompanying her—not recovery specialists—reminded her of a story she had told about her husband grinding up fertilizer, they asked if they could take the food mixer into evidence. She agreed and went straight to the kitchen cupboard where it was still sitting.

The mishandling of the search affected the way some evidence was characterized in court. Of the six most incriminating items listed in the initial affidavit supporting Nichols's prosecution, only two—the Primadet and the fertilizer receipt—constituted evidence of Nichols's guilt. The fuel meter had nothing to do with the bombing. Neither did the gas cans found in the garage or the containers of ground-up ammonium nitrate Nichols sold at gun shows. The white barrels from Nichols's garage were erroneously described as having "blue lids made from material resembling the blue plastic fragments found at the bomb scene." Actually, the barrels had no lids at all.

The government made other blunders. It *never* recovered the siphon pump, which Nichols used in the mixing of the bomb materials. And it never figured out that the duffel bag and rucksack were McVeigh's, *even though Nichols told the FBI they were.* The question of where McVeigh left his personal effects would end up consuming untold man-hours and send agents on at least one wild-goose chase into the Arizona desert. The answer was under their noses all the time.

Also undiscovered were the blasting caps and nitromethane tubes Nichols had buried beneath his crawl space. These could have had a profound impact on the investigation and trials, and perhaps led to the indictment of other coconspirators. Instead, they lay undisturbed for another ten years.

THE AGENTS AT TERRY NICHOLS'S HOUSE MADE ONE DISCOVERY THAT became a central part of the bombing investigation. It was a telephone calling card in the name of Daryl Bridges, obtained through the far-right publication *The Spotlight*. In an age before cell phones, these cards were the easiest way for people of limited means to stay mobile and still keep a single telephone account. Subscribers called an 800 number, entered a PIN number, and then used as many minutes as they had paid for.

Nichols had purchased the card, using the made-up name, when he was still living with his brother in Michigan. He maintained a ledger of payments, also found by the FBI, to keep the card solvent. There was nothing criminal about running a calling card under an assumed name, but as investigators started to dig through the card's phone records, it became clear that Nichols and McVeigh had used it to talk to each other, to talk to friends and contacts like Michael Fortier and Dave Paulsen, and to contact potential vendors of key bomb components—everything from the nitromethane to the Ryder truck.

Published accounts suggest that the Daryl Bridges investigation began when the physical card was discovered by the FBI on April 23. But forty-eight hours earlier, a Miami-based Secret Service agent named Mary Riley had already established some key links between the card and the bombing conspiracy. Riley's field notes indicate that she pulled together several pieces of the puzzle, via a maze of telephone companies, switchboard protocols, computer database interfaces, and other technological complexities. But something went wrong—so wrong that when it was time to present the case in court, all of Riley's work, and even her name, had disappeared from the record.

Riley was one of the savviest telecommunications and computer investigators in federal law enforcement. But, instead of working solely with the task force to obtain subpoenas for the relevant records, she established a second line of communication with Donna Bucella, one of Janet Reno's top aides in the Justice Department. It is not entirely clear who initiated contact with whom—neither would return messages requesting an interview. They were friends from Bucella's time as a federal prosecutor in southern and central Florida. Bucella was now deputy director of the Executive Office of U.S. Attorneys, overseeing top prosecutors around the country. According to several FBI veterans, Riley's channeling of information to Bucella broke the chain of command, which should have gone directly through the task force leadership in Oklahoma City. There was also a secondary problem of overreaching, which according to the FBI risked jeopardizing the admissibility of the phone records— the guts of the government's case against McVeigh and Nichols—as evidence in court.

Riley's big break came on April 21, when she heard that someone had called Eldon Elliott's body shop using the calling card number, 1-800-793-3377, which was traced to the Spotlight company. Spotlight, she discovered, was an MCI subscriber, and MCI's security department told her that the Spotlight account had been sold to a company called West Coast Telephone. John Kane, the entrepreneur behind WCT, was happy to look through his company's records and even called MCI to consult their confidential reverse directory to identify the subscriber.

That brought up the name Daryl Bridges and a Michigan address, matching the Nichols brothers' information. Riley then asked Kane for any calls Bridges might have made on April 14, the day Robert Kling called Vicki Beemer for a Ryder truck rental. Kane discovered that two calls had gone out in quick succession, the first to Terry Nichols's home in Herington and the second to Eldon Elliott's. It was not immediately clear where these calls originated, or whether they were made by the same Spotlight subscriber. Kane also contacted the Boston Financial Group, which handled payments on the Spotlight cards, and gave them the PIN number associated with the Bridges calls. Boston Financial reconfirmed the subscriber as Daryl Bridges and said he had $117 left on his account.

All this was privileged information with implications for subscriber privacy. It was perhaps understandable, given the speed of Riley's work and the urgency of the investigation, that she did her digging first and, to judge by her own records, worked on securing subpoenas thereafter. Not even her fiercest FBI detractors begrudged her that—they said they would have done the same, and could not imagine a judge or jury objecting, given the scale and urgency of the investigation. The executives at MCI and WCT were on stickier ground, because of their own obligations to protect their customers' privacy. But the time lag between information and legal cover was not great at this stage.

Then the information flow turned from a trickle to a flood. Already on April 21, Riley had a printout from Kane of hundreds of Daryl Bridges calls from December 1993 to April 17, 1995, two days before the bombing. These included calls to Terry Nichols's number in Herington, Lana Padilla's number in Las Vegas, and a cluster of numbers in the Philippines. Riley also learned that the all-important call to Eldon Elliott's body shop on the morning of April 14 came from a pay phone in Junction City—a discovery that would establish a significant link to McVeigh, because he had been across the street that morning, exchanging his clapped-out station wagon for the Mercury Marquis.

Riley's notes indicate that she believed her findings would move quickly into the hands of front-line investigators. She even communicated directly with some FBI agents. But the task force commanders somehow did not receive the information. Riley faxed everything to Don Stephenson, the Secret Service liaison in Oklahoma City, who should have briefed the task force leadership. While there is evidence Stephenson spoke to individual FBI agents, it's unclear if he did or did not talk to their commanders. There was definitely a monstrous communication failure. The FBI team who questioned Terry Nichols in the Herington police station would have been delighted to know about the Bridges card on the night of April 21; Riley had the information that afternoon, including evidence contradicting Nichols's assertion that he and McVeigh had had no phone contact for months before Easter Sunday.

Was the Secret Service leadership holding on to the information for itself, as some senior FBI agents have alleged? Or did something go wrong in the internal workings of the FBI? The available documentation, along with the memories of senior investigators and prosecutors, make it difficult to draw a conclusion, except that miscommunication was rampant. In one instance, Riley called a phone company in Michigan to get a subscriber name for what turned out to be James Nichols's number, only to be told that a bureau agent had already been in touch to ask the same question. (The bureau person, though, had two of the digits transposed.)

The problem with the second line of communication started on April 22, when, according to Riley's notes, Bucella asked her to send four pending subpoena requests through her. Soon, they were in regular contact by both phone and fax.

It was not a widely advertised relationship. The task force leadership was unaware of it, and remained so until some were questioned about it for this book. Weldon Kennedy said: "If I'd have known that, I would have taken her head off. I would have thrown her off the task force in a heartbeat." Another top FBI case manager was equally harsh on Bucella: "If she didn't know the basics of that, then she sure should have. She was one of the DOJ's lead prosecutors at that time."

Two days later, on April 24, Riley and the FBI were at cross-purposes again. Someone went to a pay phone near the Fort Riley command post at 3:30 A.M. and used the Daryl Bridges card to call a second pay phone nearby. Nobody picked up. This had to have been an FBI agent testing the card, but neither Riley nor John Kane at West Coast Telephone understood that, because the FBI did not tell them. They thought they might have picked up the trail of another conspirator. And so, they spent hours addressing an issue that was, in fact, no issue at all.

Later that same day, Riley contacted the Boston Financial Group and asked for the payment records of every Spotlight calling-card holder—about five thousand people in all. According to Riley's notes, she fired off a subpoena request to Don Stephenson in Oklahoma City, and Stephenson later told her the subpoena had been issued. But the FBI soon came to worry that this line of inquiry was too broad, and that it somehow threatened the admissibility of the phone records. And it was not just the FBI that was concerned. By the next day, a manager at the Liberty Lobby, the avowedly racist organization behind *The Spotlight*, called John Kane's office, demanding assurances that no information on his customers would be divulged. On April 26, the FBI decided, as one agent told John Kane, to "start at the beginning" and reanalyze the phone records as though Mary Riley never existed.

Nobody at the FBI has ever given a satisfactory explanation of what Riley did to incite the bureau's wrath. Weldon Kennedy suggested she made mistakes in the actual technical analysis of the phone records. But Riley's field notes address the points Kennedy raised. Kennedy's successor as head of the task force, Danny Defenbaugh, said more explicitly he could not talk about the subject in any detail. When asked if Riley or the Secret Service had somehow overreached in the number of records they requested, Defenbaugh replied: "That's a great theory." He also confirmed that once the FBI took control, they no longer pursued the financial records of the Spotlight card holders.

There has been no explanation, either, of why the FBI placed so much blame solely on Riley. Didn't she have bosses? Didn't someone sanction what she was up to? What about Don Stephenson, who received her field notes on a regular basis? Was the FBI entirely blame-less, given the contact its own agents had with Riley?

Riley was fired from the task force within days of her trip to Oklahoma City and ended up under internal investigation by the Secret Service—an inquiry that was not made public but resulted in Riley being cleared, leaving government service, and moving into a high-level, high-paying job with Bank of America.

Donna Bucella's career was left entirely unblemished. She was soon promoted to head of the Executive Office of U.S. Attorneys and has since occupied high-level government jobs in the FBI and cus-toms and border patrol, interspersed with stints in private practice. Interestingly, she also worked at Bank of America for a while.

Not everyone blamed Riley. John Kane, who worked equally closely with the FBI when they took over the records search, saw her as the victim of a crude power play: the FBI was jealous of her work, and wanted to take credit for it. "She was as committed to finding the answers in this case as anybody could be," he said. "Her attitude was, I don't care what badge I'm carrying in my pocket. . . . Anything that could be done to get after these guys sooner, faster, better, she was all over it."

When a couple of FBI agents visited Kane's California offices and said they were there to investigate Riley, Kane wasn't pleased. "I rolled my head and my eyes and said, fine, whatever. . . . They prob-ably spent an hour and a half asking questions that didn't seem like anything I could relate to the case," he said. "She lost, and they won."

Riley's field notes were never handed over to the defense teams ahead of McVeigh's and Nichols's federal trials—a potential violation of the rules of evidence. The task force leadership insisted it, too, never saw the notes. "This is the first time I've seen this," one senior FBI manager said when shown them. "If Judge Matsch sees this, I don't even want to be in the same country as the guy. He will blow up, he will be seething, he will go try to find heads, and I don't want him to go find mine."

A more nuanced view was offered by a member of the federal prosecution team, who did not think the notes would cause much of a stir more than a decade after the trials, because they were not exculpatory to either McVeigh or Nichols. The prosecutor agreed that the primary problem was a turf war between the Secret Service and the FBI, in which nobody was blameless.

"The Secret Service was dying to do everything they could to hold on to that piece," he said, "and they got shut out. There was a fundamental quandary whether they had the experience to do the job. But I never doubted Mary Riley."

THE FBI WENT OVER EVERY INCH OF JAMES NICHOLS'S FARM, BUT they did not find a whole lot. For Nichols, having the feds crawling over his private property was the nightmare his radical politics had taught him to fear the most. He railed that he was never shown a search warrant and he might have been right about that—the warrant was signed by a judge at 6:54 P.M., more than four hours after the raid began.

"You people have no right to be in here," Nichols remembered shouting. "I demand to see a Fourth Amendment warrant. I demand to talk with Janet Reno." An ATF agent supposedly responded: "Oh shut up. We have more rights in here than you do."

Still, Nichols answered all the feds' questions. He was not shy about his friendship with McVeigh or their shared interest in explosives. But he was quicker than his brother in understanding the seriousness of his situation, and his show of candor was almost certainly calculated to minimize the trouble he faced. Nichols told the FBI that, in 1992, he, his brother, and McVeigh made bottle bombs out of brake fluid, gasoline, and diesel fuel and detonated them on the farm, just for kicks. He also constructed small bombs using prescription vials, Pyrodex, blasting caps, and safety fuse. But he had never bought ammonium nitrate and did not know if his brother or

McVeigh had purchased any. He said Terry owned a bunch of bomb-making books. And he was "confident" McVeigh had the knowledge to manufacture one from ammonium nitrate.

Like his brother, James Nichols made insinuations about McVeigh's involvement in the bombing, without offering evidence that might smack of collusion or out-and-out betrayal. He was also careful to proclaim Terry's innocence. Since he claimed never to have visited Terry in Herington—apparently true—he could make a plausible case that he knew nothing about any interactions between his brother and McVeigh in the final days before the bombing.

The feds found no ammonium nitrate on the farm; the best they came up with were twenty-eight fifty-pound bags of fertilizer "*containing* ammonium nitrate," which was far from the same thing. They found several large tanks of diesel fuel, some nonelectric blasting caps, Pyrodex black powder, and safety fuse. None of this was evidence of collusion in the bomb plot. These were commonplace farm items; such explosives are often used to blow out tree stumps or remove boulders.

At Joe Martinolich's direction, agents divided the farm up into a grid, and went over all of it with metal detectors. But Martinolich ultimately concluded the feds had no grounds to arrest James Nichols. This was not what Louis Freeh wanted to hear, and he said so. He wanted James Nichols charged with conspiracy. Martinolich responded, as calmly as he could, that he didn't have probable cause to seek an arrest warrant.

Freeh flew into a fury and said: "If you don't do it, I'll find someone who will."

"We don't have the evidence," Martinolich told him.

"We'll sort it out later," Freeh insisted.

Martinolich shared his director's gut feeling that Nichols was somehow involved in the bombing, but he questioned the ethics and the tactical wisdom of arresting him on charges that could not be backed up by real evidence. Freeh worried that Nichols might somehow disappear if he was not taken into federal custody. Martinolich was offended that Freeh questioned his ability to keep Nichols under surveillance; he understood the pressure Freeh was under to solve the case, but he also had his professional pride. The next day, he called headquarters and offered his resignation.

The last thing the FBI needed at this moment was a high-level defection pointing the finger at Freeh's leadership skills. Bear Bryant called Martinolich at once, apologizing profusely for the way he had been treated and promising that his concerns would be addressed. The bureau then appealed to the Justice Department, which fashioned a compromise. Nichols would be arrested, but instead of bombing charges, he would be accused of conspiring to possess unregistered firearms and explosives. It was not much of a charge—who makes a bottle bomb and registers it?—and it was thrown out as soon as it was heard by a judge. Still, it provided a temporary way for all parties to save face.

The episode killed Martinolich's desire to pursue his long and illustrious FBI career. He did not leave the bureau right away; it took another botched FBI job, the investigation of the 1996 Olympic Games bombing in Atlanta, to convince him to do that. Still, the pattern was set. For the second time in a few days, Freeh had ridden roughshod over one of his most experienced managers, exactly the sort of person he should have turned to, not against, during a major investigation.

THE HIGH-PROFILE ARRESTS OF MCVEIGH AND THE NICHOLS BROTHERS were hailed at the time as great breakthroughs, but they came at a price, because they closed down avenues that could have led to other potential coconspirators. Nobody was a better candidate for more subtle treatment than James Nichols: the feds could have put him under surveillance, given themselves time to analyze his phone records, and waited to see who visited or called over the next several days. Someone important might still seek refuge in Decker, or receive a phone call from Nichols to discuss another planned attack.

That was certainly on the minds of task force leaders in Oklahoma City. "At the beginning, we were not even sure McVeigh was the one responsible," Bob Ricks recalled. "Was he part of some larger conspiracy? . . . Was he just a driver? A lot of times police arrest a driver, and the bad guys disappear."

The investigation was further hampered by its inability to prevent media leaks. If the Nichols brothers' names had not been all over the radio and television in the late morning of April 21, *both* brothers could have been put under surveillance. Lana Padilla, or Josh, could have made a monitored call to Terry to see what he might volunteer—not as a suspect in custody but as a free man. Mary Riley and the executives at West Coast Telephone could have kept monitoring the Daryl Bridges card.

The task force leadership did not understand at first why crucial leads were seeping into the public arena. Then Weldon Kennedy learned that ATF headquarters was routinely forwarding the Oklahoma City briefings to its entire staff, and so creating hundreds of potential news media sources around the country. "I blew up," Kennedy said. "I went completely nutso."

He plugged the leak as quickly as he could, but others soon developed in its place. For example, a reporter for the *Dallas Morning News* in Oklahoma City was having an affair with an ATF agent she knew from Texas and was pumping him for everything he knew. Several front-page scoops later, the agent was sent back to Dallas.

For these reasons, the early arrests were never more than a qualified success. Members of the Decker raid team became convinced that James Nichols had known they were coming and removed incriminating evidence—something Nichols himself has always denied. One odd thing Nichols insisted on was that his incarceration was somehow designed to prevent him from retrieving crucial evidence from the scene in Oklahoma City, which he said could have exonerated him, and his brother, and McVeigh, and pointed to the "real" perpetrators.

What was it that James Nichols was so anxious to do in Oklahoma City? Why, too, did he seem determined to make contact with Terry and McVeigh? Over and over, Nichols expressed a wish to talk to one or both of them face-to-face, a move he seemed to think would help clear all their names but which, to law enforcement, suggested he wanted the three of them to get their stories straight.

Such face-to-face meetings might have been very useful to the investigation, of course, if the participants could somehow have been lulled into thinking they were not being monitored or recorded. Once the feds launched their raid, however, this was no longer an option.

{ Five }

WAR FEVER

Tim McVeigh woke up on February 24, 1991, to the greatest test of his young life, the launch of the ground war to expel Iraqi forces from Kuwait. The battle plan envisaged up to 70 percent casualties, effectively turning McVeigh's company and others like it into sacrificial lambs for the next wave of tanks and ground troops. They expected to encounter mines, barbed wire, artillery and antitank fire, and maybe nerve gas. "Take your worst nightmare, then quadruple it, then quadruple it again," a Vietnam veteran who led the platoon next to McVeigh's said, "and you still won't get to where you'll be this time tomorrow."

At 3:00 P.M., a line of M1 Abrams tanks, equipped with giant blades, began plowing up the desert sand. McVeigh's job, as a gunner atop his own infantry tank, a Bradley Fighting Vehicle, was to take out enemy positions before they could fire on him. "No one knows," he later told the journalist Jonathan Franklin, "what the feeling is like to know that any second you could be hit by a bullet or shell from indirect fire or from a tank."

Once the fighting began, the Iraqi frontline units—tired, hungry, lice-infested conscripts—wanted nothing more than to surrender.

Many did not get the chance. Those who crawled out of the sand churned on top of them by the M1 tanks immediately faced Bradley gunners like McVeigh. The battlefield was a slaughterhouse. Trench by trench, the Iraqis were given sixty seconds to surrender, and those who hesitated, or did not hear the warning, were buried alive or blown to smithereens. Thousands of Iraqis were pulverized, dismembered, or burned. Many were plowed into shallow desert graves.

This went on for four straight days. When McVeigh wasn't manning his gun, he took hundreds of photographs of corpses and mangled Iraqi equipment. James Rockwell, the unit's supply sergeant, was given several as keepsakes. "One of them," Rockwell said, "was of an Iraqi soldier sitting in a deuce-and-a-half truck that had been bombed. The guy was literally burned like a piece of toast, but his hands were still on the steering wheel."

McVeigh and his comrades were high on killing. "If it's in front of us, it dies" was one infantry company's slogan. McVeigh nicknamed his Bradley "Bad Company," after the rock song he liked to blast through the vehicle. The crew sang along to the lines about killing "in cold blood," and fighting, gun in hand, " 'til the day I die." On the second day, McVeigh wowed everyone with his gunnery skills, using just a single round to hit two Iraqi soldiers dug in at a machine-gun emplacement a thousand yards away. He hit the first man in the chest, obliterating his upper body and leaving a red vapor trail where his head used to be. The episode became legendary across the 16th Infantry, earning McVeigh an Army Commendation Medal. That was one of five awards he won by the end of Operation Desert Storm, including the Bronze Star. He was described as an inspiration to his fellow platoon members and a credit to the army— the most lavish praise he had received over his brief and troubled life. And it stemmed from his skills as a killer of devastating efficiency.

EVEN BATTLE-HARDENED VETERANS OF VIETNAM AND OTHER WARS thought the rout of the Iraqi forces was particularly grim, a spilling

of largely innocent life that prompted lawyers and human rights activists to accuse the United States of war crimes. The dead were not
counted or identified, much less "honorably interred" as the Geneva
Conventions prescribed. And there were multiple reports of Iraqis
being killed after they had dropped their weapons and put their
hands up.

According to at least three of his fellow soldiers, McVeigh
breached a number of the rules of war himself. After the Oklahoma City bombing, Larry Frame, Richard Cerney, and Todd
Regier disclosed that McVeigh had shot surrendering soldiers, including four who had already been taken prisoner. Frame told
the FBI he was in the Bradley Fighting Vehicle directly behind
McVeigh's and saw him kill "several" Iraqi soldiers as they climbed
out of a trench. Cerney called McVeigh a "cold-blooded bastard"
who thought life was very cheap. When the FBI brought these
allegations to McVeigh's old company commander, Scott Rutter,
he worried he was being investigated for war crimes himself and
refused to answer their questions.

It is impossible to know how these experiences altered McVeigh's
psyche or otherwise hardened him for the slaughter he would perpe-
trate four years later. But his exposure to combat certainly changed
his outlook and behavior. Before, he always strived to be the ideal
soldier. He did not allow himself to succumb to boredom or get demoralized by the long months of waiting in the Arabian desert, as
many of his fellow soldiers did. He took the conditions as a challenge
and somehow kept his 25-mm cannon as well-greased as it would
have been back at Fort Riley. Scott Rutter felt in retrospect he was
almost *too* good. His compulsion to perform at the highest levels was
in some ways a facade, a show of bravado covering something darker
beneath.

After his return home, McVeigh lost focus. In the spring of
1991, he flew to Fort Bragg in North Carolina to try out for Special
Forces, but had to withdraw on the second day because his feet
were too badly blistered to complete a five-mile march. This should

have been only a temporary setback; everyone understood he was out of condition after his stint in the Gulf, and he was invited to come back for another shot. But McVeigh took this as a signal to get out of the army.

McVeigh had been thinking about his time in the Middle East and now recoiled at his own gung-ho enthusiasm amid the slaughter. He became convinced that the government had manipulated him into fighting an army of hapless conscripts who were not really enemies at all. "We were falsely hyped up [to kill Iraqis], and they are normal like you and me," he told Jonathan Franklin.

McVeigh's epiphany about American power was not a condemnation of neo-imperialism or of a lust for oil. He felt the military's role was strictly to defend America's domestic borders, and that the United States had been hoodwinked into a United Nations policing operation. These thoughts fed into his long-held belief that the United States' true enemy was an international cabal of money-grubbing liberals, multiculturalists, and Jews intent on stripping citizens of their basic rights, starting with the right to bear arms. This view had been ingrained in him over and over in *The Turner Diaries*, a book he discovered during his earliest days in uniform.

Politics was the means by which McVeigh forged a new identity for himself after the security of his old world—the army, and his place in it—fell apart. Most likely, his fixation on government manipulation masked a severe bout of post-combat depression, as the psychiatrists who examined him after the bombing would later postulate. James Rockwell, the Charlie Company supply sergeant, remembered McVeigh coming into his storeroom at Fort Riley and talking about having a computer chip in his backside. It was not clear if he meant this metaphorically or literally. McVeigh said he was leaving the army, because the military had done things to him he didn't like.

"Like what?" Rockwell asked.

"I think they've brainwashed me or injected me with something," McVeigh said.

Rockwell was astonished. He probably knew the men as well as anyone; he encouraged McVeigh to sit and talk whenever he came in for tank supplies or tools. McVeigh visited regularly and opened up in ways he rarely did to others. He talked about his parents' divorce when he was sixteen years old, and the bitter fights, about his mother moving to the next town with his two sisters and leaving him with his dad. Still, Rockwell saw McVeigh as the ultimate "squared away" soldier, a man so in control it was hard to imagine him encountering anything he couldn't deal with. The government conspiracy talk made no sense.

"Tim, you don't really believe that, do you?" he asked.

McVeigh replied: "Yes, I do."

Rockwell asked why he would throw away his promising military career and the recognition he had earned. McVeigh delivered a line Rockwell later recalled with a shiver. "There's things I got to do, Sergeant Rock," he said, "and I cannot do it from within here."

AFTER TRYING AND FAILING FOR THREE DAYS TO CONVINCE JENNIFER McVeigh to talk, the FBI put her on a plane back to Buffalo and got her father to urge her to cooperate. When she said no, she was taken to the FBI office and put on the phone to her mother. Still she would not answer questions about the bombing. "I didn't know what was going on," she said, over and over. She was clearly frightened.

The FBI had been through her room at her father's house and found some incendiary documents on her computer. They were written by her brother, but the feds made it clear that if she didn't speak up she would have to answer for the contents herself. The first document was a letter to the American Legion and characterized the ATF, FBI, DEA, and U.S. Marshals Service as "a bunch of fascist tyrants" and "power-hungry stormtroopers of the federal government." The second document was an unsigned one-paragraph rant about the ATF. "All you tyrannical motherfuckers will swing in the wind one day," it read, "for your treasonous actions against the

Constitution and the United States. Remember the Nuremberg War Trials. But . . . but . . . but . . . I was only following orders! . . . . Die you spineless, cowardice bastards!"

Jennifer's interviewers let her sleep on that, then upped the pressure the next morning by displaying poster-size photographs of her and Tim, along with a timeline of their movements leading up to the bombing and a list of charges they said they were considering. The agents even opened a book of federal statutes and showed her some choice paragraphs. "Whoever commits an offense against the United States or aids, abets, counsels, commands, induces or procures its commission, is punishable as a principal," one of them read. Next to the printed words, an agent had scrawled: "I.e., death." The next page had a section on treason, this time with a handwritten addendum that said: "Penalty equals death."

Jennifer began talking and didn't stop for the next eight days. She didn't know the FBI's threat to bring capital charges against her was strictly a scare tactic, or that treason can be prosecuted only in wartime. She talked until her head was spinning and she was crying so hard she was all but gasping for breath.

For the first several days, she was determined not to rat out her brother, but the FBI kept applying more pressure. "They told me he was guilty," she later testified, "and that he was going to fry." She understood that if she did not want to be prosecuted herself, she needed to tell them everything she knew. It took her a full week to do that; she reached her breaking point only after the agents forced her to look at graphic, full-color photographs of mangled babies' bodies from the Murrah Building.

"It was controversial at the time to show her pictures of dead children," Weldon Kennedy, who gave the authorization, acknowledged—so controversial that it was omitted from the official record.

But the move paid off, and Jennifer was ultimately smart enough not to throw her own life away after her brother's. "I think that was the reason, the tipping point, that made her decide she would cooperate," Kennedy added. "There's no question a lot of pressure was put on her."

LIKE MCVEIGH, NICHOLS WAS ROCKED BY HIS PARENTS' DIVORCE. As a child, he sat so quietly in class his teachers wondered if he had hearing difficulties. Long after his arrest, it was determined that he had Asperger syndrome. Still, he was smart and resourceful, and dreamed of a career in medicine. But when his mother was given the Decker farm in her divorce settlement, she ordered him to leave college and help her run it. He complied without a murmur. The farm crisis of the early 1980s was setting in, compounded by floods that turned the Michigan fields to mud. Right away, the bounties of Terry's childhood gave way to poverty and constant struggle. He hardly talked to his father anymore, and his older brother Les was an abiding worry after a horrific accident at a grain elevator, which left him with burns over 95 percent of his body. Joyce, a matriarchal figure with a propensity to drink, rammed her car into her ex-husband's tractor, and was once found by a sheriff's deputy throwing beer cans into a cornfield. When he challenged her, she turned on him with a chain saw. Mercifully, she was too drunk to start it up and threw it at him instead.

Nichols dabbled in property investment with the help of his real estate agent, then known as Lana Osentowski. She was twice divorced, with two children, and she encouraged Nichols to follow her into a sideline selling insurance. They married in 1981, and Josh was born a year later. By 1988, the marriage was in trouble, and Lana suggested that Terry enlist in the army. She filed for divorce shortly after he left for basic training, by which time she was living fifty miles away in Bay City and checking in on her three children, whom she left with various relatives, just once or twice a week. Nichols requested a discharge so he could return home and take care of Josh.

James Nichols was no luckier in his marriage to Lana's younger sister, Kelli. Their 1987 divorce was so contentious that Kelli accused her husband of molesting their son. Nichols eventually managed to rebut the charge, but he could not forgive his ex-wife, or the courts; it was a turning point in his hostility toward the government.

By the end of the 1980s, James and Terry were back on the farm. Terry wanted to get married again, so he flew to the Philippines and selected a seventeen-year-old mail-order bride in Marife Torres, the daughter of a provincial police chief. Months went by while they processed the paperwork enabling Marife to come to the United States. And when Nichols flew back to the Philippines in June 1991 to pick her up, he discovered she was five months pregnant by another man—"complicating matters some," as he later put it.

Just about the only thing Nichols did not regret was his bond with Josh. Father and son were so close that Lana could not believe Nichols would ever jeopardize the relationship by involving himself in a major criminal conspiracy. Years later, as Josh struggled with drug and alcohol addictions and shuttled in and out of the Nevada criminal justice system, Padilla could not contain her anger at Nichols for abdicating his parental responsibilities. "I truly believe [Josh] is in prison because he depended on a father who abandoned him," she said. "Not to mention a mother who abandoned him, too. But I didn't blow up a building. People get divorced every day, but their ex does not blow up a building."

EARLY IN THE INVESTIGATION, THE FBI THOUGHT McVEIGH AND Nichols might be gay lovers, or at least that they had a strong homoerotic bond. Padilla said McVeigh was certainly controlling and possessive of Nichols, almost to the point of jealousy. But that, Padilla said, was as far as it went: "McVeigh never approached Terry, you know . . . in that way. He was always high on methamphetamines."

When they met, Nichols was thirty-three, at least ten years older than most of the recruits in basic training. They saw him as a natural leader, none more so than McVeigh, a skinny twenty-year-old unsure of his physical abilities. McVeigh began working out obsessively to build up his muscle strength, and would clean and re-clean every item of his equipment while others went out drinking and partying. He and Nichols stayed on their commanders' good side, but ran in a wild crowd including a kid from Boston who once lobbed a CS gas canister into a topless bar; Mike Fortier, who was into drugs; and another troublemaker who accompanied them on secret outings to detonate black-powder bombs.

McVeigh and Nichols also delved into white supremacist literature. McVeigh read *The Turner Diaries* first, then passed it on to Nichols, Fortier, and anyone else in the unit he thought might be receptive. They were radicalized by the book's revolutionary spirit more than its breathtaking racism. Still, McVeigh and Nichols had grown up in places where there was a casual disdain for blacks, Jews, and foreigners, and they were uncomfortable around many of the African-Americans in their unit. They weren't beyond cracking jokes about "niggers" and "porch monkeys," as McVeigh freely acknowledged in his prison interviews. Before he was out of uniform, McVeigh also signed up with the Ku Klux Klan.

SENIOR CASE MANAGERS BEGAN TO SUSPECT SOMETHING WAS WRONG with the sketch of John Doe Two. They issued two versions, one bare-headed and one with the zigzag-patterned cap described by Tom Kessinger, but the leads these generated were a waste of time. By April 26, a week after the bombing, the task force brought in Jeanne Boylan, a different sort of sketch artist, whose technique did not involve showing witnesses stock facial features but rather used an idiosyncratic method of interviewing subjects to draw out their memories strand by strand. Time and again Boylan had corrected the work of conventional artists and helped crack cases. Now Danny Coulson was instructing her tersely: "Find out what's wrong with these damn drawings."

Within hours, Boylan was face-to-face with Kessinger at Eldon Elliott's shop and picking up a welter of new details. Kessinger had seen John Doe Two only from the side, not head-on as the original sketch portrayed him, and many of the facial details were wrong. Kessinger saw him only briefly, as he stood with his arms crossed in front of a poster, but noticed his muscular frame and the beginnings of a tattoo poking out from beneath his left T-shirt sleeve. Boylan started working up a brand-new sketch.

Kessinger also wanted to talk about John Doe One and offered a fascinating new detail. Robert Kling was a tobacco-chewer, and did something that made Kessinger stare and stare. "When a guy chews," he told Boylan, "he tucks the chaw over to one side or the other so he can talk, know what I mean? But he doesn't divide it in two. This guy standing at the counter had a long, thin face, blue eyes, this sorta flat-top hair like an army guy, and two puffs, two plugs of chew, one tucked over on each side of his bottom lip. Funniest damn thing I ever seen."

The FBI was working on the basis that McVeigh and Kling were the same person, but McVeigh was not a tobacco-chewer. With the other inconsistencies raised by Kessinger and his fellow employees—that Kling was five foot ten (three inches shorter than McVeigh), had a line or deformity across his chin, and rough skin (McVeigh's was smooth)—the government's case was starting to look shaky.

When Boylan told one of the top FBI supervisors what Kessinger had said, he had her escorted to a hotel room in Junction City and told her to stay put until further notice. Two agents subsequently grilled her about her interview with Kessinger. She felt she was being interrogated and told them to lighten up.

Come on, she said, we're all on the same side. They paid no attention.

An hour later, one of the agents returned to her room. "Ms. Boylan?" he said, looking straight at her. "The information you produced this afternoon does not exist."

Boylan was stunned. "Wh-what information?" she stammered.

"Very good," the agent replied. He nodded once, turned around, and left.

IN THE WINTER OF 1991–92, TERRY AND JAMES NICHOLS BEGAN FOL-lowing Ralph Daigle, a local extremist preacher, who persuaded Terry to max out his credit cards on the quaint theory that the banks were not backing up their money with silver or gold, and so were defrauding the American people every time they made a loan. Daigle—who was later prosecuted and convicted of tax evasion—was a common-law advocate who argued that the government and the banks were an offense to the Constitution. Daigle derived many of his ideas from a notorious racist preacher James Wickstrom, who once argued that "Jew money barons" created the farm crisis of the 1980s and were "financially and morally rap[ing] the white Christian-American people." Credit card bills, Daigle preached, merely needed to be re-turned with the phrase "dishonored with due cause," and the banks would have no option but to cancel the debt.

The Nichols brothers certainly liked the idea of fleecing the banks, especially now Terry was married and starting a new family, and signed up to the ideology that went with it. Terry ran up credit card bills of more than $26,000 with Chase Manhattan and the First Deposit National Bank of Pleasanton, California, and then tried to challenge his creditors in court, acting as his own counsel.

It did not go well. Nichols argued that the court had no jurisdiction and the banks should pay him damages of $50,000, or 14,200 ounces of silver, for "fraud and misrepresentation." He also attempted to invalidate his own signature as a way of nullifying the pledge he made on his credit card applications to honor his debts. He was a no-show when the First Deposit National case came up for trial. And in the Chase Manhattan hearing, he refused to recognize the Chase lawyer and said he wanted the bank's whole board of directors to come and face him instead. He refused to approach the microphone recording the proceedings, saying he didn't want to acknowledge the court by walking all the way into the room. The judge threatened to throw him in jail for contempt.

By June 1993, even Nichols realized his quixotic adventures in court were futile. His only choices were to conjure up more than $30,000 in debt and accumulated interest, or drop out of the system. He chose the latter. "I was pissed at Ralph [Daigle], the banks, and myself, and I decided not to pay the judgment," he said. "I went on a cash basis with everything. . . . And I decided not to put my name on anything that would be on a database to where the banks could track me down." And so Nichols sabotaged any remaining chance of a normal life.

McVEIGH WAS ALSO COMING UNSTUCK FROM MAINSTREAM SOCIETY. Quitting the military left him with few enviable options. It was not a good time to be a white working-class man. The Buffalo area was depressed, and the only work he found was as a minimum-wage security guard. On the side, he joined the National Guard reserves and found a part-time job at a gun store.

For more than a year, McVeigh wavered between depression and anger. He read comic books and spent money he did not have betting on the Buffalo Bills. With thoughts of suicide in his head, he called a Veterans Administration hospital in Florida and asked about mental health counseling. But he let the idea go when he was told he had to give them his name. He dropped his memberships to the Ku Klux Klan and the National Rifle Association because he could not afford them. But he was still absorbed by politics and read radical right-wing periodicals and books voraciously.

In early 1992, he wrote a revealing letter to the local paper, expressing his belief that stable employment and anti-Communism seemed to be giving way to social incoherence and political corruption. "America is in serious decline," he wrote. "We have no proverbial tea to dump. Should we instead sink a ship full of Japanese imports? Is a civil war imminent? Do we have to shed blood to reform the current system? I hope it doesn't come to that, but it might."

This is when McVeigh started spending weekends at gun shows. He was interested in firearms and thought he could generate a little extra income by selling blast simulators, smoke grenades, and copies of *The Turner Diaries*. Principally, though, the shows offered McVeigh a new social network, one where taboo ideas like white supremacy, nostalgia for the confederate South, and radical antigovernment action could be discussed openly. William Pierce, the author of *The Turner Diaries,* described the gun shows as a "natural recruiting environment" for his brand of race warriors; the number of shows, and of firearms changing hands outside the context of licensed gun dealerships, increased so rapidly in this period that both the government and the gun-control lobby lost count.

The militancy of the shows escalated decisively after the Ruby Ridge incident of August 1992. What began as a misguided attempt to dismantle the Aryan Nations turned to needless tragedy, as the man the ATF tried to recruit as an informant, Randy Weaver, refused to play along and slowly grew in agents' minds into a Rambo-style menace.

Weaver reacted angrily when an undercover ATF agent sold him an illegal weapon and tried to trap him into ratting out his friends in the white supremacist movement. He became angrier still when the government pressed charges, retreating up his mountain and refusing to come down no matter how many times he was summoned to court. Weaver's wife, Vicki, then raised the stakes by writing a letter to the local U.S. attorney, whom she described as "the servant of the Queen of Babylon," and declaring that a war was imminent.

Eventually, a small army of federal agents surrounded the Weavers' cabin to bring matters to a head. Shooting began when the Weavers' Labrador heard the surveillance team and started barking.

Minutes later, the dog, fourteen-year-old Sammy Weaver, and a U.S. marshal were all dead. The next day, an FBI sharpshooter, operating under hugely controversial rules of engagement authorizing him to shoot to kill on sight, hit Vicki Weaver in the face while she was cradling her fourteen-month-old baby. She died instantly. Randy Weaver and a family friend were wounded, and it seemed they were all destined to die before the siege was over. The feds, though, revoked the rules of engagement they had imposed, and open hostility gave way to more psychological forms of confrontation.

After nine days of negotiation, the surviving members of the Weaver household gave up peacefully and were later absolved of murder and multiple other charges. The government walked away shamed and humiliated.

The mainstream media hardly covered Ruby Ridge, but its impact on the populist right was profound. On the radical fringe, it inspired a widely publicized meeting of the country's top neo-Nazis and antigovernment agitators, who vowed to resist a federal government "gone mad"—Louis Beam's words—with bloodlust for its own citizens. "Over the next ten years you will come to hate government more than anything else in your life," Beam told his fellow Patriots in Estes Park, Colorado. "If you think that this generation of men will maintain its present freedoms without also having to fertilize the tree of liberty with the blood of both patriot and tyrant, then you are mistaken."

McVeigh was as transformed by the moment as anyone. The "tree of liberty" line would, of course, end up on the T-shirt he wore when he was arrested. He was also deeply influenced by an essay Beam had republished earlier that year, which advocated a revolutionary strategy of "leaderless resistance." If the soldiers of the radical right worked autonomously or in small cells instead of taking orders from a centralized command, Beam argued, law enforcement agencies and their informants were less likely to find out about their plots in advance and could never catch up with the entire movement. "Let the coming night," he declared, "be filled with a thousand points of resistance."

McVeigh was determined to be one of those resistance points and started cutting many old ties. He had already quit the National Guard. In September 1992, he sold a rural plot of land near Buffalo he had bought in his more narrowly survivalist pre-army days and used the $9,000 proceeds to travel more extensively, including his first trip to the Nichols farm in Decker. He also built a file of newspaper and magazine clippings pointing to egregious abuses of government power—a list of grievances that would feed his growing rage for the next two and a half years. Usually the episodes involved federal agents acting on faulty information, who burst into the homes of innocent citizens: a computer executive from San Diego shot three times by customs and DEA, or a Washington housewife slapped in handcuffs while the feds tore the place apart, leaving her twenty-one-month-old daughter alone in a bathtub.

In early February 1993, McVeigh piled some possessions into his trusty 1987 Chevy Geo Spectrum and left New York for good. He later told Michel and Herbeck that the spur for leaving was losing a thousand-dollar bet he made on the Buffalo Bills in that year's Super Bowl. But McVeigh had quit his security guard job on January 26, five days before the game, and had been selling off anything he could not comfortably fit in his car.

A more likely motivation was an invitation to go into business with a rich gun dealer in his late fifties, whom he had met at a recent show in Fort Lauderdale. The dealer was known to McVeigh as Bob Miller, but his real name was Roger Moore. He would play a pivotal role in the events leading to April 19, 1995.

The FBI agents questioning Jennifer McVeigh were intrigued by a December 24, 1993, letter from her brother that suggested he was funding his revolutionary enterprise through bank robberies. The letter denounced the banking system as the financial arm of a corrupt and evil government, echoing the "common law" language Ralph Daigle had used with Terry Nichols. And it cast robbers, credit fraudsters, and illegal arms traffickers as romantic heroes fleecing the rich to champion the poor. McVeigh said he and his unnamed friends were justifiably breaking the law to fight against a "higher evil." He continued: "We are at war with the system, make no mistake about it. . . . We have to fund our war efforts with, sometimes, 'covert' means."

Jennifer could not, or would not, say what those covert means were. McVeigh referred to a "friend who knocks over banks," and a credit scam of some sort. "In the past," McVeigh wrote, "you would see the news and see a bank robber, and judge him a 'criminal.' But, without getting too lengthy, the Federal Reserve and the banks are the real criminals, 'cash' as we know it is counterfeit, and a dollar is just worthless paper, so where is the crime in getting even . . . ? I guess if I reflect, it's sort of a Robin Hood thing, and our gov't is the evil king."

On the third day of Jennifer's questioning, one of the agents asked the FBI crime lab in Washington to check McVeigh's and the Nichols brothers' fingerprints against evidence left behind at a string of unsolved bank heists across the Midwest. This was the beginning of an attempt to tie McVeigh to the Aryan Republican Army. It was never discussed in court, but it would consume untold man-hours over the next several months.

CHRISTOPHER BUDKE, AN FBI AGENT FROM KANSAS CITY, WAS IN line at the Fort Riley Burger King when a man in uniform approached and asked: "How long are you all going to be here?"

Budke was startled and initially brushed him off. But the man approached again and introduced himself as Sergeant Rick Wahl. He explained how he had gone fishing at Geary Lake with his son the day before the bombing and had seen a Ryder truck with a second vehicle. Wahl knew right after the disaster that his information could be important, and he put in a call to the FBI's tip line. A dispatcher said someone would get back to him, but nobody had in days.

Budke scrawled a few notes in pencil and promised to follow up. Wahl would soon prove invaluable, telling the FBI where and when the bomb was built and leading them to the exact site. A more alert FBI could have started working on all that on April 19 or 20. As it was, only a chance encounter almost a week later prevented them from missing it altogether.

TIM MCVEIGH WAS WEARING HIS FULL GULF WAR BATTLE DRESS and carefully polished black boots when he encountered Roger Moore for the first time. Moore had never seen combat duty, but he was fascinated by anyone who had. So he and McVeigh started talking about McVeigh's service in Desert Storm and his political ideas. They became fast friends.

Ostensibly, Moore should have been enjoying his retirement but he was also driven by an abiding anger against the government, if not the world. He had made a fortune in the boat-building business in the 1970s, and now divided his time between Arkansas and southern Florida. He had a wife, who generally stayed in Florida, and a girlfriend he kept openly in Arkansas. He ran an ammunition supply business with his girlfriend, because it gave him an excuse to travel to gun shows and meet fellow right-wing radicals. Officially, the company was called the American Assault Company, but more commonly it went by the nickname, The Candy Store.

After the bombing, Floyd Hays, an FBI agent in Arkansas, spent many hours with Moore and described him as "infatuated" with McVeigh. That Desert Storm uniform clearly spoke volumes, because everything else about McVeigh was down-at-the-heels that

January weekend at the National Guard Armory in Fort Lauderdale. He barely had money for gas, slept in his car, and was never sure where to find his next meal. Moore's wife, Carol, took pity on him and fetched some sandwiches. Later, Moore invited him to split the costs of a table at an upcoming gun show in Miami's Coconut Grove. McVeigh was thrilled. A few weeks later, Moore called McVeigh at his sister's house near Miami to confirm the invitation. They worked the show together, then planned to meet again for another show in April.

At the end of February, McVeigh's antigovernment fire was further fueled by the botched ATF raid on the Branch Davidian compound outside Waco. The ATF believed the community had built an armory of automatic weapons, grenades, assault weapons, and 50-caliber Barrett rifles and launched a full-scale assault on the property. The Davidians, though, were forewarned, and soon four ATF agents and six Davidians lay dead, with two dozen others injured. The FBI moved in, for what would turn into a fifty-one-day siege. Unlike Ruby Ridge, this grim spectacle was prime-time news on every station, confirming to citizen militias and the Patriot Movement every suspicion they had harbored about the government's propensity for waging war against its own citizens. The FBI borrowed hardware from the military, including a line of Bradley Fighting Vehicles, which were particularly shocking to McVeigh, because he knew firsthand how much damage they could do.

McVeigh drove to Waco in the middle of March. He could not get within three miles of the compound, because of police barricades and checkpoints, so he parked his car in a field alongside dozens of others and laid out a bunch of bumper stickers. FEAR THE GOVERNMENT THAT FEARS YOUR GUN, one read. WHEN GUNS ARE OUTLAWED, I WILL BECOME AN OUTLAW, read another.

Although McVeigh never said so, one person he probably met in Waco was Louis Beam. Beam arrived as a credentialed journalist for the far-right magazine *Jubilee* and drew immediate attention

when he likened the ATF to the Nazis and the KGB at a press briefing on March 14 and asked if a police state was on the way. Beam
was swarmed by police and security guards, who checked him for
outstanding warrants before letting him go. Three days later, when
he tried to return for another briefing, he was slapped in handcuffs
and arrested for trespassing. Beam relished the attention, telling
every television reporter he was being punished for asking "the forbidden question."

McVeigh almost certainly heard about Beam's misadventures,
and would have had plenty to talk about if he sought him out. Was
this where the godfather of "leaderless resistance" passed on some
lessons to his most ruthless disciple? FBI and ATF agents worried
about the radical far-right at the time were in no doubt about Beam's
potential for fomenting violence on an alarming scale. Jim Cavanaugh of the ATF described him as "the most dangerous man in
America." Beam and his blisteringly charismatic speaking style were
to the Patriot Movement, Cavanaugh said, what Reinhard Heydrich,
Hitler's pitiless protégé, had been to the planning of the Holocaust
at Wannsee.

THE FBI KNEW MICHAEL FORTIER WAS TROUBLE WHEN HIS FRIEND
and neighbor, Jim Rosencrans, came at them screaming and waving
an SKS assault rifle. That was on April 21. They couldn't help noticing, too, the coiled-snake flag in the front yard of Fortier's trailer
home bearing the Revolutionary War slogan DON'T TREAD ON ME.
This guy did not love the federal government.

The agents grilled Fortier for four days while he continued to say
he knew nothing and that McVeigh was not capable of slaughtering so
many innocent people. The FBI became ever more suspicious that he
had foreknowledge of the bombing or that he had played a direct role.
The more they delved, the more obvious it became that Fortier was
lying. He said, for example, that McVeigh had not visited Kingman

before February 1995, but the FBI knew McVeigh had been using a Kingman address for his correspondence for close to two years.

The FBI asked Fortier to take a polygraph test. He agreed to be asked about his whereabouts leading up to the bombing, but not about his knowledge of the plot itself. Having first pleaded ignorance, he now pleaded fear. "If I tell you what you want to know," he said on the fourth day, "I'm a dead man." The agents were unimpressed. Kenneth Williams (who would later become known as the author of the "Phoenix Memo," one of the disregarded pre-9/11 warnings about Middle Easterners enrolling in flight schools) called Fortier a "baby killer" and tried to scare him straight. It didn't work.

When Fortier and his wife, Lori, were home alone after their interrogations, they tried to rid their house of incriminating items. Even before the FBI first came, Lori realized her typewriter ribbon still bore the imprint of the name Robert D. Kling, which McVeigh had typed onto his fake driver's license. As soon as she heard the news that Kling had rented the Ryder truck, she ripped out the ribbon and burned it. Michael had taken a 50-caliber rifle and some explosive components and hidden them inside a kit car at his brother's house on the other side of town. He still had to worry about a half-empty bag of ammonium nitrate, which Fortier and McVeigh had used to make test explosives; some galvanized steel tubing typically used to make pipe bombs; and a .22 Hornet rifle and scope left over from the stash of weapons he had obtained from McVeigh the previous December.

Fortier did not dare carry any of the items off his property himself, so he passed them over the fence to his meth-head buddy Rosencrans, who agreed to dispose of them. Rosencrans buried the ammonium nitrate in the desert, where it was recovered three months later, and he pawned off the rifle for cash and another weapon. Fortier also handed Rosencrans a paper grocery bag with a miscellany of smaller items from McVeigh, including books, two videotapes on Waco, an army supply catalogue, and a copy of the radical right-wing

Patriot Report. Rosencrans took these to the safest place he knew, a house shared by his mother and his half-brother Chuck, who—improbably—was also his stepfather.

The only drug-related object the feds found at the Fortiers' house was an old tinfoil pipe containing marijuana residue, raising the question of whether they had ditched drugs, too. Michael Fortier denied any attempt at concealment when he took the stand in McVeigh's trial; he wanted the jury to believe his house had been empty of any illegal narcotics since the eve of the bombing, when he spent all night tweaking on crystal meth with Jim Rosencrans. Had they really smoked their way through everything? The feds did not pursue this. The FBI was itching for a member of McVeigh's inner circle to come forward about the bomb plot, and Fortier seemed the most likely candidate. So Weldon Kennedy sent Danny Coulson, one of the bureau's most experienced agents, to turn one or both Fortiers around. Coulson first applied for a warrant to search the Fortiers' home, and then he drew up a proffer letter, a take-it-or-leave-it deal under which Fortier was invited to talk without risk of self-incrimination as a prelude to a plea bargain. The one condition was that he could not lie.

With the warrant in hand, Coulson invited Fortier to meet him and his colleague Bob Walsh at a sheriff's substation near his house. They promised the search would be as noninvasive as possible. Fortier was welcome to stick around and watch. Coulson, who was intimately familiar with the mentality of right-wing radicals, also did his best to disarm any notion that the search constituted an assault on Fortier's fundamental rights. "This is not a war," he told him. "You and your friends may be at war with your government. Your government is not at war with you."

Coulson wasn't just making a fine speech; he was also playing for time, because he knew that agents were already swarming over the Fortier property. The media was right outside, tipped off by the local police scanner. So, too, was Jim Rosencrans, who was again brandishing his SKS rifle and doing a little dance up and down McVicar Avenue. He was raving about the "fucking FBI" and telling anyone willing to listen that the sheriff's department was stockpiling ammunition under the Kingman hospital for the United Nations and its New World Order shock troops. When he strapped on a gas mask and announced he was going coyote-hunting, sheriff's deputies and the FBI chased him into a field and disarmed him. The FBI search team, meanwhile, took advantage of Fortier's temporary absence to bug the phone and place listening devices around the house. Coulson's kid glove concealed a sharp fist.

McVEIGH'S FIRST TRIP TO KINGMAN IN THE SPRING OF 1993 WAS A quick one. He dropped in on Michael Fortier and scouted for gun-show material. He also set up a mailbox, signaling his intention to return. But soon he was off again to a big gun show in Tulsa a thousand miles to the east. He was supposed to meet Roger Moore there, but ended up introducing himself instead to Moore's girlfriend, Karen Anderson, who was working their table alone. The next day, McVeigh brought his things and asked if he could share the space. Clearly, they got along, because by the end of the weekend, Anderson and Moore invited McVeigh to follow them back to the ranch for several days.

First, McVeigh made another significant acquaintance. Andreas Strassmeir, fresh in from Elohim City, wandered by the table and ended up buying McVeigh's Desert Storm battle uniform for $2—a terrific bargain, he later told Justice Department lawyers—as well as a pair of gloves. Even better, he sold McVeigh a knife he'd been trying to offload all day. The two men talked and found they had similar views on Waco.

McVeigh joked around with Strassmeir, who wore a black leather jacket and camouflage pants. "I was a little worried, because you looked like a Nazi," he said. "I'm glad you're not a Nazi." Strassmeir said he was relieved that McVeigh was not a "right-winger," apparently meaning he was not an overt racist. "He definitely was not a right-wing guy, I would not say that. And he liked the fact that I was not one," Strassmeir insisted. "Tim was not antigovernment. He was against certain agencies making war against their own citizens."

There is an irresistible streak of comedy in two adherents of radical right-wing ideology insisting that neither was right-wing at all. Clearly, though, they found each other memorable, far more so than Strassmeir was willing to admit after the bombing. According to McVeigh, Strassmeir called over the two friends he was with— most likely Pete and Tony Ward, or Dennis Mahon—and told them: "This guy feels the way we do." The feeling was mutual: McVeigh thought he and Strassmeir were "brothers in arms."

When reporters and investigators asked Strassmeir about the encounter two years later, he told them he could barely remember it and had not recalled McVeigh's name until it was plastered all over the news. But his pinpoint recollection of their Nazi banter and the exact terms of the purchases they made from each other suggests otherwise.

Another indicator that Strassmeir felt a kinship with McVeigh was that he gave McVeigh a business card with the Elohim City address and phone number, and an invitation to drop by any time. Grandpa Millar had given Strassmeir some cards mostly to ensure he would not forget the Elohim City phone number; he certainly did not want him passing them out indiscriminately. "I was very careful handing out the Elohim City business card," Strassmeir later acknowledged.

SOMETIME IN LATE APRIL, STEVE CHANCELLOR, THE ARMY CID man in Oklahoma City, noted the FBI's interest in Elohim City and in Strassmeir. Chancellor had just come home from an undercover narcotics case in Hamburg, which was the last place Strassmeir had been stationed before coming to the United States. Chancellor told his colleagues: "I have a fantastic German informant from Hamburg. I'm telling you, he could talk the underwear off Mother Teresa. He's that good. If you want, I'd be glad to introduce you guys."

At this stage, the FBI had Carol Howe's reports about Strassmeir's threats to blow up buildings and wage war against the federal government. And the Daryl Bridges phone records indicated that one of the card users had made a two-minute call to Elohim City on April 5, two weeks before the bombing. At least some government agencies— the State Department, Immigration and Naturalization Service, and ATF—also knew that Strassmeir had overstayed his visa.

Chancellor persuaded his army superiors to fly his informant in from Germany. "I had him meet with the FBI and ATF, and I made arrangements for him to work up a cover story [to go into Elohim City]. I think he would have been very successful," Chancellor said. But the task force turned down his offer. Perhaps the investigation leadership was counting on Carol Howe to come back from Elohim City with some actionable intelligence. The State Department's diplomatic security section had asked after Strassmeir's criminal record, and reported back to the task force that he was clean.

Chancellor was surprised. "My feeling was, they didn't believe this guy, which was too bad," he said. "I offered it to the FBI. They chose to go a different way, or maybe they thought it wasn't important. I just moved on."

On April 19, 1993, McVeigh was at the Nichols farm in Decker and loading up his Road Warrior to take both brothers down to Waco, when Terry yelled at him to come inside. The television news was showing flames licking up around the Branch Davidian compound.

It was the fifty-first day of the siege, and the FBI had decided to choke the Branch Davidians out with CS gas. When that did not work, they punctured big holes in the property with M728 combat engineer vehicles on loan from the army. Soon, three separate fires fueled by sixty-mile-per-hour winds were raging in the main building, consuming everything.

Seventy-five people died, including twenty-five children. Some were burned to death, while others, including David Koresh, were found with gunshot wounds. In his own account, McVeigh was speechless and felt tears running down his cheeks. He and the Nichols brothers convinced themselves that the FBI had set the fires—not the Davidians, as the government and a number of subsequent official inquiries would conclude.

WHEN THE FBI SEARCHED McVEIGH'S MAILBOX IN KINGMAN, THEY found an extraordinary unopened letter sent from Little Rock, Arkansas, nine days before the bombing. Written in a near-illegible scrawl, it was signed by "Bob" and written to Tim Tuttle. There was no return address. Next to Bob's signature, in block capitals, was the word BURN. The letter appeared to be answering a previous letter from McVeigh, and that made it even more difficult to decipher. One particularly alarming line read: "Plan is to bring the country down, and have a few more things happen, then offer the 90 percent a solution. (Better Red than Dead)." The letter referred to a robbery, to worries about security being compromised, and to a plan for May that Bob said should now be dropped. It also mentioned someone named Karen, who was "not interested in risks" and "not interested in the slightest at this point."

The FBI's linking of this letter to Roger Moore was one of its more inspired pieces of detective work. Agents had been working for days to figure out the significance of two safety-deposit keys found in Terry Nichols's garage. One was traced to a Union Bank of North Carolina branch in Florida and the other to the Arkansas Bank & Trust in Hot Springs. The banks said the keys belonged to Moore and reported that a few months earlier he had changed safety-deposit boxes because of a security problem connected to the loss of the keys.

A check on Moore revealed he had a live-in girlfriend named Karen Anderson, who was a plausible fit for the Karen in the letter. They also learned that the previous November Moore had reported a robbery at the ranch, in which he said he lost $60,000 in guns, precious stones, gold and silver bars, photographic equipment, and rare artifacts, as well as almost $9,000 in cash. Among the missing items were the two keys. Moore had volunteered the three names he thought most likely to have pulled off the robbery, and one was Tim McVeigh.

The FBI was perplexed. It had strong grounds to suspect McVeigh and Nichols of carrying out the robbery. But Roger Moore was also exchanging cryptic messages with McVeigh months later, suggesting that the two men still trusted and confided in each other. Was the Moore robbery intended as a fund-raiser for the bombing? Or was the robbery a scam orchestrated by Moore as well as McVeigh, either to defraud the insurance company or to create some plausible distance between them as they plotted an antigovernment revolution? Investigators initially worked on both scenarios.

Moore was extremely indignant when he was brought in to meet with the FBI at the Garland County Sheriff's Office in Hot Springs. "I obviously was lied to and fooled," he said about the bombing. "I almost shit when I saw it on TV." He gave the first of many accounts of the robbery, describing how a masked man with bad body odor, full camouflage dress, and Israeli combat boots confronted him with a shotgun fitted with a garrote. The intruder trussed him up like a turkey and spent ninety minutes ripping through the house in search of valuables before taking off in one of Moore's own vans. In this iteration—the details would change over the next two and a half years—the man had a dark complexion and a beard visible beneath his ski mask. His accomplice stood ready to pounce at the slightest sign of struggle, and later helped load the wares. Moore said neither man was McVeigh—the intruder was shorter and thicker-set—but he suspected that whoever robbed him had done so at McVeigh's behest. When the FBI showed Moore the safety-deposit key from the Arkansas Bank & Trust, he exclaimed: "He robbed me!" Moore assumed the FBI had recovered the key from McVeigh; he didn't know about the Terry Nichols connection.

Moore became discombobulated when he was shown the letter he had sent to McVeigh shortly before the bombing. He acknowledged he had written it and said "Bob" was a shortened version of his alias Bob Miller. But he insisted that most of the letter was about the gun-show business and the robbery. His aim was to lure McVeigh back to the ranch and figure out if he had been responsible. He said the line about security being compromised was a reference to the robbery and the fact that someone clearly knew he had a large number of valuables in the house. When he wrote that Karen was not interested in risks, he was referring to their efforts—which Karen no longer wished to make—to track down their stolen weapons in the militia movement.

Moore was winging it. When asked about the lines "the important thing is to be as effective as possible" and "let's let May go," he said he couldn't remember what they meant. But the FBI was more inclined to believe him than not. In the official write-up of that first interview, the agents did not mention the most startling line in the letter, the one about the "plan to bring the country down." They also appear to have forgotten to ask why he wrote BURN in upper case next to his signature.

Moore insisted he had nothing to do with the bombing and was never told anything about it. McVeigh was smart, he said, but probably it was the other guy—John Doe Two—who was the brains of the operation.

ONE MONTH AFTER WACO, MCVEIGH ORDERED A BOOK CALLED *Homemade C-4,* published by Paladin Press in Boulder, Colorado, a fertile source of how-to books on guns, ammo, and explosives. It was sent to his mailbox in Michigan at a time when he was traveling extensively, so it probably sat around for several months before he read it. Over time, though, it would prove almost uncannily influential on the Oklahoma City bomb plot.

The term "homemade C-4" has nothing to do with plastic explosive; it is paramilitary slang for ammonium nitrate bombs, so called because they pack a big wallop and because their ingredients are readily available to ordinary citizens. Ragnar Benson, the book's pseudonymous author, suggested purchasing the AN at farm-supply stores, which is exactly what McVeigh and Nichols ended up doing. He talked about the standard blend of AN and fuel oil commonly used by miners and farmers, but he also suggested using nitromethane. "The stuff is a real pisser," he wrote, "as fast as TNT, with just as high a brisance. It is useful for cutting steel and other paramilitary survival applications." The best way to find nitromethane, Benson went on, was at drag strips and stock-car races. Sometimes, it could be found in hobby shops. McVeigh and Nichols would explore all of those options to obtain their own nitromethane.

All of that still lay some way off, however. McVeigh settled in Kingman for a while, finding a place of his own and a new job as a security guard. He was still doing gun shows, and sometime in June or July, he came across a videotape titled *Waco: The Big Lie,* which restoked the radical fire within him because it purported to show that the government had used tank-mounted flamethrowers to start the blaze that consumed the Branch Davidians at Mount Carmel.

The video gave McVeigh grounds to believe the incident was a premeditated crime. "No convincing will come close if you don't actually see it for yourself," the film's promotional teaser said. "But be warned, you may not be able to sleep again." McVeigh brought a copy to Kingman to show Mike Fortier. It was his new *Turner Diaries,* the call-to-arms he felt compelled to share with everybody.

• • •

JENNIFER MCVEIGH WANTED TO LOOK OUT FOR HER BROTHER'S IN-
terests, but her resolve was no match for the FBI's pummeling. On
the eighth day of questioning, after her mother was flown in from
Florida to plead with her, she finally spilled her guts. "Tim is fried
anyways, so I might as well tell you," she said. She was scared and
exhausted and looking for a way out.

Her most startling stories concerned a visit McVeigh made to
Pendleton in November 1994 to help settle the affairs of their grandfather, who had died a few weeks earlier. Jennifer said he had a wad
of $100 bills, three of which he asked her to exchange for other
banknotes. When she asked where the money came from, he said it
was his take from a bank robbery. Jennifer's impression was that the
robbery had taken place recently. Her brother told her he had not
participated but knew the people who had. Her affidavit refers to
"participants," indicating more than one.

The affidavit also describes a time when Jennifer found her
brother in a "fuming" rage. On the spur of the moment, Tim told her
to leave him alone, but the next day he said that someone he knew
had failed to carry out a murder as planned. "I believe my brother
was then trying to decide what to do about the individual who had
failed to carry out these orders," the affidavit said. "I recall that prior
to this revelation he had been awaiting a telephone call, and I now
believe that this call was directly related to this murder plan."

The intended murder victim was most likely Roger Moore.
Maybe the robber was supposed to carry out the killing, or maybe
someone was supposed to come in afterward to kill Moore. Michael
Fortier testified at McVeigh's trial that the motive for the robbery was
to find a list of names of people Moore had threatened to turn over
to the federal government if he ever got into trouble. That doesn't
sound like a persuasive motive for a robbery—Moore would have
been more likely to go to the feds, not less, if he felt under attack—
but it could have been a plausible motive for murder.

Jennifer left the FBI office on May 2 determined to find a

lawyer and negotiate an immunity deal in exchange for her testimony. The FBI came away with an impression of McVeigh as a multifaceted criminal more akin to a mafia boss than a lone-wolf domestic terrorist.

"I believe that my brother was more involved as a leader in his group rather than as a follower," Jennifer said in her affidavit. The bank robbery and the attempted murder were, in her eyes, an indication that he had moved past the propaganda stage of his revolution. "My assumption," she said, "is that my brother was now taking some kind of action in support of his political beliefs."

Six

THE GREAT JOHN DOE TWO DISAPPEARING ACT

By September 1993, McVeigh's antigovernment fury had grabbed the attention of law enforcement. Operating under his alias Tim Tuttle, he was at the Crossroads of the West gun show in Phoenix, when Al Shearer, an undercover hate-crimes investigator with the Maricopa County Attorney's Office, started up a conversation. McVeigh began telling him how to convert flares into rudimentary explosive shells and said: "It's great for shooting down ATF helicopters." Shearer was alarmed and called the local offices of both the ATF and FBI.

To his amazement, the feds said they couldn't do anything because selling a flare gun was not illegal. Technically, this was correct, but after Waco the assumption was that the feds were more attuned to trouble from the radical right. As Shearer's supervising attorney put it: "The issue wasn't so much that this guy was trying to sell flare guns. It's that he was a nut."

It was, in retrospect, a tantalizing early opportunity to put McVeigh on the law enforcement radar. But Shearer's instinct for danger was overlooked.

• • •

OKLAHOMA CITY WAS THE CASE DANNY COULSON HAD BEEN PRE-
paring for all his life. He knew his way around right-wing radicals.
He had managed tricky arrests and potentially explosive stand-offs,
had set up the FBI's elite Hostage Rescue Team, and had a reputation
for doggedly following leads, no matter how difficult or politically
inconvenient. He knew Weldon Kennedy was about to be replaced
and assumed he was in the running for his job. But, shortly after he
left Kingman in early May, he was called off the case completely.

"I was absolutely shocked," he said. "I should have been given the
job of commander. *I* would have given the job to me."

First Bob Ricks, then Joe Martinolich, and now Coulson: the
body count of senior bureau figures was mounting. Coulson abilities
were impressive, even if he was not a universally loved figure. His
maverick streak, and periodic insistence that he knew better than his
bosses, did not always sit well. And he was definitely no "Friend of
Louie."

Louis Freeh chose this same moment to appoint Larry Potts, one
of his closest associates, as the bureau's permanent deputy director—
despite his controversial role in drafting and approving the rules of
engagement at Ruby Ridge. Everybody thought Potts's career would
be stalled until the Justice Department finished its investigation and
determined whether or not he was responsible for the shoot-to-kill
policy that led to Vicki Weaver's death. But Freeh believed the media
was now distracted, and Potts was earning plaudits for his work directing the Oklahoma investigation's day-to-day operations.

Freeh's faith in Potts—stemming from their days working a
mail-bombing case in Georgia in the late 1980s—was not misplaced.
He was a bureau golden boy, an investigator of extraordinary talents
with a glittering future. Still, Freeh had to expend much political
capital to get his way. Congress had reacted poorly to an internal
FBI investigation that rebuked Potts only for poor oversight at Ruby
Ridge, and was considering hearings. And Jamie Gorelick, the tough-

as-nails deputy attorney general, reacted to the proposed promotion with a flat no.

Freeh told Gorelick that if he did not get his way, relations between the Justice Department and the bureau would be irreparable. A game of political brinksmanship followed. The Justice Department had completed a report on Ruby Ridge in June 1994 in which it found that Potts and another senior FBI commander were responsible for drawing up the controversial rules of engagement; the report also found "numerous shortcomings" in the FBI's oversight of the operation. This report was not made public, but releasing it was an option the Justice Department had up its sleeve. Freeh, meanwhile, knew that Potts had observed Gorelick and Janet Reno closely during Waco, when he served as the bureau's liaison to the attorney general's office. In the end, Reno blinked first, publicly praising Potts as "the very best the FBI has" and announcing the appointment herself at one of her regular post-bombing news briefings.

The Potts promotion created an immediate backlash. Gene Glenn, who had been the FBI's on-scene commander at Ruby Ridge and was given a demotion and a fifteen-day suspension, complained to the Justice Department that he was being made the scapegoat even though Potts had conceived, drawn up, and approved the altered rules of engagement. Glenn accused the FBI's internal investigators of asking skewed questions to reach predetermined conclusions, adding that they were more interested in protecting senior management than in unearthing the truth. Glenn's reaction drew the ire of Freeh's general counsel, Howard Shapiro, who called his allegations "absolutely irresponsible and destructive to the FBI" when the bureau was engaged in a vast criminal investigation. Shapiro was right that the controversy was a dangerous distraction from the Oklahoma City case. But the distraction originated with Louis Freeh.

Potts remained nominally in charge of the bombing investigation, but he spent most of the next six weeks fighting for his job and reputation. The Justice Department's Office of Professional Responsibility opened an investigation into Glenn's allegations, and an incandescent Republican majority in the House of Representatives monitored it all closely.

Over time, it became clear that the bombing investigation's high points had already come and gone by May 3, 1995, the day the Potts furor broke. Individual street agents continued to do sterling work and make important breakthroughs, but for the institution it was all downhill from there.

RICK WAHL, THE ARMY SERGEANT WHO WENT FISHING AT GEARY Lake on April 18 with his son, did not see the Ryder truck and pickup arrive or leave. Neither he nor a second witness who drove by, Bob Nelson, spotted anyone inside. So the feds set up a roadblock on Route 77, by the Geary Lake turnoff, and asked passing drivers if they had seen anything.

The results were notable, but not for reasons the government might have expected.

More than twenty witnesses said they had seen a moving truck at the lake, and at least five said they had seen it *in the week before Easter* as well as the Tuesday after. Georgia Rucker, a Herington real estate agent who helped Terry and Marife Nichols purchase their house on South Second Street, drove Route 77 twice a day to take her son to and from school. She saw a Ryder truck on Monday, April 10, and said it was still there on the next two days. She did not drive the route from Thursday to Monday. On Tuesday, April 18, she saw the truck shortly before 8:00 A.M.; but that afternoon it was gone. At times, Rucker saw the Ryder with other vehicles, but she could not recall what they looked like. Seeing the truck by the lakeshore was so odd, she and her son started to look out for it. "We joked that those people must have a real big fish to pack away," she said.

James Sargent told a similar story. On April 10, he retired from the army and instantly went fishing at Geary Lake. He remembered the day clearly, down to the pear he brought for a snack. He arrived in the early afternoon and spotted a Ryder truck on the shore. After a couple of hours, he saw a white car and a rust-colored pickup drive up. He saw the Ryder again on April 11 and 12, and he probably saw it on April 13, although he was not certain. Sargent said he enjoyed a drink or two on these outings, but he was also sure that alcohol had not distorted his memory. "It's pretty hard for someone to forget something when they have seen it four days in a row," he testified.

These accounts all bolstered the theory, which the FBI and prosecution considered, that a second Ryder truck was involved in the bombing. Lea McGown and her son Eric said they had seen McVeigh with a Ryder on Easter Sunday, more than twenty-four hours before the one used to destroy the Murrah Building was rented from Eldon Elliott's. Other witnesses later came forward with similar stories, notably three dancers from a Tulsa strip club, whose voices were captured on a security tape on April 8 as they discussed an obnoxious client matching McVeigh's description. "On April 19, 1995," the client said, "you will remember me for the rest of your life." A yellow moving truck was parked out back at the time. Now two new witnesses who seemed credible were talking about a Ryder truck popping up in the very place where McVeigh and Nichols would later mix the bomb.

What purpose could a second truck have served? Was it the bomb truck, but broke down or otherwise failed to meet the plotters' requirements? Was it a decoy? In the end, the government chose not to address these questions. Some members of the prosecution thought they were too difficult to answer with any certainty; others were incensed that the FBI erected the roadblock at all, because it developed material they might now have to argue against in court. "It only undermines the proof," one prosecutor said impatiently. "We already had Wahl. We didn't need all this other junk."

Bob Ricks, for one, disagreed with this vigorously; it was not enough to wish a difficult problem away. "Some things that were reported were obviously physically impossible," he said, "but you have to weigh all of that. . . . That's the nature of eyewitness testimony.

"The roadblock also led to people we believe were highly credible, who could give us valid descriptions of what was taking place there at Geary Lake. It doesn't have to be consistent with the theory. What we are trying to find are the facts."

This episode highlighted a growing tension between the Justice Department's more aggressive lawyers and many of the task force's top managers. While the prosecutors wanted to tie up loose ends and secure convictions, the FBI's gut instinct was to keep digging and figure out what happened. The friction was not without its complexities: some prosecutors were more willing than others to let the case head in unforeseeable new directions, and some investigators were more fearless than others in standing up to the Justice Department's pressure. On this, though, the hardliners prevailed: the second Ryder truck was soon dropped as a subject for investigation.

IN THE FALL OF 1993, MCVEIGH CONTINUED TO ATTEND GUN SHOWS and told his sister he was establishing a "network of friends." It is likely that these included Richard Guthrie, the wild man of the Aryan Republican Army. Pete Langan later said that Guthrie met McVeigh on the gun-show circuit, and one plausible venue was a big show in Knob Creek, Kentucky, that October. McVeigh attended, and it would have been an easy commute for Guthrie from his hideout in Cincinnati. After the show, Guthrie and Langan made plans to rob an armored truck in the Fayetteville area in northwestern Arkansas. McVeigh's previous work as a security guard on an armored truck made him the right sort for Langan and Guthrie to approach for help.

If McVeigh and Guthrie did not meet at a gun show, they could have been introduced by Thom Robb, a Ku Klux Klan leader based in Harrison, Arkansas, near Fayetteville. Guthrie was in regular contact with Robb from about 1992, and Nichols supplied evidence suggesting McVeigh knew him, too. When Nichols and McVeigh drove through Missouri and Arkansas in October, Nichols remembered being surprised by how well McVeigh knew the area, and how he talked about a KKK sign just north of town before they had driven past it. This was Robb's property.

Nichols later claimed he made this trip because he was thinking of moving his family to the Ozarks, and he was looking for land suitable for a blueberry farm. But it is also remarkable how close they skirted to Elohim City, including one documented instance when McVeigh was pulled over and cited for illegal passing less than ten miles away. McVeigh had held on to Strassmeir's business card after meeting him six months earlier. This was also the period when Mike Brescia, Kevin McCarthy, and Mark Thomas's teenage son Nathan all moved to Elohim City—and all but Nathan would later be deeply involved with the Aryan Republican Army.

Nichols denied knowing these people, but he did suggest someone else that he and McVeigh met: George Eaton, who was friendly with the Elohimites and lived in the next town. Eaton was the publisher of the *Patriot Report,* which McVeigh and his sister Jennifer read enthusiastically. McVeigh mentioned Eaton as the two of them were driving around. Nichols added: "Tim definitely knew the area and some people who lived there." McVeigh also described an ideal place, a "safe haven" where someone could lie low for a while. "This place was on the border of the Oklahoma and Arkansas state line," Nichols recalled. This had to be a reference to Elohim City.

Eaton, Strassmeir, Brescia, Guthrie, Robb—all were plausible members of McVeigh's "network of friends." And, in the fall of 1993, they all had revolution on their minds.

IN ARIZONA, THE FBI WAS TOLD THAT STEVE COLBERN, A FEDERAL fugitive with a biochemistry degree and a fascination with explosives, kept a mailbox with the same service McVeigh used in Kingman.

The tip was not correct, but by the time the FBI established that, it had learned that Colbern had been under ATF investigation for months, because he was suspected of possessing a .50-caliber Browning machine gun. And the more the FBI dug, the faster he shot up their suspect list.

The previous November, a Metropolitan Water District employee had found a mysterious note attached to a power utility pole near Needles, on the California-Arizona border. It was addressed to "S. C." and appeared to be a recruitment letter. Its most inviting line was: "A man with nothing left to lose is a very dangerous man and his energy/anger can be focused toward a common/righteous goal." It also included this line: "I'm not looking for talkers, I'm looking for fighters."

When the FBI agents saw the note, they immediately recognized McVeigh's handwriting and saw it was signed "Tim T.," a shortened version of Tim Tuttle. Was "S.C." Colbern? And, if so, had he joined McVeigh's bomb plot? Colbern had the qualifications to build a bomb and, as the FBI soon learned, the ideological inclination as well.

The FBI soon learned, too, that in November 1994, one day before the robbery at Roger Moore's ranch, Colbern was in Texarkana, no more than two hours' drive from Moore's property, and mailed a resignation letter to his boss at Cedars-Sinai hospital in Beverly Hills, California, where he did DNA research. Colbern also owned a 1975 brown Chevy pickup, the same vehicle associated with McVeigh multiple times on April 19.

The feds found Colbern's pickup in Bullhead City, Arizona, in the yard of a double-wide vacation trailer belonging to his family. He lived there in the early 1990s with an Armenian wife he had since divorced. The neighbors said he was a freak in military fatigues, who lived in abject squalor and had snakes and other animals crawling all over the house.

The vehicle was not quite the jackpot the FBI had hoped for. It had not been driven in years, ruling it out as one of the vehicles seen in Oklahoma on April 19. But inside the car, the agents did find two bags of ammonium nitrate, one full and one glaringly empty.

BY LATE 1993, McVEIGH HAD COME TO REGARD TERRY NICHOLS AS some combination of friend, ideological soul mate, and open-door hotelier. Nichols had a robot-like habit of doing whatever he was told, and McVeigh—like Joyce Nichols, Lana, and Ralph Daigle—took full advantage. Earlier in the year, when McVeigh was flitting between the Midwest and Arizona, he asked Nichols to drive to Pendleton, a ten-hour round-trip, and pick up his television set, a baseball glove, some cooking utensils, and a batch of sandbags. Nichols agreed without a murmur. Now McVeigh decided to base himself at the Decker farm, doing no more than occasional chores and begging off farmwork altogether, because, he said, the hay bothered his sinuses.

This arrangement came to a halt on November 22, when Marife found Jason, the Nicholses' two-year-old son, unconscious on his bedroom floor with a plastic grocery bag over his head. At the time, Terry and Marife were preparing to move to Las Vegas. Marife immediately assumed that Jason had climbed out of his crib to play with some packing materials left in the middle of the room. Terry and James, she later recalled, were in the fields, and McVeigh was still asleep. She picked up Jason, removed the plastic bag, and banged frantically on McVeigh's door. While McVeigh administered CPR, she ran out of the house screaming for her husband. Nothing, though, could revive the boy.

Local officials ruled Jason's death an accident, as there was no evidence to suggest anything more sinister. But the medical examiner refused to talk to Terry and Marife after the funeral, and Marife was herself riddled with doubts, mostly about her husband. She was convinced that Terry told the 911 dispatcher about the plastic bag before she had a chance to tell him about it. And it was Terry who had insisted on storing the packing materials in Jason's room. Had he harbored a plan to kill Jason? Was McVeigh in on it too?

Jason had been a cause for distress ever since Marife confessed to Terry in June 1991 that the child she was carrying had been conceived with her old boyfriend, Jojo Angelito Florita. She told Nichols it was too late for an abortion and would understand if he divorced her. Nichols chose to accept the circumstances, signed the birth certificate as Jason's father, and, by all accounts, treated the boy lovingly enough. Marife later complained that other members of the Nichols family refused to accept Jason, and even told Terry to use cloth diapers on him, because the boy wasn't good enough for disposable ones. Terry, for once, paid no attention.

After the bombing, the FBI reexamined Jason's death, wondering if they could pin one more murder on McVeigh or Nichols. They suspected that McVeigh might have killed the boy in some grotesque experiment, to see if he could snuff out a child's life, as he planned to do many times with the bomb. But, in the end, the feds found no more evidence than the county authorities.

Marife realized her initial suspicions might have been the result of shock, and the need to blame someone. But she found it impossible to trust her husband again. When Nichols purchased *The Poisoner's Handbook,* she wondered whether he intended to murder her and Nicole to collect the life insurance. Bills from the hospital, the ambulance company, and the doctor who treated Jason kept arriving, and Nichols ignored them for so long they started coming in Marife's name.

To escape their creditors, the Nicholses moved to Las Vegas at the turn of 1994. Yet Marife still felt trapped and desperate. Twice, she dreamed she was on a boat landing, walking toward a small craft containing the entire Nichols family, when she heard Jason's voice begging her to go no farther. She could only interpret it as a warning from her dead son to get out of Terry Nichols's life before it was too late.

THE EVIDENCE RECOVERY TEAMS AT THE MURRAH BUILDING HAD picked the place pretty much clean, but a huge pile of rubble, two stories high and thirty feet across, still covered one of the building's key structural supports. It was impossible to tell how solid that support still was. Engineers warned that if the rubble pile was disturbed, the rest of the structure could tumble and bury everyone. The teams painted the pile red and left it alone; it became known as the red pyramid.

Right after the bombing, the White House had directed the General Services Administration to preserve and rebuild the building, as a gesture of defiance against those who had destroyed it. But that was no longer realistic. "More than once," Weldon Kennedy remembered, "we had pretty serious thunderstorms and had to evacuate the building on the advice of the engineers."

Demolition was the only option. The evidence teams wanted to sort through the red pyramid, but couldn't as long as the building's shell was still standing. The fire department was sure two or three more bodies remained buried, and pressure was mounting to pull them out. Criticism would later fly that, by knocking down the building, the task force was effectively burying evidence about the size and composition of the bomb. Actually, demolition was the only way to extract the remaining evidence.

From an investigative standpoint, the bomb site continued to be as chaotic as it had been in the first few days. For nearly two weeks, there were reports of government agents sneaking out automatic weapons, ammunition, and small packages that looked, to trained eyes, like C-4. Some reports were probably accurate; others were fueled by a mounting distrust pitting federal agencies against each other. "It was comical in a way, because the ATF didn't want the

Secret Service to see them remove things, and DEA didn't want the others to know what they were doing," Oscar Johnson, an elevator technician who stayed on site as a volunteer, recalled. "They all acted like little kids hiding stuff from each other."

One senior ATF agent, Harry Eberhardt, was eventually asked to leave the task force, because Danny Defenbaugh, who arrived in Oklahoma at the end of April and soon took over from Weldon Kennedy, suspected he had entered the building without authorization to remove a possible weapon. "He had a device, and he went back into the building to get it," Defenbaugh said. Eberhardt denied any wrongdoing and said he felt Defenbaugh victimized him because of an unconnected grievance between the FBI and the ATF. But Defenbaugh insisted: "He was seen, he lied about it, and then he was investigated."

AMONG THOSE OPPOSED TO DEMOLISHING THE MURRAH BUILDING was Stephen Jones, the newly appointed chief defense counsel for Tim McVeigh. Jones was a loquacious Southern gentleman, an inveterate Anglophile, a man of breeding and eclectic tastes, and a wily, well-connected political operator with a residual admiration for Richard Nixon, for whom he had worked as a young man. He seemed an incongruous fit for McVeigh, with his blue-collar roots and spiky resentment of privilege in all forms. Sure enough, they got along horribly.

Jones was not McVeigh's first choice. After his two court-appointed public defenders recused themselves, McVeigh wanted Gerry Spence, the flamboyant Wyoming lawyer who claimed he'd never lost a case and rubbed the government's face in the dirt when he defended Randy Weaver. When Spence was ruled out—it is not clear if he said no or was never asked—McVeigh pursued Dick DeGuerin, a similarly flamboyant Texan who had represented David Koresh. But DeGuerin turned down the case as well. Representing the most hated man in America was not an assignment to take on lightly.

Jones got the job because he was law-school buddies with David

Russell, the federal judge in charge of finding legal representation for McVeigh and Nichols, and also because he was brave, or rash, enough to take it on. Criminal defense was not his specialty, although he had worked more than two dozen capital cases over his career; he called himself a county-seat lawyer, occupied mostly with clients like a local religious college or his hometown newspaper, the *Enid News and Eagle*. Just prior to the bombing, he had served as special counsel to Frank Keating, the newly elected governor of Oklahoma and a former FBI agent. Jones and McVeigh were out of step immediately. "I haven't been brainwashed," McVeigh said at their first meeting. "I did this for the movement, and no one else paid for it."

Jones was intending to base his defense on the existence of a broader conspiracy, in which McVeigh was just a bit player. But now his client was telling him he was not willing to go along with a search for coconspirators. It was a problem he would not resolve for as long as he was on the case.

Jones's opening gambit in federal court, to forestall the demolition of the Murrah Building, was equally inauspicious. Every civic leader from the state congressional delegation to the mayor had endorsed the General Services Administration's finding that the wreckage posed a significant safety hazard. Jones, though, described the building as "the single most important item of evidence in this case" and asked for time to conduct an independent analysis.

The request was granted, and demolition was postponed for almost two weeks so Jones could send in a bomb expert and a small team of lawyers. They found nothing. Staff for John Coyle, one of the public defenders who represented McVeigh for the first two weeks, felt a bittersweet twinge as they watched the new defense counsel go about his business. "You watch," a Coyle clerk who knew Jones was overheard saying, "he'll make it all about himself." McVeigh certainly came to believe that he did.

● ● ●

DURING THE FIRST WEEK OF MAY, THE FBI BECAME CONVINCED
that the second person at the Ryder truck rental was twelve-year-old
Josh Nichols. The Oklahoma City command post even told division offices around the country to stop looking for anyone else. This
made little sense, because Josh was not tied in any way to the acquisition of materials, and he had a rock-solid alibi for April 19. Even
if he looked a little like the sketch of the second man seen at Eldon
Elliott's, he wouldn't have gone there without his father, and Terry
Nichols was not there. The FBI essentially mistook Josh's knowledge
of the bomb plot—of which there were many tantalizing clues—for
actual criminal involvement.

Until he was confronted directly with his resemblance to the
mystery co-conspirator on May 6, Josh had been willing to answer
just about any question thrown at him. He even made phone calls
to Agent Calhoun after hours to tell her what was on his mind. The
FBI, though, preferred to ratchet up the pressure to see if Lana, Josh,
or Terry might crack and disclose something new. But they didn't;
they just lawyered up.

Twice, agents asked Padilla to fly out to Oklahoma City to testify
before the grand jury. The first trip was canceled at the last minute.
The second time, there was still no grand jury hearing, only reporters and camera crews at the Oklahoma City airport, who had been
tipped that Josh was now a John Doe Two suspect and ambushed
her with questions. Padilla was appalled, but she still continued to
cooperate. The FBI asked her to repack the bag Josh had taken to
Kansas for his Easter trip, so the clothes could be tested for bomb-
making residue. She did so, and they were clean. A few days later, the
FBI asked her for every baseball cap in Josh's collection so they could
be compared to witness sightings of the cap worn by John Doe Two.
Again, Padilla complied.

For about eight days, the FBI allowed the circus surrounding
Josh to bring the hunt for John Doe Two to a complete standstill.
According to the Secret Service, up to 150 new leads were held back

from investigative field offices around the country. When it finally became clear, on May 11, that no joy was to be had from Josh, they were sent out again.

IN EARLY 1994, McVEIGH PAID AN IMPROMPTU OVERNIGHT VISIT TO Karen Anderson at the Arkansas ranch while Roger Moore was in Florida for the winter. Anderson cooked him a steak, and they talked about Waco. But did something else happen? Anderson, in one of her early FBI interviews, said McVeigh slept in her bed that night. She quickly added that she moved to the other bedroom, the one usually occupied by Moore (they kept separate rooms). Hers was next to the bathroom and she thought McVeigh would be more comfortable there. But this was a rather odd explanation. Had she really given up her bedroom, the government wondered, or had she invited him to join her?

Anderson denied any such thing; she thought of McVeigh "as a son." Still, many of McVeigh's friends and acquaintances noticed a pattern: McVeigh would form strong, almost obsessive attachments to his closest male friends and then hit on their wives or girlfriends behind their backs.

A few months later, McVeigh began dropping in regularly on Michael Fortier's then-fiancée Lori at the tanning salon where she worked. At the same time, McVeigh and Michael Fortier were so tight that Jim Rosencrans teased his neighbor about having a "second wife." Rosencrans had a similar dynamic with McVeigh; his girlfriend Patty complained about being treated like a second-class citizen, but she also recalled a time Rosencrans walked in on one of her own conversations with McVeigh and accused him of making a move on her.

There are two schools of thought about McVeigh's sexuality. The first says he was a highly ascetic person who sublimated whatever sexual energy he had into his war on the government. Sex either did not interest him or it scared him because he was unsuccessful at it. Much later, when he was on death row in Indiana, his fellow inmates nicknamed him "Virgin McVeigh."

But there is also evidence he was highly interested in sex, and grabbed at it wherever he could. Beyond his flirtations, he almost certainly had a brief affair with Marife Nichols in the summer of 1994. Marife testified about it at trial, and Terry Nichols subsequently confirmed he had been betrayed by his wife and his best friend.

McVeigh seems to have viewed sex much as he viewed his need for food, as a craving to satisfy efficiently so he could get on with something more interesting. To stave off his appetite, he often resorted to military MREs, or Meals Ready to Eat; to assuage his interest in sex, he looked for people he could use quickly and discreetly.

Rosencrans told the FBI McVeigh was always talking about "getting a piece of ass" and was even willing to pay for it. Rosencrans described him as "a weird, quiet, and clean guy."

On May 10, a rural property broker in southwestern Missouri named Bill Maloney contacted the FBI and said he had met McVeigh, Nichols, and their presumed coconspirator. Maloney saw news reports about two drifters getting arrested thirty-five miles away in Carthage, Missouri, and recognized one of the names, Robert Jacks. The man he had met with McVeigh and Nichols was called Jacks, too, though he spelled it Jacques or Jocques. And he was very different from the drunken drifter—quickly dismissed as a suspect—who had been found with a bunch of discarded beer bottles and pizza boxes.

Maloney said that McVeigh had called the previous October from Kansas in response to an ad offering a forty-acre parcel "in the middle of nowhere." Two weeks later—the date was later fixed as November 2—two men walked into Maloney's office and introduced themselves as Jacques and Nichols. Someone had already made an offer on the forty-acre parcel, but Maloney offered them a larger one bordered on three sides by national forest. They were interested in that, too. After ten or fifteen minutes, a third man entered, wondering what was taking so long. The others called him Tim.

Maloney's ability to recall the tiniest detail seemed almost too good to be true. He described, for example, how McVeigh was drawn to a green Remington shotgun shell on Maloney's desk. Maloney said he used those to hunt coyotes, and McVeigh opened his mouth to laugh. Maloney recounted: "I could see a discolored eyetooth on the upper right side of his mouth. He had a filling showing through the enamel. I also remember that he had unusual hands that were deep set between the thumb and the forefinger. His hands looked like they could break if they were gripped very hard."

Maloney was an ex-serviceman who had conducted eyewitness recall exercises with naval intelligence and was proud of his razor-sharp recall. He remembered that Jacques wore olive-colored hiking boots with little suction cups and cleats on the soles. Jacques, he said, was a muscular man with large biceps and a bulging neck, about five foot eleven, swarthy complexion, possibly American-Indian, with a tattoo on his left forearm showing wings or some other insignia. He also had an unusually pointed, narrow nose, unlike the sketch.

All three were military types, Maloney said, and carried themselves confidently. Their inquiries suggested they were looking for a place to hide, but they did not have a vehicle appropriate for the terrain, only an old sedan, which Maloney would later recall as a Chevy Monte Carlo. Maloney became suspicious enough that he asked Jacques to handle a brand-new topographical map of the area and then put it in his safe, in case the FBI ever needed fingerprints. He handed it to his first FBI interviewer.

Maloney's uncanny command of detail was counterbalanced, over time, by indications that news reports were distorting his memory. Investigators did not know quite what to make of him. "Either Bill Maloney had fallen from the sky as a pure gift from the heavens, or he was completely certifiable," said Jeanne Boylan, the sketch artist, who interviewed him and produced a John Doe Three drawing based on his recollections. It is curious that the description Boylan got from Maloney was an almost exact match for a sketch she developed from Debbie Nakanashi, a downtown post office worker injured in the explosion. Nakanashi remembered seeing a Jacques look-alike, complete with tattoo on his left arm, with a tall, wiry blond guy, not unlike McVeigh, a day or two before the bombing. Investigators also found the name "Jacques" scrawled, in a number of different spellings, in Marife Nichols's address book. If Jacques was a phantom, he certainly had a way of popping up all over the place.

The easiest of Maloney's observations to check was the discolored tooth. Bill Teater, an Oklahoma City–based FBI agent, looked up McVeigh's military health records and discovered he had had a procedure, probably a root canal, on his right lateral incisor. A few weeks later, Teater observed McVeigh in person, when a gaggle of agents and lawyers met him at the federal courthouse in Oklahoma City, ostensibly to obtain handwriting samples. Teater's job was to watch his mouth. "I got him to smile," Teater recounted, "at which time I saw the tooth with a root canal."

The Jacques investigation would go on for close to five years. It generated just enough promise to keep going: a pair of Jacques brothers who went to school with McVeigh; and a Robert Jacquez, now apparently dead, who once shared a mailbox with Jim Rosencrans in Odessa, Texas. But certain FBI agents and federal prosecutors, especially those who felt confident of where the case was going, suspected it might also be a colossal waste of time.

In the end, their biggest problem was not with Robert Jacques, whose existence remains a question, but with Danny Defenbaugh, the new task force leader, who kept Jacques on his priority list long after the prosecution team had lost interest. Defenbaugh, they felt, did not command the respect necessary to fulfill his responsibilities. He had spent most of his FBI career as a bomb technician, traveling the world to investigate attacks from Puerto Rico to Beirut. He had been in charge of violent crime investigations in Miami and had served as the number two in Mobile, Alabama. But he had never commanded a field division or occupied a high position in headquarters.

Most seriously, he was not seen as a leader with the authority to corral rival agencies, push for what he needed from his own bosses, and find a coherent path through a torrent of information. Defenbaugh was the straightest of straight arrows, but he was also impulsive, gruff, and had a volcanic temper. He made enemies as easily as he made friends, and freely acknowledged he was an investigator at heart, not a manager.

"The common view was that he was not the right choice that would get us to where we needed to be," said one senior agent who might have expected the job for himself. Another overlooked candidate was blunter. "When I heard they'd made Defenbaugh commander, I just about crapped out," he said. "He's the last person I would have picked." I. C. Smith, the top agent in Arkansas at the time, concurred that Defenbaugh was not highly regarded, and said: "The only thing he had going for him was that he was a butt-boy to Bear Bryant." (Smith used the term "butt-boy" in a strictly figurative sense to imply that Defenbaugh did Bryant's bidding in a sycophantic or servile way.) Bryant, the head of the National Security Division at headquarters, indeed became Defenbaugh's champion and maintained close contact throughout the investigation.

Louis Freeh had already shown he was more interested in imposing his leadership stamp than in promoting harmony in the ranks. "My gut feeling is, they couldn't control [Kennedy]," Smith said. "They wanted people there who were pliable." Defenbaugh would defer to Bryant, because he did not have the political wherewithal to push his own agenda, and Bryant would make sure the task force did the director's bidding. Defenbaugh all but acknowledged this when he characterized his role as "making a coordinating effort to make sure that certain things get done, that certain things do not fall through the cracks, that *somebody doesn't make an independent decision on their own* that may or may not be approved by others."

The result was that an enormous amount of energy was expended on certain investigative strands—beyond Robert Jacques, the FBI collected more than 13 *million* paper motel registration records—while other topics, such as Elohim City or Roger Moore, were not investigated enough because Defenbaugh did not have the clout to insist. Some people, including members of the prosecution team, accused him of overreaching when he tried to broaden the case in one direction or another, while others accused him of lacking the nerve to do what it took to find McVeigh's coconspirators. The experience eventually left Defenbaugh burned and embittered.

"What they needed was a highly centralized investigation with clear lines of authority," Smith observed. "It didn't happen here."

AFTER A WEEKLONG SEARCH, THE FEDS FOUND STEVE COLBERN IN the semi-abandoned mining town of Oatman, about twenty minutes west of Kingman, where he shared a filthy trailer with three other drifters and he manufactured crystal meth in an outhouse. At first, he denied knowing McVeigh or having any involvement in the bombing. But he broke down quickly, especially when pressed for an alibi for April 19. "If I, like, tell you everything I know, can I, like, make a deal and get a break on my charges?" he asked.

Since his arrest in California, Colbern had spent several months in the Arizona desert, including extended periods in abandoned mineshafts. Most likely, he had also been on the road in his red Volkswagen Bug, as attested by the Texarkana postmark on his resignation letter to Cedars-Sinai hospital. His whereabouts on April 19 were uncertain. Preston Haney, the owner of his trailer, said he had been holed up for days, watching television and subsisting on a diet of spaghetti, beans, and vitamins. But agents had also accumulated reasons to wonder if he was not hundreds of miles away with McVeigh. The

Louis Beam, the far right's devastatingly eloquent propagandist and advocate of "leaderless resistance" against the government, being apprehended at Waco in 1993 after asking the "forbidden question" at a news briefing about America turning into a police state. *AP Images*

Fed Up With the Government?

DETONATOR

WAR - Box 65 Fallbrook, CA 92088
www.resist.com

A typical early 1990s anti-government propaganda image, from Tom Metzger's group White Aryan Resistance.

Robert Millar, the patriarch of Elohim City, who excused the regular presence of fearsome violent criminals by saying they came from Jesus. *From the collection of J.D. Cash*

Carol Howe, the ATF's secret informant at Elohim City, sported a large inky swastika tattoo on her left shoulder (partially visible) and loved to take provocative pictures. Andreas Strassmeir dismissed her many years later as a "dress Nazi."

A rare photo of Roger Moore, an irascible ammunition dealer who knew Tim McVeigh from the gun-show circuit. Many senior law enforcement officials were disappointed Moore was not pursued more aggressively as a bombing suspect. (He's seen here outside the Oklahoma courthouse where Terry Nichols was tried on state murder charges.) *AP Images*

McVeigh in what he described as his biker disguise. *Courtesy of the Oklahoma National Memorial & Museum*

The white-supremacist bank robber Pete Langan had a secret life as a preoperative transsexual.

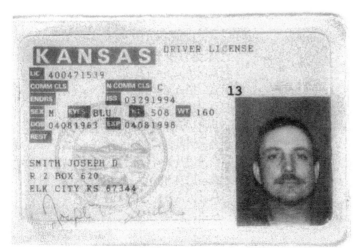

A fake driver's license made by Langan's volatile sidekick, Richard Guthrie, who thought the Oklahoma bombing would trigger a civil war. *Evidence entered into trial*

A bag of ammonium nitrate prills similar to those used to build the bomb. *Courtesy of the Oklahoma National Memorial & Museum*

96-CR-68-M
Government Exhibit

70

Date _____

A locker at the Marion Marietta quarry, which McVeigh and Nichols robbed in October 1994 to obtain blasting caps and Tovex detonators. *Courtesy of the Oklahoma National Memorial & Museum*

96-CR-68-M
Government Exhibit
745
Date_____

Hell on earth: the immediate aftermath of the bombing, when the streets of down-town Oklahoma City were choking in smoke and debris and the cars parked for blocks around were reduced to mangled wrecks. *Courtesy of the Oklahoma National Memorial & Museum*

ATF Agent Luke Franey holds up a sign in the window of the ATF's top-floor offices; his account of that morning raises a lot of unanswered questions. *J. Pat Carter*

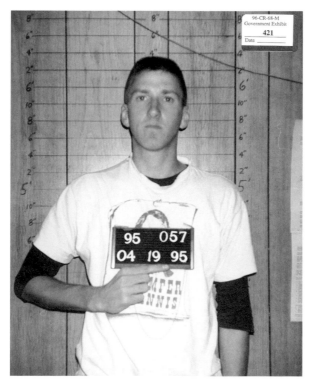

McVeigh's mug shot following his arrest on gun and traffic charges shortly after the bombing. *Courtesy of the Oklahoma National Memorial & Museum*

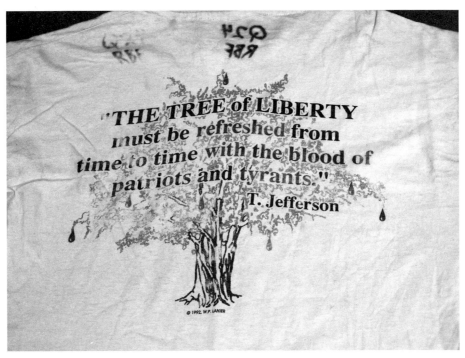

The T-shirt worn by McVeigh when he was arrested; the line about refreshing the tree of liberty with blood echoed a line in an incendiary speech of Louis Beam's two and a half years earlier. *Courtesy of the Oklahoma National Memorial & Museum*

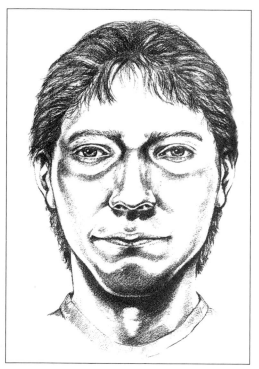

A sketch developed from the memory of Jeff Davis, a Chinese-food-delivery boy who insisted the man who opened the door of Room 25 at the Dreamland Motel was someone other than McVeigh. *Courtesy of the Oklahoma National Memorial & Museum*

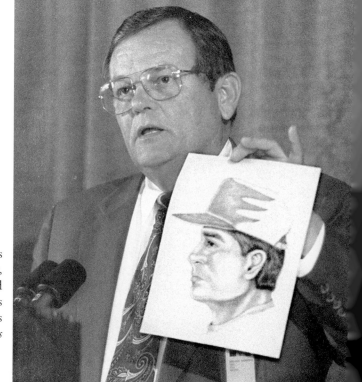

Weldon Kennedy, the FBI's first on-scene commander, brandishes an amended sketch of the mysterious John Doe Two at a news conference. *AP Images*

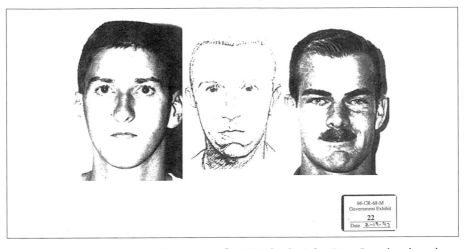

A triptych of images presented in court of McVeigh, the John Doe One sketch and Sergeant Michael Hertig. The government argued that McVeigh was John Doe One, and that any inconsistency was due to witnesses at Eldon Elliott's body shop confusing him with Hertig, who rented a Ryder truck almost exactly twenty-four hours later. There are grounds to doubt both of these assertions. *Courtesy of the Oklahoma National Memorial & Museum*

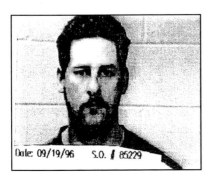

The Ward brothers, Pete *(top left)*, Tony *(top right)*, and Sonny *(bottom)*, after their arrest in Oregon in 1996. Carol Howe told the FBI Pete and Tony were a match for John Does One and Two. The FBI spoke to Pete Ward, but none of the brothers was considered a suspect in the Oklahoma City bombing. *Oregon police files*

PM 3:57:18

McVeigh, captured on video at the Junction City McDonald's on the day the Ryder truck was rented. He left McDonald's no sooner than 3:57 P.M. but managed, according to the government, to walk more than a mile uphill to Eldon Elliott's in time for the rental agreement to be printed at 4:19. It was raining at the time, but the man who rented the truck was dry. *Trial exhibit*

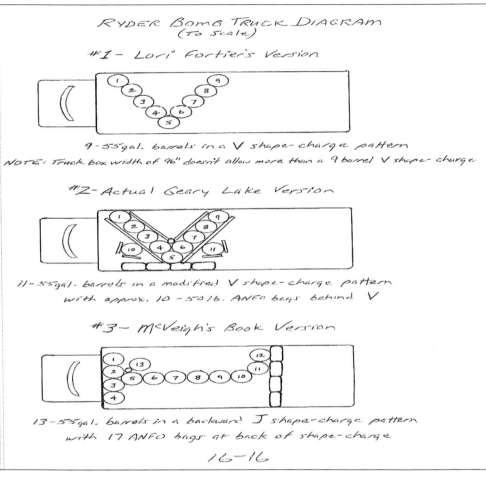

Diagrams drawn by Terry Nichols showing Lori Fortier's description of how the bomb was built (supposedly based on what McVeigh told her), his own memory of the construction of the bomb, and McVeigh's version as described in *American Terrorist*. Explosives experts put most credence in Nichols's version, raising questions of who was the true bombing mastermind. *From Nichols correspondence*

McVeigh with his lawyers Stephen Jones (right) and Rob Nigh (left). *AP Images*

① HEARd About
CAulburn on the
NEWS. WAnt to see
his picture. MAy be
I could be of help.

② Talking to Attourny
TodAy. ~~the~~ he mAy
wAnt to see A copy of
the proffer. Is it possible
To get copy?

The message Michael Fortier scrawled on the back of a Kit Kat candy wrapper to tell the FBI he was now willing to cooperate. *Courtesy of the Oklahoma National Memorial & Museum*

Andreas Strassmeir in Civil War costume in 1994. *Courtesy of Kirk Lyons and Andreas Strassmeir*

Andreas Strassmeir, Berlin, 2010. *Photograph by Andrew Gumbel*

Oklahoma Ku Klux Klan leader Dennis Mahon doing a Nazi salute in front of a Ryder truck, some time after the bombing. Mahon's very public statements that associated him with McVey ended his career as an aircraft mechanic, but did not attract more than token investigative interest.

SHORT BARREL FIREARMS	ILLEGAL EXPLOSIVE DEVICE	TITLE III	ALCOHOL / TOBACCO
OTHER (Explain)	OTHER (Explain)	OTHER (Explain)	OTHER (Explain)

EXPLAIN/JUSTIFICATION

This investigation involves the Bombing of the Murrah Bldg. in Oklahoma City, OK. It is suspected that members of Elohim City re/involved either directly or indirectly through Conspiracy. It is suspected that suspect #2 may be at the location. Fund. be used for CI-subsistence, expenses travel. Re 53200-95-0005W

PART II - SUB CASHIER FUNDS REQUEST AND APPROVAL

In connection with the above investigation, I request that an advance of funds, in the sum of $ _250.00_ be issued to me by the sub cashier to be used for confidential expenditures, the purchase of information, and/or the purch of evidence.

SPECIAL AGENT	DATE	TOTAL FUNDS EXPENDED IN THE CASE TO DATE	
Angela Finley	05 18 95	$ 4 452.99	
GROUP SUPERVISOR OR RESIDENT AGENT IN CHARGE	DATE	AMOUNT APPROVED (Write out)	$
David E. Roberts	05 18 95	Two Hundred Fifty	250.00

PART III - DISBURSEMENT / RECEIPT OF FUNDS

The ATF authorized Carol Howe to return to Elohim City after the bombing to look for co-conspirators, hurriedly reversing their previous determination that she was mentally unstable. The text, in Angie Finley's handwriting, says: "It is suspected that members of Elohim City are involved either directly or indirectly through conspiracy. It is suspected that suspect #2 may be at the location."

29 Nov. 2007

MORNING OF APRIL 18, 1995

> I woke up about 5:30 A.M. on Tuesday, April 18th, got dressed, and was ready to head out the door to meet Timothy McVeigh at the Herington Storage Units about a mile away just off of Highway 77 at 6 A.M., but I procrastinated. I sat down at the dining room table debating with myself whether to go or not. I was resisting to go but McVeigh's recent threats, beginning on Easter Sunday, of harming my family was still fresh on my mind as

The beginning of Terry Nichols's detailed description of building the bomb, written in 2007; he had not previously confessed it.

Nichols's federal trial lawyers, Ron Woods (*left*) and Michael Tigar, on their way into court. Every day Woods would turn to Tigar and say: "Time to go throw up." *AP Images*

Joe Hartzler, the government's chief prosecutor in the McVeigh trial, in the wheelchair he utilized due to multiple sclerosis. *AP images*

Larry Mackey, Hartzler's number two who went on to run Terry Nichols's federal trial. *AP Images*

Niki Deutchman, the jury foreman in the Nichols federal trial, gives an impromptu news conference after finding Nichols not guilty of first-degree murder in January 1998. She formed a special courtroom bond with Nichols's lawyer Michael Tigar and described him as "one heck of an attorney." Soon after, she was receiving death threats. *AP Images*

day before his arrest, his most recent girlfriend, Barbara Harris, had produced a letter he wrote the previous fall—also postmarked Texarkana and dated November 4—in which he talked about his desire to avenge Waco. On the day of his arrest, the ATF showed his picture to Lynda Willoughby, the manager of the Mail Room on Stockton Hill Road, and she said she recognized him as someone who had come in to pick up McVeigh's mail in the month before the bombing.

Extraordinarily, the FBI appeared indifferent to this information, disregarding not only the new leads from the ATF but also the unresolved question of the Browning machine gun.

Some iteration of the usual interagency rivalry was probably at work here. The FBI had a bombing to investigate, and apparently regarded the firearms violations as distractions from their goal of coaxing Colbern into talking about McVeigh. But they were also oddly quick in dismissing Colbern as a suspect, relying on information from Colbern's uncle, a retired orthopedic surgeon from California, that he was a paranoid schizophrenic. But Dr. Edwin Colbern had said more than that: he also had been afraid, from the time Steve was a teenager, that his nephew would one day become a "mad bomber."

Asked specifically about Oklahoma City, Dr. Colbern said he "believed Steven was capable of being involved." The FBI not only disregarded this; the information was not handed over to the defense teams representing McVeigh and Nichols. "They even knew what Colbern smelled like," Nichols's lead defense lawyer, Michael Tigar, complained many years later, "but didn't think to let us see the evidence against him."

WHEN MICHAEL FORTIER HEARD ABOUT COLBERN'S ARREST, HE jumped into his Jeep Wrangler and drove over to one of the FBI agents keeping him under surveillance a block and a half away. Fortier passed him a Kit Kat candy wrapper, on which he had scrawled in block letters: "Heard about Caulbern [sic] on the news. Want see his picture. Maybe I could be of help."

He also let the agent know he was at last willing to accept the government's offer to consider a plea deal in exchange for his cooperation. "Talking to attorney today," the Kit Kat wrapper added.

ON MAY 17, THE *NEW YORK TIMES* FEATURED A FRONT-PAGE STORY that said McVeigh had claimed responsibility for the bombing. For a man planning to plead not guilty in a death penalty case, it was not exactly ideal headline material. Many people assumed that prison guards at El Reno must have overheard something. But the source was McVeigh's lawyer, Stephen Jones.

Jones had had a busy first week on the job. He initially wanted to strike a plea-bargain deal to save his client's life. In his account, he lobbied for a meeting with Janet Reno, telling Justice Department officials he might be able to offer up John Doe Two if, in exchange, the government took the death penalty off the table. McVeigh never publicly acknowledged the existence of a John Doe Two, so we have only Jones's word on that. In any event, McVeigh had an apparent change of heart and told Jones to cancel the meeting. "I would have argued for his life," Jones said, "but he withdrew that authority."

What McVeigh wanted, Jones said, was to plead a "necessity defense"—to admit his guilt but claim his actions were justified. Jones told him such a defense would never fly in court, but McVeigh would not accept his advice. Jones worried that McVeigh would make some glaringly public confession making him impossible to defend. And that was when the story appeared in the *New York Times*.

In the revised 2001 edition of his memoir *Others Unknown*, Jones acknowledged his responsibility for the leak but described it as a form of damage control, a way to satisfy McVeigh's itch for notoriety while minimizing the risk that he would call *60 Minutes* or ABC News and offer a lengthy, on-the-record disquisition. He and

McVeigh discussed making a public admission but went back and forth on how it should be done. "It was incumbent on me," Jones wrote, "to find a way to protect Tim and at the same time assuage his craving for fame."

It was never clear how this protection was achieved by a front-page confession in the country's most authoritative newspaper, but Jones insisted he had McVeigh's full permission to speak to the *Times*. His book reproduces a letter of authorization initialed at every paragraph and signed by McVeigh on May 18—the day *after* the *Times* story appeared. Another lawyer on the defense team reported that Jones was very pleased with himself when he secured McVeigh's signature. "Jones talked to Tim alone when he got that paper signed. He had a chalk-striped suit on," the lawyer recalled. "He was patting the lapel of his suit and bragging . . . that he'd gotten it."

Jones also wrote that he agreed to the leak on condition that McVeigh not do any leaking of his own. "I wanted his pledge," he said. "No more." But there was no evidence McVeigh had made any attempt to talk to the press, so the "no more" line is a little baffling. Rob Nigh, Jones's number two on the defense team who got to know McVeigh better than anyone, directly contradicted Jones's premise. "I don't believe he [McVeigh] was itching to say anything," Nigh said. "If he had been, he would have said it."

Nigh also said McVeigh was not only interested in a necessity defense. He was also willing to sit back and say nothing, while the government struggled with the holes and contradictions in its evidence and—with luck—failed to prove its case, as was then happening in the O. J. Simpson trial in Los Angeles. "If you wanted to embarrass the federal government," Nigh said in an indication of his client's mind-set, "what better way than to be found not guilty?"

McVeigh later complained that Jones leaked the *Times* story entirely on his own. "S.J. gave that to 'em, my own attorney!" he told Michel and Herbeck. "I don't get this. I tell my attorney something, and it goes into the newspaper." When asked about this, Jones first offered no comment and then, a few days later, said he had McVeigh's oral permission before speaking to the *Times* reporter. But the other member of Jones's defense team questioned the accuracy of this, saying that Jones leaked the story by himself and sought permission only subsequently.

Jones, the lawyer said, was trying to push a different talking point in the *Times* story. "The strategy was to get out in front on the subject of the kids. That's item number two in Tim's sworn statement and also in [the] story. The line Stephen wanted to push was that McVeigh had been past the building but not in it, and didn't know about the day-care center." Sure enough, the *Times* reported that McVeigh had no idea there were kids in the building and was "surprised" to learn that many of them had been killed. In the authorization letter, which Jones drafted in his own handwriting, McVeigh signed off on a similar sentiment—"that I am saddened children were killed 4/19/95."

This strategy would mean that, barely a week into his tenure as McVeigh's lawyer, Jones had all but given up on seeking an acquittal and was now hoping to soften the public's view of McVeigh by characterizing the children's deaths as an unfortunate mistake.

Jones was certainly smart. If he had to cajole McVeigh into signing the authorization letter, he most likely appealed to McVeigh's desire to protect his friends and coconspirators. McVeigh's claim of sole responsibility sent a reassuring message to the people under the most pressure from the FBI. Jones wrote in his book that this was never explicitly discussed, but he acknowledged it might have been a motivator for McVeigh.

"If Mike and Lori Fortier and James and Terry Nichols knew he was not 'ratting them out,'" he wrote, "they wouldn't be inclined to turn against him." They could also do what it took to limit their own exposure to prosecution, in the knowledge that they had McVeigh's blessing and protection.

● ● ●

AFTER THE FBI BUGGED THE FORTIERS' HOUSE AND PHONE, THEY overheard one indiscretion after another. Michael laughed at the idea of being called as a witness in federal court and said he would "sit there and pick my nose and flick it . . . and kind of wipe it on the judge's desk." He said he would sell his story to the tabloids, and bragged in the cockiest way imaginable about being "the key" the government needed to crack the case. Investigators found this insufferable, but they knew Fortier was right. They needed an insider to testify against McVeigh, and he was it.

Michael and Lori were taken to Oklahoma City and began providing rich and interesting material, though it was hard to tell how much of it was true. And the FBI seemed afraid to ask. They were interviewed together rather than separately, and afforded an hour of complete privacy to go over what they intended to say.

Fortier did most of the talking, focusing mainly on the trip he and McVeigh took to Oklahoma and Kansas in December 1994. McVeigh said he had a lot of guns to pick up in the Midwest, and Fortier was welcome to resell them for his own profit. The only thing McVeigh wanted in exchange was a wooden gun stock from Fortier's collection. Fortier suspected something fishy, but McVeigh handed him an AR-15 rifle and said he could keep it as long as he accompanied him to retrieve the rest. The deal was on.

The guns were in Kansas, but McVeigh detoured to Oklahoma City to show Fortier a building he intended to blow up. Fortier said the target was tall, U-shaped, with glass frontage—an adequate description of the Murrah Building but one he could easily have picked up from the news after the bombing. Fortier said they did a quick drive-by and left—a statement contradictory to the eyewitness reports of McVeigh walking into the Murrah Building that same day and asking unusual questions.

The next day, Fortier rented a Crown Victoria sedan to transport the guns back to Arizona. They headed to a nearby storage locker—he did not remember the exact location—where McVeigh gave him twenty-five or thirty rifles and shotguns. Fortier asked where they'd come from, and McVeigh told him: "Bob in Arkansas." Fortier asked if they were stolen, and McVeigh winked. Fortier did not take this entirely as a yes; he told the FBI he thought "Bob in Arkansas" was John Doe Two and that the guns somehow tied him and McVeigh together.

Fortier said that McVeigh repeatedly attempted to recruit him for the bombing. At one point he asked McVeigh why he was targeting Oklahoma City, and McVeigh answered: "Because it's easy." McVeigh asked what would persuade him to join the plot, and Fortier said he would not act until he saw a United Nations tank in his front yard.

Fortier and the prosecution team later agreed that the tank-in-the-front-yard conversation took place in August 1994. But if McVeigh had told him about the Oklahoma City plan then, why did Fortier characterize it as a revelation when they were en route to Kansas four months later? Fortier would acknowledge under cross-examination in the trial that he lied to the FBI that day. And the FBI did not call him on it.

By the spring of 1994, McVeigh appeared to be living a normal life in Kingman, working a stockroom job at True Value Hardware, earning extra money as a gardener, and continuing to peddle his wares at gun shows. But this was all a cover for his true passion: heading out to the desert for target practice and trial runs with pipe bombs and other explosives.

He was putting himself through a rigorous training program for his future as an outlaw. Jim Rosencrans remembered several occasions when Lori Fortier drove her husband and McVeigh to the middle of nowhere and left them, with full backpacks and weapons over their shoulders, for two or three days at a time. Other times, they would all go out with Ruger mini-14s and Glocks and shoot the crap out of rocks and empty cans.

They also experimented with explosives but had little success. Their pipe bombs were not much better than giant firecrackers. Fortier testified that on one occasion McVeigh placed a large pipe bomb under a boulder, hoping it would split apart, but the boulder merely trembled and rolled a little.

McVeigh's first forays into criminality were equally unimpressive. One night, he and Fortier headed to the National Guard armory to check a rumor that United Nations troops were massing in Kingman. When a diesel truck pulled in with its headlights blazing, they stole some tools from the undercarriage of two Humvees and fled. This was hardly the way to start a revolution.

Around this time, they met Walter "Mac" McCarty, a grizzled former marine who shared much of their antigovernment fervor. Fortier first spotted the pistol on McCarty's hip as he was walking the aisles of True Value. Soon the three men were regularly discussing the Trilateral Commission and the New World Order and going to McCarty's house for handgun shooting lessons. McCarty liked the young men, particularly McVeigh, but did not see them as sophisticated thinkers, or leaders. "They are both frustrated men and great brainwashing material, very impressionable," he said after the bombing. "They remind me of recruits I had in boot camp. You could feed them, teach them the Marine Corps hymn, creeping and crawling and 'yes sir, no sir,' lull them into becoming fighting machines, and send them overseas to kill."

Another person McVeigh almost certainly encountered—though both later denied it—was Jack Oliphant, the leader of a right-wing revolutionary gang called the Arizona Patriots, who attempted an armored car robbery in Nevada in the 1980s and plotted a string of bomb attacks across the Southwest. The Patriots were, in many ways, a knock-off of The Order, the notorious white supremacist gang from the Pacific Northwest, who pulled off a string of assassinations and a spectacular armored car robbery before going down in flames in a showdown with the FBI near Seattle in 1984. The worst damage Oliphant ever caused was to himself, shooting off his right arm in a misadventure with a shotgun. Still, his armored car robbery plan, involving a staged traffic accident and sleeping gas to neutralize the guards, earned him four years in prison.

Oliphant's remote Hephzibah Ranch was a gathering spot for local skinheads and an ideal place for weapons or explosives training. The caretaker of the Lazy L ranch next door, Dyane Partridge, told the FBI after the bombing that she regularly heard gunfire, although no explosions. She also remembered seeing McVeigh, Nichols, and another man chop wood with Oliphant sometime during the winter of 1993–94. (Nichols had just moved to Las Vegas, ninety miles away.) She remembered the encounter because Oliphant had made it clear that she and her dog should not get too close.

When Oliphant's wife, Margo, spoke with the FBI, she referred fondly to "Timmy," leaving the interviewing agent skeptical of her claim that she did not know McVeigh. Oliphant kept a mailbox at the same office as McVeigh. And McVeigh acknowledged that one of his favorite shooting spots was right around the Oliphant ranch.

If McVeigh did, in fact, know Oliphant and sought to learn from him, the chances are he did not get too far. The Arizona Patriots veteran Tom Hoover described Oliphant's crowd as "a ragtag bunch of dipshits from the weeds with shoulder weapons" and remembered only one explosives expert, a character named Lefty, who accidentally blew his thumb off while fooling around with a grenade.

The Fortiers' social circle was no more promising for fomenting a bomb plot, because it was as much about crystal methamphetamine as it was about revolution. Jim Rosencrans told the FBI: "Getting high is the only thing left we can do in America." While McVeigh used the drug himself, especially to stay awake on cross-country car journeys, he also understood that if he wanted to complete his mission, he would need to find other friends.

• • •

PERHAPS THE MOST INTERESTING THING STEVE COLBERN TOLD FED-eral prosecutors was that he was put in touch with McVeigh by Roger Moore and Karen Anderson. Colbern was a regular customer of the couple's ammunition business, the Candy Store, and in late 1994 he asked if they knew of a hard-core antigovernment group he could join. Anderson mentioned McVeigh by his alias Tim Tuttle, and gave Colbern his P.O. box number.

Colbern and McVeigh corresponded to set up first one, then another meeting, but McVeigh never showed. When Colbern learned—from Roger Moore—about the message McVeigh left on the power utility pole, he was too scared to pick it up. In the end, he said, he never met McVeigh, and gave up on the idea of joining a radical group.

The attorneys accepted this, despite the ATF's evidence that Colbern and McVeigh were acquainted. This was likely influenced by Lori Fortier, who told the FBI three days earlier that McVeigh had not been interested in reaching out to Colbern. The prosecutors—led by Janet Reno's top aide, Donna Bucella—either ignored or were never given the countervailing evidence. Dennis Malzac, one of Colbern's roommates at the Oatman trailer, told the ATF he had heard Colbern talking about making an ammonium nitrate bomb and adding nitromethane to "step it up a little." If the FBI had talked to Malzac, they might have pressured him to say what he told a California detective five years later—that a clean-cut man with blond hair and a military bearing had visited Colbern at the trailer a week or two before the bombing. Malzac was 90 percent sure the visitor was McVeigh. Around the same time, he remembered Colbern asking an odd question: he wondered how big a bomb it would take to destroy the federal building in Oklahoma City.

This material does not create a criminal case against Colbern, because he could have been interested in ammonium nitrate bombs independently of McVeigh, and Malzac could have been exaggerating or lying. But the FBI and the Justice Department did not pursue this, just as they did not pursue the possibility that Colbern owned an enormously dangerous 50-caliber machine gun. The deal that prompted Colbern's release as a bombing suspect did not say anything about this gun, despite evidence he had bought ammunition for it from Moore and Anderson. The gun never came up in *any* of Colbern's subsequent dealings with the criminal justice system, and was never recovered. Colbern's lawyer, Richard Hanawalt, called it "the eight-hundred-pound elephant in the room."

Colbern served less than four years for the charges arising from his 1994 arrest in California, and he was barely mentioned in any of the Oklahoma City bombing trials. According to Bob Sanders, a former deputy director of the ATF, Colbern could—and probably should—have been sentenced for life, given his serious weapons violations and links to McVeigh. "I'm very surprised," Sanders said, "that this guy is walking the streets today."

CAROL HOWE RETURNED TO ELOHIM CITY FOR THREE DAYS IN EARLY May and reported that someone there had talked about a "big secret" connected to the bombing. She had not been able to figure out what this secret was. As the government's sole eyes and ears in the community, she was debriefed by both the ATF and the FBI in Oklahoma City—the FBI never produced a paper trail connected with the meeting—and then returned home.

Only on May 18, when she was formally reinstated as an ATF informant and paid $250, did she agree to have another go at penetrating the community. But she never made it back. Within days, Howe called her handler, Angela Finley, and said she'd received two separate warnings to stay away. The ATF later learned that Grandpa Millar had fingered Howe as a government snitch, a potential death sentence. They never sent her to Elohim City again.

• • •

MICHAEL TIGAR, THE LEAD COUNSEL APPOINTED TO REPRESENT Terry Nichols, won his client's confidence with an immediate string of courtroom victories. Tigar was one of the more brilliant defense attorneys in the country—dogged, erudite, charming, and a scourge to underprepared prosecutors and law enforcement agents. On May 25, he poured out a torrent of indignation at the treatment not only of his client but also his client's wife, who had been held in "protective custody" at a variety of motels in Kansas and Oklahoma for thirty-four days. Marife Nichols, he charged, was being kept "virtually incommunicado and without counsel" even though she was accused of no wrongdoing. She was interrogated continuously, denied access to her husband's lawyers—never mind her husband—and subjected to search and seizure of her personal property, including her journal. Tigar said this was grossly unfair, and reflected the "lamentably thin" case against Terry Nichols.

Some of this was lawyerly bombast, calculated to secure his client's cooperation as much as it was a shot at the Justice Department. But his description of Marife's predicament was on point. Shortly after Nichols's arrest, Marife learned she was pregnant, but did not dare tell her husband right away. She was still hoping to catch a flight to the Philippines on May 10. When that became impossible, she begged the FBI for the $5,000 they took from her bedsprings so she could make new plans to leave. They refused.

Once Tigar got involved, she and Nicole were allowed to visit Nichols. She was also given the $5,000 and allowed to book a flight to the Philippines. Still, she was mad that the FBI had transported her to Oklahoma City but now would not pay for a hotel or take her back to Kansas. She left a scathing voice-mail message with Gene Thomeczek, an FBI agent who had questioned her extensively back in Kansas. "I'm still in Oklahoma City and everything is going bad," she said. "I mean, thanks a lot . . . for leaving me here. I just feel like, you know, this is a great time really. You really are a nice guy, but I can't believe these people are doing this to me."

She and Nicole flew to the Philippines the next day.

JUST AS THE FBI WAS TIRING OF THE HUNT FOR JOHN DOE TWO, AN army sergeant newly based in Fort Benning, Georgia, came forward with information suggesting he might never have existed. Sergeant Michael Hertig told agents that he and a friend had rented a Ryder truck from Eldon Elliott's the day before the Oklahoma City bombing. He thought he should mention this, because his friend Todd Bunting looked a bit like John Doe Two and, at the time of the rental, was wearing a multicolored Carolina Panthers ball cap, not unlike the one in the composite sketch.

Agents viewed this as a near-providential answer to one of their biggest problems. The man calling himself Robert Kling had rented his Ryder truck on April 17, one day before Hertig and Bunting, and at almost exactly the same time in the afternoon. Had Tom Kessinger and his colleagues confused John Doe Two with Bunting, and, if so, did that mean McVeigh had come into the shop alone?

The FBI tracked down Private Bunting at Fort Riley, and he was indeed a plausible fit for the composite sketch—muscular, with tattoos on both biceps. Bunting said he was a smoker and might have lit up at the body shop, just as Vicki Beemer remembered. Bunting allowed the agents to photograph him wearing the Carolina Panthers hat and the same T-shirt he had worn on April 18 so they could gauge the precise way the tattoos jutted out from below the sleeve. The look was remarkably close to Tom Kessinger's description.

After this, the FBI held firm to its belief that the events Kessinger and the others described seeing on April 17 had actually occurred a day later. The match was far from perfect. The body shop witnesses remembered John Doe Two being shorter than Kling, but Bunting was five foot ten, about the same height or slightly taller than Hertig. And Hertig did not look like John Doe One, because he had a bushy mustache on the day of the rental; Kling, everyone agreed, was clean-shaven. There were two other major flaws in the government's theory. First, Eldon Elliott was away on the afternoon of April 18, so he could not have confused Bunting with the second man he saw accompanying Kling. Second, Vicki Beemer knew Michael Hertig and recognized him when he came in on April 18. For that reason, she was certain she did not confuse him with Kling.

What really happened? Tom Kessinger probably did confuse some of Todd Bunting's features with what he remembered of John Doe Two—particularly the arm tattoo sticking out from beneath the sleeve of his T-shirt. But that did not mean he was wrong about his recollection of how many people came into the body shop on Monday, April 17.

Many people saw the Todd Bunting theory as a genuine break-through. Danny Coulson thought so at first, until he heard the objections raised by Elliott and Beemer and determined that the FBI was hiding the John Doe Two problem instead of getting to the bottom of it. "The bureau ended up undercutting its own witnesses," Coulson said. "They wanted only one guy." He felt this constituted a violation of the FBI's fundamental mission. "If I was a commander and they were coming up with invented stuff," he said, "I'd be pulling their tongues through their butts."

Bunting caused some friction among the FBI's higher-ups, too. I. C. Smith, back in Arkansas after his stint in Washington, remembered asking Bob Blitzer of the bureau's counterterrorism section about "Unsub Number Two"—their term for John Doe Two—and being surprised when Blitzer said he did not exist. "Is the issue that he doesn't exist," Smith countered, "or that you couldn't find him?"

• • •

MICHAEL FORTIER WAS BECOMING A REGULAR LAW ENFORCEMENT tour guide. He took the FBI to the storage locker where McVeigh had stashed blasting caps and other explosive components at the end of 1994, and showed them where he and McVeigh liked to camp and shoot. He also told them about a duffel bag full of supplies that McVeigh buried in the desert so he could hide out after the bombing.

The feds had a few theories on where McVeigh would have gone if he had not been arrested. The one that intrigued them most had him heading to a major airport, either in Wichita or Kansas City, and flying to Arizona—even though this would have forced McVeigh to go through airport security.

Fortier told the FBI he thought McVeigh had filled up several bags with food, money, guns, and ammunition, and stashed them all over the desert. And he mentioned one instance in which he had driven McVeigh into a box canyon and waited for an hour while his friend dumped a green duffel bag somewhere in the wilderness. The feds asked Fortier for directions, and started hunting. "We had the army, the FBI—every method known to man—searching by grid and by rock, but we never found that duffel bag," Weldon Kennedy said. "I presume it's still out there."

Fortier could easily have fabricated the whole thing. But the FBI did not seem to consider that. "Why would Fortier make up a story like that?" Kennedy asked, years later. "There was no reason for him even to tell us that." No reason—other than Fortier's desire to tell the feds what they wanted to hear, and the pleasure he would get from wasting their time. The question of where McVeigh was heading after the bombing has never been resolved.

BEYOND THE JOHN DOE TWO DILEMMA, THE FBI HAD TO STRETCH the evidence to prove that McVeigh was John Doe One. Not only did they lack physical evidence putting him in the Junction City body shop, they could barely figure out how he arrived in time to sign the rental contract.

A video surveillance camera at a McDonald's just over a mile away captured McVeigh at 3:57 P.M. on April 17, the day the Ryder truck was rented. McVeigh no longer had a car and, according to the government, was alone, so he presumably walked to Eldon Elliott's, a good twenty minutes away. In the FBI's narrative, he made it there in time to enter, introduce himself, and have Vicki Beemer print out the rental form, which was time-stamped at 4:19 P.M. It was raining at the time—a "light mist," as Elliott later testified—but when Kling arrived at the body shop, he was dry. The FBI assigned an agent from the Kansas City bureau to reproduce McVeigh's movements and see if he could make the journey in time. Agent Gary Witt left McDonald's at 3:57—perhaps a touch earlier than McVeigh's actual departure—and arrived at 4:16, with three minutes to spare. One can assume he didn't dawdle; one of his colleagues conceded he walked "at a brisk pace."

When McVeigh talked to Michel and Herbeck, he felt compelled to give a more elaborate explanation of how he got to Eldon Elliott's. About three-quarters of the way there, he said, a young man pulled over and asked if he needed a ride. In the car, he "ran a hand through his brush cut, drying off his hair." No man has ever come forward to match McVeigh's account, and even the FBI gave it no credence. That leaves two other possible scenarios. Either McVeigh was not alone at the body shop, and was driven there by John Doe Two; or he never went at all, and John Doe One was an associate who looked a little like him but was shorter, with rougher skin and an odd way of chewing tobacco.

Most agreed that the best evidence tying McVeigh to the Ryder rental was not the eyewitness testimony, or the John Doe One sketch, but the name Kling, a known alias for which McVeigh had prepared a fake ID with the help of Lori Fortier's typewriter and iron. But McVeigh could have given this ID to someone else so the rental could not be traced directly to either of them. College students, after all, lend their driver's licenses—both real and fake ones—to underage friends. This would not be much different.

McVeigh left no fingerprints at Eldon Elliott's, on the counter or on the rental form. And the handwriting on the rental papers was also inconclusive. A prominent handwriting expert consulted for this book said that the evidence presented at trial linking McVeigh to the Robert D. Kling signature was too weak to determine they were the same. Linda James, the president of the National Association of Document Examiners, said the signature was clearly disguised writing, and "only indications at most" suggested that the originator was McVeigh. Even the backward slant that had excited Agent Mark Bouton did not prove anything, she said, because seven out of eight people who disguise their writing—as was the case here—slant it in a different direction.

By early June 1995, the investigation was driven by two deeply flawed principles. The first was that the eyewitnesses were unreliable and could be dismissed if their contentions clashed with the government's theory of the case. This became a circular argument, to the extent that testimony was then cherry-picked to reinforce a predetermined viewpoint. Of course, assessing eyewitnesses' reliability is important, but there is little evidence it was done dispassionately or fairly in this case.

Prosecutor Scott Mendeloff gave a revealing illustration of the mind-set when he insisted that the Dreamland witnesses must have been mistaken about seeing a second Ryder. "They got their timing off," he said. "There is no indication McVeigh rented a second truck. There's one truck." Perhaps the most instructive way to understand Mendeloff's argument is to read his sentences in reverse, beginning with the last one. He *started* from the premise that there was only one truck—a notion that four eyewitnesses, interviewed separately, all challenged. Rather than allowing himself to challenge the premise, he challenged the eyewitnesses.

The second flawed principle was that the Daryl Bridges phone records could track anything and everything related to the bomb plot. Certainly, a lot of things could be—the hunt for bomb components, the attempt to secure help from people like Dave Paulsen, the frequency of communications between McVeigh and Nichols, and their movements around the country. But the phone records were elevated beyond an investigative tool. "There is absolutely, unequivocally, no way there could have been other conspirators, because the phone records would have shown that," Weldon Kennedy argued. "We interviewed every single recipient of a phone call from Nichols or McVeigh." Kennedy rejected the notion that Elohim City, for example, had not been properly investigated—he called the idea "bullshit." "There was no extensive investigation of Elohim City," he said, "because there was only one call there, which lasted a few seconds."

This reliance on phone records lost sight of a number of things. First, the records could not identify who was making a call. (At least three people—McVeigh, Nichols, and Marife—had the PIN code, and they could have passed it to others.) Second, even though Nichols purchased the card, McVeigh could have used it to set his friend up as a fall guy. And, third, the dependence on the Bridges records assumes that McVeigh and Nichols had no other means of making phone calls away from home.

The last assumption seems particularly perilous. Roger Moore and Karen Anderson told the FBI about phone calls they received from McVeigh, none of which appeared on the Bridges records. Anderson testified, for example, that he phoned just hours ahead of his overnight visit in early 1994; it was not a Bridges call. Years later, Terry Nichols described how it was a constant source of irritation that McVeigh kept using the card, and he badgered him to get one of his own. According to Nichols, when they met in Kansas on April 14, 1995, McVeigh had obtained a prepaid debit card, and showed it to him to end the argument. There may have been other cards besides.

In June 1995, the investigation had been going just over a month and already, despite the FBI's protestations about leaving no stone unturned, the shape of the government's case was set. It was as notable for what it left out as it was for the oddly truncated version it presented as the whole story.

Seven

The Many Mysteries of
"Bob from Arkansas"

When Roger Moore was asked by investigators about his relationship with Tim McVeigh, he described it as a catalogue of disappointments and betrayals. Moore had welcomed the young man into the gun-show business, he said; he had fed him, let him share hotel rooms, and invited him to the ranch in Arkansas. In return, McVeigh sponged off him, embarrassed him in public, stole his idea for converting flare guns into rudimentary rocket-launchers, and set him up for a robbery in which Moore lost tens of thousands of dollars' worth of cash, precious stones, and firearms, as well as personal keepsakes—rare curios from his travels and a .22 Hornet Winchester rifle given to him by his father—which no amount of money could replace.

As FBI agents broadened their investigation, they understood that Moore and his girlfriend, Karen Anderson, had played down both the number of times they had met McVeigh and the length of their encounters. The couple described big, blow-up arguments, including one at the Soldier of Fortune Convention in Las Vegas in 1993, in which McVeigh got into Moore's face "like a top sergeant" before storming out. But they offered no explanation of why they continued to extend invitations to him. This seemed particularly puzzling, since the couple was intensely private and had offered hospitality to only three or four other people in their ten years in Arkansas.

Moore described McVeigh as paranoid to the point of instability. On an April 1994 visit, he had insisted on sleeping near a window with his Glock .45 under his pillow. He spent hours feeding bullets into his Ruger mini-30 and cranking them out again on Moore's gravel driveway, apparently convinced that the government was after him and likely to pounce at any moment. Such bizarre behavior did not deter Moore from continuing to write to McVeigh and, as we have seen, using a near-impenetrable private language to convey sensitive information.

In the run-up to the trials, the government largely accepted Roger Moore's account and groomed him as a prosecution witness. But the government's own information, along with previously unpublished research by defense investigators and a firsthand account from Terry Nichols, all suggest that Moore could as easily have been a participant in the plot, not only facilitating the supposed robbery but also offering valuable instruction on bomb-building.

Moore and Anderson said the April 1994 visit was McVeigh's last, but McVeigh's defense team later obtained information suggesting that he returned once or twice more that summer to pick up batches of Kinestik, a binary explosive kit whose components were ammonium nitrate and nitromethane—the very ingredients later used to blow up the Murrah Building. Moore, according to this information (later deemed genuine by McVeigh in his interviews with Michel and Herbeck), had cases of the stuff and did not sell it "to just anybody." Terry Nichols said Kinestik packs supplied by Moore were used as boosters for the ammonium nitrate barrels he and McVeigh mixed at Geary Lake. According to Nichols, Moore also gave McVeigh blasting caps and cannon fuse.

Nichols is not a neutral source, of course. Since 2005, when he first started talking about his own role in the bomb plot, he has pushed to have Moore arrested and prosecuted as a coconspirator. He told the FBI they could find Moore's fingerprints on a box of nitromethane tubes, originally components from Kinestik kits, which were hidden beneath his house in Herington. When Nichols's accusations first surfaced, Moore not only denied any wrongdoing; he accused Nichols of acquiring the Kinestik himself because he was an "angry man" with his own agenda. The FBI found fingerprint traces on the box Nichols was talking about, but they did not test them for almost three years and then concluded that the prints were unreadable.

McVeigh certainly obtained Kinestik from somewhere. He told Michel and Herbeck he possessed "a couple of small cylinders," one filled with white powder and the other a red liquid—an exact description of Kinestik, even if he chose not to call it that. (The white powder would have been the ammonium nitrate, the red liquid nitromethane.) According to Nichols, McVeigh had bragged about having Kinestik since mid-1993; in September 1994, they detonated a kit in a creekbed in Kansas.

We also know that, before then, McVeigh's trials with explosives had come to naught. Afterward was a different story.

BY THE SUMMER OF 1994, TERRY NICHOLS WAS WORKING AS A FARM-hand outside Marion, Kansas. The work was tough and offered little financial reward. And it did nothing to improve his marriage: Marife had taken Nicole back to the Philippines earlier in the year, and was planning to attend college there in the fall. Nichols still dreamed of starting a blueberry farm and settling down properly, but he had hardly shaken off the radical antigovernment ideology he developed in Michigan. One of the first things he did when he moved to Kansas was to walk into the local county clerk's office and, using a lot of the pseudo-legal language he learned from Ralph Daigle, renounce his U.S. citizenship. The clerk remembered him as polite but "not friendly."

One day, McVeigh showed up on one of his frenetic cross-country road trips and suggested they go full-time into the gun-show business together. Immediately, McVeigh suggested buying fifty-pound bags of ammonium nitrate, ostensibly to sell to survivalists and home-made explosives enthusiasts. Nichols paid no attention to this red flag. Following McVeigh appealed to his romantic spirit of rebellion, and he gave his employer a month's notice.

Nichols had about $12,000 in cash, from the sale of a farm he and Lana had owned, plus another $12–15,000 in gold coins he bought with the proceeds of his credit-card scams. He turned almost all of it over to McVeigh, who assured him he would get it all back once the business was up and running. McVeigh, though, wanted the money to purchase bomb components. He was essentially leeching off Nichols and relying on his naive willingness to do whatever he was told.

McVeigh didn't just take Nichols's money. He also slept with his wife over several days in September 1994, while Nichols was still working in the fields and she was preparing to leave for the Philippines. McVeigh's motivation—absolute ownership over Nichols—was a lot clearer than Marife's. She later said McVeigh had simply "taken over," helping himself to her like he did to everything else. Nichols concurred: "McV was clearly in the mind-set of using everything I had—my home, my phone, my food, my truck, my trust, myself, and even my wife! And [he] did it all as a means of setting me up to take the fall as part of his goal to achieve his mission."

Nichols, though, did not know how to resist McVeigh's demands, and McVeigh seemed to derive sadistic pleasure from pushing him ever further. Prosecutors would later argue that Nichols unambiguously crossed the line between coercion and cooperating with McVeigh, but the evidence suggests that he did not always understand the difference. One day McVeigh wanted to demonstrate what it was like to be shot at, as he had been in the Gulf War. So he took Nichols into the fields, told him to crouch behind a big rock, and opened fire, most likely with his Ruger assault rifle. "When I count, you roll," he ordered. Nichols was terrified, but did exactly as commanded.

INVESTIGATORS WORKING FOR THE NICHOLS DEFENSE TEAM SPENT two years unearthing everything they could about Roger Moore. And the more they dug, the more bewilderingly complex the man became. He had spent years working for the federal government he later professed to hate, first for the Social Security Administration in Iowa, and then for the air force. In the 1960s, he and his wife, Carol, had jobs and top-secret security clearances at North American Aviation. From there, they moved to Florida, where they made a fortune in the boat-building business, cashing out in 1977 to settle into a long retirement.

The impression Moore gave to his neighbors and acquaintances in Arkansas was of an angry, suspicious, conspiracy-spewing, tight-fisted gun nut who did not know how to make friends or observe basic rules of civility. He would fire high-powered rifle-rounds and mortars on his ranch after dark, which even in rural Arkansas was regarded as eccentric. Once, he let off a smoke bomb and knocked one of his neighbors unconscious for twenty minutes. He never apologized.

His aversion to having people in the house went back at least to 1986, when a housekeeper ran off with thousands of dollars in cash, and a friend he and Anderson invited to house-sit committed suicide in their garage. He didn't even like attending gun shows much. Bill Stoneman, a local gunsmith, who was the closest thing Moore had to a best friend, said Moore usually let Karen Anderson go by herself so he could stay home with the horses, ducks, geese, parrots, and cats.

When he did tag along, Anderson would lug all the gear and do most of the selling. "I hate this shit," Moore himself acknowledged to defense investigator Roland Leeds. "It bores me to death."

Still, rumors about Moore abounded. Some of the more fantastical—and unverified—stories that circulated after the bombing suggested he might have taught sabotage techniques for the CIA at the Camp Peary military base in Virginia, or had been a participant in the Reagan administration's illicit efforts to sell arms to the Nicaraguan contras, or had manufactured pontoon boats used by the CIA to mine three Nicaraguan ports in 1984, or had funneled information to the government on Barry Seal, a former CIA pilot who organized drug transports to Central America from Mena, Arkansas, not far from Moore's ranch.

The Nichols team did not know what to make of such stories, but they found more reasons of their own to question Moore's connections and activities. Despite his background as a successful businessman, and the existence of at least two bank accounts in his name, they found he had almost no credit history. They never figured out why. They also puzzled over a line Moore had given to Rodney Bowers of the *Arkansas Democrat-Gazette* shortly after his first FBI interviews became public.

"Whatever I was doing for the FBI," Moore said, "is fucked up, because they blew my cover." Bowers later told defense investigators that Moore had called him in a fury when he saw this quoted in the paper. But he would not elaborate on what he meant.

FBI AGENTS WITH THE BOMBING TASK FORCE ALSO FOUND REASONS to raise questions about Moore's past. They learned that, in 1988, he was caught up in an FBI sting operation, code-name Operation Punchout, which tracked the theft of equipment and supplies from Hill Air Force Base near Salt Lake City. Items as big as F-16 engines—worth about $2 million each—were disappearing and ending up in the hands of private military surplus dealers. So the FBI set up a fake storefront staffed by a team of undercover agents and handed out flyers at gun shows to lure the thieves into doing business with them. Among the first people to respond to the flyers were Roger and Carol Moore.

Hidden cameras recorded the Moores as they sold $2,100 worth of .223-caliber ammunition and said they could also come up with explosives and a large number of bootlegged porn videos. The agents asked about their suppliers and they said they were plugged into an "underground" network.

A major investigation appeared to be warranted, but none ever took place. The ammunition rounds the Moores sold were reloads, which made it less likely they had been stolen from the air force. The FBI did not pursue this or any other angle, according to the available records, so the U.S. attorney in Salt Lake City had no grounds to prosecute. A member of the Arkansas State Police Intelligence Unit later said he and a Garland County police lieutenant had looked into the porn distribution issue and could not substantiate it. Oddly, the Garland County Sheriff's Department kept no paperwork on the investigation and, when asked, said there was none.

Moore caught another lucky break in 1989. Using his gun-show alias Robert Miller, he struck a deal with a man in Florida, who said he wanted a hundred pounds of C-4 plastic explosive. They exchanged addresses and phone numbers, and Moore said he would send the C-4 by UPS once he was home in Arkansas. But the man was an undercover informant for the ATF, and he passed Moore's personal information to his handlers. Then something strange happened. The same Arkansas State Police Intelligence Unit officer who found no evidence of wrongdoing in the porn investigation started to pursue a different Robert Miller, a young gangbanger involved in drugs and sex crimes. The officer, Don Birdsong, said he never received Moore's contact details or other information that would have told him he should have been looking for a middle-aged arms dealer.

Four years later, the ATF was on Moore's tail again, this time in response to an alert that Moore and Anderson were selling incendiary ammunition rounds and flares to an ex-convict in Oregon. Federal law forbade out-of-state sales to anyone without a federal firearms license, much less a convicted arsonist and attempted murderer who could not legally buy weaponry at all. The ATF considered bringing a case but ultimately decided not to.

Did this history of abortive investigations indicate that Moore enjoyed special protection? Bill Buford, the head of the ATF in Arkansas in the early 1990s, did not exclude it. He cited other possible reasons—evidence rules and gun lobby pressure not to enforce federal firearms license regulations—why the two ATF-related cases did not go forward. Buford would not confirm that the ATF faced political obstacles beyond these procedural difficulties. But he also did not deny it.

ON SEPTEMBER 13, 1994, PRESIDENT CLINTON APPROVED A TEN-YEAR assault weapons ban, and McVeigh wondered if he hadn't been plunged into the opening chapter of *The Turner Diaries,* in which passage of a repressive new gun law inspires the beginnings of a white supremacist resistance movement. Nichols said McVeigh experienced the weapons ban as a "prophecy . . . coming true before his very eyes." There and then, McVeigh started driving around Kansas looking for bags of ammonium nitrate. He needed eighty or ninety bags for his bomb, but he never found more than a few at a time. Nichols chalked this up to McVeigh's "city mind," and told him to go to a farm co-op. He even told McVeigh how to look one up in the yellow pages.

They ended up going together to the Mid-Kansas Co-op in McPherson, immediately after Nichols finished his last day's work on the farm. But McVeigh had apparently decided he did not want to be seen making the purchase. As they were approaching the co-op, he jumped out of Nichols's pickup, saying he needed to make some phone calls. Nichols bought forty fifty-pound bags of ammonium nitrate on his own, in cash, and told the salesman, Rick Schlender, that he was planning to spread them on some freshly planted wheat fields.

Schlender found that odd, because the weather was not good for planting and most wheat farmers used liquid fertilizer. Schlender had no strong memory of the man—or men—who made this purchase; he told the FBI he remembered two of them. Since it was raining, Nichols bought a light-colored camper shell to fit over his truck bed—a feature many witnesses would pick up in the months to come.

He and McVeigh dumped the ammonium nitrate in a storage locker in Herington, where Nichols had originally intended to store his furniture. Now he noticed that McVeigh had not rented the space in his name, as he requested, but under the alias Shawn Rivers. It was another warning sign about McVeigh's intentions that he failed to pick up on until much later.

That night, McVeigh pushed Nichols further into criminality by suggesting they scope out a nearby mining quarry and take whatever explosives they could find, just for fun. McVeigh presented it as something similar to his misadventure with Fortier at the National Guard armory in Kingman. But, this time, he and Nichols conducted a thorough reconnaissance and made plans to come back the next night. They brought Nichols's Makita drill to break the padlocks and took care to park McVeigh's Chevy a quarter-mile away on the far side of a field.

They hauled away enough material to build several large bombs: 299 sticks of Tovex, 544 electric blasting caps, and 93 lengths of Primadet shock tube fitted with nonelectric caps. Even now, Nichols would not see what trouble McVeigh was leading him into. "I was in denial that this one act would suck me into worse things that McVeigh had up his sleeve," he wrote in 2010.

They were remarkably lucky they weren't caught. A trucker named Craig Knoche usually parked his vehicle outside the quarry at midnight so he could catch a few hours' sleep before loading up in the morning. That Saturday, though, he was out late and did not pull in until about 4:00 A.M. He spotted lights from a stationary vehicle half a mile away, but nodded off to sleep when he saw no signs of people moving about. When the local sheriff, Ed Davis, investigated, he found four padlocks missing but recovered a fifth, which had been drilled through and abandoned—possibly because McVeigh and Nichols heard the truck coming.

Sheriff Davis drew up a list of suspects, but Nichols and McVeigh would not have crossed his radar, because they did not have criminal records. Besides, Nichols and McVeigh were gone the next day—off to Arizona with eight and a half boxes of Tovex beneath Nichols's camper shell and the blasting caps in the trunk of McVeigh's Spectrum. Any obvious trace in Marion County was gone with them.

IN OCTOBER 1993, ROGER MOORE WAS SLUNG IN JAIL IN WAGONER, Oklahoma, for pulling a loaded gun during a road-rage incident. The Oklahoma Highway Patrol could never prove that Moore opened fire, as the occupants of the other vehicle alleged. But they still charged him with illegal possession—of the gun, and of "controlled dangerous substances" they found in his car.

As soon as Karen Anderson heard, back in Hot Springs, she started digging for $50,000 in cash she had buried at the ranch and sped to Oklahoma to bail him out. She tried to hand the money in great wads to the sheriff's office, but the desk officer wouldn't accept it and sent her to a bail bond agency across the street. Anderson befriended the agent, and was soon in touch with the best-connected lawyer in town, Richard McLaughlin. Soon after, Moore walked away with just $303 in fines and court costs.

The story might have ended there, except that six months after the Oklahoma City bombing Moore reappeared in McLaughlin's office and complained he had been overcharged. He was so obnoxious that McLaughlin lost his temper and told Moore he hoped the FBI indicted him for the bombing. Moore said the feds would not touch him, "because he was a protected government witness." McLaughlin either missed the significance of this or did not believe it. Instead, he accused Moore of financing the bombing. Moore, in McLaughlin's account, "got a funny look on his face." Sensing that things were about to get violent, McLaughlin reached for his gun, pointed it at his client, and told him to get out. He kept an eye on Moore all the way to the parking lot.

When McLaughlin told this story to Moore's bail agent, Dianna Sanders Burk, he heard an even stranger one in return. In April 1995, right after the bombing, Burk learned that Moore had been trying to reach her to get someone out of jail. In fact, he drove to Wagoner just to see her. She had sold her business by then and did not see him or speak to him for several days. They maintained regular contact over the next few months, and Burk became ever more intrigued when Moore started talking about his friend Tim McVeigh, who he said was "not a bad guy" but had been set up by the feds.

Even before she swapped notes with McLaughlin, Burk became convinced that Moore had come looking for her in April to bail McVeigh out of the Noble County jail.

BACK IN KINGMAN, MCVEIGH AND NICHOLS COULD NOT WAIT TO test their new explosives, so they went to the desert to detonate an improvised ammonium nitrate and nitromethane device inside a gallon milk jug. It did not work. Nichols thought McVeigh did not allow enough time for the liquid to soak in. McVeigh was too embarrassed to talk about it, and just kept experimenting. A few days later, he went back to the desert alone and this time, he said, the mixture blew without a hitch.

McVeigh used some of the new materials that he and Nichols

had stolen from the quarry, but the bulk of the Tovex and blast-ing caps were now in a storage unit in Kingman, which McVeigh rented as soon as he arrived. Then, on October 11, McVeigh called Nichols back from Las Vegas, where he was visiting Josh, and in-sisted they move the blasting caps—just the caps—right away to a new storage unit 140 miles away in Flagstaff. Ostensibly, McVeigh did this to spread the risk of discovery, but Nichols said there might have been another purpose. "McVeigh had to hand about half of those blasting caps off to someone," he said, "because only about half were ever recovered." The FBI never looked into it, because they never knew about the Flagstaff storage locker; Nichols did not disclose this until 2007.

On October 16, the tension between the two men exploded into open animosity. They were driving from a gun show in Colorado Springs back to Kansas when McVeigh gave the order to buy a second ton of ammonium nitrate. Nichols asked what it was for, then tried to say no when McVeigh spelled it out for him. "He became very angry," Nichols recounted. "As he spoke, he shifted his body, turning toward me a bit, lifted up his left arm over the top of the seat back, which caused his plaid flannel shirt to swing back . . . , and exposed his Glock .45 handgun."

McVeigh said he knew where Nichols's son Josh lived, where his brother James lived, where his mother lived, and would have no problem "eliminating them" if necessary. If he even suspected Nich-ols of running to the authorities, he would put a bullet in his head. "No one is going to stop me carrying out my plans," he said.

This was the turning point, Nichols said, the moment when he finally understood how much trouble he was in. But he was too scared by McVeigh's volcanic moods and too confused to know how to back out. So he kept doing as he was told.

The next day, McVeigh extended the contract on the Herington storage locker, still using his alias Shawn Rivers, and told Nichols it was no longer available for his furniture. Nichols found another space and lugged his things without a protest. A day later, Nichols bought the second ton of fertilizer at the Mid-Kansas Co-op.

Next, McVeigh demanded another $4,000 to pay for the rest of the bomb components. Nichols said the only way he could get the money was to sell off part of his gold coin collection. McVeigh ordered him to do it and accompanied him to his coin dealer in Wichita to make sure it happened.

So it went with the rest of the shopping spree. When McVeigh and Nichols visited a stock-car race south of Dallas the next weekend, they had no problem acquiring three fifty-five-gallon barrels of nitromethane; the salesman was happy to take the cash—Nichols's cash—and ask no questions. That left just a dozen barrels to complete the bomb components. McVeigh was so particular about what he wanted that it took almost a week of driving around Kansas to find them. They eventually picked up six refurbished black steel barrels with removable lids from a recycling center, and six white plastic barrels from a dairy processing plant. The total cost of all twelve: just $54.

McVeigh and Nichols stored everything in the Herington locker and headed back to Kingman. Despite Mike Fortier's later testimony, it seems unlikely McVeigh had picked out a specific date or target city yet. Nichols was sure he was planning a bombing for Thanksgiving, Christmas, or New Year's. Either way, his intention was set. He told Fortier he intended to inflict mass casualties, which he rationalized by likening his targets to storm troopers in *Star Wars*. "They may be individually innocent," he said, "but they are guilty because they work for the Evil Empire."

Nichols headed back to Las Vegas to visit Josh, and to put some distance between himself and McVeigh's plans, but within days McVeigh was ordering him to come back to Kingman again. McVeigh was going to New York because his grandfather just died and he wanted to give Nichols instructions before he left. Nichols was afraid of what those would entail, so he blew off the meeting and headed to Kansas where he did not think he could be discovered.

To his astonishment, McVeigh showed up the next morning at the Geary Lake camping ground where he had pitched his tent—a favorite spot that was probably not all that difficult to guess—and told him the new assignment had to do with "Bob from Arkansas." Nichols thought McVeigh was going to suggest bringing Roger Moore into their gun-show business; he had mentioned in the past that "Bob" was interested in providing sale items to help get them going.

But McVeigh had a completely different proposal. "We are going to rob him," he said. Or, more specifically, Nichols was going to rob him. "It will be much easier than you think," McVeigh said. "He will be like a kitten and give you absolutely no trouble at all. Just trust me."

ON THE MORNING OF SATURDAY, NOVEMBER 5, ROGER MOORE WAS wandering out to feed the animals when a masked man pointing a pistol-grip shotgun ordered him to lie flat on the ground. Soon he was lying trussed up on the living-room couch while the intruder picked the house clean. Nichols, who carried out the robbery, felt it was all too easy and couldn't help wondering if it had been prearranged with Moore's consent. He was not the only one who thought the whole thing stank.

Moore told many different versions of the story, and they all begged a lot of questions. According to most of his accounts, he was initially immobilized with plastic police ties but successfully sweet-talked the gunman into replacing them with duct tape, because they were cutting off the blood circulation to his hands. The unusually indulgent robber was also thoughtful enough to leave an opened penknife on an end table next to the couch, enabling him to slice through his bonds once the robbery was over. Moore described the intruder as a ruthless Special Forces type, but the man's behavior seemed neither ruthless nor especially careful. Beyond the penknife, he also left a loaded stainless-steel revolver sitting in a magazine box just a few feet from his purported victim.

Moore said the robber took more than seventy firearms, but the insurance adjuster noticed that the closets where the guns were supposedly kept were too small to hold that many. Bill Stoneman told investigators that Moore and Anderson usually kept their cash and jewelry buried on the property, but the robber found silver and gold coins and bullion, precious, and semiprecious stones, pre-Columbian jade from Costa Rica, and close to $9,000 in cash all lying openly around the house.

Moore's uncanny memory of the robber's appearance was also suspect. In his court testimony, he described a swarthy man, just under six feet tall, who stank like a "pig yard" and was wearing a black serge ski mask with generous eye and mouth openings, and unusual gray Israeli combat boots. Terry Nichols later contradicted this by saying he wore 1990s-era camouflage gear, ordinary brown jersey gloves, and standard-issue black boots. He had a nylon stocking over his head, not a ski mask, with holes cut out for his eyes and his glasses perched on top.

"My glasses on the outside should have been obvious to Moore, but he never describes the robber as wearing glasses," Nichols wrote in 2010. Nichols's lawyers suggested in court that Moore had taken his description of the black mask from a photograph on a gun-show flyer, which the FBI found in his van.

If Moore's description was wrong, could it have been an attempt to protect Nichols, or to incriminate someone else? Richard Guthrie, the Aryan Republican Army bank robber, was one of the few people on the radical right who had a pair of Israeli combat boots and he was also known to neglect his personal hygiene. Had he done something to anger Moore? Intriguingly a Robert Miller driver's license and several Kinestik packs were recovered after Guthrie and Pete Langan, his fellow ARA ringleader, were arrested in early 1996. But the FBI never made serious inquiries into this link.

• • •

McVEIGH TOLD NICHOLS THAT ROBBING MOORE WOULD BE HIS reward for fronting so much money over the previous two months. All McVeigh wanted were the guns and a $2,000 cut of the cash; Nichols was welcome to the rest. In the run-up to the robbery, McVeigh told Nichols with great precision where to find everything—including Moore's camper van, which was parked by the back door for easy loading. McVeigh said the robbery had to take place on November 5, because Karen Anderson would be away at a gun show—something she had told almost nobody, according to an interview she later gave the FBI. McVeigh also knew that Moore would walk out of the house around 9:00 A.M.

Nichols found everything as McVeigh described, except the cash, which was not in a filing cabinet but—even more obviously—on Moore's desk. Nichols, ever the stickler for following instructions, had to ask Moore for help locating it, prompting a sarcastic comeback from Moore. He took nothing of value from Anderson's room, as instructed, although he did help himself to two pillowcases to carry some smaller items, and removed the quilt from her bed so he would have something to cover the loot in the back of Moore's camper van. The quilt later showed up on the Nicholses' bed in Herington.

ROGER MOORE'S NEIGHBOR VERTA "PUDGE" POWELL THOUGHT HE was playacting from the moment he rang her doorbell and said he had been robbed. His phone lines had been cut, and he barged past her, demanding to use the phone. She glowered when she saw a revolver sticking out of his sweatpants.

Pudge said Moore talked in a suspiciously low voice on his calls. When her husband came home, they found out Moore had not even phoned the police. Moore said something about the government trying to shut down a movement he was leading and suggested he had been robbed to keep him "in check." When the sheriffs arrived, at Powell's insistence, they asked Powell if he thought the robbery was genuine. He, like the rest of the family, did not believe any of it.

Farmers Insurance was also skeptical. The company adjuster handling Moore's claim thought the story sounded like a "rehearsed script." He would have launched a full investigation, but the caps on Moore's policy left more than 90 percent of his claim uncovered. Quibbling over a $5,900 settlement was not worth the company's time, so he let it go unchallenged.

Moore had no apparent problem with the money—he had deliberately underinsured himself because he didn't want anyone, even his insurance company, to know how many valuables he kept on his property. But he was oddly upset not to have the robbery investigated. He made an angry phone call to his insurance agent and told her daughter, who answered the phone, he would "smear [her] all over the counter."

On the evening of the robbery, McVeigh called Michael Fortier and told him that "Terry did Bob." He also advised him to watch his back. "He thought that Bob would send private investigators out to Arizona to look for him," Fortier later testified. "And if those investigators would be in Kingman, they would find me, because I'm associated with Tim."

Curiously, McVeigh knew all about the robbery before Nichols had a chance to tell him. The Daryl Bridges records show that Nichols did not call McVeigh that day; Nichols said he did not contact McVeigh until Monday, November 7, after he had dumped the robbery loot in a new storage locker in Council Grove, Kansas.

If Nichols did not tell McVeigh the robbery had gone off smoothly, then someone else must have, possibly Moore himself. McVeigh was at a gun show in Akron, Ohio, and not easy to reach, but he could have waited by a pay phone at a prearranged hour, or used an intermediary at the gun show to take a message for him. The FBI preferred to believe that the phone call to the Fortiers did not take place until several days later—even though it is in the Bridges records at 8:09 P.M. Eastern Time on November 5.

• • •

ONCE NICHOLS HAD SECURED THE GUNS, HE DROVE TO LAS VEGAS with the rest of the stolen goods. He had decided he wouldn't tell anyone where he had stashed everything; he had a feeling that if McVeigh found out, the loot would not remain his for long, But he found himself telling McVeigh about the guns anyway as soon as he was asked. He was angry with himself about that, and determined not to let anything else elude his grasp.

Nichols's plan was to fly to the Philippines and stay until the New Year so he could not be blamed for any catastrophes over the holidays. The Philippines was not exactly a risk-free destination; he was deathly afraid of Marife's ex-boyfriend, and far from convinced that Marife still wanted to be married to him. But that was a chance he would have to take.

He arrived at Lana Padilla's house beside himself with paranoia. He was terrified about being drawn into a criminal conspiracy and did not know how to share his troubles without burdening Lana or Josh with guilty knowledge. Lana thought his strange behavior was a sign of suicidal depression. Nichols had been out of touch for the second half of October, and while he hadn't told Lana about quitting his farm job, she suspected it, because he was no longer answering his phone there. Eventually, she sent a note to his post office box in Kansas, which said: "Call me. It's urgent. We need to talk about Josh."

Nichols needed to devote some proper time to his son, so he postponed his flight to the Philippines until November 22—the anniversary of Jason's death—and started planning the disposal of his property in case he didn't make it out of Southeast Asia alive. In context, the "Go for it!" note from Nichols to McVeigh takes on new, or at least more shaded, meanings. This phrase follows on from a paragraph describing locker #37 in Council Grove, the one with Moore's guns in it. Nichols explained—and it seems plausible—that the line

"As for heat, none that I know of" refers to the Moore robbery, not the purchase of bomb components. And "Your on your own, go for it!!" could mean: if I'm out of the picture (because I'm dead), take the guns and do what you will with them.

Nichols barely made it out of the country. As he boarded the first leg of his flight, from Las Vegas to Los Angeles, a security guard spotted a stun gun in his hand luggage. He had packed two as gifts for Marife's family. Although carrying an offensive weapon on a passenger aircraft was a federal offense, the episode was treated, amazingly, as no big deal. Nichols repacked the stun guns in his checked luggage and was allowed to proceed.

ONCE McVEIGH REALIZED NICHOLS WAS OUT OF THE COUNTRY, HE turned to his other best friend, Michael Fortier, and used the loot from the Moore robbery as leverage to try to talk him into helping carry out the bombing.

His promise of a $10,000 payday certainly concentrated the Fortiers' minds. Lori ironed the plastic cover on McVeigh's fake Robert Kling ID and disguised the blasting caps from the quarry robbery by wrapping them in Christmas paper. According to Lori, McVeigh also performed a little demonstration, taking a pile of soup cans from the Fortiers' kitchen cupboard and arranging them into the configuration he had in mind for the ammonium nitrate and nitromethane barrels. The prosecution used this story at McVeigh's trial to show a high degree of premeditation, but there are grounds to doubt its veracity. When Michael Fortier was asked on the witness stand if Lori had told him the story before she shared it with the FBI, he said she had not.

Either way, McVeigh lured Michael Fortier into traveling with him to Kansas and Oklahoma with two boxes of blasting caps in the trunk. But he could not convince him to carry out the bombing then and there. A frustrated McVeigh drove on to Michigan, but on the way, his car was hit hard from the rear on the I-90 highway. "In 1/2 a second," he later wrote, with his customary blend of fact and self-dramatization, "I restarted the car, floored it and popped the clutch." With his front wheels spinning and his back wheels dragging against the smashed fender, he maneuvered himself out of danger in the nick of time.

The stark reality, not lost on McVeigh, was that the thump could have set off one or more of the blasting caps and blown him to smithereens. By the time McVeigh wrote about the accident—to Roger Moore, of all people—he had convinced himself that the accident was intentional, most likely the work of a government agent. "This makes me real nervous. Has anyone else had anything happen to them?" he asked in his letter, dated January 10, 1995.

Why was Moore still corresponding with the man he saw as the lead suspect in the robbery? Moore said he wanted to draw McVeigh back to the ranch and confront him face-to-face. "I could kill that motherfucker for robbing me," Moore later railed to a defense investigator. "I didn't need this." The surviving correspondence, however, suggests that Moore and McVeigh were on remarkably good terms, writing cryptically but unmistakably about starting a revolution against the government. "The important thing is to be as effective as possible," Moore wrote in the letter recovered from McVeigh's mail drop after the bombing. Was he really just talking about recovering his guns?

AFTER THE BOMBING AND THE INITIAL ROUND OF INTERVIEWS, THE FBI assigned Mark Jessie, an agent out of the Hot Springs office, to keep an eye on Moore. But Moore did not get along with Jessie, and he was replaced with a softer agent, Floyd Hays, who struck up an unlikely friendship with Moore that earned him repeated—and unheard of—invitations to the ranch. "Roger was a person who wanted everyone to like him," Hays said years later. "He was a little bit different. But he was not a mean guy or a bad guy."

This was hardly conventional wisdom in Hot Springs. But it was not an uncommon view in the FBI, where Moore was being considered as a prosecution witness, and any suspicions about him were increasingly viewed as an inconvenience. Jon Hersley, an agent from Oklahoma City who helped interview Moore and Anderson and later helped prepare the case for trial, believed everything Moore said and, in a book he cowrote, argued that Moore's association with McVeigh was the consequence of an overly trusting nature. "Moore had learned over the years that being in the gun-show business meant meeting all kinds of people," Hersley wrote. "Some were wonderful— and there were some whose intentions were not so noble." Somehow, Roger Moore had morphed into a poor, fragile flower of a man. "He was nervous about being suspected," Hays concurred, "almost to the point of crying." Within months, all investigative interest in him evaporated.

NARROWING THE INVESTIGATION'S FOCUS WAS NOT MET WITH UNI-versal approval, even within the government. "There was intense discussion inside the prosecution team, in terms of . . . whether McVeigh and Nichols were the only two responsible," said Larry Mackey, one of the prosecutors most open to new avenues of investigation. Some of Mackey's colleagues were willing to give up on John Doe Two and accept the Todd Bunting theory, while others remained skeptical. Some were intrigued by Robert Jacques. The possible link to the bank robberies grew more enticing after a newspaper article about the Murrah Building bomb was left at the scene of an ARA heist in Missouri in August 1995.

John Magaw, the ATF director, spent the summer expecting Roger Moore to be indicted, along with at least one or two others. "Any investigative effort worth its salt would have pursued it, and pursued it hard," he said of Moore. "That may be one of the people I felt all along was culpable—involved in one way or another."

Broadening the investigation's focus, however, became unlikely once the Fortiers struck a deal on August 4 to testify against McVeigh and Nichols. Michael Fortier pled guilty to charges of transporting and selling stolen weapons and failing to alert the authorities to the bombing in advance. In exchange, the government promised to go easy on his sentence, provided he held up his side of the bargain on the witness stand. Lori Fortier, who was four months pregnant, was given immunity.

The indictment, which appeared six days later, set the start of the conspiracy at September 13, 1994, but did not explain why. This led to speculation in some quarters that the date was somehow connected to Elohim City, because McVeigh checked out of a nearby motel in eastern Oklahoma that morning. The date, though, had nothing to do with the evidence. It was the day President Clinton signed the Violent Crime Control and Law Enforcement Act, which first introduced the death penalty for using, or conspiring to use, a weapon of mass destruction. Prosecutors worried that if they put the start of the conspiracy any sooner, the capital charges might get thrown out. It didn't mean that evidence before that date was inadmissible; plenty was admitted, in both trials. It was a technicality—"legally relevant," in Mackey's words, "but factually irrelevant."

The indictment was not entirely blind to the continuing investigation and referred to "others unknown" besides McVeigh and Nichols. But it did not point fingers at anybody else by name. It was, in essence, a promissory note on the outcome of further investigation, which never materialized.

{ Eight }

OKLAHOMA'S OWN PRIVATE AFGHANISTAN

Even before Carol Howe learned Andreas Strassmeir's full name, she had him marked for a dangerous man. They met when she and Dennis Mahon drove up to Elohim City for weekends in the fall of 1994, and she was immediately startled by the vehemence of Strassmeir's antigovernment rhetoric. "His plans," she wrote in her notes, which she later passed on to the ATF, "are to forcibly act to destroy the U.S. government with direct actions and operations. Assassinations, bombings, mass shootings etc. He believes we cannot outbreed the enemy so we must use mass genocide against them and of course the biggest enemy—the U.S. government."

Howe saw Strassmeir and his ragtag security team on their regular patrols around the perimeter of Grandpa Millar's community, and she heard him talk about converting an SKS rifle to full automatic using a piece from a food can. When he boasted he was stockpiling weapons and might have access to an M60 machine gun—a serious piece of military hardware unavailable on the open market—her handlers' ears pricked up and they told Howe to find out as much as she could about the strange, belligerent man she knew as Andi the German.

As an attractive blonde in a predominantly male world of gun nuts and would-be revolutionaries, Howe did not have to try hard to coax Strassmeir, or anyone else, to open up. She accompanied him to a nearby swimming hole, giving him a good look at her inky-black swastika tattoo, and flashed her knowledge of military hardware. Howe knew she had Strassmeir's attention when he shoved his hand down her shirt, although she later wondered if he was feeling for a wire. By Christmas 1994, she had his full name and birth date, enabling the ATF to check his immigration status and establish he was an overstay on his visa.

Howe was equally efficient in collecting evidence against Mahon. She gave him grenade hulls, which she obtained from Angela Finley, her ATF handler, and induced him on at least two occasions to fill them and detonate them in the woods. She recovered shrapnel pieces to pass on to the ATF, and she also reported with glee how he "hauled his fat butt" to safety after he had pulled the grenade pin, then demanded sex, or at least a back rub, as a reward for what he had done. "You realize we just committed a major felony here," she reported him saying with obvious elation. Howe rejected his advances and said that if he found her cold, it was because good terrorists needed ice in their veins; he had told her so himself.

Nothing in Howe's file suggests she came across Tim McVeigh or Terry Nichols at Elohim City, but she provided plentiful information pointing to threats of violence from within the community. As 1995 dawned, she told her handlers about a sermon in which Millar gave his blessing to a war against the ATF and the rest of the government. Patriots from Texas, Missouri, Arkansas, and Oklahoma would join forces for the coming fight, Millar predicted, and carve out a swath of independent territory. She also reported Mahon boasting about a five-hundred-pound ammonium nitrate bomb he set off in Michigan.

Several people in and out of government have attempted to discredit Howe as a fantasist and a liar. Strassmeir dismissed her, with the benefit of hindsight, as a "dress Nazi"; Kirk Lyons, apparently taking umbrage at the way she flirted with Strassmeir to win his confidence, called her "a very screwed up little vamp." But her work proved to be right much more than it was wrong. Bob Sanders, a former deputy director of the ATF, was impressed when he reviewed her file in 1997, and saw no reason to think she attempted to fabricate information, deceive anyone, or exaggerate. Dave Roberts, Angela Finley's boss at the ATF's Tulsa office, told a grand jury hearing in 1998: "I felt that Carol Howe was being effective as an informant, and I felt that she was sincere in her efforts."

And yet her information did not lead to a broader investigation, or even to explosives and weapons charges against Strassmeir and Mahon, as Howe and her handlers expected. Bob Sanders thought this was an outrage. "The entire manpower devoted to this investigation seems to have been nothing but one trainee agent [Finley]," he wrote incredulously in a report for Howe's legal representatives. "If the information provided by [Howe] is to be believed, as it clearly was, then the lack of investigation by BATF amounts to gross nonfeasance per se. . . . This was amateur hour in Oklahoma."

It was not the first time the federal government had tiptoed around Elohim City, only to lose its nerve and shy away. Nor would it be the last. After the Oklahoma City bombing, many people in law enforcement wanted to know what had gone on there, and felt there was a strong chance it had some connection to McVeigh. But they were either reluctant to investigate, or ordered not to.

JACK KNOX KNEW ELOHIM CITY WOULD BE A PROBLEM AFTER THE bombing, because he had come unstuck in his own efforts to investigate the place eight years earlier.

At that time, he was still an FBI agent, based in Fort Smith,

Arkansas, and he had a very personal reason to be suspicious of Grandpa Millar, because he had been targeted for assassination by Millar's friends Jim Ellison and Wayne Snell. Both of those men were now serving hard time, but Knox and the U.S. Attorney's Office in Fort Smith had ambitious plans to retry them, along with their most prominent brothers in arms, for the rarely prosecuted crime of sedition. It was only the third time in the country's history that such a charge had been brought, but the government was determined to eradicate the threat from the radical far right once and for all. Many of the defendants in the case were in prison already but some, including Louis Beam, now started appearing on FBI Wanted posters.

One fugitive of particular interest to Knox was James Wallington, who had been a peripheral figure in The Order, the most dangerous of the 1980s white supremacist gangs. Wallington was suspected of having transported and hidden millions of dollars from a spectacular armored-truck robbery in northern California in 1984. And now the word was that he was hiding out at Elohim City.

Knox had Millar's blessing to visit the community, but when he arrived with a full FBI search party, he was greeted by a posse of teenagers with semiautomatic and fully automatic weapons. "We radioed down for Millar and an assistant of his to come before there was an incident," he recalled. The teenagers backed off.

Knox was disinclined to ruffle community feathers by sending armed agents into the Elohim City church, so he told Millar they would stay away as long as he had his word that Wallington was not inside. Millar assured him he was not. "I didn't think they would disrespect God so much that they would hide a fugitive in there," Knox said.

But Knox heard a few days later that Wallington was in the church after all. He had been living in a disused bus under the alias Charlie Green and raising a daughter, Sarah, who later married Dave Hollaway of the CAUSE Foundation. Sarah had vivid memories of spending part of her itinerant childhood sleeping on a sack full of banknotes from the California robbery in the back of a truck. The money was never recovered.

The sedition trial did not go well, either. Jim Ellison was the star prosecution witness, but he had no credibility, because he was so manifestly in it to reduce his prison sentence at everyone else's expense. The defendants hated him for ratting them out, and the jurors were little better disposed. In the words of one observer, he came across as a "lying, deceiving sociopath."

The dock included former members of The Order and Ellison's Covenant, the Sword, and the Arm of the Lord, plus the radical right's three most recognizable national leaders: Richard Butler of Aryan Nations; Robert Miles, an incendiary Ku Klux Klan leader from Michigan accused of plotting to put cyanide in the nation's water supply; and Beam, who was arrested at a lakeside hideout in northern Mexico after a dramatic shootout with the federal police.

To the government's dismay, Judge Morris "Buzz" Arnold dispensed with the usual jury selection procedure and handpicked an all-white jury who knew nothing about the defendants' crime sprees and previous trials. One juror flirted openly with David Lane, who was involved in the murder of the Denver radio host Alan Berg, and another ended up marrying David McGuire, one of Jack Knox's suspected would-be assassins. "The judge," Knox complained, "was dredging right at the bottom of the barrel."

After seven weeks of testimony, the jury acquitted everybody—a humiliation for the government and an unalloyed triumph for the radical right. The defendants marched from the courthouse to a nearby Civil War memorial and raised a Confederate flag. "The message was the same one God told Pharaoh," the Arkansas Klan leader Thom Robb crowed. " 'Let my people go.' "

The FBI conducted an agonizing postmortem. "The bottom line was, the jury couldn't understand how a dozen people could get together and overthrow the country," Horace Mewborn of the bureau's domestic terrorism unit said. The FBI decided that if it ever tried another case against white supremacists, it would keep the evidence as simple as possible: no subplots, no overreaching, and no attempts to tie individual crimes to a broader movement.

"We learned that the hard way with Fort Smith," Mewborn said. Inevitably, this influenced FBI thinking after the Oklahoma City bombing and accounted for some of the reluctance to take the case beyond McVeigh and Nichols.

Soon, the FBI was further hamstrung by a scandal over its monitoring of CISPES, a left-wing group opposed to the Reagan administration's policies in Central America. Since Watergate, the Justice Department had insisted that the bureau focus only on bona fide crime investigations, to the exclusion of more speculative intelligence-gathering. But when the FBI director was forced to admit to Congress that the bureau's lengthy investigation into CISPES was groundless, the rules were tightened, and any subject that risked blurring the line between violence and legitimate political speech was suddenly deemed radioactive. That included investigations into the far right. "Everybody just walked in fear of domestic terrorism cases," Mewborn said. "They were positive they were going to blow up in their face."

The FBI never went back into Elohim City. Mewborn lobbied for a new warrant on Wallington and won the backing of the FBI's Little Rock division. But Bob Ricks, then a deputy assistant director, killed it in Washington. "I don't even remember if he gave me a reason," Mewborn said.

The decision was almost certainly not Ricks's alone, nor was it necessarily the wrong one at the time. "I was told that everybody was armed in there," Ricks said in a 2010 interview. "The element of danger was extremely high. . . . A lot of people would have gotten killed, more than likely, all for a potential witness. It seemed to me that other means needed to be deployed."

Sooner or later, though, the notion that the FBI would do nothing about Elohim City *because* it was dangerous risked looking like a dereliction of its fundamental responsibilities.

• • •

By the time Andreas Strassmeir crossed paths with Carol Howe, he assumed he was going to die in a firefight with the FBI or ATF. Years later, he made the extraordinary admission that he was more afraid of being sent back to Germany than of getting shot to pieces by the feds. "I wished they had come," he said in a 2010 interview. "Why didn't they?"

Since the Waco siege, the Elohim City elders had been jumpy about being next on the government's hit list, and Strassmeir made it his business to ensure the community would not go down without a fight. He attended gun shows—where he befriended McVeigh—and arranged purchases of weaponry and ammunition. He organized platoons of young men, set up a shooting range, and showed them how to handle grenades and Claymore mines. With his military-trained eye, he surveyed the hilly terrain and saw in it "a mix of the Afghani mountains and the Vietnam jungle."

"Helicopters are useless, tanks are useless," he said. "It's all about infantry."

At different times, his crew included Pete Ward, Kevin McCarthy, and Mike Brescia, with whom he shared a house. He taught Cheyne Kehoe to shoot and remembered him as a "rebellious spirit" and a "cool guy." Once, a sheriff's department narcotics officer dropped in unannounced and walked straight into an armed exercise. "He was impressed," Strassmeir recalled. "The message was: We're not some Jesus freaks on the mountain. It won't be a cakewalk."

Grandpa Millar placed greater confidence in Strassmeir and his military experience than in Zera Patterson, his nominal security chief, who had been Strassmeir's host when he first arrived. Strassmeir's ambition was to equip every adult with at least two firearms, and Millar gave his blessing to acquire SKS assault rifles, AR15s, and Ruger mini-14s.

Since nobody at Elohim City had any money, the budget did not permit a lot of frills. Strassmeir purchased Chinese SKS knockoffs by the crateload, and ammunition to go with them. "You get the rifle, bandolier, stripper clips, and folding bayonet for fifty dollars," he said. A crate of 7.62 × 39–mm ammo, containing more than a thousand rounds, ran to just $90.

The ATF eventually caught up to his cut-price suppliers, warning thirty-five leading importers and all federal firearms license-owners in early 1994 that the government now regarded the ammunition as armor-piercing and therefore illegal. Strassmeir and his friends raced around every tackle shop they could find to snap up the dwindling supplies of "Chink" ammo.

Strassmeir was walking a dangerous line between defensive maneuvers and outright provocation. He knew he could not provide real protection from a full-on federal raid, but that did not deter him. "The funny thing," said Dave Hollaway, who was furious when he found out about his friend's activities, "is that Andi can't shoot *himself*. He's prehistoric, man, prehistoric! . . . You can only keep people out of trouble if you can command respect yourself. Andi was a quarter-eyed guy."

It didn't help that, as a foreign national, Strassmeir was not legally permitted to purchase firearms, or that he had ignored the stamp in his passport limiting his last entry into the United States to three months. Before he went to live in Elohim City, in 1991, he had kept his immigration status in order, either by flying back to Germany or hopping over the Mexican border. Now, though, he was an overstay, at risk of deportation at any time.

He was appropriately cautious about one thing, and that was the risk of informants. "Betraying the right wing in America," he said, "is a career, not a death sentence." He was forever telling Grandpa Millar not to trust outsiders, but Millar, to his endless frustration, paid no attention, repeating only that everyone came to him from Jesus.

This Strassmeir, the paramilitary radical, was very different from the young man who impressed the Israeli army and talked a seasoned CIA operative into considering him for a high-risk job on the Mexican border. He had been sucked into the far right during his time with Lyons and Hollaway in Texas and immediately felt comfortable mixing with weekend-warrior types. One place he visited was a gunnery range that Louis Beam co-owned in the mosquito-ridden rice fields east of Houston. Hollaway was married at the time to the daughter of Beam's business partner, a Korean War veteran named Bob Sisente, whom Hollaway himself described as a "freakin' gangster" with a "concrete head, neck, and shoulders, and a body of metal." Lyons fell in love with the sister of David Tate, a member of The Order serving a life sentence for murdering a Missouri state trooper, and married her in a double ceremony with his best friend Neill Payne, who paired up with another Tate sister. The ceremony was at Aryan Nations headquarters in Idaho, with Richard Butler officiating and Louis Beam as best man.

Strassmeir was so enamored of this world that it did not occur to him that Lyons and Hollaway sent him to Elohim City to get rid of him. He said he loved the frontier spirit of rural Oklahoma, and loved being able to get by on just a few days' construction or wood-chopping work each month. He lived for long stretches off home-made bread, garden cucumbers, poached deer jokingly known as "wild goat," and expired almond butter supplied in industrial quantities by Tony Alamo, an eccentric preacher later convicted of child abuse and pornography crimes in Arkansas.

Strassmeir needed no money for everyday transactions, because Elohim City operated on a barter currency based on glass beads known as "glows." Until the advent of a phone line, which the Elohimites rigged up by digging a trench and extending the public line, the only way to communicate with the outside world was to walk a mile and a half to a phone in a padlocked shed, nicknamed "EC phone home." Strassmeir marveled: "We were like the first settlers on the continent, with a gun rack in the church. . . . It was like going back three hundred years."

Strassmeir's rural idyll was not without its deeper oddities. In February 1992, Pete Ward borrowed his car to buy some chewing tobacco, only to be pulled over by a state Highway Patrol trooper who had been on the lookout for Strassmeir for some time. Trooper Vernon Phillips issued Ward with two tickets—for driving without Oklahoma plates and failing to produce a license—and had the car impounded and searched. When Strassmeir found out, he had "an absolute fit," according to the tow truck driver, Kenny Pence, and demanded his car back, claiming diplomatic immunity.

A flurry of phone calls followed—from Kirk Lyons, and from people saying they were officials from the state police, the military in North Carolina, and the State Department in Washington. Pence found the whole thing a "really strange deal." One caller told him the governor was involved and urged him to release the vehicle without delay. Pence, assuming these people were who they said they were, complied.

Strassmeir gave the impression, once again, of having friends in very high places.

The FBI talked to Robert Millar on a regular basis before the Oklahoma City bombing, but could never tell if he was a stand-up guy or just stringing them along. Horace Mewborn said his domestic terrorism unit in Washington would funnel questions through the Muskogee resident agent, but would never receive helpful answers. "I don't know who was playing whom," he said. "Sometimes I got the feeling Millar was playing the resident agent, and feeding us a bunch of poop. It was all general information, of no help to us."

The ATF also kept an eye out, liaising with the Oklahoma Highway Patrol to watch the roads so they could track who was coming and going. Periodically, the ATF and FBI would get together for informal meetings to pool their knowledge on Elohim City. But Bill Buford, who was the ATF's top agent in Arkansas at the time, said these were a joke, because nobody knew much, and nobody was willing to give away what little they had. "If the FBI had information," he said, "they wouldn't share it with us. And when we got information, we wouldn't share it with them."

This was a crucial period in the development of Louis Beam's "leaderless resistance" movement, and Elohim City was as regular a meeting point for revolutionary fighters as anywhere in the country. Among those known to have sought shelter and support in the community at the time were Willie Ray Lampley, who was plotting bomb attacks on abortion clinics, gay bars, and antiracist groups; Chevie Kehoe, who murdered a gun dealer and his family in Arkansas in early 1996; and, of course, Mahon and most of the Aryan Republican Army.

Yet the feds were only dimly aware of the danger these men posed and—with the exception of just a handful of agents—did not think it worth the trouble to find out. Buck Revell, a veteran of the FBI's top brass, felt the bureau knew "almost nothing" about the radical right, because of its aversion to intelligence-led investigations. Certainly, if McVeigh had visited—one of the persistent unknowns of the Oklahoma City investigation—there was no direct channel of communication to let them know, or to tip them off to what it portended.

Millar was a slick operator, rarely turning down an invitation to talk to law enforcement, or to the media. Each time, he drew on the pacifist rhetoric he had learned from his father, a Canadian Mennonite preacher, to depict Elohim City as a wholly innocent place of close-knit family values, hard work, and self-sufficiency. His credit with the feds went back to 1985, when he helped the FBI negotiate a peaceful end to a siege at Jim Ellison's compound at Bull Shoals Lake, Arkansas. Danny Coulson, the head of the FBI's Hostage Rescue Team who oversaw the operation, remembered Millar as a spindly figure who strolled up the road "dressed as if a pretty widow had invited him to an ice cream social," in a vanilla suit and shiny alligator shoes.

To many in federal law enforcement, Elohim City seemed more pleasantly quirky than dangerous. The Elohimites ran their clocks on sundial time, used the Hebrew calendar, organized daily services at high noon in a church with only circular walls, spoke in tongues, and healed the sick by laying on hands. To earn a living, they had a sawmill and a trucking company, which were run by two of Millar's sons. On his business card, Millar proclaimed his community "a city of the universe."

But there was a darker side. Millar was fascinated from an early age by theories of racial separation and the apocalypse. When he first settled in the United States, he established a community school in rural Maryland, whose brochure depicted him with a pencil mustache and arm outstretched in a Nazi salute over the caption: "Heil Hitler."

He not only befriended Jim Ellison but anointed him "King James of the Ozarks," the direct heir to King David. Two nasty child-custody disputes from this time, the early 1980s, elicited testimony depicting Elohim City as a cultlike community in which obedience was all, polygamy and incest ran rampant, and the Millar clan routinely took the law into its own hands. When one father showed up with a custody order to demand his daughter, he was beaten back by men with guns. The neighbors testified they were afraid of being "burned out" if they crossed the Millars in any way. A Canadian court, where one of the cases was heard, denounced a "lifestyle that reeks of hypocrisy and self-indulgence."

Much of this history was overlooked or forgotten by the mid-1990s. Tim Arney, the FBI's agent in Muskogee, drove to Elohim City several times—part of a nationwide initiative to sound out isolationist communities for signs of trouble after Waco—and never saw anything he found disturbing. "Most of them were pretty sweet people," he recalled. "They didn't flash guns, or throw up roadblocks. . . . Millar certainly attracted a lot of nutcases and right-wingers, but I think he left them disappointed."

Arney was taking direction from his boss in Oklahoma City, Bob Ricks, who also appeared to view Millar as a reasonable man; he felt Millar would neither encourage violence nor do anything to provoke a government attack. According to Danny Coulson, Ricks and Millar talked once a week.

Was the FBI too indulgent? Arney and Ricks both bridled at the suggestion. "Don't get me wrong," Arney protested in a 2010 interview, "I'm not saying Millar is an innocent guy. He always looked unhealthy when I visited." Ricks said it was an "overstatement" to say, as Coulson had, that he felt Elohim City was under control. But he acknowledged he had been reassured by Millar's repeated undertakings to cooperate in the event of a crisis. "Anything you want to see," Ricks remembered him saying, "we're open."

Regrettably, the FBI never properly took him up on that offer.

THE ATF HAD TWO REASONS NOT TO GO AFTER DENNIS MAHON after Carol Howe delivered the shrapnel pieces and the descriptions of him making grenades. The better reason was that the agency was investigating Mahon for as many as ten attacks on people and property since the early 1980s, and did not want to stop building its case for the sake of two harmless detonations in the woods. The less good reason was that the ATF did not want to share its information with the FBI.

The ATF needed the FBI's help to make its case because of the bureau's broader experience of criminal prosecutions. But it also knew the FBI was unlikely to help, because the bureau had looked at Mahon, too, and concluded he was all talk, a provocateur too unstable to be trusted with a real mission. And so the ATF decided to keep its information to itself.

After the bombing, the FBI was furious not to have been informed when Howe first reported on Mahon and Strassmeir. And Tommy Wittman, the ATF's assistant special agent in charge in Dallas who

kept a supervisory eye on Howe, said the bureau was right to be furious. The layers of bureaucratic infighting, as he described them in a
2010 interview, were almost too dizzying to comprehend.

"The thinking was, we don't want to talk to Mahon, because,
if we did, he'd know we're super-interested in him and he might
change his activities," Wittman said. "But of course he already knew
we were interested. The thinking was also, we don't know if the FBI
or another agency may be looking at him, so *we* won't. If we make
an inquiry, they'll want to know what we know, and we don't want
others to know, because they'll know we are interested and won't
share information with *us*."

This was Milo Minderbinder logic straight out of the pages of
Catch-22. "In hindsight," Wittman acknowledged, "a lot of things
should have been done very differently. A lot of things that made
sense then look very different now, from the outside."

The government tried to argue after the bombing that Howe's
evidence against Mahon did not amount to much. One federal prosecutor called it "crap." But it wasn't seen that way in the ATF. Tristan
Moreland, an ATF agent who eventually arrested Mahon on bombing charges in Arizona in 2009, said the decision not to go after
him was purely strategic. "If they had prosecuted him then for weapons manufacture and possession," he said, "I have no doubt Mahon
would have gone to prison."

The awkward truth was that the ATF's confidence was shot in
the wake of its disastrous mishandling of Ruby Ridge and Waco, and
senior managers did not want to confront another group of heavily
armed survivalists with a grudge against federal agents.

"Elohim City, to me, was a situation [where] we had to be very
delicate," the head of the ATF's Dallas field division, Lester Martz,
later testified. "I specifically told Angie [Finley], Dave Roberts,
and ASAC Wittman that I do not want any overt, covert, on-the-
property surveillance—nothing done in Elohim City without my
prior approval."

The ATF knew, too, that the last thing the FBI wanted was to bail them out of another botched raid, as it had in Idaho and Texas. As the saying in bureau ranks had it at the time: "We're not taking a bite out of that shit sandwich."

In some ways it is remarkable, given the ATF's pervasive fear of another armed standoff, that the Carol Howe investigation went as far as it did. Dave Roberts kept going mostly because of Howe's report about the M60 machine gun. Roberts gave preliminary briefings to the U.S. Attorney's Offices in Tulsa and Muskogee, and sought advice on whether Howe's sexual history—particularly her liaisons with people she was investigating—might affect her credibility in court.

Finley asked the Immigration and Naturalization Service for a formal certificate that Strassmeir was in the country illegally. She also invited the INS to participate in a raid the Tulsa office was planning to arrest Strassmeir—an invitation they took under advisement.

All the while, Howe's work continued unabated. In January 1995, she accompanied Grandpa Millar and a group of elders on a trip to Oklahoma City, where they met, incongruously, with the pastor of a mixed-race Baptist church. Howe said Millar and the pastor talked about going into the weapons business—another potential violation of numerous gun laws.

The ATF also continued to talk to the Oklahoma Highway Patrol. In early February, Wittman and Finley decided they should join an OHP flight to conduct aerial reconnaissance over Elohim City and see the extent of Strassmeir's preparations for war. Ordinarily, the ATF would use its own planes, but Wittman understood that if he asked Lester Martz for one, he would be turned down. So he, Finley, and an ATF photographer hitched a ride with pilot Ken Stafford on his Highway Patrol plane and scoured the landscape for signs of military defenses, gun positions, trenches, or razor wire. "It doesn't stick out in my mind that [the flight] was overly productive," Wittman recalled.

That was the moment the Strassmeir investigation started falling apart. Somehow, the Elohimites heard rumors of an impending raid. Most likely, this was from a trooper safety notice put out by the OHP in mid-February, describing Strassmeir as an illegal alien who carried a .45. Millar was alarmed enough to visit Tim Arney in Muskogee and demand an explanation. Arney didn't have one. But he did alert Bob Ricks, and Ricks was staggered by what he heard.

"My thought was, Jimminy Christmas, are we going to do that again?" he said. Ricks chewed out the ATF office in Tulsa, demanding to know if they really were contemplating a raid. They said no. Still, he wanted to know what information they had. Did it warrant an FBI investigation?

The ATF told Ricks nothing—about Howe, or Mahon, or Strassmeir. Ricks said he arranged a lunch with Lester Martz, because he had a feeling the ATF was stonewalling. But Martz insisted there was nothing going on. "He passed off what I was hearing as greatly exaggerated," Ricks said. "It was not a lengthy meeting. I tried to make it unequivocal, that if there was going to be a raid, we wanted to know about it. I didn't want to be called upon to clean up their mess."

AS SOON AS TERRY NICHOLS WAS BACK FROM THE PHILIPPINES IN mid-January, McVeigh pressed him to keep helping with the bomb plot. Nichols wanted to say no: Marife was returning to America, he was looking for a house to buy, and he had started attending surplus auctions at Fort Riley to get back in the gun-show business, as a solo operator this time. But something about McVeigh, once again, proved too strong to resist.

McVeigh gave Nichols the impression he had changed his intended date or his intended target, but he offered no specifics. All McVeigh said—following the plot of his second-favorite book, *Hunter*—was that he was acting at the behest of a high-level government handler who had switched the mission. McVeigh called this handler "Potts," after the FBI's acting deputy director, Larry Potts. An overtrusting Nichols believed the handler really *was* Potts. But the name was most certainly symbolic, an indication that Waco was in the forefront of McVeigh's mind and he had now chosen April 19, the day David Koresh's compound went up in flames, as his new day of action.

Meanwhile, McVeigh was out of money. He told Nichols he needed $2,000 to pay for a Ford Ranger truck, which, in reality, he had already purchased. (This was the mystery vehicle for which the FBI subsequently found title documents but no other trace.) Simultaneously, he told Michael Fortier he needed $2,000 to repay Nichols; he didn't mention that Nichols already had the Roger Moore loot to compensate him for everything he had fronted in September and October.

In short, McVeigh lied to both of them.

Fortier said he was broke, too, so McVeigh asked what he had done with Moore's guns. When McVeigh learned they had not yet been sold, he drove straight to Kingman and dragged Fortier to gun shows in Reno and St. George so he could start offloading them and generating some cash. Fortier later went to a third show to sell the rest.

McVeigh understood at this point that he probably needed new recruits. Investigators on his defense team found witnesses who said that, around this time, he made repeated contact with Dick Coffman, a leading neo-Nazi in Arizona, and through Coffman introduced himself to a Utah skinhead leader named Johnny Bangerter.

McVeigh also made an offer to Jim Rosencrans. He needed someone, he said, to drive him a long way across the country and drop him off at an airport. If Rosencrans was willing to do this, he could have the car, plus $300 in cash and a rifle. Rosencrans, who was even more broke than McVeigh, discussed the offer with his girlfriend, Patty Edwards, but she was immediately suspicious. Why would McVeigh offer his car so freely? She told Rosencrans if this was something dangerous, he would have to make a choice between the job and her.

He chose her.

IN FEBRUARY 1995, HOWE TOLD HER HANDLERS SHE COULD NOT SUB-stantiate the M60 story, knocking the legs out from Dave Roberts's best justification for pursuing Strassmeir. Then she failed to return to Elohim City as expected and cut back dramatically on her contacts with Finley. Finley stalled as long as she could, telling her bosses Howe "had personal matters to attend." Howe herself claimed she was infiltrating a skinhead group in Tulsa at Finley's direction, but the ATF later accused her of associating with the skinheads without authorization. Given how quickly their relationship soured, it is hard to say who was right.

In mid-March, Finley unexpectedly heard from Howe's land-lord, who said he knew about Howe's informant work—a serious security breach in itself—and also that she had been admitted to a mental institution. Howe had gone to Parkside Mental Health Center with a police escort, on February 8, after officers found her with self-inflicted cuts on her face, neck, arms, and hands. They described her as "out of control." Howe later confirmed the bulk of this, saying she felt under enormous pressure because of her ATF responsibilities. She spent just four hours at Parkside before transfer-ring to a regular hospital.

On March 19, the Tulsa police told Finley that Howe was back in the hospital, this time because she had been pistol-whipped by an African-American man while out on paramilitary night exercises in the woods. The next day, the ATF severed its relationship with her, saying she was "no longer loyal or competent to operate."

The ATF later made many excuses for failing to follow up on the leads Howe had established at Elohim City. One was that Howe had been a nightmare from start to finish and her information unusable—an argument undermined by the reliability of much of what she reported back. Another was that they were ordered by Bob Ricks to back off. That, too, appears to be untrue. John Magaw, the ATF director at the time, said the decision to stop almost certainly came from within his agency, before Ricks had a chance to express an opinion.

"I wanted to make sure that before we conducted any more raids of those kinds of places, we were properly retrained, had the right equipment, did really good intelligence, and had done very good practicing and planning," Magaw explained in a 2010 interview. "We weren't ready at that time."

Magaw could not remember exactly how the decision was made, but Lester Martz most likely brought the problem to him, and he and his assistant director for operations supported Martz's inclination to close Howe down. Remarkably, Magaw also acknowledged that the decision might have cost the federal government an opportunity to prevent the bombing.

When reminded of the human toll at the Murrah Building, Magaw blanched visibly, and did not deny that it might have had something to do with the decisions he made about Elohim City. He said his room for maneuver was constrained by the culture of the time: the aversion to domestic intelligence work (even though the ATF did not operate under the same restraints as the FBI), the frustrating reality that the ATF did not know how to handle volatile standoffs with extremists, and a generalized inability to assess threats from the radical right.

"It was a situation where everyone was hands-off," he said. "Would Waco happen now? Absolutely not. Would the Oklahoma City bombing have occurred? Probably not. We would have moved in on that group [at Elohim City]. But at the time I wasn't about to take chances I didn't need to take."

A case has been made over the years that Howe gave the government enough material to see the Oklahoma City bombing coming.

But that is not corroborated by the available documentary evidence of her informant work. Howe certainly reported on Strassmeir, Mahon, and Millar expressing a desire to set off bombs and attack government buildings, but she offered nothing more specific than that before April 19, 1995. (Afterward was a different story.)

Were there grounds to follow up on these threats anyway? Bob Sanders, the former deputy director of the ATF, certainly thought so, and so did Tristan Moreland, the agent who pursued and ultimately arrested Dennis Mahon. "If they had looked into the files, they would have seen Mahon had a predisposition to blowing up buildings," Moreland said. If Howe's information was deemed to be solid and the concern was about her stability, Moreland argued, the logical thing to do would have been to replace her, not shut down the entire operation.

In the heat of the bombing investigation, the government took the line that the threats were not a big deal because such talk was part of the rhetoric of the radical right and did not, on its own, imply anything. That was Finley's line of defense when she was questioned in court in 1997. She confirmed she had heard threats to blow up government buildings, but only "in general."

It was also the official position of the Justice Department once news of Howe's existence became public in early 1997. Don Thrasher, a producer with ABC News who was working on pieces about Howe and Elohim City, remembered being warned by Leesa Brown, the department spokeswoman, about the danger of jumping to conclusions based on threats alone.

"If you go beyond the story of an informant in a white supremacist compound hearing all of these stories," he quoted Brown saying, "what have you got? This happens all the time."

"Yeah, but there's one difference here, Leesa," Thrasher responded.

"What?"

"The goddamn building blew up, that's what."

The government, of course, had every reason to be defensive. The ATF had had a pair of eyes and ears in Elohim City and pulled her out, not because she was failing to pick up indications of serious criminality—she was—but because the agency was too afraid to act on them. It adopted a posture of studied ignorance and hoped for the best.

After the bombing, the ATF wanted desperately to avoid talking about Elohim City. Even after the FBI was given the Carol Howe file, Bob Ricks and Danny Defenbaugh never quite believed they had the full story. "Shame on them," Defenbaugh said. "In upper case—SHAME ON THEM. Sometimes dealing with other players in this is like pulling teeth from a toothless tiger. Ask them why [they didn't tell everything they knew]. They didn't ever give me a good reason." A contrite Magaw did not say a lot in the ATF's defense. "He's right," he responded when Defenbaugh's words were read back to him. "If we did know something and didn't bring it forward, then shame on us."

The FBI was far from blameless itself, having avoided looking into Elohim City for years. The decision to expend only token energy on the community after the bombing was the bureau's alone. That mystified some of the FBI's old pros, none more than Danny Coulson, who had spent his career chasing right-wing radicals and found the idea of shying away from Elohim City offensive and ridiculous.

"You still do your job, I'm sorry," Coulson said. "You've taken an oath. You're a professional, you figure out a way to do it. They're afraid of another Waco. . . . If that's your attitude, get out of the business. Go into the shoe business. Be a chef. By its nature it's risky. You've got to be smarter than that."

LATE ONE NIGHT IN FEBRUARY 1995, TIM MCVEIGH WAS WALKING across the Colorado River bridge from Nevada to Bullhead City, Arizona, when a man in a Ford Mustang slowed down and asked if he wanted a ride. McVeigh had no better idea how to get back to Kingman, which was thirty miles away, and offered him $5. The man, whose name was Richard Rogers, laughed off the offer; he was looking not for payment but for casual sex. He had spent the evening at a casino in Laughlin and, as he later told the FBI, was feeling "a little horny."

McVeigh's camouflage fatigues and combat boots did not exactly fit the sexpot mold. But Rogers recognized him from an earlier hitch-hiking encounter and remembered how McVeigh played with his penis and asked if he wanted to party. Rogers hadn't been interested at the time, because he was on his way to meet another friend.

The conversation quickly turned to sex, and McVeigh asked Rogers, as he had six months earlier, if he wanted to party.

Rogers responded: "What do you mean?"

McVeigh spread his legs and groped himself. "We could have a really great time," he said. McVeigh started rubbing Rogers's penis through his clothes.

An hour later, the two of them were in Rogers's trailer ten miles north of Kingman, sizing each other up and half-wondering if this was really a good idea. McVeigh talked about Waco, nobody's idea of good foreplay, and peppered Rogers with questions about an airstrip in the desert hills. At 3:00 A.M., McVeigh grabbed his crotch again and said it was time for bed.

They took their clothes off and went at it. McVeigh's tongue and throat action, Rogers later told the FBI, was "incredible": "He was good at what he did." McVeigh expressed an interest in anal sex, but Rogers turned him down, because he didn't have a condom. According to Rogers, they were both too tired to reach orgasm. In the morning, Rogers made McVeigh eggs and bacon, and drove him into Kingman. Apart from brief sightings in the grocery store, they never saw each other again.

Assuming this story is broadly true—the FBI found Rogers credible enough to interview him seven times—it suggests that McVeigh, like Pete Langan, had some personal baggage he was not in a rush to share with the rest of the Patriot Movement. Rogers thought it unlikely he was actually gay, just fooling around. He told the FBI McVeigh was most likely bisexual.

Intriguingly, this is the one intimate encounter of McVeigh's anybody has ever come forward to describe—either in the graphic detail offered by Rogers, or any other way.

OF ALL THE MYSTERIES SURROUNDING ELOHIM CITY, NONE IS MORE vexing than the question of whether McVeigh visited and, if so, whether he derived any part of the bomb plot—inspiration, training, manpower—from the contacts he established in the community. Nobody has come forward with definitive evidence that McVeigh spent time at Elohim City. On the other hand, a large number of people—from law enforcement, the federal prosecution team, the radical far right, and even Elohim City itself—have dropped hints that he was there, that the government either knew or strongly suspected he was there, and that the information was kept quiet to prevent the criminal case spiraling out of control.

We know McVeigh called Elohim City for just under two minutes on April 5, 1995, because there is a record of it on the Daryl Bridges card. Millar's daughter-in-law took the call and later said the young man on the line was looking for Andi the German. McVeigh told her he was thinking of visiting in the next few days, and Joan Millar replied that, as a friend of Strassmeir's, he was welcome any time.

The timing of the call was interesting: McVeigh had just spoken to a Ryder truck rental agency in Lake Havasu City, not far from Kingman, and was presumably making his bomb delivery plans. Was Strassmeir, or his planned visit to Elohim City, part of the calculation? Was he, as an FBI teletype later surmised, looking for new recruits because he did not think he could count on Nichols or Fortier?

The FBI files contain a reference to a second call from McVeigh to Strassmeir at Elohim City, this one on April 17, the day the Ryder truck used in the bombing was rented from Eldon Elliott's. The information on this call is sketchier, because it was never linked to a specific set of phone records. According to an FBI teletype discovered in 2003, the bureau heard about the call from the Southern Poverty Law Center, the anti-extremist campaign group, but the SPLC has been reluctant to vouch for its authenticity ever since. Richard Cohen, the group's president, said it was possible that the line in the teletype referring to a call "two days prior to the OKBOMB attack" could have been a clerical error and that the line should have read "two weeks." In other words, just another reference to the April 5 call.

Over the years, the SPLC has backtracked from a lot of information connecting McVeigh with Elohim City. Twice in the 1990s, the group's founder, Morris Dees, was quoted saying that he had information that McVeigh visited numerous times. He said it in answer to a reporter's question at the Denver press club in May 1996, and he said it in an interview with the Indiana State University criminologist Mark Hamm in 1999. But when he addressed the issue again during a talk at Southeastern Oklahoma State University in 2004, he played down his previous statements. "McVeigh probably was at Elohim City, based on evidence we've been able to pick up—stuff I really can't go into," he said. "But I don't think the entire connection is really there."

If Dees was suddenly tentative on the question, other SPLC officials were emphatic: as far as they knew, McVeigh never went to Elohim City. "[Dees] may have said it," a surprisingly dismissive Mark Potok, editor of the SPLC's *Intelligence Report,* said in 2010, "but I very much doubt it's true." Both Potok and Cohen sought to minimize Dees's role in the organization's intelligence-gathering, and refused to make him available for interview.

All of this was starkly out of character for the SPLC, which usually broadcasts any sinister connection involving the radical right as loudly as it can. One possible reason for its reticence was its close relationship with the Justice Department, which had every reason to play down links between McVeigh and Elohim City. (Its official position throughout the federal trials was that no such link existed.) If the government had information, even secondhand information, placing McVeigh at Elohim City, failing to hand it over to the defense teams could have constituted a serious violation of the rules of evidence.

Did the government have such information? Bill Buford, the former ATF chief in Arkansas, said he was briefed on both verbal and written reports putting McVeigh at Elohim City. The material was not handed over in discovery, he said, but was put into a summary report written by the FBI and sent to the Justice Department. "I'd heard it by word of mouth and it was also in the report," Buford said. "There's a lot of information in there that has not been made available to the public."

Buford could not remember the specifics, but the information referred to an actual visit, not just the April 5 phone call. How sure was he about this clamorous revelation? "I'm sure," he said.

A number of other senior law enforcement officials were approached about Buford's information, and none denied it. Bob Ricks said the FBI had found no evidence that McVeigh spent evenings or nights at Elohim City, but acknowledged: "He was always passing through." Danny Defenbaugh said he could not remember what was in the FBI reports sent up to the Justice Department, but did not exclude it. Perhaps the most revealing line came from Scott Mendeloff, one of McVeigh's prosecutors, who sought to argue forcefully that Elohim City was irrelevant to the investigation. "It's not like we didn't think he was there," he said testily. "So he visited, but so what?"

When McVeigh's own legal team asked about Elohim City, he did not acknowledge having been there, but he seemed to know all about Strassmeir patrolling the perimeter and standing guard in the driveway when visitors pulled up. McVeigh told his defense lawyer Randy Coyne that Elohim City was "pretty fucking hard-core." And he said that Strassmeir and he were "brothers in arms."

When would McVeigh have been at Elohim City? He received a traffic ticket just over the Arkansas state line in the fall of 1993, and spent the night in a nearby motel on September 12, 1994. Those have to be strong possibilities. Another intriguing date is November 1, 1994, when Tom Metzger, one of the godfathers of the radical right, paid a visit to Elohim City with Dennis Mahon. As Metzger remembered it, he spoke for half an hour in the church, watched the kids perform a dance, shook a few hands, and left again. But he also dropped a hint of more. "Those stories about sitting in another room and talking about stuff," he said, without prompting, "that didn't happen." Was this Metzger pointing to the very thing he sought to deny? It is tempting to think McVeigh would have been there to take lessons from the master, and it was not far out of his way—he was driving from Kansas to upstate New York at the time. It would also have been an opportunity to meet Strassmeir, McCarthy, and Brescia.

The last time McVeigh could have visited—following the intentions he announced in his phone conversation with Joan Millar— was during the two weeks before April 19. This would put Elohim City at the center of the bomb plot. The timing would have been tight: McVeigh checked out of the Imperial Motel in Kingman on April 11, bought an oil filter in Arkansas City, Kansas—just over the Oklahoma state line—on April 13, and arrived at the Dreamland in Junction City on April 14. But it is also possible that he made a quick trip to the Midwest between April 7 and April 11. He was checked into the Imperial Motel on those dates, but the owner later said he did not see him, he used no towels, and his bed was undisturbed. There was a flurry of Daryl Bridges calls from the Imperial up to April 6, then nothing. Would McVeigh have wanted to keep paying for an empty motel room? He might have done if, say, he was transporting blasting caps, or the second Ryder truck seen by Lea McGown and her son on Easter Sunday. It was one way to cover his tracks and minimize the risk of exposure.

If all that sounds speculative, it is. The first two weeks of April are a big mystery when it comes to McVeigh's movements, activities, and associations. On Saturday evening, April 8, a dancer at the Lady Godiva strip club in Tulsa was told by someone she later believed to be McVeigh that on April 19, 1995, she would remember him for the rest of her life. He was with two other men. Did they travel from the club to Elohim City? Kirk Lyons, of all people, did not exclude it—and he would have had an opportunity to know, because he was Strassmeir's lawyer and confidant. "It's possible he went through there on a weekend before the bombing," Lyons said of McVeigh. "That's possible."

Grandpa Millar also did not exclude that McVeigh had been to Elohim City. A defense investigator who spoke to him in 1995 reported Millar saying "it was possible that he could have met Mr. McVeigh once or twice and that it was also possible that Mr. McVeigh could have visited Elohim City." Millar was fiercely protective of his community, more interested in damping down speculation about criminal associations than in talking them up, so the indiscretion was unusual. In 1997, he was strikingly forthcoming once again when asked by the journalist Jonathan Franklin if any Elohim City residents were involved in the bombing. "There are legitimate questions to be asked, though I don't know the answers," he said. "I don't mind an honest investigation."

By that point, of course, Millar knew that no investigation had taken place, and after the trials there was little danger of one starting up. He had played the government masterfully for more than a decade. Jim Ellison's disenchanted former deputy Kerry Noble summarized it neatly. "Two things the government doesn't want," he said, "another sedition trial that fails, and another Waco that fails. What have you got with Elohim City? A possibility of another sedition and conspiracy trial that fails, and another raid that fails. That makes Elohim City, unfortunately, have the upper hand."

{ Nine }

ARYAN PARADISE LOST

One day after McVeigh and Nichols were indicted, Larry Potts was booted out as deputy director of the FBI and Danny Coulson was dismissed as special agent in charge in Dallas. They and three other senior agents associated with Ruby Ridge were placed on indefinite administrative leave. They were never told why they were suspended, nor were they formally accused of anything—not even by the Justice Department, which continued to hold on to its 1994 report holding Potts jointly responsible for the change in the rules of engagement at Randy Weaver's cabin. Over time, it became clear that their removal was Louie Freeh's way of being seen to do something to address a scandal that refused to go away. But it also had a chilling effect on the bombing investigation.

"They took out my unit chief, my section chief, the assistant deputy, Danny [Coulson], and Larry Potts. I lost the next four levels above me," said Horace Mewborn, an agent with the FBI's domestic terrorism unit, who specialized in the radical far right. "I thought, God, this couldn't happen at a worse time."

Buck Revell, who had recently retired as associate deputy director, called it an unprecedented abuse of authority and said: "At least Senator Joe McCarthy confronted his victims with his misplaced suspicions, hearsay, and innuendo, and they had an opportunity to respond."

Coulson and Potts were eventually absolved and allowed to retire. But for the next two years, they were forbidden to talk to each other—about Oklahoma City or anything else. Coulson never lost the feeling that parts of the bombing investigation were dropped when he and his colleagues were removed. "I've been involved in thousands of investigations, but I've never seen that before—that the bureau would shut down an investigation to focus guilt on one person," he said. It was something that he and Potts would never have tolerated.

NICHOLS'S LAWYER, MICHAEL TIGAR, BELIEVED THE ONLY WAY TO guarantee a fair trial—to provide a "sanctuary in the jungle" for his client, as he put it—was to move proceedings out of Oklahoma. Wayne Alley, the Oklahoma City judge who had been assigned the case by lottery, did not agree, and would not recuse himself even when Tigar pointed out that his offices were right next to the Murrah Building and the windows of his chambers had shattered in the bombing. "I have experienced greater loss of courtroom time because of water leaks and utility failures," Alley said.

Tigar found this response cavalier and irresponsible, and his fury only grew when Alley announced that the trial would take place in Lawton, a town a hundred miles from Oklahoma City, which presented considerable logistical and security challenges. Tigar won the argument: the Tenth Circuit appeals court moved the trial to Denver and assigned Richard Matsch, a judge with previous experience of trying right-wing revolutionaries, whom Tigar had wanted all along.

Tigar had to make this argument alone, though, because Stephen Jones did not want to ruffle judicial feathers in his home state and would not join him on the appeal. They argued about the reasons for years, but for Tigar, at least, this was the moment when their relationship soured decisively.

Tigar did not respect Jones, and Jones found Tigar to be insufferably sure of himself. To some extent, the tension reflected the conflicting interests of their clients: Tigar's team argued that McVeigh had manipulated Nichols and set him up, while the McVeigh team portrayed Nichols as a conniver and a liar. But it also had to do with the differences in their assignments.

Tigar had the easier case. His client was not in Oklahoma City when the bomb went off, had voluntarily answered the FBI's questions, and was now talking in great detail to his legal team. From the beginning, Tigar formulated the mantra he would take to court: that in April 1995 Terry Nichols had been building a life, not a bomb.

Jones, on the other hand, did not like or trust his client and was not sure he could construct a viable defense for someone who was both manifestly guilty and unwilling to tell his full story. "I could file all the procedural motions I wanted, but ultimately, when the trial started, I had nothing with which to defend him," Jones later wrote. He became so exasperated he forced McVeigh to undergo a polygraph and tried to confront him over the signs of evasion he showed when he was asked about the involvement of others besides Nichols.

Jones took more pleasure in building relationships with news reporters, sharing his thoughts, and parts of the evidence, in exchange for any information or leads to witnesses they had. The strategy was unceasingly controversial, and at one early hearing, Judge Matsch rebuked Jones for trying the case in the press. "We don't want to be talking about the evidence outside," Matsch told him sternly. "It's not productive."

Jones understood he needed to court Matsch's favor assiduously, and made every effort not to upset him again. But he never stopped talking, or sharing documents with the media.

• • •

In late summer 1995, Grandpa Millar took Andreas Strassmeir aside and told him he had to leave Elohim City immediately, because the feds were after him. A government informant had recently spotted Strassmeir at a gun show with an SKS rifle and revolver, and Millar had enough to worry about after the bombing without answering for Strassmeir's illegal weapons. As Strassmeir and others later understood it, Millar reached an agreement with his law enforcement contacts that Elohim City would not be raided as long as he got rid of the troublesome German.

Strassmeir hitched a ride to Black Mountain, North Carolina, the new home of Kirk Lyons's CAUSE Foundation, because he didn't know where else to go. "I figured I would find a way to get back and straighten things out with Millar," he said. "I had no alternative plan."

But when he returned to Elohim City for his things, he found them either stuffed haphazardly in the back of his car, the Suburban he had bought from Scott Stedeford, or abandoned on a roadside. Strassmeir struggled to come to terms with the many ways that Elohim City rejected him or played him for a fool. Once he had left, Grandpa Millar and the other elders told the media that Strassmeir might well have been involved in the Oklahoma City bombing. They repossessed the stone house Strassmeir thought he had bought. And he learned, much later, that the car he had purchased was "hot," because Stedeford had used it in the bank robberies. He had even been the unwitting recipient of stolen money: a $100 bill Mike Brescia had given him as a thank-you for hosting Stedeford and McCarthy over Easter, which also came from a bank job.

"I'm over it now," Strassmeir said fifteen years later, "but it took many, many years. . . . I got exiled from Paradise. The Garden of Eden is gone for me."

The FBI's interest in Elohim City was so low after the bombing that Millar came to them, not the other way around. He traveled to Oklahoma City in June 1995, after news stories began linking his community to the bomb plot, and seemed to work his way around every question the feds asked him. He remained entirely in the clear, in fact, until Richard Reyna, a defense investigator for McVeigh, started visiting Elohim City and learned it was Strassmeir McVeigh had asked for when he called on April 5.

Reyna's motivation was straightforward: if he could incriminate Strassmeir, it might diminish his own client's guilt. So he threw himself into the task, interviewing Strassmeir in Black Mountain and concluding that Strassmeir's relationship with McVeigh extended well beyond the one meeting they both acknowledged in Tulsa in 1993. When Reyna made his next trip to Elohim City, Millar fueled his suspicions by telling him that Interpol was interested in Strassmeir. Strassmeir, he said, was either a German government agent, or McVeigh's accomplice, or perhaps both. Reyna reported that Millar "did not think [Strassmeir] could orchestrate something so big such as the bombing in Oklahoma City, but . . . [he] could be depended upon to follow orders with precision."

Kirk Lyons knew Strassmeir was in trouble, because reporters started calling him and asking about Reyna's findings. The mounting suspicions dealt an immediate blow to the CAUSE Foundation's credibility, especially its efforts to sue the government on behalf of some of the Waco survivors and family members, which had earned Lyons and Hollaway unprecedented mainstream respectability. The Strassmeir controversy "put the CAUSE Foundation out of business," Lyons said. "If I ever committed actionable malpractice, it was allowing Andi to talk to Reyna."

Shortly before Christmas, Strassmeir told Hollaway he had not only met McVeigh but owned his Gulf War field jacket. "Oh come on, Andi," Hollaway remembered saying. Strassmeir became angry that his friend wouldn't believe him, and pulled a duffel bag from his closet. "There it was," Hollaway said, "with the insignia of the Big Red One on the frickin' sleeve and the name McVeigh on the front.

. . . I said, 'Holy fuck!' You can quote me on that. Holy fuck! I almost had a fucking heart attack."

Lyons and Strassmeir insisted there was no McVeigh label on the jacket, but Hollaway was absolutely sure. "The only reason I was struck dumb was because it had the frickin' name on it," he said. "All sorts of things flew through my mind. I wondered, maybe he really was John Doe Two." He said Lyons cut the tags off as a precaution. "I called Kirk right away," Hollaway recalled. "Holy mackerel, man. . . . What are the odds, what are the frickin' odds?"

Lyons and Hollaway realized that if reporters were asking questions, the FBI could not be far behind. When they received a tip, in mid-December, that Strassmeir was on a government watch list, they decided he needed to leave the country immediately, before a warrant went out for his arrest. One of their most loyal donors FedExed $7,000 overnight, and Lyons pulled Strassmeir out of the lunch shift at the Berliner Kindel restaurant, where he worked as a short-order cook. He was given just ten minutes to pack before Hollaway started driving him toward the Mexican border.

There was no time to formulate a plan. Strassmeir had recently obtained a valid passport, but it was an open question whether he could present his ID at any U.S. Customs post without risking arrest.

THE DEFENSE TEAMS STRUGGLED TO MAKE PROGRESS ON THE CASE, BE-cause the government would not hand over its witness interview reports and other crucial discovery documents. In theory, the prosecution team had an "open file" policy, allowing the defense to look at anything, but over the first eight months the Jones and Tigar teams received only a handful of lab reports, without accompanying explanations. They tried to interview key witnesses themselves, only to learn that the FBI had issued instructions telling them not to talk. The government said repeatedly that it needed more time. Stephen Jones described the attitude as "the prosecutorial equivalent of 'the check is in the mail.'"

In December 1995, Judge Matsch agreed the government needed to hand over material from the investigators more quickly and also catalogue and explain it. He would not tolerate an indiscriminate document dump, a "go fish" approach to discovery, which courts almost always frown upon.

The two sides hammered out a deal that should have clarified everyone's responsibilities. Ron Woods, the chief negotiator for the defense and Tigar's deputy on the Nichols team, had been an FBI agent and a federal prosecutor and knew the culture he was dealing with. He persuaded the government to hand over all its witness interview reports, with an index, all shorter investigative memos known as inserts, plus handwritten lead sheets and the agents' original notes. This was far from usual practice in criminal cases, and the prosecution wanted to know what it could expect in return. Woods agreed the defense would hand over its own investigative reports—another departure from usual practice—except those on the defendants themselves and their families.

In January 1996, the government unloaded an initial eleven thousand FBI witness interview reports, or 302s. The number would eventually balloon to more than eighteen thousand, and the total number of discovery materials would rise to about a million pages. Still, defense lawyers never stopped feeling the government was holding out and noticed one thing after another that appeared to be missing. Early on, Jones had to badger the chief prosecuting attorney, Joseph Hartzler, for 302s on the body shop witnesses, the Fortiers, Lea McGown, and other key players. Later, there were complaints about missing documents on Elohim City, Steve Colbern, and witnesses who saw other people with McVeigh and Nichols. The delays and omissions were always most pronounced on the issue of possible coconspirators. "It's about the worst I've ever seen," said Rob Nigh, McVeigh's number two lawyer, who had worked as a federal public defender before entering private practice. "It didn't matter how specific we were, the government's response was that everything had been provided."

The government had its own pressures: an almost unimaginable avalanche of material, close public scrutiny of its every move, and a basic lack of experience in disclosing so much. The stakes were almost impossibly high. "If you convicted [McVeigh] but did not get the death penalty, that would not be okay," prosecutor Scott Mendeloff said. "A lot of the victims were pinning some sense of resolution on us getting justice for this guy. We couldn't lose this. . . . It was like a pressure cooker."

Nigh acknowledged that, culturally, the disclosure requirements were difficult for the prosecution. But he and Ron Woods both expressed astonishment at how little the discovery agreement was respected. "We thought we were dealing with honorable people," Woods said. When asked who was least honorable on the prosecution team, he answered, cautiously: "I think that Larry Mackey and Joe Hartzler were honorable people."

By the time Danny Defenbaugh became interested in Andreas Strassmeir, it was already too late. A report from the Southern Poverty Law Center, sent to the task force on December 21 from the FBI's field office in Mobile, where Defenbaugh had recently been posted, described Strassmeir as an "associate" of McVeigh's and also appeared to disclose—the redactions make it less than clear—that McVeigh visited Elohim City shortly before the bombing. But, by then, Strassmeir had already left Black Mountain.

Two weeks later, a second FBI report based on SPLC information reported that Strassmeir was now planning to leave the country via Mexico. The bureau issued an alert to the Immigration and Naturalization Service, urging them to arrest Strassmeir on sight. "Subject is possibly armed and may be dangerous," it said. But Strassmeir slipped across the border anyway.

• • •

DAVE HOLLAWAY CALLED HIS ESCAPE PLAN OPERATION NACHT UND Nebel—a Nazi-inspired name also used by President Nixon's Plumbers. Hollaway thought it was a mistake to try to cross the border quickly, while any alert was at its highest. So he drove Strassmeir to Port Aransas, near Corpus Christi, and left him with a friend for Christmas while he returned to his children in Houston. Really, his plan was to have no solid plan at all.

Just after New Year's, Hollaway persuaded Strassmeir to give an interview to Rick Sherrow, the former ATF agent turned reporter for *Soldier of Fortune* magazine. "I wanted something on the record that would show Andi was not involved in the bombing," Hollaway explained. Sherrow did as asked, publishing his piece long after Strassmeir was gone, but he also took a photograph that was reproduced across the Internet and probably did more than anything to fuel the rumor that Strassmeir was John Doe Two. "It pissed me off that Sherrow was brought in," Kirk Lyons said. "We never heard the end on that stinking picture."

Strassmeir and Hollaway did not cross the border until mid-January 1996. They chose Nuevo Laredo, just 130 miles from Corpus Christi, but Hollaway decided that driving there would be too obvious. He told Strassmeir to book a plane ticket to join him in Houston, and then book another flight from Houston to Laredo. He also promised Strassmeir he wouldn't need to present an ID on a domestic flight, which was not true, even in the pre-9/11 era. Strassmeir cursed Hollaway as he approached the ticket counter in Corpus but somehow managed to think on his feet. He had his host in Port Aransas, Claud Brown, purchase the ticket and walk with him through security, as though Brown were the traveler and he was a friend accompanying him to the gate. Strassmeir had to show his driver's license but was not obliged to have a ticket to go with it. Once through the metal detectors, he took the ticket and traveled under Brown's name, while Brown turned around and left. Strassmeir's ID was not checked again.

In Laredo, he and Hollaway took a taxi from the airport and talked the driver into taking them through to Mexico. At the crossing, Strassmeir noticed no other taxis were in line and said he wanted to walk across the footbridge, leaving Hollaway to bluff his way past the border police. But Hollaway told him to stay put.

U.S. Customs immediately ordered everyone out of the car. Strassmeir and Hollaway were asked to produce their passports, and uniformed officers went through their luggage. "Shit," Strassmeir thought, "we're fucked." The first thing that grabbed the officials' attention were some charcoal pills Strassmeir had handy in case of diarrhea. Hollaway, being Hollaway, turned them into a joke. The officers were briefly charmed, taking him and Strassmeir for a harmless gay couple. Then they found a copy of *Playboy* in Strassmeir's bag, they weren't gay any more, and the mood turned.

Strassmeir shot a panicked look at Hollaway as if to ask, should I run for it? Hollaway shot a look back that said: relax. He later claimed he had known they would be all right, because Strassmeir's name was spelled wrong in the FBI computer files. In fact, the INS alert had the spelling right, but in Strassmeir's German passport the double "s" was rendered with the Germanic ß, which to American eyes would look like a capital B. Customs most likely ran a check on Andreas STRABMEIR and didn't come up with anything. Their passports were returned, and they were waved through.

In Nuevo Laredo, they lingered just long enough to eat *cabrito,* the local goat specialty, then jumped on a bus to Monterrey, which was in turmoil, because the local drug lord's lawyer had just been shot dead over lunch with the state police chief. The distraction was perfect for Hollaway and Strassmeir, who took two taxis to a fleapit hotel on the edge of town. Hollaway checked in regularly with Kirk Lyons, using an untraceable AT&T card. "We used the same codes that the French Resistance used in World War II," Hollaway said. "If Kirk had said, 'John has a long mustache,' I would have hung up the phone and gone underground. If he said, 'The chair is against the wall,' it would have been really ugly. As it was, he just said, no developments."

From Monterrey, Hollaway and Strassmeir flew to Mexico City, and Hollaway picked another fleapit. When Strassmeir protested—he called it "the crappiest hotel I've ever been in"—Hollaway spun the story that it was a former CIA safe house he frequented in the 1980s when he worked as a pilot making secret runs to Central America for the Nicaraguan contras. It is unclear if that story was true.

After two days, they flew to Cancun, then took an Air France flight to Paris, and from there the night train to Frankfurt. This was the most nerve-racking part of the trip, because the conductor collected their passports and did not return them until they were close to their destination. If Strassmeir's name was on a watch list, he could be arrested on arrival. It was unlikely that Germany would apprehend one of its own citizens so quickly for crimes committed in the United States, even with an international warrant out for his arrest. But Hollaway and Strassmeir were too panicked to think this through clearly.

In Frankfurt, they were met by Strassmeir's mother, who fed them at one family house and put them on a train to the principal Strassmeir residence in Berlin. Hollaway stayed for several more days, most of them in bed with the flu, before buying himself a plane ticket home. Strassmeir suspected Hollaway was just along for the ride, enjoying Berlin as the capper after Cancun and Paris. But Hollaway was also out of money for the return journey, and had to wait for Lyons to wire him more.

They never spoke again. Hollaway called Strassmeir an "ungrateful yahoo" who never appreciated how much time and money had gone into bailing him out of trouble. Strassmeir felt deeply nostalgic for Elohim City, but hardly gave Kirk and Dave another thought. "When I got back to Germany," he said, "I dreamed of the hills of Oklahoma." Knowing he would never go back, he reflected, was the greatest devastation of his life.

● ● ●

By the beginning of 1996, the Aryan Republican Army wasn't generating enough income from its robberies to justify the risk of being arrested or shot. The gang's ambition to hold up an armored truck—where, in Richard Guthrie's words, "the big *bolitas* were at"—had gone nowhere. They tried to expand, but their newest member, Michael Brescia (who had been Strassmeir's Elohim City roommate), was thought to be a liability for mishandling a smoke grenade, and he was dropped almost as soon as he was recruited. Intriguingly, Brescia went by the alias "Tim," which could have been a nod to McVeigh, if not also an acknowledgment that another "Tim" had helped the gang in the past.

The rest of the gang quickly turned on each other. Guthrie was marginalized because of his drinking and volatile behavior. McCarthy and Stedeford lost the will to carry on without Brescia, their friend and Nazi punk bandmate. Langan was torn between waging a revolutionary war and exploring his gender identity.

The final unraveling came when Guthrie tried to recruit an old friend from Cincinnati, Shawn Kenny, without realizing he was a government informant. As Guthrie drove to meet Kenny at a suburban Italian restaurant, he noticed a "secret admirer" on his tail and tried to get away. After a short chase, he slammed his Ford van, the Blitzenvagon, into a snowdrift and soon had a clutch of federal agents "piled on top of my back like they were tackling Joe Montana while he was throwing the winning touchdown in Super Bowl XXII."

Within three days, Guthrie had led the feds to Langan. A posse of federal agents moved in on an ARA safe house in Columbus, Ohio, and pumped dozens of rounds of semiautomatic weapons fire into Langan's white van. Amazingly, Langan survived; he had dived into a wooden toolbox in the back of the van and took no direct hits—although he had a shotgun shell pad lodged in his left cheek, and other injuries. When paramedics cut off his clothes to look for bullet wounds, they noticed his chest, legs, and pubic hair were shaved, his fingernails were two inches long, and his toenails bore traces of pink polish.

The Oklahoma bombing investigation showed little interest in Guthrie and Langan, which was surprising, given their earlier inquiries into McVeigh's possible involvement in bank robberies. But they were also not properly briefed. They were not told, for example, about a batch of electric blasting caps wrapped in Christmas paper, which were recovered from the Columbus safe house. These would have triggered an immediate association with the Christmaswrapped caps McVeigh had in his Spectrum when he was rear-ended in Michigan. But, as an FBI explosives expert later disclosed in court, the caps were destroyed by the Columbus Fire Department. Danny Defenbaugh did not learn this until eight years after the fact, and then only because a journalist told him. "I was definitely lied to," he told Leslie Blade of *Cincinnati CityBeat*.

Other things Defenbaugh never saw from Columbus included a driver's license for Bob Miller, Roger Moore's gun-show alias, and video footage of several properties, which, according to Langan, included Moore's and Anderson's ranch. These things did not make a rock-solid case for the ARA's association with McVeigh, but they cried out for further investigation. The bombing task force was never given the chance.

DEFENBAUGH WAS DETERMINED TO INTERROGATE STRASSMEIR, AND contacted the U.S. legal attaché in Germany about sending an FBI team to Berlin. But before he could obtain clearance, the FBI needed to alert Strassmeir about another issue—a death threat from Dennis Mahon—which slowed everything down and ultimately worked in Strassmeir's favor.

Mahon had threatened to have Strassmeir kneecapped and executed, after being told by the amateur investigative reporter J. D.

Cash that Strassmeir was a government informant. Cash's assertion was little more than guesswork, a deliberate provocation intended primarily to elicit an unguarded reaction from Mahon. And he certainly got one. "Sweet Jesus I'm fucked!" Mahon exclaimed on hearing the news. He jumped on the phone, first to Mark Thomas and Mike Brescia to warn them, then to a neo-Nazi contact of his in Germany. Through his German-speaking twin brother, he said Strassmeir should be hunted down and forced to confess before being killed.

It is doubtful whether the Mahons' interlocutor took this seriously. But Cash shared his interview notes with McVeigh's defense team, and they notified the FBI. A day or two later, Strassmeir was summoned by the Bundeskriminalamt, the German equivalent of the FBI, who briefed him on the threat and indicated that the FBI wanted to talk to him about the bombing. Back in the United States, Kirk Lyons and Dave Hollaway decided the best way to ward off a full interrogation was to release a lengthy statement in Strassmeir's defense. It worked. Somewhere between FBI headquarters and the Berlin embassy, Defenbaugh's request for a sit-down interview was turned down.

Defenbaugh next heard about Strassmeir three months later, when he walked in on two federal prosecutors and an FBI agent on the phone to him in Germany. Defenbaugh had not been informed in advance, let alone asked for approval. He also understood this was not the full interrogation he intended, just a perfunctory walk-through of Strassmeir's earlier written statement. Strassmeir later dismissed the interview as a "joke." "They didn't want to know anything," he said.

There were other signs that some of Strassmeir's official history in the United States was being rewritten. Two weeks before the prosecutors' call, the State Department reissued a list it kept of his entries into the United States. The document incorrectly said he had come in on two separate tourist visas—in reality, he had a multiple-entry visa. And this version of the document also excised the intriguing code letters "A O," which had previously appeared under the rubric "special status." These had generated speculation that Strassmeir was under some sort of official protection; now they were gone.

The Justice Department never publicly acknowledged Defenbaugh's suspicions about Strassmeir's involvement in the bombing, and, shortly before McVeigh's trial, flat-out denied their existence. "At no time," prosecutor Beth Wilkinson wrote to Stephen Jones, "did the FBI consider Andreas Strassmeir . . . a subject of the Oklahoma City bombing investigation."

AFTER MONTHS OF AGONIZING OVER A STRANGE DISCREPANCY IN ITS tally of severed body parts found in the rubble of the Murrah Building, the Oklahoma state medical examiner's office realized it might have stumbled on evidence of a possible coconspirator among the dead. Early on, the office was at a loss to match a lower left leg, with a military boot attached, to any of the known victims. Extensive DNA testing revealed that the leg belonged to Lakesha Levy, a twenty-one-year-old air force recruit now buried in New Orleans. Levy had previously been matched with an entirely different left leg, whose provenance was now in question.

This was a professional embarrassment, but also an investigative conundrum. The authorities had one more left leg than they had right legs. Who could it belong to? Stephen Jones brought this problem to Dr. T. K. Marshall, the chief state pathologist for Northern Ireland, and Marshall told him that, in the Western world, there was no such thing as an unclaimed innocent victim. Marshall had seen dozens of cases of IRA "mules" who died when bombs exploded in their laps. This looked similar to him—a conspirator so close to the source of the blast that the rest of his body simply vaporized.

Lakesha Levy's body was exhumed in February 1996, and the leg mistakenly associated with her analyzed by one of the country's leading forensics experts, Dr. Clyde Snow. Snow concluded it probably belonged to a dark-skinned white man measuring five foot six, or a slightly shorter woman. The chief medical examiner later testified that his office never found a match, but two people closely involved in the investigation said this was not exactly right. The FBI was confident the leg belonged to a Secret Service agent named Cynthia Campbell Brown, but did not want her remains tested. Doing so could raise the question of whose leg *she* was buried with—and perhaps set off an uncontrollable chain reaction of exhumations and mistaken body-part reidentifications.

Dr. Snow said he was not told about Brown. He blamed the original mistake on the evidence recovery team, saying they disregarded instructions to bag every body part separately and just assumed that the leg found next to Lakesha Levy's body must belong to her. A senior FBI source said this was far from the only such mistake. The FBI liaison to the medical examiner's office was dismissed from the task force, because, the source said, it became impossible to present detailed body-part evidence at trial. If the extra leg did belong to a coconspirator, he was never investigated, much less identified.

AT THE END OF MARCH 1996, ANGIE FINLEY TOLD CAROL HOWE her identity had been compromised. An FBI agent forgot to redact her name in a debriefing document before releasing it to the McVeigh and Nichols defense teams, and now her life was in danger from the white supremacists whose confidences she had betrayed. Finley offered to put Howe up for the weekend, but she declined. She was far from sure the federal government had her best interests at heart.

Ever since her removal from the Elohim City beat in March 1995, the paperwork on Howe had been a study in contradictions. At first, the ATF declared her mentally incompetent, but two months later, when they needed her to go back to Elohim City to investigate the bombing, they said she was "stable and capable of working in this investigation." In January 1996, Finley and her supervisor, Dave Roberts, wanted to remove Howe a second time, because they found her unreliable. But when her name leaked out, they switched gears again. "This informant," Finley wrote, "has not been overly paranoid or fearful during undercover operations."

Finley acknowledged in court that the reason she had said nice things about Howe in May 1995 was that she needed to write whatever it took to get her reinstated. Journalists and lawyers who championed Howe were equally suspicious that the negative assessment just two months earlier was prompted by a political decision to get her out of Elohim City as fast as possible.

With her name in the open, Howe started complaining about strange phone calls and people following her. Rather than trust the FBI or ATF, she associated herself ever more closely with the radical right—in an effort, she said, to rebuild her credibility. It was a highly dangerous game.

The evidence recovered from the ARA safe house in Columbus revealed an interest in bomb-making going far beyond the hoax devices the gang liked to leave behind at bank robberies. It included pipe bombs, blasting caps, timers, switches, Semtex, nitromethane and Kinestik packs. But the FBI did not see this as evidence of a possible link with the Oklahoma City bombing until Pete Langan suggested it to them.

By the summer of 1996, Kevin McCarthy and Scott Stedeford were also in custody—they were traced through McCarthy's uncle, a Philadelphia city policeman—and Langan was concerned about McCarthy testifying against him as part of a plea deal he had been offered. So Langan decided to throw a wrench into the government's plans. He told Agent Ed Woods: "You're going to have problems with your witnesses, because they have the blood of Oklahoma City on their hands." Woods responded: "You certainly have my attention now."

Langan was told that if he spilled everything he knew about

the bombing, he could qualify for a plea deal, too. Langan, though, was suspicious; the negotiations broke down and the offer was withdrawn. In the end, the government chose not to question McCarthy's credibility by looking into his alibi for April 19, 1995, or any of the other bombing-related "liabilities" Langan accused him of having. The immediate priority was to send Langan away for life, and they knew McCarthy could help them do that with his testimony. A fishing expedition to explore whether he played a role in the bombing conspiracy seemed too uncertain to be worth the risk.

The strategy for prosecuting the bank robberies became clear after Guthrie—the other key witness the government was grooming to testify against Langan—hanged himself in his jail cell in mid-July. Guthrie had described his crimes in extraordinary detail and given up his best friend, only to be told the U.S. Attorney's Office in Cincinnati would still insist on him serving thirty years behind bars. Even the FBI agents who had questioned him found this a "draconian" decision. But the prosecutors were adamant. Guthrie reluctantly signed the plea deal, and immediately drafted suicide notes to his brother and his lawyer. He even went on a crash diet to minimize the risk of his noose snapping.

According to Matthew Moning of the Cincinnati Police Department, the FBI also questioned Guthrie about the bombing and threatened him with the death penalty if money from the robberies was ever tied to the financing of McVeigh's plot. If the questioning was intended to shock Guthrie into making revelations, though, it did not work. Guthrie's lawyer, Kelly Johnson, said his suicide had nothing to do with threats from the FBI. It was a "final tweak of the nose" at the government he despised. If he harbored any secrets, they died with him.

In September 1996, the three Ward brothers and a fourth man were arrested in Oregon. A state trooper caught them filching gas from a service station, and soon established that they had stolen their car in northern Canada two days earlier. Too broke to make bail, they stewed in jail for four days, until an FBI agent turned up and interviewed Pete Ward—just Pete—about the Oklahoma City bombing. Within hours, all four were released.

The FBI agent, Kerry Larsen, did not explicitly deny paying the $60,000 in bail money, saying in an interview: "I don't know anything about it." (This was moments after his wife, who answered the phone, could be overheard saying: "Just tell him you don't remember anything.") Larsen was similarly cagey when asked if Pete Ward might have been recruited as an informant. "That would generate a lot of paperwork," he said. Asked if that was a yes or a no, he responded: "I don't want to get into who's an informant and who's not an informant."

The FBI had grounds to be suspicious of all three Ward brothers. Carol Howe had named Pete and Tony as possible matches for John Does One and Two. Pete was a tobacco chewer, and Tom Kessinger, the mechanic at Eldon Elliott's, said he remembered John Doe One chewing tobacco in an unusual way. Sonny had been brought to the attention of the Oklahoma Highway Patrol as a possible bombing suspect.

Pete Ward's interview with Agent Larsen offered further leverage for the FBI, because it contained obvious contradictions with the known factual record—about the timing of his departure from Elohim City, about the number of weapons in the community, and about his grandfather, who he said was a retired FBI agent. But there is no evidence that the bureau challenged him on any of these things.

FOR MUCH OF 1996, STEPHEN JONES TRAVELED EXTENSIVELY, SEARCH-ing for expert witnesses and alternate explanations of who was behind the bombing. Some of these trips, like his visit to T. K. Marshall in Northern Ireland, led to witness appearances at trial. Jones argued that it was almost impossible to find qualified pathologists or bomb analysts in the United States willing to take the stand, because they either worked for federal law enforcement or would not help defend the country's most notorious criminal.

Jones traveled to London (four times); to Northern Ireland, Wales, and Scotland; to Israel and Syria, Hong Kong and the Philippines. Sometimes he talked to obvious experts, like Dr. Jehuda Yinon, an Israeli bomb-trace analyst, who gave an authoritative critique of the FBI crime lab. Other choices were more difficult to understand, like the side trip he made to the Polish ambassador in Damascus, Stanisław Pawlak, to ask about Terry Nichols's contacts in the Philippines and the likelihood that he had met Ramzi Yousef. Pawlak was an odd man in an odd location for this, and none of the material about the Filipino terror connection—from him or anyone else—made it to open court. Jones himself likened the Filipino connection to the Virgin Mary's "unrevealed third secret" in her apparition at Fatima, prompting his legal team to nickname his Far Eastern trips the "Fatima Project."

Despite some complaints that he was globe-trotting at government expense, these trips did not cost a lot—around half a million dollars, out of $15 million in total defense expenditures—and were all approved by Judge Matsch. But it was not exactly clear what they achieved. One of Jones's lawyers, Ann Bradley, flew to Amsterdam to chase a report that John Doe Two was in the custody of Dutch police. He was not. Jones acknowledged that a lot of what he learned was about global terrorism, not leads related to the Oklahoma bombing. He described Yitzhak Rabin's former chief of staff, Amos Eilan, as being on the "must-see list," without saying why. He described a contact at Israel's National Police Headquarters as "someone who might have been of assistance to us." In Hong Kong, he said he visited retired CIA operatives "who assisted."

On the eve of McVeigh's trial, Jones distilled much of what he had learned into a lengthy brief, called a writ of mandamus, in which he said a foreign power, probably Iraq, brought down the Murrah

Building. This power, he went on, hired a Middle Eastern engineer with the skills to make a bomb that could be transported and detonated safely, and then contracted the job out to the American neo-Nazi movement. He also suggested the FBI was looking into a possible bombing suspect in the Philippines, whom it had not named but who had links to Ramzi Yousef. Jones wanted the government to produce more discovery material—on subjects including Elohim City, Carol Howe, Dennis Mahon, and Andreas Strassmeir—and the writ was no doubt written broadly to obtain the broadest possible results. It failed to do so.

The government's chief prosecutor, Joseph Hartzler, had already spent months attacking people who peddled "wacky theories"—a line widely interpreted as an attack on Jones. Certainly, Hartzler was as anxious to bury some of the legitimate questions about the government's role as he was to poke fun at the criticisms and alternate theories that clearly departed from plausible reality. But the more Jones chased seemingly incredible connections to the Middle East and other parts of the world, the easier Hartzler's job became. The Nichols team, after all, did not travel the world in search of expert witnesses, or engage in learned conversations with ambassadors and far-flung university professors.

McVeigh made no secret of his disapproval, describing his attorney's trips as "a waste of time, defense resources, and taxpayer money."

THE PROSECUTION TEAM HAD ITS OWN DISAGREEMENTS AND STRONG personalities to contend with. Its members had fundamentally different views of the case—from the hawks, who wanted to paint McVeigh and Nichols every shade of black, to more subtle minds, who questioned the degree of Nichols's guilt and wondered who else might be involved. They had one "knock-down, drag-out fight" over the fuel meter found in Terry Nichols's garage, with one lawyer wanting to introduce it as evidence on the grounds that it *could* have been used to mix the bomb, and everyone else arguing that it was broken and proved nothing. And they fought again, in the fall of 1996, over the question of whether to hold separate trials for McVeigh and Nichols. "It was not a merry trial team," one prosecutor said. "I was very proud of the job we did. We were very efficient. But it's not like we had fun doing it."

Instinctively, the prosecution preferred a single trial in which the guilt of one defendant could more easily spill over and taint the other. But Judge Matsch refused to admit Terry Nichols's eight hours of voluntary questioning at the Herington police station as evidence unless the trials were separated. It would be wrong in a joint proceeding, the judge argued, not to give McVeigh's lawyers the opportunity to question Nichols about what he said. But if Nichols did not take the stand, that would not be possible. Matsch offered the prosecution a choice: hold a single trial but omit the Herington testimony, or fall in line with the defense teams and agree to separation.

In the end they agreed to two trials. But it was a bitter argument, and years later Larry Mackey said they—and he personally—made the wrong decision. "If they had been tried together," Mackey acknowledged, "Nichols would have been convicted by the first jury and executed."

ON DECEMBER 13, 1996, THE FBI ARRESTED CAROL HOWE WITH her new boyfriend, James Viefhaus, and accused them of fomenting bomb plots at their Tulsa home. The agents did not appear to know that Howe had worked as a government informant, even though one of them was Angie Finley's husband. They were responding to a telephone hotline message delivered by Viefhaus, which warned of bombs hitting fifteen American cities on December 15. When the FBI agents searched the house, they found bomb-making paraphernalia, including black powder, cannon fuse, and sections of pipe fitted with "nipples," or connector pieces common in bomb assembly.

The arrests were understandable: Bill Morlin, an investigative reporter specializing in the radical right, alerted the FBI as soon as he heard the hotline message, which referred to the Oklahoma City bombing and said innocent civilians should be considered "expendable if necessary." But the evidence was problematic, because the most sensitive materials were either given to Howe by Finley to help with her undercover investigations, or had been gathered by Howe as evidence for the ATF.

Viefhaus was indicted almost immediately on charges of making threats and possessing an unregistered explosive. Howe's fate remained uncertain until March 1997, two weeks before the start of McVeigh's trial. The decision to indict her, too, dealt a huge blow to her credibility as a would-be defense witness for McVeigh, and raised the question of whether the government had pressed charges expressly to keep her out of the bombing trial. The jury hearing her case could never shake this suspicion.

IN LATE 1996, DAVE HOLLAWAY FOUND AN AGITATED MICHAEL BRESCia and his girlfriend holed up at his house, saying the feds were after him for a string of bank jobs. Hollaway wanted to know how many bank jobs he was talking about.

"I think the boys committed about twenty-six."

"Twenty-six! How much did you make?"

"About nineteen hundred bucks."

Hollaway was incredulous. "You could have worked at the CAUSE Foundation and made more money."

The FBI had been sniffing around Brescia for months, asking questions about McVeigh's April 5 phone call to Elohim City as well as the bank robberies. He had fled Elohim City after getting into a fistfight with one of the elders and was living back in Philadelphia, where he enrolled in night school and worked as a bookkeeper for a computer company in a bid for normality. But supporters of a militia leader from Alabama were waging a publicity campaign against him, based on his supposed resemblance to John Doe Two, and affixing UNWANTED BY THE FBI posters on telephone poles around Philadelphia.

Hollaway suggested he give himself up. Brescia understood, and did not resist when he was arrested in Philadelphia—on robbery charges only—on January 30, 1997. He later agreed to a plea deal under which he admitted participating in one bank robbery in Madison, Wisconsin, and helping to plan six others.

Also on January 30, Mark Thomas was arrested at his farmhouse near Allentown. He, too, seemed to be expecting the feds, and made sure the house was full of television cameras and journalists. "I was afraid," he said, "if they didn't know the cat was out of the bag, they might try to kill the cat."

The FBI spent five hours searching Thomas's farmhouse for weapons or explosives, but didn't find anything. Thomas had an old blue bus concealed on the farm, where he stashed his explosives, weapons, and ammunition, but the FBI did not unearth it for another three months. They also failed to follow up on Thomas's ex-girlfriend, Donna Marazoff, who had reported him boasting about blowing up a federal building during the day, or on Thomas's allegation that Kevin McCarthy had "taken out the Murrah Building"—a line he said he heard from Richard Guthrie.

Michael Schwartz, one of the U.S. attorneys who prosecuted the ARA, said in an interview that he was sure the bank robbers and McVeigh had "at least crossed paths." Why wasn't this link investigated? Schwartz did not answer directly, saying only that if evidence had emerged of the ARA's involvement in the bombing, they would surely have been prosecuted for it. His focus, though, had been elsewhere. "We went to bat for McCarthy at his sentencing," he said, "because he had cooperated with the government in the investigation. He was instrumental in his cooperation, and he received a significant sentence reduction. Had he been involved in the Oklahoma City bombing, we would not have done any of that."

The prosecutors felt no pressure, either, to explore Brescia's resemblance to John Doe Two. One day before Brescia's arrest, the Justice Department unsealed a brief laying out the Todd Bunting mistaken-identity theory and declaring, as a matter of public record, that John Doe Two did not exist.

McVeigh's prosecutors were nervous about relying too heavily on testimony from Jennifer McVeigh and the Fortiers, but many of the other witnesses either could not identify McVeigh or had seen things—extra conspirators, or more than one Ryder truck—that the government did not want mentioned on the stand. So the prosecutors, along with a handful of trusted FBI agents, set about making the problems go away.

They interviewed and reinterviewed witnesses, looking for weaknesses in their stories or ways to get them to change their minds. Lea McGown would not back down from her story that she had seen a second Ryder truck at the Dreamland Motel, but her son Eric conceded that his memory might not have been reliable. He took the stand; she did not. They could not sway Jeff Davis, the delivery boy who brought Chinese food to room 25 at the Dreamland on April 15 and was adamant someone other than McVeigh opened the door. The FBI thought Davis was being obstinate and grilled him for twelve hours over two days when he arrived in Denver for trial. But Davis insisted he saw a shorter, fuller-built man than McVeigh, with tousled hair and rounder facial features. He never testified.

Daina Bradley, the young woman who endured the most harrowing of rescues and lost her mother and two children, was a little easier to work with. She threatened to be a powerful defense witness because of her vivid physical description of a second man stepping out of the passenger side of the Ryder truck moments before the explosion. But she also remembered the truck being parked backward, against the one-way system, which had to be wrong—if only because it would have put the passenger side of the truck on the far side, as she looked out. This was a new observation; in her first two interviews right after the bombing, she made no mention of the incorrectly parked truck. But the prosecution ran with it, blaming her confusion on memory-loss problems associated with her medication.

They relied on similar inconsistencies to neutralize Bill Maloney, the Cassville real estate agent, who had been so precise about McVeigh's discolored tooth and might conceivably persuade a jury that the mysterious Robert Jacques, with his take-charge demeanor, was the real bombing mastermind. Jon Hersley, the FBI case agent who worked most closely with the prosecution to prepare the case for trial, undermined Maloney by arguing that the vehicle Maloney said he spotted in November 1994 was "eerily similar" to the yellow Mercury McVeigh was arrested in—a vehicle McVeigh did not buy until five days before the bombing. Maloney even said the vehicle was a Mercury in his later interviews, reinforcing the impression that media coverage had scrambled his memory. Earlier, though, he had been sure it was a Chevy Monte Carlo.

Hersley was the prosecution's go-to person to resolve many of the holes in the case. Notably, he and Scott Mendeloff made extensive efforts to convince Tom Kessinger that John Doe Two was a phantom. For close to two years, Kessinger would not budge from his contention that two people rented the Ryder truck on April 17. He could not have mistaken John Doe Two for Todd Bunting, he said, because Bunting's face was wrong, and so was his Carolina Panthers hat. But Mendeloff and Hersley won him over—or wore him down. First, they convinced him the arms and the tattoo poking out from his left arm sleeve were the same as Bunting's. Then they presented him with evidence that his recall in 1997 was inconsistent with what he told the FBI sketch artist on April 20, 1995. The face was Kessinger's last line of resistance. "That's him [Bunting]. I must have made a mistake," Mendeloff remembered him saying.

Such methods were not universally condoned by the prosecution team. "My rule of thumb is, never trust an identification that got better over time," Larry Mackey said. "I was far more ready to rely upon other evidence, without trying to hammer people." Ironically, the government never called Tom Kessinger, because they knew he had a dubious past that could cloud his credibility, and they were also worried about how solid his identification of McVeigh as John Doe One really was. The main purpose of the Mendeloff-Hersley effort was to neutralize him as a potential witness *for the defense,* all the better to keep the John Doe Two issue out of the trial. When asked about this, Mackey would not criticize a colleague. But he did say: "I think it's fair to say there was a lot of hammering. But I wasn't the one on the other end of the hammer."

Mackey was not the only one who felt uncomfortable. Danny Defenbaugh was appalled at Hersley, not least because, he said, Hersley often acted without his authority or approval. "We had to watch over Jon," Defenbaugh said. "If the prosecution said, we want that leak covered, he'd do it. He'd go around trying to stop viable investigations, especially if they involved other people in the conspiracy. Every time we caught him, I had to bring him in the woodshed to paddle him. Then he'd go right back at it."

Defenbaugh was not against going back over the evidence and plugging holes. He had a whole team he left behind in Oklahoma to take care of exactly that—making sure the FBI had an answer for any question that might come up in court, or in the media. But it was one thing to find answers, and another to distort the evidence, which he thought Hersley was doing. He was particularly exercised by Hersley's characterization of the Cassville material. "It wouldn't be the first time Mr. Hersley was inaccurate," Defenbaugh thundered. "He wasn't there, he didn't investigate it, but he's going to try to tell you that he did."

Defenbaugh even accused one prosecutor, whom he would not name, of "trying to undermine the investigation." Scott Mendeloff, speaking for all his colleagues, took vigorous issue with this. "What he is saying is categorically false," Mendeloff said. "Nobody tried to shut down anything. We had every incentive to explore wherever the leads took us, and we did. And he wouldn't know, because he was not involved in the day-to-day investigations I conducted with the case agents."

No one on the prosecution team would say more on the record. Off the record, though, one of them pointed to a lack of respect for the FBI's top investigator. "None of us did anything to undermine him," he said of Defenbaugh. "We just didn't want to work with him."

ON FEBRUARY 28, 1997, THE *Dallas Morning News* RAN A FRONT-PAGE story saying McVeigh had admitted responsibility for the bombing and took pride in the "body count" he had inflicted. Even more damaging, the source was a trove of documents the paper said had emanated from the defense team.

Stephen Jones learned about the piece shortly before it appeared on the newspaper's Web site. He tried to scare the reporter, Pete Slover, into holding it, without success. He knew this story could render his client indefensible and he briefly contemplated filing a lawsuit against the paper. But he contented himself with a waiver from Judge Matsch allowing him to disregard a court-imposed gag order and defend himself in public.

It was not easy. First, Jones told the media that the *Dallas Morning News* had been the victim of a hoax. Then he changed tack and accused the newspaper of stealing documents—legitimate documents—thereby breaking numerous federal laws. In a third iteration, he announced that the *Dallas Morning News* had perpetrated both a hoax *and* a theft. The supposed confession, written up by one of Jones's investigators, was a concocted document drawn up to secure some unspecified advantage with the radical far right and not, as he put it, a "legitimate defense memorandum." The media's response was unforgiving: the *Rocky Mountain News* accused Jones of weaving a "tangled web" that pushed against the limits of legal ethics.

The real story is not easy to discern. According to members of Jones's team, Slover had swiped tens of thousands of documents off a defense investigator's laptop. Either the investigator was careless, as one account had it, or he deliberately left a document on his computer for Slover to read while he left the room, never suspecting that Slover would download everything. It is also conceivable that the investigator or another member of the defense team gave Slover the files, inadvertently or otherwise. Jones later filed a bar complaint against Slover, who was a fully qualified lawyer in Texas as well as a news reporter, to press his contention that the documents were essentially stolen. But it was Slover who prevailed in the closed-door disciplinary hearing, suggesting he had done nothing seriously wrong.

It was also unclear to what extent the headline-grabbing McVeigh material was bogus. The most damning items in the *Dallas Morning News* piece came from write-ups of interviews McVeigh purportedly gave to Richard Reyna. But Reyna—according to both Jones and his number two, Rob Nigh—never spent time alone with McVeigh. The lawyers had no idea Reyna had written up these interviews until the leak fiasco broke.

Still, the defense had a secret it didn't want revealed. McVeigh might not have told Reyna the killer line: "We needed a body count to make our point." But he said something similar to Stuart Wright, a Waco expert from Lamar University in Texas, whom Jones had invited to talk to McVeigh on numerous occasions. When Wright asked why he blew up the building during the day, McVeigh answered: "Because in order to really get the attention of the government there has to be a body count." Beyond its frankness, this was an almost exact echo of Jim Ellison's rationale for attacking the Murrah Building in 1983.

Most likely, the rest of Reyna's memos were based on real material, too, including an admission by McVeigh that he had purchased Kinestik from Roger Moore. McVeigh himself confirmed the veracity of the material in his interviews with Michel and Herbeck. "Behind the scenes, the thinking in the defense team was that these documents did have credibility, that this was real stuff," Wright recalled. "Everything in that [*Dallas Morning News*] report looked spot-on to me."

A few days later, with jury selection looming, the *Playboy* magazine Web site posted a detailed defense chronology of McVeigh's movements, deepening the gloom in the McVeigh camp. The authenticity of the document was never questioned, although Jones argued it was out of date and far from definitive. Clearly, the defense had lost control of its confidential materials, and Judge Matsch indicated he was willing to give McVeigh a new legal team and a new trial. But McVeigh preferred to proceed, requesting only that the jury pool be expanded to lessen the potential impact of the leaks.

The McVeigh defense team would make further serious mistakes before the trial was over. But, to Jones, this was the moment the enterprise slipped "beyond redemption by even the most skilled of our craft."

{ Ten }

TRIAL AND PUNISHMENT

Stephen Jones's best hope for salvaging the case from the *Dallas Morning News* disaster was to construct an entirely new narrative in the courtroom from the moment he began interviewing prospective jurors. Jury selection, which can often seem dry and tedious to the casual observer, is always regarded as an important opportunity to shape perceptions, sound out initial reactions to the evidence, and, in a capital case, eliminate jurors disinclined to settle for a lesser punishment than death. Under the circumstances leading into this trial, it became crucial.

Jones and his colleagues were still optimistic about poking significant holes in the government's evidence and sowing real doubt that McVeigh had conceived and carried out the bombing alone; enough, anyway, to take the death penalty off the table. But jury selection caused some of the most experienced members of the team to change their mind.

Jones asked so many questions about the *Dallas Morning News* leak and the political views of the potential jurors that he antagonized as many as he won over. The *American Bar Association Jour-*

nal described his questioning as "inept" and needlessly hostile; even Judge Matsch felt compelled to comment.

Jones cracked jokes and flashed his learning and tried to find common ground, but one of his fellow defense-team members said he was ultimately "ineffective at accomplishing anything." The colleague added: "If you read through the transcript looking for evidence of a systematic process, you're not going to find one."

Jones's approach, his colleagues said, was to think that jurors with a military background and a fondness for guns would find an affinity with McVeigh. He picked a navy veteran who managed real estate, a Mormon woman from a military family, and a former liquor-store attendant who was once held up at gunpoint. He also picked an air-force-veteran-turned-business-owner, who attended gun shows and believed firearm ownership should be mandatory. He had written in his questionnaire: "Penalty of death is justified in all cases in which someone has been killed by a criminal act."

Unless Jones could somehow convince this juror that McVeigh was not in Oklahoma City on April 19, he was a surefire vote for execution. A Nichols defense lawyer whispered to Richard Burr, Jones's designated point man on arguing against the death penalty: "Dick, your penalty phase is fucked right here."

Burr chalked a lot of the problems in jury selection up to his side's inexperience. The team never challenged a ruling from Judge Matsch barring them from asking prospective jurors whether they could consider a sentence lesser than death; it made some of them feel they could only shoot for acquittal, a daunting prospect. "We knew nothing about voir dire," Burr acknowledged. "We didn't have a real death-penalty trial lawyer on the team, and we suffered from that. . . . It's a delicate matter, and it takes some real skill that none of us had."

The government's lawyers did much better at assessing the jury pool and testing out parts of the case that made them nervous. Revealingly, prosecutor Pat Ryan asked juror candidate number 947 how he would feel if he suspected other people were responsible for the bombing, besides McVeigh. Outside the courtroom, the prosecution was insisting that McVeigh acted alone and that nobody else was involved. But the team realized this would not go unchallenged and, privately, they had doubts, too. "Sometimes, perhaps, the investigation simply hasn't uncovered every last detail," Ryan said. "My question to you is, is it going to cause you any pause in returning a guilty verdict?"

Number 947 responded: "I don't think it would be a problem." His selection went unopposed.

IN THE MIDST OF JURY SELECTION, THE JUSTICE DEPARTMENT released a much-delayed report lambasting the work of the FBI crime lab, including a comprehensive takedown of just about every aspect of its work in Oklahoma City. The focus was on Dave Williams, the FBI's top explosives analyst, who was accused of failing to base his conclusions on the forensics of the bomb scene, working instead from evidence gathered by other investigators and passing off the findings as his own.

Williams concluded, for example, that the bomb was an ANFO device, but he based this solely on the ammonium nitrate receipt found in Terry Nichols's house, not on actual ammonium nitrate traces from the crime scene. He also said the bomb components were contained in fifty-gallon barrels, just like the ones found in Nichols's garage, but the Justice Department inspector general said it was impossible to estimate the size, because no measurements had been made of the curvature of the barrel fragments at the bomb site. Williams suggested Primadet was used as a detonator, but the I.G. said the only indications of this were the Primadet boosters found in Nichols's house. Williams was also accused of mishandling tests on McVeigh's knife and clothing, making it impossible to determine if they bore traces of pentaerythritol tetranitrate, a telltale sign of contact with Tovex.

The Justice Department report was a 530-page declaration of no confidence in almost every aspect of the FBI's work, in this and six other major cases. John Lloyd, a fellow of the Royal Society of Chemistry in Britain who examined the bombing lab reports on behalf of the defense, said: "It is impossible to determine from them the chain of custody, or precisely what work has been done on each item, or the reliability of the reported results."

JOE HARTZLER, THE GOVERNMENT'S CHIEF PROSECUTOR, HAD BEEN diagnosed six years earlier with multiple sclerosis, and delivered his opening statement from a motorized wheelchair. The handicap, and its visible manifestation, resonated immediately with bombing survivors. He began with the anguish of a mother, Helena Garrett, who had dropped off her sixteen-month-old son, Tevin, at the day-care center as she would on any other morning. Hartzler's rhetoric was restrained; he didn't bandy words like "callous," or "evil," or "monstrous." To elicit revulsion, he highlighted little details—notably, the earplugs McVeigh popped into his ears as he was walking away from the Ryder truck, a luxury his victims were not afforded. He promised the jury: "We will make your job easy."

Hartzler built a simple and straightforward narrative, touching on McVeigh's ideological fervor, his purchase of books on explosives, the Daryl Bridges card, the evidence tying him to Junction City and the Ryder truck, and, finally, the many indications that he personally detonated the bomb. Hartzler, like Pat Ryan, anticipated the jurors' consideration of "others unknown" and sought to detach it from McVeigh's guilt. "We don't bear the burden in this trial of proving whether there is or is not another person with McVeigh," he said.

Hartzler demonstrated his knowledge of the jury by drawing a clear distinction between people who espoused the right to speak their minds and purchase firearms unhindered, and those, like McVeigh, who used the ideals of the American Revolution to justify criminal violence. "Our forefathers didn't fight British women and children," he said. "They didn't plant bombs and run away wearing earplugs."

WITH HIS OPENING SENTENCE, STEPHEN JONES PROMISED HE WOULD not just raise reasonable doubt but would demonstrate "that my client is innocent of the crime that Mr. Hartzler has outlined to you." The statement was bold enough to elicit gasps. Minutes later, Jones was reading out the names of all 168 people who died in the bombing. Jones thought this would communicate his appreciation of the crime's enormity, but to many it came across as rank opportunism. The head of an Oklahoma City survivors' support group called it "dishonorable." A bereaved stepfather was disgusted.

For the next two and a half hours, Jones delved deep into the minutiae, with little of Hartzler's smoothness or narrative vision. The *ABA Journal* said his presentation was rambling and disjointed. He never plainly stated his strongest argument: that the government could not prove McVeigh was John Doe One, let alone say for sure that John Doe Two did not exist. Instead, he walked through every statement Tom Kessinger had made to the FBI over the previous two years at a level of detail the jury found confusing and dull.

Jones did better when he mentioned the crime-lab disaster and highlighted the prosecution's questionable reliance on the Fortiers, saying the case stood or fell on their credibility. By then, though, many of the jurors were no longer following.

THE PROSECUTION MOVED SWIFTLY THROUGH THE EVIDENCE, INTER-spersing the drier, more technical parts with carefully paced eyewitness accounts of the bombing's horrors. The Jones team had expected the trial to be a slog lasting several months, but it turned into a sprint and many of the witnesses they were hoping to grill were not called at all. "We underestimated, and underestimated grossly, the extent to which the government would rely on emotional testimony about the bombing, and the impact it would have," Rob Nigh said years later.

Pointing out that the government had no witness to place McVeigh in Oklahoma City on April 19 could not compete with distraught parents describing how they said good-bye to their toddlers for the last time. In retrospect, Nigh felt his team should have seen this coming, because the emotional material was the prosecution's "best evidence."

BEHIND THE SCENES, THE PROSECUTION WAS TRYING TO DECIDE whether to call Roger Moore. Some believed that Moore had an important story to tell; others didn't want to expose the jury to a witness with so little credibility.

The issue exposed a fault line between the hardliners on the team, who never doubted the official story that McVeigh robbed Moore and wanted the evidence aired, and pragmatists like Larry Mackey, who had their doubts about the robbery and did not believe it had financed the bombing.

The argument grew heated, drawing in Danny Defenbaugh, who thought the only place in a courtroom Moore belonged was in the dock. He felt so bruised by the argument that, years later, he would not discuss the details. Still, his side won, and Moore was not called to the stand.

THE FEDS' ONLY PHYSICAL EVIDENCE POINTING TO AN AMMONIUM nitrate bomb was a book-size chunk of the Ryder truck with painted fiberglass on one side and partially burned plywood on the other. An FBI scientist, Steven Burmeister, claimed to have found ammonium nitrate crystals embedded in the plywood side about a month after the bombing. The discovery was initially hailed as brilliant, but McVeigh's team referred derisively to "magic crystals" and asked how they had survived the heavy rainstorms in Oklahoma City on the night of the bombing. Fred Whitehurst, a whistle-blowing chemist at the FBI lab who triggered the Justice Department investigation, testified for the defense and told the court he did not believe they could have survived, because ammonium nitrate liquefies on contact with moisture.

The FBI argued that the plywood side of the piece was facing down and so protected the crystals from the rain. Burmeister said that chemicals coating the ammonium nitrate prills—aluminum, silicon, and sulfur—helped with the preservation. Whitehurst said this made no scientific sense.

The defense won a rare victory here, sowing genuine doubt about the FBI's credibility beyond the Justice Department's findings. But it made little difference, because jurors never doubted that an ammonium nitrate bomb destroyed the Murrah Building, regardless of the chemical evidence.

So it was with much of the rest of the case. Jones hammered away at the Fortiers, doing a passable job of demonstrating that they continued to lie long after they promised the FBI to tell only the truth. But the jury believed enough of their testimony, particularly the parts about McVeigh's bomb plans, to make the rest seem secondary.

THE JONES TEAM PLACED ITS HOPES, INSTEAD, ON A DRAMATIC courtroom appearance by Carol Howe. Not only did Howe's defense attorney, Clark Brewster, convince her to take the stand; he also passed on information from Howe's criminal case, which the government had withheld from discovery in the bombing trial.

The trial judge in Tulsa, Michael Burrage, was deeply worried that evidence from his courtroom could affect the McVeigh case, but he allowed Howe to fly to Denver as long as she was transported on a government plane and held in shackles. He also forbade Jones and Nigh to talk to her directly, obliging them to sit down with Brewster instead to prepare a proffer—a rundown of her testimony explaining how Mahon, Strassmeir, and Millar had talked about blowing up federal buildings and waging war.

Judge Matsch was also skeptical about taking her evidence on Elohim City in isolation, and ruled that the proffer was "not sufficiently relevant to be admissible"—a controversial decision that provoked some criticism in the legal profession.

Howe was put back on her Learjet and returned to Tulsa; Jones, who had hoped to broaden the case into the sort of terrain he had been exploring for two years, could only face the inevitable.

SITTING SILENTLY AT THE CENTER OF THE TRIAL, MCVEIGH WAS fully engaged, taking notes and exchanging comments and jokes with his attorneys. The world might have remembered his steely stare outside the Noble County courthouse, but the jurors and witnesses saw a more relaxed man, who cracked an occasional smile.

In the run-up to trial, McVeigh had some second thoughts about the bombing. He told Michel and Herbeck he was so impressed by the novel *Unintended Consequences,* a potboiler about violent revolution, in which the protagonist chooses assassinations over bombings, that he now regarded it as a better book than *The Turner Diaries.* "It might have changed my whole plan of operation if I'd read that one first," he said.

But McVeigh felt no remorse. "To these people in Oklahoma who lost a loved one," he told his biographers, "I'm sorry, but it happens every day. You're not the first mother to lose a kid, or the first grandparent to lose a grandson or granddaughter. . . . I'm not going to go into that courtroom, curl into a fetal ball, and cry just because the victims want me to do that."

Often, during the trial, he felt prickly and defensive. He hated Joe Hartzler calling him a coward and dismissing his political beliefs as a "manifesto." He winced at Jones's performance, particularly his cross-examination of the Fortiers, which departed from the script he and Rob Nigh had worked on. He had to fight off his fury when one witness, the nitromethane salesman Tim Chambers, said he had the face of a possum.

John R. Smith, the psychiatrist who examined McVeigh most extensively, said McVeigh had created a vivid fantasy life in which he saw himself as the cartoon superhero, righting all wrongs and taking up arms on behalf of an oppressed world. In court, he took solace in the role of lone warrior, defiantly confronting his uncomprehending enemies.

THE PROSECUTION HAD ONE MORE SURPRISE, WHICH THEY SLIPPED into Larry Mackey's closing statement, leaving the defense no time to respond. The subject was Robert Kling's handwriting, which Judge Matsch had disallowed as a subject for witness examination. The defense, having successfully argued against the scientific validity of handwriting analysis, assumed it was a dead issue. But the prosecution was anxious to address arguably the biggest hole in its case and provide some physical evidence, however tentative, that McVeigh was at Eldon Elliott's to pick up the Ryder truck.

Mackey showed the jury examples of McVeigh's cursive script, pulled them together letter by letter, and declared that they were a match for the Kling signature. Mackey did not cite a single authority for his assertions, which professional document-examiners found questionable, but that no longer mattered. Jones told the jury: "I can't cross-examine his closing argument." It was the lawyerly equivalent of a white flag.

In his summation, Jones was unable to counter Mackey's central assertion that he had failed to prove his client's innocence. Other than a last-ditch attempt to discredit the Fortiers—he likened them to Tarzan and Jane, swinging from one disconnected clump of government evidence to another—he steered clear of the evidentiary nitty-gritty. He quoted old-fashioned authors—Edmond Marjoribanks, George Bernard Shaw, James Gould Cozzens—unlikely to resonate with the jury. And he all but conceded that his client would be found guilty. "McVeigh," he said, "was convicted in the court of public opinion . . . before the first witness had testified, before the first piece of evidence had been introduced, even before his lawyer was appointed." The jury deliberated for only three and a half days before convicting McVeigh on all counts.

The penalty phase was equally one-sided. This was when the defense team stood the best chance of reaping any rewards from the holes they had poked in the government's case, but they were divided in their approach and had little to work with. The character witnesses for McVeigh could do little more than echo a gloriously tone-deaf line of Michael Fortier's from the evidence phase of the trial: "If you don't consider what happened in Oklahoma, Tim is a good person."

Dick Burr, an experienced Texas jurist who had helped pioneer the art of giving jurors reasons to spare the life of convicted criminals in death-penalty cases, said he could have done more—even at this stage—to talk about McVeigh's traumatic experiences in the Gulf War, his post-combat depression, and the influence of others on his fragile sense of self. But he was instructed not to delve too deeply into McVeigh's psychology and family background, or into the aberrant behavior of adherents of the radical far right. "At almost every turn," Burr said, "when we started getting to that sort of information, we got pulled back. . . . [It was] because of an ideological notion that it was somehow dishonorable to Tim to portray him as someone vulnerable and shaped by things beyond his control." It was no secret on the defense team that Burr and Jones did not get along; other members of Burr's mitigation team said—and Burr did not deny—that he came very close to quitting.

In the end, Jones conceded that his client was guilty, a stunning reversal from his earlier position. McVeigh, he now said, had "killed more people in Oklahoma City than all of the American dead in the

Persian Gulf War." The jury deliberated for just three hours before voting unanimously for death.

Rob Nigh agreed with Burr that this had not been inevitable. Ramzi Yousef, after all, did not receive the death penalty for the 1993 attack on the World Trade Center, and neither did the Unabomber; no prisoner had been executed in the federal system since 1963. "Of course it would have been possible for [McVeigh] not to get the death penalty," Nigh argued, years later. "It was a very realistic possibility. It was difficult—but doable."

Everyone on the team knew this meant that McVeigh would go to his grave without divulging the identities of any others involved in his bomb plot. He had no motive to talk now. The trial had validated him as the bombing's lone mastermind, and he was happy to take full credit.

THE TRIALS OF CAROL HOWE AND JAMES VIEFHAUS, WHICH TOOK place back-to-back at the end of July and the beginning of August, were a disaster for the government. Viefhaus was convicted of making threats and possessing an unregistered explosive, principally because Howe testified against him. And that put Neal Kirkpatrick, the prosecuting attorney, in an impossible position. How could he portray Howe as hostile to the government when she had just turned in her own boyfriend? Did this not show she was still interested in helping out, as she had when she worked as an informant and gathered up the very bomb components now being used as evidence against her?

The jury acquitted Howe on all charges. Afterward, Kirkpatrick was frustrated that the court never saw her swastika tattoo, which was always artfully covered by her courtroom dresses. "She looked pretty in pink," he said. "I got outlawyered on that case."

The defeat had a devastating effect on Howe's former handlers at the ATF. Even before the verdict, Dave Roberts and Angie Finley felt they were being set up, because the U.S. Attorney's Office refused to grant Finley access to her full files ahead of her testimony. They saw themselves as scapegoats for running a promising, potentially game-changing operation at Elohim City that their superiors were not anxious to advertise—or apologize for closing. "If it weren't for me," Roberts said of his protégée, "she'd be totally flapping in the wind." Roberts was soon targeted and transferred out of his job as resident agent in Tulsa. He retired from the ATF, against his will, in April 1998.

McVEIGH WANTED NOTHING MORE TO DO WITH STEPHEN JONES, but getting rid of him was not so easy. Jones was on vacation for several weeks after the trial. McVeigh grew impatient and called Lou Michel of the *Buffalo News* to dump all over his defense attorney. Jones had screwed up and "screwed up badly," he charged. "You would not believe some of the things that have occurred in this case. The man has repeatedly lied to me in the past." He wanted Congress to investigate.

Some of McVeigh's allegations were demonstrably false, for example a charge that Jones had lied to the judge so he could stay on the case after the *Dallas Morning News* leak. (Court records showed McVeigh had indicated his consent to proceed independently.) But that made no difference, and an outraged Jones immediately announced his intention to withdraw.

First, though, they had to endure the formal sentencing hearing. As Jones and McVeigh entered court together for the last time on August 14, 1997, they avoided eye contact and did not shake hands, as they had every day during trial. Jones said nothing on his client's behalf, and McVeigh offered only a line from Justice Brandeis: "Our government is the potent, omnipotent teacher. For good or ill, it teaches the whole people by its example." The passage goes on to say more about government law-breaking, but McVeigh stopped and said: "That's all I have." Having never spoken in court before, he now withdrew into silence as Judge Matsch condemned him to die.

Within two weeks, Jones was out of McVeigh's life. Rob Nigh

took over as lead counsel, and Dick Burr became cocounsel. Jones, though, could not resist letting McVeigh know exactly what he thought of him. In a formal communication to the Tenth Circuit Court of Appeals, he said his client "has raised the definition of the term 'ingratitude' to new meanings," with an outburst that was "small, graceless, and petty." He said he hoped his withdrawal would cause McVeigh to "come to his senses."

THE PROSECUTION TEAM PLANNED TO LEAVE THE NICHOLS TRIAL TO Scott Mendeloff, but his unapologetically belligerent manner had made him a deeply polarizing figure, and some of his fellow prosecutors could no longer work under him. That alarmed the top echelon of the Justice Department—especially now that Mendeloff's main champion in Washington, the Criminal Division chief, Merrick Garland, had left to take up a federal judgeship.

Garland's replacement, Bob Litt, flew to Denver one weekend when Mendeloff was away, so he could assess the situation firsthand. Mendeloff was not fired, but was told on his return that his appointment to head the Nichols team was now in question. Mendeloff quit to take a long-promised position in the private sector. He felt deeply aggrieved to have worked so hard on the case, and on a modest government salary, only to be abandoned by his colleagues.

Larry Mackey, meanwhile, received a phone call from Janet Reno, asking if he would consider taking on Nichols. Mackey said he had a family to get back to, but Reno flew to Denver to convince Mackey and his wife, Ann, at a secret meeting at the airport. By the time of the first pretrial hearing on Nichols, on August 6, 1997, Mackey was ready for another long round in Judge Matsch's courtroom.

FROM THE FIRST PROSPECTIVE JUROR, IT WAS CLEAR THE NICHOLS trial would be very different than McVeigh's. Her name was Niki

Deutchman, and she was a forty-seven-year-old nurse and midwife interested in energetic healing and world travel. She appealed to the prosecution, because she was a dues-paying supporter of the Southern Poverty Law Center and a convert to Judaism. But a childbirth practitioner seemed an unlikely advocate for the death penalty, and Michael Tigar, Nichols's chief counsel, could not imagine a more ideal juror.

Tigar won her over almost immediately with a learned discussion of the Lamaze method. He was already thinking ahead to evidence Deutchman knew nothing about, a book on Lamaze that had been recovered from Nichols's house. As he asked his questions and flattered her intelligence, their voir dire gave way to something akin to a Spencer Tracy–Katharine Hepburn movie.

Deutchman's questionnaire said she distrusted lawyers, so Tigar asked for an example of an attorney manipulating the system. "It's okay," he said playfully. "I can take it."

"I haven't seen *you* manipulating the system," Deutchman responded.

"We hardly know each other."

"Right. No."

This was the courtroom equivalent of love at first sight, the formation of a special bond between lawyer and juror that the prosecution would not detect until too late. Not only did Niki Deutchman end up on the jury; she became the foreman.

TIGAR AND HIS COLLEAGUES HAD THE ADVANTAGE OF WATCHING THE prosecution work in the McVeigh trial. They also had an easier client to defend, and significantly less public scrutiny. But Michael Tigar and his cocounsel Ron Woods also put on a masterful performance full of energy, purpose, and wit that embarrassed the government time and again.

Tigar was not shy about challenging Judge Matsch and argued, successfully, that jurors overtly itching for the death penalty should be thrown out by the judge (a provision that would have got rid of that obvious death juror in the McVeigh trial). He persuaded Judge Matsch to set strict limits on the use of emotional victim-testimony—which had been so effective against McVeigh. And he even extracted a rare apology from the judge for losing his temper with a jury candidate.

"All that," Tigar explained many years later, "was a way of saying to the judge: 'Everyone's looking. There's an enormous premium to do this right.'"

Some on the prosecution side felt Judge Matsch was tipping his hand and deliberately sparing Nichols the death penalty. But Tigar said Matsch could not be accused of leaning. "We argued for everything by going toe-to-toe with the other side," he said. "We earned it."

WHEN LARRY MACKEY AGREED TO RUN THE NICHOLS TRIAL, HE told Janet Reno he wanted to resolve the case on whatever terms he thought best. Although the official line remained that all the bombing perpetrators had been caught, he went to Nichols in late summer 1997 and offered him a deal in exchange for naming other coconspirators. Nothing came of it. "He was not realistic," Mackey recalled, "about accepting his own responsibility."

Privately, Mackey never stopped wondering if others were involved, and he said many of his colleagues felt the same way. "If you had said to us, 'Anybody in the room 100 percent confident that McVeigh was alone, raise your hand,' we would have all kept our hands in our laps," he said.

Mackey also wondered if Nichols really deserved the death penalty. "There's an interpretation one can make that, by the end, Nichols was withdrawing from the conspiracy," he said. "He was clearly not as committed by April 19."

In some ways, the prosecution of Nichols was more straightforward than McVeigh's, because he was tied directly to the two tons of ammonium nitrate, the loot from Roger Moore, and other physical evidence. But the government's challenge was that Nichols was being tried for murders he did not directly commit. At times, the government was tentative; at other times it came across as overconfident. The defense exploited both weaknesses to withering effect.

In his opening, Mackey told the jury Nichols "was there at the beginning, and he was there at the end." But Mackey knew Nichols was probably *not* there at the beginning—waging war on the government had been McVeigh's idea—and he was *not* there at the end, when the bomb actually went off.

Michael Tigar addressed this right away. The only evidence that Nichols was in on the plot early on, he said, came from the Fortiers. "Here is the prosecutors' problem," he went on. "Neither Michael Fortier nor Lori Fortier ever heard Terry Nichols say he was going to bomb anything, wanted to bomb anything, planned to bomb anythin. . . . All they know is what Tim McVeigh told them. And the evidence will be that what Tim McVeigh told them was a series of lies, provable lies."

TIGAR AND WOODS SCORED AT LEAST FIVE SIGNIFICANT COURTROOM victories, and each one eroded more of the jury's confidence in the FBI's evidence-gathering, and in the government's commitment to the truth. In contrast to the Jones team, which repeatedly hinted that the real story lay outside the parameters of the prosecution case, they engaged the government entirely on its own terrain and pulled the evidence apart, piece by piece.

While questioning Louis Hupp, the FBI's top fingerprint specialist, they got him to admit that 1,034 latent prints collected from McVeigh's car, his room at the Dreamland Motel, and the Ryder rental agency had never been checked against the FBI's computer databases. Hupp said the task force leadership made sure the prints did not match a list of known potential suspects, but decided that a broader computer analysis "would not be necessary." The FBI did not even do an intercomparison—and figure out how many of the 1,034 fingerprints belonged to the same people.

The prosecution was so surprised that it could not come up with an explanation. So, Tigar provided one, which went unchallenged: "They didn't care."

Next, the defense wrong-footed Karen Anderson. The government knew it would be uncomfortable to have her and Roger Moore on the stand, but felt there was no choice this time, because of the many guns of theirs that ended up in Nichols's possession. Anderson testified that, after the robbery, she found an old list of Moore's fire-arms that she provided to the FBI. But defense researchers, checking each firearm against ATF records, discovered that one of them was a Ruger mini-30 legally registered to Nichols since 1993. Tigar moved in for the kill.

"Isn't it a fact," he asked Anderson, "that this list that you pre-pared is a fraud?"

"No, sir, it is not," she responded weakly.

Anderson was not Tigar's main target here, so he left it there, but in his summation, he said: "There is only one place in the world she could get [the list], and that's because the Federal Bureau of Inves-tigation showed her a bunch of guns that had been recovered from Terry Nichols's house, told her what the serial numbers were so that they could make up this phony document and then pretend to find it and bring it in to you." The government could only fold. Wilkinson told the jury: "We are not asking you to rely on that list in any way."

Defense triumph number three involved embarrassing FBI agent Stephen Smith about the notes taken during the nine-hour inter-rogation of Nichols in the Herington police station. Ron Woods knew from his own experience as an FBI agent that any discrep-ancies between the notes and the official 302 write-ups could be fertile ground, and he asked Smith to read his twenty-two handwritten pages, critiquing him line by line and in particular noting their relative skimpiness. "This is a disgrace," Tigar thundered later in the trial. "The top law enforcement agency in the world, the large criminal case, and this is their evidence of what they obtained from the suspect?" This was highly influential with the jury.

Victory number four concerned the prosecution's attempt to tie some plastic fragments found at the bombing scene to empty barrels found at Nichols's house. Its key witness, an employee of the Smurfit plastics company named Theodore Udell, was such a disaster the defense recalled him later and forced him to acknowledge that much of his previous testimony had been incorrect. Judge Matsch threw out almost everything he said.

The government claimed that at least one fragment found at the bomb scene was made by Smurfit, and had been made according to a proprietary formula that clearly identified its origin and created a link to the barrels belonging to Nichols. The premise was dubious to begin with, since between 1992 and 1995 Smurfit made about 2.5 million barrels just like the ones at Nichols's house. Then Tigar got Udell to admit that the formula was no longer proprietary but was freely available to Smurfit's competitors.

Then came the biggest bombshell: the FBI agent working with Udell disclosed that the whole plastic-fragment theory had come from Scott Mendeloff, who circumvented the FBI chain of command and instructed him not to file any 302 reports—a violation of bureau protocol. Had Mendeloff still been on the case, this might have crippled the prosecution team.

Tigar used this moment to accuse the government of working backward from Nichols's Smurfit barrels with the intent of incriminating him. "Why didn't they test the barrels in Michael Fortier's house?" Tigar asked. "Why didn't they test any of the other hundreds of pieces of plastic? Well, it's just like Agent Hupp's 1,034 fingerprints: because they didn't care."

●　●　●

THE JURY BEGAN TO LOOK FORWARD TO THESE PERRY MASON moments. Tigar used students from the University of Texas as his research assistants, and put his former student Jane Blanksteen, the
fourth Mrs. Tigar, in charge of whittling down information and putting it on index cards, which she placed in a box on his desk. One
juror was overheard observing: "Have you noticed, whenever Mrs.
Tigar puts a purple card in the box, that means Mr. Tigar is going to
beat up on the witness some more?"

For all the fun they appeared to be having, Tigar and Woods
knew the trial was a high-wire act. Woods would turn to his colleague as they walked in each morning and say: "Time to go throw
up." Tigar was appalled by what he saw as the prosecution's desire to
get the death sentence at any cost, and later accused the government
of "some of the most unprofessional conduct I have witnessed."

One example—and their fifth significant victory—occurred
during Tigar's cross-examination of FBI agent Christopher Budke,
who bumped into Sergeant Rick Wahl and discovered he had seen
the Ryder truck at Geary Lake the day before the bombing. Tigar
and his team had looked for an FBI 302 from Budke's encounter
with Wahl in the Fort Riley cafeteria, but never found one. Tigar
asked Budke directly if he had written a 302.

"No, I did not," Budke replied.

"Did you ever memorialize—that is to say, write down—'Sergeant
Wahl told me about a Ryder truck and a pickup truck'?" Tigar asked.

"Yes I did."

This admission meant that Tigar had caught the government
withholding a document, so he approached the bench, persuaded
Judge Matsch to halt proceedings, and asked the prosecution to produce it immediately.

The document turned out to be a handwritten lead sheet, and
Larry Mackey had a copy of it in his briefcase. This sheet showed
that Sergeant Wahl had initially described the second vehicle as a
gray Chevy pickup. Only later, once it became known that Nichols
owned a dark blue GMC, did Wahl say his memory was of a dark-

colored vehicle. When the cross-examination resumed, Budke tried to save himself by suggesting Wahl had told him the pickup was "dark-colored . . . possibly gray"—in other words: both things at once.

"Sir, do you see the words 'dark-colored' anywhere on this document that you wrote?" Tigar asked.

Budke said it might not have been what he wrote down, but it was what Sergeant Wahl had said. Tigar retorted: "Is it your habit, sir, to write down something different from what witnesses tell you when you're conducting investigations?"

The broader significance of this was not the evidence—Wahl had seen Nichols's truck. But it showed that the government had never handed over a large library of handwritten lead sheets, later estimated to number forty thousand, despite promising to do so in its discovery agreement with the defense. Matsch ordered the release of about twelve thousand lead sheets after Nichols was convicted, and the rest were contested all the way to the end of his Oklahoma state trial in 2004. They included McVeigh's and Nichols's old army buddies offering ideas on the identity of John Doe Two, which both federal defense teams could have found useful.

Mackey argued that withholding lead sheets was not as serious as Tigar made out, because the differences in Wahl's testimony were insignificant. But Tigar was not satisfied. The whole point of the discovery agreement, he said, was to go beyond the federal rules of evidence established by the Supreme Court's 1963 *Brady v. Maryland* decision. "What the government agreed to hand over was independent of *Brady*," Tigar argued. "If we had just wanted *Brady*, we would not have made an agreement."

TIGAR AND WOODS ENDURED ONLY TWO REAL SETBACKS. They talked Judge Matsch into allowing Carol Howe to testify this time, but her appearance was a net gain for the prosecution. Howe, her swastika tattoo now lasered off her shoulder, said she had seen McVeigh at Elohim City in 1994, something she had not claimed before. Beth Wilkinson did an adept job of casting doubt on her truthfulness, the judge precluded any mention of her work as an informant, and she was not brought up by either trial team again.

Even more damaging was Marife Nichols, who was called to cast her husband in a positive light but never looked at him, could not remember their wedding date, and provided details of a coded letter from McVeigh to her husband indicating not only that they were in touch before Easter Sunday 1995, but that they were getting ready to "shake and bake"—a line that seemed to refer to the bombing.

Wilkinson gave as red-blooded a closing argument as she could muster, but she had to acknowledge problem areas. Tigar, in his closing, played directly to Niki Deutchman's suspicions about the legal profession. "Ask yourself," he instructed the jury, "was that lawyer guessing, does that lawyer have evidence . . . , or is that just a guess, is that a leap, is that speculation?"

As the jury retired, they were given something the McVeigh jury did not have—instructions on considering a guilty verdict on lesser charges. When the jurors returned after five days, they upheld just one of the listed charges, conspiracy to use a weapon of mass destruction. They found him not guilty of carrying out the bombing, and reduced each of the eight murder charges (one for every federal employee) to involuntary manslaughter.

The death penalty was not yet off the table, because of the guilty verdict on the conspiracy charge, but the prosecutors now faced a much bigger challenge to talk the jury into it. Tigar, in his final appeal, did something utterly unexpected: he physically embraced Nichols and called him his brother, evoking the way Joseph, in the Old Testament, had revealed himself to his brother Benjamin when he stood in judgment over him. The point, Tigar explained, was not to negate the loss of all the brothers, mothers, fathers, and sisters in the bombing, but rather to understand something fundamental about Western civilization. "He reached out," Tigar said of Joseph, "because even in that moment of judgment he could understand that this is a human process and that what we all share looks to the future and not to the past. My brother is in your hands."

Beyond the rhetorical power of this closing—perhaps the crowning moment of his career—Tigar was also addressing a particular audience, an audience as small as one. He knew Niki Deutchman would appreciate his appeal, because she was a student of Judaism. Hence the reference to Joseph, and also to the old Israelite court, the Sanhedrin, which Tigar described moving out of the Temple in Jerusalem specifically to avoid passing death sentences. Many people later complained that the entire case swung on the connection Tigar forged with Deutchman. But it takes just one jury member to vote down a death sentence, so why not court just one?

Ultimately, five jurors were against death, more than enough to bounce sentencing back to Judge Matsch. Some jurors who had advocated execution were in tears. In Oklahoma, "Hangin' Bob" Macy, the district attorney of Oklahoma County, vowed to retry Nichols on capital charges for the 160 dead not covered by the federal indictment. A lot of people were angry with Deutchman, especially after she held an impromptu news conference on the courthouse steps. "The government didn't do a good job of proving that Terry Nichols was greatly involved in all of this," Deutchman told the media scrum around her. She found the FBI "arrogant" for thinking it did not need to record its interviews; the evidence-gathering had been "sloppy." Deutchman denied that Tigar had singled her out, or that she had smiled at him every morning as he walked into court. But when a reporter asked what she thought of the defense team, she couldn't help herself. "Michael Tigar," she said, "is one heck of an attorney."

Within hours, she and her family were receiving death threats.

Judge Matsch and the prosecution gave Terry Nichols one final chance to name the "others unknown" cited in the indictment. "If the defendant in this case comes forward with answers or information leading to answers to some of these questions," Matsch said in a post-conviction hearing in March 1998, "it would be something that the court can consider in imposing the final sentence."

Nichols would not play ball. "My attorney," he later wrote, "recommended to me to keep my mouth shut because Bob Macy . . . was on the warpath to get me to Oklahoma and get me executed." And so Judge Matsch sent Nichols away for life without possibility of parole. Matsch urged the government to keep investigating the bombing but was pessimistic this would actually happen. "I don't know that there is an ongoing federal investigation," he said from the bench. "If the government can provide us with any information about whether there is, we will gratefully receive it."

Officially, the government was still investigating, but had little to show for it. Kathy Wilburn, the grandmother of two of the youngest bombing victims, remembered telling Jon Hersley, the FBI agent who liaised most closely with the prosecutors, that she was upset about the 1,034 uninvestigated fingerprints. "Kathy," she remembered Hersley saying as they both attended one of the Nichols hearings, "don't worry about that. We're not going to give Michael Tigar any more ammunition to point the finger at someone else. When this is over we're going to run those prints." It didn't happen. Hersley later told Wilburn she had misunderstood him, but she was adamant. "I'd be happy to take a polygraph test," she said.

McVEIGH WAS MOVED TO THE SUPERMAX PRISON IN COLORADO after his sentencing and housed in the same wing as Ted Kaczynski (the Unabomber), Ramzi Yousef, and Luis Felipe, a Cuban gang leader from New York. The guards nicknamed the wing Celebrity Row. When Michael Fortier and Terry Nichols showed up, they were kept in another part of the prison. Nichols wanted nothing to do with the friend who, he felt, had ruined his life. Fortier spoke to him just once.

McVeigh had not given up on embarrassing the government. His new legal team filed an appeal, raising everything, from the government's failure to hand over documents to Judge Matsch's decision not to call Carol Howe at his trial. One filing was so long Rob Nigh and Dick Burr were fined $10,000 for excessive wordiness. The appeal failed anyway.

McVeigh, meanwhile, did his best to blend in with prison life, forming perhaps the most surprising friendship with Kaczynski. They may have been from different places on the political spectrum, but they were both ideologues who believed in violence. Kaczynski was intrigued to learn about McVeigh's Gulf War service. McVeigh commented: "Yes, sir. Ironic, isn't it? In Desert Storm I got medals for killing people."

Kaczynski thought the Oklahoma City bombing had been "unnecessarily inhumane." But he found McVeigh more intelligent than he imagined, and more open to other people and other cultures. "I suspect that he is an adventurer by nature," Kaczynski later wrote, "and America since the closing of the frontier has had little room for adventurers."

In July 1999, their association came to abrupt end when McVeigh was handcuffed, chained, and flown, with nineteen other prisoners, to a new federal death row facility in Terre Haute, Indiana. This was the real-life version of the popcorn Hollywood movie *Con Air,* with heavily armed federal marshals watching nervously over the likes of Anthony Battle, a mentally disturbed serial offender from Georgia, and David Paul Hammer, a brilliantly devious con man and murderer who inspired both Cyrus the Virus, the John Malkovich character in *Con Air,* and Thomas Harris's man-eating evil genius, Hannibal Lecter.

The first time McVeigh spoke to Hammer, who was feared by almost all his fellow inmates, he bragged about the destruction in Oklahoma City, saying: "The official score is 168 to 1. I'm up." To which an unimpressed Hammer replied: "Well, I guess they can't kill you more than once."

Gradually, McVeigh, Hammer, and a third inmate, Jeffery Paul, began holding meetings they nicknamed "Klan rallies," because they were the only whites on death row. They were not friends, exactly, but they looked to each other for companionship and protection. McVeigh was called "baby killer" by his fellow inmates, and teased for his dearth of sexual experience, but Hammer was his insurance policy against enduring anything worse.

Hammer also helped McVeigh move up the date of his execution by waiving all final appeals on his own death sentence. Hammer did not want to die, although he vacillated about that for years; his principal goal was to set a legal precedent McVeigh could follow. "I'll be glad to leave this fucked-up world," McVeigh told Michel and Herbeck. If his last habeas corpus petition was turned down, as he was almost sure it would be, he wanted to close down the legal process. The problem was, he knew of nobody on federal death row who had done this before. So Hammer put in his own request. It was accepted, and McVeigh had his precedent. Later, Judge Matsch quizzed McVeigh to make sure he understood the consequences of his decision. Once Matsch was satisfied, he set the execution for May 16, 2001, and McVeigh began saying his good-byes.

Everything was thrown into doubt again eight days before the execution date, when McVeigh's lawyers were suddenly told that the FBI had found several hundred new 302s, inserts, and other documents that should have been handed over in discovery. The media, which was about to descend on Terre Haute en masse, sniffed a major scandal. The families of the bombing victims were appalled, and McVeigh let it be known he was considering a legal challenge to his execution after all. On May 11, Attorney General John Ashcroft announced he was postponing the execution for a month to give the attorneys time to conduct a "careful study" of the new material.

Rob Nigh and his colleagues raced through the new documents in search of exculpatory material they could use in an appeal. Then, two weeks later, seven hundred documents became more than a thousand, raising questions about what else might still be out there. The final inventory and analysis presented by the defense has never been unsealed by Judge Matsch, but the discovery files themselves have become available, and they make it possible to reconstruct a list of the most troubling items. These included some significant Steve Colbern material—a videotape of him brandishing a machine gun, and the letter he wrote to his girlfriend in November 1994, saying he wanted to join a movement to avenge Waco.

Other items included testimony from a previously undiscovered Dreamland guest, who never saw a Ryder truck or a Mercury Marquis. They included an entire file on Dave Shafer, an Indiana seed salesman who claimed to have heard James Nichols talking about a plot to attack the Murrah Building as far back as 1989. And they established possible links between Terry Nichols and members of the radical Posse Comitatus movement in western Kansas, most notably the entourage of a Wichita militia leader named Brad Glover. One of the 302s described a person fitting Glover's physical characteristics, who said that in February or March 1995 "someone was going to smoke some Okies . . . wait until Timmy V. does his job."

Most of the rest of the material was entirely useless, and a defense team would have had a hard time extracting much from it at trial. Nonetheless, the failure to disclose the documents earlier was taken very seriously. The government was forced to acknowledge it had failed to meet its legal obligations. Louis Freeh, the FBI director, had to explain himself before Congress. And the Justice Department launched an investigation.

The issue, as the Justice Department inspector general later wrote, went beyond complying with the rules of discovery, touching on the FBI's "troubled" information-management systems and their likely impact on future investigations. In December 2000, the FBI archivist had suggested a way of consolidating the bombing records and preparing them for long-term storage. To that end, he asked the FBI's field offices to eliminate duplicate files and send the rest to Oklahoma. When they did, agents started noticing things they had never seen before. Danny Defenbaugh, by then the FBI's special agent in charge in Dallas, became aware of the new documents at the end of January but did not raise the alarm for three more months—a delay the inspector general said was due to his "lack of attention," "lack of direction" to his review team, and "lack of follow-up" until the last possible moment.

It is not clear if Defenbaugh was as negligent as the report made out, or if he was being directed by his superiors in Washington to take responsibility. The experience clearly embittered him, especially after he was faced with getting disciplined and kicked back to Washington or retiring. He chose retirement. He also said: "Whenever they issue an I.G. report, even if it is politically charged, they always allow for the person being accused . . . [to respond] and include the response in the final report. Mine was not. I did respond. They failed to put in my response."

In his autobiography, Louis Freeh spun the episode as a triumph for his organization. "The FBI did exactly what the public should expect," he wrote. "It gave full disclosure." But Rob Nigh and his colleagues argued the exact opposite in their last-ditch petition to Judge Matsch. They itemized sixteen separate occasions when government lawyers told the court that they had handed over everything, only to be upbraided by the court for some oversight or omission or delay. On November 14, 1996, a government lawyer stated: "We have disclosed our entire investigation in this case." Nigh's brief showed that wasn't true.

McVEIGH'S FINAL DAYS SAW ANOTHER DISPUTE WITH STEPHEN JONES. The catalyst, this time, was the publication of *American Terrorist* by Lou Michel and Dan Herbeck. Several reporters had courted McVeigh for in-depth interviews, and initially he refused them all. He said his mind was changed by the publication of Jones's book

Others Unknown, in 1998, which "enraged him to the point of action." *American Terrorist* hit the bookshelves on April 3, 2001, weeks before his scheduled execution.

The first edition of Jones's book had included nothing of his interactions with his client, as he was bound by a professional obligation of confidentiality. But once he knew McVeigh was planning a tell-all book, Jones decided the attorney-client privilege no longer applied. The second edition of *Others Unknown* appeared on April 27, 2001, three weeks after *American Terrorist,* and included an open letter "to my colleagues at the bar" justifying his position. Jones said he had found as many as forty precedents to support the view that McVeigh had ended the attorney-client privilege before he did. The decision to break his silence about his client was "unquestionably among the most difficult . . . I have ever had to make," but the upshot was clear. "It was critically important," he wrote, "that the record be set straight, and who really in the final analysis could set it straight more fully than I?" Jones even called his decision an act of bravery. "To remain silent," he suggested, "would have been cowardice. How could I live with myself?"

Many lawyers were stunned by Jones's actions and by how few critical statements McVeigh actually made about Jones in *American Terrorist.* In his open letter, Jones objected to descriptions of himself as "befuddled" and "craving notoriety and the spotlight," along with McVeigh's complaint that he had failed to provide the "necessity" defense McVeigh wanted. McVeigh had said much worse in his habeas appeal, where he accused Jones of defending him for the sole purpose of writing a book.

Michael Tigar was appalled by Jones's "ratting out his client" and wrote to Judge Matsch arguing that McVeigh's execution should be stayed on the grounds of ineffective assistance. The letter has never been made public, but Tigar described it as saying: "You have a chance here not to kill this guy. Here are the reasons you ought to think about it." Jones said he was never told about Tigar's attack. "I was not aware of any such letter," he said, "and frankly doubt it was written."

Judge Matsch saw nothing in the late discovery materials to shake the validity of McVeigh's conviction, and rejected the argument, made by Rob Nigh, that a delay would create the opportunity to investigate people who helped McVeigh bomb the Murrah Building. The pressure on Matsch was, of course, enormous, and the decision he made was both legally and politically a lot safer than denying the execution that the government and McVeigh both desired. Did he have any room, really, to rule differently? "He could have," Rob Nigh opined. "I don't think he was happy about it, by any stretch."

McVEIGH WAS NOT HANGED FROM THE GALLOWS IN THE TOWN square, but his death by lethal injection on June 11, 2001, broadcast via closed-circuit television to the media and relatives of the victims, was the closest thing to a public execution in modern American history. McVeigh called it "Bloodstock."

Inside the prison, and especially in the death row wing known as Dog Unit, the first federal execution in thirty-eight years was met with a sense of unshakable gloom. McVeigh had a knack for making himself popular, and found a way of laughing and joking even about his own death. "Still breathin'," he signed off his last letter to Jeralyn Merritt, a Denver-based lawyer on his trial team with whom he had formed a close bond. David Hammer remembered McVeigh forming his hand into a noose and making a yanking gesture whenever anyone asked how he was. "I will grieve for what Tim once was, and for who he is now, because no man ceases to be a human being, no matter his actions or how horrid those actions were," Hammer wrote in his journal three days before the execution.

Many of the inmates had difficulties eating and sleeping. They were put on lockdown, and the prison authorities replaced the usual menu of cable television programs with comedy films to alleviate the tension. Hammer, a diabetic, gave himself an insulin overdose the night before McVeigh's death. "I did so hoping to die," he later wrote.

McVeigh was wheeled into the execution chamber looking significantly thinner than he had at trial. Hammer said he deliberately undernourished himself so he would look like a concentration camp victim. He stared the same hard stare the country remembered from his perp walk outside the Noble County courthouse six years earlier, and held it as the poisonous chemicals pumped into his leg. He left behind the poem "Invictus," by William Ernest Henley, to speak for him. "I am the master of my fate; I am the captain of my soul," the last lines ran—an echo of McVeigh's belief that his execution was something he was inflicting on the government, not the other way around. He died, unflinching, with his eyes open.

The bereaved in Oklahoma City expressed satisfaction that he was gone. President George W. Bush, who had approved a record number of executions as governor of Texas, said the bombing victims had been given "not vengeance, but justice." He then uttered a line that indeed credited McVeigh with being captain of his soul. "One young man," Bush said, "met the fate he chose for himself."

Rob Nigh was given the excruciatingly difficult task of paying homage to the moment, and to the devastation that the bombing wrought, while at the same time finding appropriate expression for the many misgivings he felt about the way the story had ended. "To the victims in Oklahoma City, I say that I am sorry that I could not successfully help Tim to express words of reconciliation that he did not perceive to be dishonest," he said. "I do not fault them at all for looking forward to this day or for taking some sense of relief from it." But he also questioned what kind of justice had been done exactly. "We have made killing a part of the healing process," he said. "In order to do that, we use such terms as 'reasoned moral response.' But I submit there's nothing reasonable or moral about what we have done today."

This was not his client's perspective, but it was an eloquent plea that went beyond simple opposition to the death penalty. Nigh's words were an appeal to light over darkness, to truth over obfuscation and lies, to the importance of seeking a fuller understanding of the bombing in all its complexity, not just settling for a distorted account and hoping for closure from one more cold-blooded killing. Nigh knew the story of the bomb plot better than anyone, because McVeigh had told him things he hadn't shared with anybody else. He knew much more than what had come out in court, or in books, or in the wilder speculations in cyberspace. Nigh's knowledge, though, could not be passed on. McVeigh was his client, and this time, attorney-client privilege would extend beyond the grave.

McVeigh's secrets died with him. The rest of us can only seek to reconstitute them from the broken pieces that he and his terrible act left behind.

VENGEANCE AND TRUTH

"I want him dead! I want his family dead! I want his house burned to the ground! I wanna go there in the middle of the night and I wanna piss on his ashes!"
—ROBERT DE NIRO AS AL CAPONE
IN *THE UNTOUCHABLES* (1988)

Almost four years after McVeigh's execution, and close to ten years after the bombing, Terry Nichols revealed the secret of the missing explosives under his house in Kansas. He did not tell a lawyer, or the FBI; rather, he confided in his two closest cell mates in the Supermax prison.

Gregory Scarpa Jr. was a member of New York's Colombo crime family, forever on the lookout for information to trade. Nichols saw him as someone to whom you give a scrap of truth and "he will twist it, weave in lies, and fabricate a story that sounds very convincing." Tito Bravo was a man of equally low scruples, whom Nichols trusted more but whom Scarpa described as "an almost pathological rat, a double-crosser who would say anything to anyone for a ham-and-cheese sandwich." The three of them were locked down in individual soundproof cells for twenty-three hours a day, but they managed to communicate through the plumbing.

Nichols told Scarpa he could produce evidence that might get Roger Moore arrested for involvement in the bombing, but he was concerned the feds might destroy it if they got to it first. Then he hinted he knew the whereabouts of explosives left over from the Oklahoma City plot. Scarpa promised Nichols $450,000 for his information. An overtrusting Nichols believed him and made arrangements for Scarpa to send the money to his church minister. Soon, he told Scarpa the full story of the boxes beneath his old crawl space in Herington.

Scarpa contacted Stephen Dresch, an investigator he knew in Michigan, and said he had a tip about an imminent bomb threat. Dresch guessed that Scarpa must be talking about Terry Nichols and, suspecting that a tenth-anniversary plot might be in the works, notified the FBI and the office of William Delahunt, a Massachusetts congressman on the Homeland Security subcommittee.

That was on March 1, 2005. On March 3, an FBI polygraph expert flew to Colorado and talked to Scarpa, and determined that he was not credible. Next, Scarpa turned to a forensics expert named Angela Clemente. She and Dresch came to the Supermax and were given astonishing detail on the Herington cache—the boxes' exact dimensions, a description of the contents, even specifics on the insulating wrap. According to Scarpa, Nichols was talking because he, too, was worried about an anniversary attack and did not want any more blood on his hands. Nichols later said he was worried about no such thing.

The only thing Scarpa wouldn't disclose was the address where the materials could be recovered; he wanted a deal first. Dresch, however, found the address on his own, using his Homeland Security contacts. They agreed on a plan: Homeland Security would recover the materials, and Scarpa would be appropriately credited. But when Dresch traveled to Herington, he found no sign of government or law enforcement presence. The deal had gone sour.

Dresch's next move was to cajole the FBI into looking under the crawlspace, the exact outcome Nichols did not want. The feds did nothing until two big news stories—Pope John Paul II receiving the last rites and Terri Schiavo, the brain-dead Florida woman being taken off life support—broke on the same day, giving them the cover they wanted from the media. After digging deep enough to see that the tip was valid, the FBI called in a bomb squad from Topeka and worked all night to recover everything.

Nichols ended up with nothing for his disclosure. The Roger Moore fingerprints never materialized, and neither did the $450,000. Still, the episode was significant, because it marked the first time Nichols admitted his role in the bomb plot. By scrambling the information Nichols was interested in pushing, Scarpa did everyone a grave disservice.

The one public official who took significant action was Dana Rohrabacher, a conservative Republican congressman from southern California, who visited Nichols in June 1995 and wrote a report for the House International Relations Committee. Rohrabacher's focus, though, was on establishing a foreign connection to the Oklahoma City bombing, which did not interest Nichols. "I don't believe Congressman Rohrabacher will be much help," Nichols wrote afterward. In 2006, Rohrabacher offered to see Nichols again. "If he's only interested in a Philippine connection," Nichols recounted, "tell him not to waste his time, because there is none."

Nichols had many other valuable things to say about the Oklahoma City bomb plot. His writings, to the authors of this book and to others, went into great detail about his relationship with McVeigh, how they built the bomb, and other matters. Rohrabacher missed the chance to glean that information, as did the FBI, which wanted to know if he was willing to name names of possible coconspirators other than Roger Moore, in whom they continued to show no interest.

Nichols might have spoken out a lot sooner if it had not been for the determination of the Oklahoma authorities to retry him after he was spared the death penalty in federal court. Bob Macy, Oklahoma County's gung-ho district attorney, wanted to see him executed at all costs and, in late 1998, indicted him on 160 counts of first-degree murder, plus one count of manslaughter of an unborn fetus, later upgraded to a 161st murder charge.

In May 1999, Macy had his funding for the prosecution pulled and redirected to tornado victims. Eighteen months later, Macy was ordered off the case altogether after a judge blasted him for "blatant violation of the rules of professional conduct," including breaking a gag order and showing unseemly enthusiasm for killing Nichols.

Just when prosecution seemed to be off the table, Macy's successor, Wes Lane, surprised everyone by announcing that he wanted to go ahead. Nichols's talented state defense team strove to carry on where Michael Tigar and Ron Woods had left off, accusing the government of withholding documents and failing to conduct an adequate investigation into other suspects. One of the new lawyers, Mark Earnest, did some remarkable legwork to establish that the FBI had researched phone calling cards used by Pete Langan and the other bank robbers and checked for possible connections to the bombing. The ARA had made a striking number of calls from a rest area on I-35, just north of the spot where Charlie Hanger arrested McVeigh, suggesting—at least to Earnest, and perhaps also to the FBI—that the robbers might have been waiting to pick him up there.

Judge Steven Taylor dismissed the ARA connection as "melodrama and hyperbole" and would not allow Langan, Mark Thomas, and other ARA witnesses to testify. The jury in rural McAlester, ninety miles south of Tulsa, took just five hours to conclude that Nichols was guilty of first-degree murder on all counts. When it came to the penalty phase, however, they deadlocked. No more than eight jurors voted for the death penalty. Some were impressed that Nichols had embraced Christianity in prison and, as they heard it, prayed so hard during the trial he wore out four Bibles. Others thought a life sentence was worse punishment than death for a man who now believed he was going to heaven. The effort to "correct" the outcome of the federal trial proved futile, and cost Oklahoma taxpayers—who had consistently expressed their misgivings—more than $10 million.

Even before it was over, Terry Nichols wrote to Attorney General John Ashcroft, offering to tell everything he knew if the Justice Department would take his allegations against Roger Moore seriously. The letter was more threatening than respectful. "If you want this to work in a positive way," Nichols wrote, "then I strongly suggest that you contact me as soon as possible." Ashcroft never responded. That's when Nichols wondered whom else he could tell about the whereabouts of the explosives boxes.

For ten years, Nichols did not tell his family that he helped McVeigh build the bomb. It was cathartic when he finally confessed to the crime, but also a shock to those he loved the most. Josh, whose young adult life was already marked by alcohol and addiction, was deeply affected. Josh had always defended his father, and now his worst fears about him were confirmed. For Terry, the knowledge that he had betrayed his family weighed almost as heavily as the 168 people who died as a consequence of his actions.

THE VETERAN ATF INVESTIGATOR JIM CAVANAUGH HAD A SAYING HE would share whenever he worked high-profile cases: "We've got to run this lead *De Niro—dead.*" It was a reference to *The Untouchables,* and expressed the idea that law enforcement agents should keep digging until they are quite sure there is nothing left to check, second-guess, or look at from another angle. "It's a failure not to do that," Cavanaugh said. "People will always be tempted to say about one piece of information or another: 'We don't need it for the prosecution.' The way it worked on a lot of these cases, we would have to run all these leads out, even if we thought we'd come to a dead end. And that's how it should be."

The "De Niro–dead" principle operated at many levels in the Oklahoma City investigation. At Danny Defenbaugh's behest, agents took copies of more than 13 million hotel and motel records to track McVeigh's movements. The bureau impounded more than 6 million rental records from Ryder, covering every vehicle rented nationwide between January 1, 1994, and the day of the bombing. They ran 160,000 license plates. The FBI crime lab shipped the entire counter from Eldon Elliott's body shop to headquarters. A pay phone outside a McDonald's in Junction City was shrink-wrapped, uprooted, and opened so forensics experts could check every coin inside for fingerprints.

But they may also have lost sight of the big picture. Investigators never made more than a token effort to investigate Elohim City— much less follow through until every lead was De Niro–dead. They did not touch Louis Beam, despite indications he had knowledge of a bomb plot and of the young man who would carry it out. They did not properly investigate the historical connection between Jim Ellison, Wayne Snell, the 1983 plot to blow up the Murrah Building, and Grandpa Millar. Snell wound up dead, but far from De Niro–dead.

The feds talked to Andreas Strassmeir, eventually, but challenged him on nothing of significance. The same was true of Grandpa Millar. They did not question Dennis Mahon, even though they had material for an indictment against him. They gave a free pass to the Ward brothers, even though their movements around the time of the bombing were suspect, and Pete and Tony Ward were identified as possible John Does One and Two.

The feds showed little interest in running down the Aryan Republican Army bank robbers, because they were more interested in Kevin McCarthy's testimony against his fellow gang members than they were in investigating his two bogus alibis for April 19. The investigators who pursued the robberies did not share crucial evidence with the bombing task force, sabotaging any chance of making a meaningful link between the two cases.

The prosecution could never prove that McVeigh rented the Ryder truck in person, or that he—or his surrogate—had done so alone. Whatever one thinks of Todd Bunting and the theory of eyewitness mis-association presented at trial, the story left room for objections; it was not De Niro–dead. Prosecutors could not explain why two dozen witnesses had seen McVeigh in Oklahoma City on the morning of the bombing with at least one other person. They could not explain the brown Chevy pickup sightings, or the second Ryder truck seen at the Dreamland Motel on Easter Sunday, or the voices heard in McVeigh's room while he was in Oklahoma City dropping off the Mercury, or the identity of the man who took the Chinese food delivery the night before. The multiple suspicions about Roger Moore were simply left hanging, making him perhaps the luckiest man in the entire investigation.

One of the prickliest problems with the government's case was its failure to explain how McVeigh and Nichols could build a huge destructive device without advanced explosives training and be confident it would go off. The government claimed the pair learned from books, fooled around on James Nichols's farm in Michigan, and conducted experiments in Arizona once they had begun to assemble their bomb components. But the narrative was still missing huge chunks. The government had McVeigh detonating a pipe bomb—nothing to do with ammonium nitrate—in the desert outside Kingman in the summer of 1994, with modest results. Then, a few months later, they had him mixing ammonium nitrate and nitromethane in a gallon-size plastic jug and setting that off, too. According to Terry Nichols, the experiment was a failure. How did the bombers go from amateur hour in October 1994 to mass murder on a horrific scale six months later? The official record is silent.

The missing explosives were never properly run down, either.

Since the FBI crime lab could not figure out the composition of the bomb, it was difficult to know which of the known components assembled by McVeigh and Nichols were used to destroy the Murrah Building and which were left over. The topic was certainly a cause for concern: Defenbaugh pushed unsuccessfully for an eleventh-hour FBI interview with McVeigh to ask him about it. According to Terry Nichols, he and McVeigh exhausted the supply of ammonium nitrate and nitromethane, but not the Tovex or the blasting caps. Nichols said they used just one case of Tovex to mix the bomb, leaving another seven and a half cases unaccounted for, along with about 60 Primadet nonelectric blasting cap systems and 340 electric blasting caps. Where did this material end up?

This book has examined how institutional failure, lack of nerve, turf wars, and a political imperative to prosecute the Oklahoma City bomb plot swiftly and cleanly all impeded the FBI and the other investigative agencies from meeting the standards expected of them. Ironically, by the time McVeigh and Nichols went on trial, the leaders of each prosecution team, Joseph Hartzler and Larry Mackey, were more willing to acknowledge the possibility of other coconspirators than the FBI. This wasn't just about serving justice; it was about the FBI's need to defend its reputation, at the expense of the truth.

"Two evil men did this and two evil men paid," Frank Keating, the FBI agent who became governor of Oklahoma, declared in 2004. That's the story the bureau has told itself for fifteen years.

McVeigh certainly helped the FBI make this argument. His desire to be recognized as the lone mastermind of the bombing converged with the FBI's desire to say that nobody else was involved. In 2002, Louis Freeh wrote in his autobiography: "It was Timothy McVeigh himself . . . who persuaded me that the conspiracy didn't go beyond what we had uncovered." Freeh was too smart not to see this as an argument of convenience as much as investigative fact. But he was not the only one who made it. "Reading the interviews with McVeigh [in *American Terrorist*], I was astounded how close to the truth we were," said Weldon Kennedy, the FBI's first on-scene commander who later served as Freeh's deputy. How astounding was it, though, that McVeigh dovetailed his account with the government's? He was familiar with the official narrative of the bombing, having read all the discovery materials and sat through more than a month of court testimony. Was it not *more* astounding to think that the perpetrator of the worst domestic bombing in American history—a man who lied to his friends, made sexual advances to their wives, was prone to self-aggrandizement, and thought the bereaved of Oklahoma City should stop whining and just get over themselves—would give a book-length account of his crimes and tell nothing but the truth?

There is, as both Rob Nigh and Michael Tigar intimated, a fundamentally antithetical relationship between vengeance and truth. One has a tendency to block out the other. Nobody can fault the bombing victims for the desire to pin their grief and rage and loss on readily identifiable culprits, and to see those culprits punished swiftly and severely. But when law enforcement agencies and higher government institutions allow that same emotional response to guide their actions—or, worse, allow themselves to exploit the victims' raw emotions to cover up mistakes and lash out dishonestly at their critics—then the truth suffers, and with it the most salient qualities of a civilized society.

SOURCES

Prologue

Matsch quote from a March 25, 1998, post-conviction hearing in the Nichols federal trial; quote from Kerry Noble, Jim Ellison's sidekick in the 1980s paramilitary sect the Covenant, the Sword, and the Arm of the Lord (CSA), from a never-released documentary made by a production company named MGA (Made for General Audiences); transcript of interview, dated March 22, 1999, obtained by authors. Ashcroft turned down FBI requests for $50 million in new counterterrorism funds the day before 9/11; see Richard Clarke, *Against All Enemies*, p. 254, and Dan Eggen, "Ashcroft's Pre–9/11 Priorities Scrutinized," *Washington Post*, April 13, 2004. He faced at least two high-profile lawsuits, *Raich v. Ashcroft* and *Santa Cruz v. Ashcroft*, because of his opposition to California's medical marijuana laws. Infamously, Ashcroft paid $8,000 to cover up a nude female statue, the *Spirit of Justice*, in the Great Hall of the Main Justice building in Washington. "Curtains for Semi-Nude Justice Statue," BBC News, January 29, 2002. Janet Reno on deadbeat dads, see Justice Department news release of December 22, 1994, "Attorney General Reno Announces Plan to Crack Down on Dead-Beat Parents Who Fail to Pay Child Support"; Danny Defenbaugh said in an April 5, 2011, interview (Gumbel) that this priority was met with consternation at the FBI, because it tied up resources the offices wanted to expend on serious crime. Reno did not respond to interview requests. The Department of Homeland Security study, prepared in coordination with the FBI, is *Rightwing Extremism: Current Economic and Political Climate Fueling Resurgence in Radicalization and Recruitment*, published April 7, 2009. Most controversial was its finding that neo-Nazis, skinheads, and other white supremacists were learning combat skills in the army and that "rightwing extremists will attempt to recruit and radicalize returning veterans in order to exploit their skills and knowledge derived from military training and combat. . . . The willingness of a small percentage of military personnel to join extremist groups during the 1990s because they were disgruntled, disillusioned, or suffering from the psychological effects of war is being replicated today." Jonathan Franzen, *Freedom*, p. 445; James William Gibson,

Warrior Dreams, p. 12.Sign on prosecutors' door related by Larry Mackey, interview (Gumbel), April 28, 2011; Joe Hartzler remembered the sign reading: "Don't hide the crime in the clutter," interview (Gumbel), June 2, 2011. Keating quoted in Jon Hersley, Larry Tongate, and Bob Burke, *Simple Truths,* p. 10; Michael E. Tigar, *Nine Principles of Litigation and Life,* p. 161; the last two sentences take their inspiration from a similar sentiment expressed by Michael Tigar in his opening argument in the Nichols trial on November 3, 1997. Tigar said: "To the living, we owe respect. To the dead, we owe the truth."

Chapter 1

EOD team:

Interview (Gumbel and Charles) with confidential source familiar with Mogg and Humphries, May 13, 2010; Mogg partial travel records released by Defense Finance and Accounting Service, letter to Roger Charles, February 10, 1998; Mogg phone interviews with Don Devereux, June 6, 2001, and Mary Mapes, June 17, 2001, graciously shared with authors. Mogg's words to Devereux, when asked what he was doing in Oklahoma City, were: "You'll have to ask the FBI about that." A number of senior FBI agents responsible for domestic security or for Oklahoma said they knew nothing about the EOD team or its mission.

McVeigh and Nichols meet to build the bomb:

Terry Nichols handwritten account, "Morning of April 18, 1995," November 29, 2007; Nichols's written answers to author questions, March 20, 2010; McVeigh's version in Lou Michel and Dan Herbeck, *American Terrorist,* pp. 214–20.

Wayne Snell predicting a bomb:

Prison official Alan Ables's interview with Canadian Broadcasting Service *Fifth Estate* program, broadcast October 22, 1996. Also quoted in Howard Pankratz, "Blast blamed on revenge attack linked to militant's execution," *Denver Post,* May 12, 1996, and in John Solomon, "Government had information suggesting Oklahoma City attack weeks before McVeigh struck," Associated Press, February 12, 2003; Ellison quoted in Kerry Noble, *Tabernacle of Hate: Why They Bombed Oklahoma City,* pp. 134–35.

Walter Reed Army Institute of Research:

Interviews (Charles) with Karyn Armstrong and Adolph Januszkiewicz, February 6, 1998. Dennis Dutsch, Governor Frank Keating's chief of security, said he was sure the query did not originate with his office. The governor's office would never go through the Pentagon for a request of this nature. (Interview with Gumbel, June 22, 2011.)

Steam-generating plant incident:

Trigen log quoted in Richard Sherrow, "Aftershocks and Subterfuge: Cloud of Doubt Lingers Over Government Cover-Up," *Soldier of Fortune,* April 1996; Glenn Wilburn's conversations with Charles Gaines and Harvey Weathers quoted in Kathy Sanders, *After Oklahoma: A Grieving Grandmother Uncovers Shocking Truths About the Bombing . . . and Herself,* pp. 89–90; Wilburn also interviewed by Tom Jarriel of ABC's *20/20,* November 18, 1996. His account is corroborated by Harvey Weathers in his FBI FD-302 interview of May 15, 1996, file no. 14935, and by Oklahoma City fire chief Gary Marrs in his FBI FD-302, May 21, 1996, file no. 15006. The sarin gas alert story is also from Marrs. See also Judy Keen, "An Army of Agents, Experts Following Hundreds of Leads," *USA Today,* April 20, 1995.

McVeigh and Nichols at Geary Lake:
Terry Nichols's handwritten account, "Morning of April 18, 1995," op. cit. McVeigh's line about sacrificing himself if necessary, from Nichols's answers to author questions, February 21, 2011. McVeigh's account, from Michel and Herbeck, *American Terrorist,* pp. 216–20; expert opinion on explosives: interviews with, among others, Special Agent Tristan Moreland of ATF, November 5, 2009, and February 4, 2010 (Gumbel), and noted explosives expert and government consultant Pharis E. Williams, September 21, 2010 (Gumbel and Charles, by e-mail); Andrew Macdonald [William Pierce alias], *Hunter,* pp. 176–79.

Links between Snell, Beam, and others, etc.:
Jack Knox interview (Gumbel), May 10, 2010; Bruce Campbell interview (Gumbel), October 21, 2009; Cheri Seymour interview (Gumbel), July 22, 2009; confidential informant reporting Beam meeting Mary Snell in April 1995, contained in January 29, 1996, FBI insert, file no. E 7453; Mary Snell, interviewed by the FBI on August 12, 1995, FD-302, file no. 9384, said her husband had no advance knowledge of the bombing; FBI interview with Roy L. Byrd, Florence, Arizona, January 25, 1996, FD-302, file no. 13856; Bill Buford interview (Gumbel), May 11, 2010; Mary Snell letter to Michigan militia, quoted in Daniel Levitas, *The Terrorist Next Door: The Militia Movement and the Radical Right,* p. 5.

Odd departures from Elohim City:
Millar quoted in interview with MGA documentary crew, May 23, 2000; Andreas Strassmeir, interviews (Gumbel), June 30–July 3, 2010; "Field marshal of Elohim City" line from Dave Hollaway interview (Gumbel), July 10, 2010; information on Aryan Republican Army robberies/meeting to disband from FBI FD-302 interview with Richard Lee Guthrie, case no. 91A-CI-63809 (MC-124), dated March 4–15, 1996, esp. p. 17 for this time frame; and also Guthrie's unpublished handwritten prison memoir, *The Taunting Bandits,* aka *Banks for the Memories,* esp. p. 155; on Thomas getting money from the Des Moines robbery and giving Stedeford a fake driver's license, see Mark S. Hamm, *In Bad Company: America's Terrorist Underground,* p. 221; Stedeford's and McCarthy's movements, see McCarthy's FBI FD-302 interviews, June 17, 1996 (not in the bombing case file), and September 20, 1996; Mark and Nathan Thomases' movements, per FD-302 interview with Mark Thomas, April 17, 1997 (not in the bombing case file). Information on Nathan Thomas at Elohim City from Carol Howe, see ATF report of investigation for November 1994, op. cit.; Sonny Ward leaving Elohim City for elsewhere in Oklahoma, then Valdosta, Georgia, see FBI FD-302 interview with Oklahoma Highway Patrol trooper John Haynie, April 28, 1995, file

no. 389; Priscilla Ward's Sunday-school teacher Kennilee Mooney, see her FBI FD-302, file no. 14818, April 27, 1996; on Pete Ward and the Ward parents, see FBI FD-302 with Pete Ward, September 23, 1996, file no. 16069.

Ken Stern report:
Militias: A Growing Danger, published in *Issues in National Affairs,* vol. 5, no. 1 (New York, American Jewish Committee, 1995); cover memo provided to Gumbel by e-mail, December 23, 2009, along with information on researcher group pooling information; LaPierre and Liddy quoted in Kenneth S. Stern, *A Force Upon the Plain,* p. 222.

Dave Hollaway's strange phone call:
Dave Hollaway interview (Gumbel), May 6, 2010, FBI FD-302; interview with Hollaway, August 12, 1996, file no. 15886; Kirk Lyons interviews (Gumbel), March 23, 2010 and May 27, 2010.

McVeigh traveling from Kansas to Oklahoma:
McVeigh's account told to defense lawyer Jim Hankins in May 1995 and quoted in a confidential defense memo dated January 22, 1996, written by Amber McLaughlin and Bob Wyatt. The memo was first obtained by freelance reporter Ben Fenwick and subsequently released by producer Martin Smith of PBS's *Frontline.* See http://www.pbs.org/wgbh/pages/frontline/documents/mcveigh/; J. W. Odom, interviewed by the FBI, April 28, 1995, file no. 17075; Ingrid Mae Willmurth, interviewed April 24, 1995, by Agent Mario Reyes of ATF, see FBI FD-302, file no. 207; Cattle Baron's Steakhouse sighting and Jackie's Farmers Store sighting cited in Arnold Hamilton, "Ryder Truck, Trail of Food Take Bomb Inquiry Along Back Road; Reported Sightings of Suspects Studied Up and Down U.S. 77," *Dallas Morning News,* November 27, 1995.

Wilburn household breakfast:
Glenn and Kathy Wilburn, interviewed by Tom Jarriel of ABC's *20/20,* November 18, 1996. Quotes taken from ABC internal transcript.

Bill Grimsley and the bomb squad truck:
Grimsley FBI FD-302, file no. 15426, dated July 8, 1996; FBI interviews, file nos. 11607 and 11735, with bomb squad captain Bob Heady and his squad, dated November 7, 1995; Heady reinterviewed May 20, 1996, file no. 15002; witnesses include Dan Adomitis, interviewed by Tom Jarriel of ABC News, November 19, 1996 (information taken from raw ABC transcript); J. D. Reed, who wrote an account titled "Wednesday, April 19, 1995, A Black Day for Us All," in *Workin' Interest,* a company newsletter of Parker & Parsley Petroleum USA Inc., vol. 96, issue 3; and Norma Joslin, quoted in Laura Vozella, "Pair See Conspiracy in Blast; Government Tipped Off, Couple Say," *Fort Worth Star-Telegram,* March 31, 1996. Joslin's insistence on being driven into underground garage for grand jury hearing taken from notes (Charles) from her meeting with Oklahoma State Representative Charles Key, October 3, 1997; Sheriff J. D. Sharp denying presence of bomb squad downtown to local Oklahoma media cited in Petition for Writ of Mandamus of Petitioner-Defendant, Timothy James McVeigh and Brief

in Support, filed in the Tenth Circuit Court of Appeals on March 25, 1997; bomb squad in blue jeans, quoted in *NBC Extra,* March 19, 1997; interviews (Gumbel) with bomb squad members Kyle Kilgore and Stanley D. Brown, September 21, 2010.

Bomb squad/sniffer dogs:
Renee Cooper FBI FD-302, file no. 11474, November 22, 1995; see also Sanders, op. cit., pp. 66–67; private investigator Claude Criss interviewed by Tom Jarriel of ABC News, November 19, 1996; interview (Gumbel), August 18, 2010; Debbie Nakanashi told congressional investigator John Culbertson that her bosses and the U.S. Attorney's Office had put limits on what she, as a federal employee, could say in court. In her exact words: "They also said that if I had seen, like, for instance . . . if I had noticed bomb dogs on the outside of the building as I was coming to work on the day of the bombing, that was something that I could not testify as to that I had seen that." The interview was recorded and entered into the congressional record July 27, 2000, at a hearing of the House Subcommittee on Commercial and Administrative Law. See http://commdocs.house.gov/committees/judiciary/hju67342.000/hju67342_0.htm; Randall Yount interview (Gumbel), September 30, 2010; John Haynie, FBI FD-302, dated May 20, 1996, file no. 15004. Surveillance training explanation from his testimony before the Oklahoma County grand jury, January 28, 1998, obtained by authors; Haynie quotes from interview (Gumbel), December 17, 2010, the culmination of three months of phone calls and e-mail correspondence; OHP time logs obtained through an open records request; Rick Stephens interviews (Gumbel), October 12, 2010, February 1 and February 14, 2011.

Ryder truck/other vehicle sightings after 8 A.M.:
McVeigh arriving in Oklahoma City at 8:50 A.M., see Michel and Herbeck, op. cit., pp. 223, 229. Leonard Long, interviewed by J. D. Cash, November 14, 1995, tape obtained by authors. See also J. D. Cash and Jeff Holladay, "Startling New Evidence: At Least 4 People Directly Involved in Bombing," *McCurtain Daily Gazette,* January 23, 1996; Morris John Kuper, FBI FD-302, interviews on October 24 and November 1, 1995 file nos. 10935 and 11356; Kyle Hunt, quoted in Sanders, op. cit., pp. 87–88; Mike Moroz, FBI FD-302, file no. 68, dated April 21, 1995, also quoted in Peter Gelzinis, "FBI Turns Tragedy into 'Nightmare,'" *Boston Globe,* May 13, 2001; Dave Snider, interviewed by MGA documentary crew, March 27, 1999. Transcript obtained by authors; James Linehan, FBI FD-302, file no. 1645, dated April 25, 1995, also interviewed by MGA documentary crew, April 13, 1999, transcript obtained by authors. Danny Wilkerson's story told by Jannie Coverdale, interview April 2001, see Andrew Gumbel, "Timothy McVeigh: A Deadly Silence," *The Independent* (UK), April 17, 2001; Danny Coulson, quoted on BBC television program *The Conspiracy Files,* March 2, 2007. Also, interview (Gumbel), May 19, 2010; the "innocent" Ryder truck, see Billy Holdson's FBI FD-302, file no. 17699, April 16, 1997. *The Turner Diaries* passage describing FBI headquarters bombing, see Macdonald, op. cit., pp. 36–42; Jane

Graham, public statement, "Murrah Building Bombing/Information and Mis-Information," November 15, 1996; Dave Hollaway, interview (Gumbel), May 6, 2010. Underground parking lot story also related by Andreas Strassmeir, interview (Gumbel), July 3, 2010; Kirk Lyons, interview (Gumbel), May 27, 2010; sighting of Ryder truck attempting to enter alley behind federal courthouse, interview (Charles) with former Oklahoma Highway Patrol trooper Steve Newby, citing fellow OHP trooper Mike Stroud, September 12, 1997; interview with the head of Federal Protective Service, Tom Hunt (Gumbel), December 16, 2010, and with John Magaw (Gumbel), June 22, 2010.

Prank call to Justice Department:
Jones and Israel, *Others Unknown*, pp. 3–4, 242–50; in *The Turner Diaries*, a character called Henry uses a public phone booth to call the *Washington Post* one minute before a truck bomb destroys FBI headquarters. See Macdonald, op. cit., p. 40.

Fax to Steve Stockman's office:
Statement, with text of fax, put out by Stockman's staff, April 24, 1995. More information in Richard Whittle, "Fax to Congressman on Day of Blast Explained by Sender; Woman Says She'd Hoped to Limit Disinformation," *Christian Science Monitor*, April 26, 1995; and in Bennett Roth, "Oklahoma City Tragedy: Threat or a Promise? Stockman Reveals Fax Author's Taped Vow to 'Go Ballistic,'" *Houston Chronicle*, April 27, 1995.

Final minutes before the explosion:
Gary Lewis, quoted in J. D. Cash, "Eyewitness to Bombing Saw McVeigh, Smiling Mideasterner," *McCurtain Daily Gazette*, August 11, 1995; Glenn Grossman FBI FD-302, file no. 198, dated April 23, 1995; second FBI FD-302, file no. 14843, dated April 30, 1996; Daina Bradley, see McVeigh trial transcript, May 23, 1997; Rodney Johnson, from MGA documentary transcript, interviewed March 18, 1999. Leah Moore, see J. D. Cash, "The Final Moments Before the Oklahoma City Bombing," *McCurtain Daily Gazette*, January 24, 1996. (Leah Moore misspelled Lea Mohr.) Levoid Jack Gage, FBI FD-302, file no. 7221, July 27, 1995; McVeigh's description of putting in earplugs and walking away, Michel and Herbeck, op. cit., pp. 229–31; Secret Service timeline obtained by authors, timeline entry on Grossman at 1930 on April 24, 1995; Richard A. Serrano and Ronald J. Ostrow, "FBI Re-Creates Events Leading to Bomb Blast," *Los Angeles Times*, October 25, 1995.

Chapter 2

Oklahoma Military Academy:
Stanley Brown, contemporaneous notes, written April 19, 1995, and revised April 20, 1995, made available to authors. Also, interview (Gumbel), September 21, 2010.

Federal courthouse:
Gary Knight, interview (Gumbel), September 1, 2010; more details in John Perry, "A Day of Terror," *Daily Oklahoman*, April 23, 1995.

Rear axle hits Richard Nichols's car:
Nichols testified in the McVeigh trial, May 14, 1997. Nichols is no relation of
Terry or James Nichols.
Glenn Wilburn on scene:
From transcript of interview with ABC's *20/20,* November 18, 1996.
Murrah Building:
Some details of America's Kids day-care center taken from Rick Bragg, "Tender
Memories of Day-Care Center Are All That Remain After the Bomb," *New York
Times,* May 3, 1995; on the mini-scandal concerning Danielle Hunt's work as
operator, see notes to chapter 3. According to inspection reports from the Okla-
homa Department of Human Services, obtained by Gumbel, attendance at 9:00
A.M. was consistent at about thirty kids in the first three months of the year, nine
or ten more than were present on April 19. On Dana Cooper's educational quali-
fications, see "Those Who Were Killed" section of the Oklahoma City National
Memorial Web site, http://www.oklahomacitynationalmemorial.org; story of
Brandon and Jessica Denny from Tom and Danielle Hunt, interviews (Gumbel),
December 16 and 17, 2010. On Brandon Denny's medical travails, see Arnold
Hamilton, "Life Goes on for Young Survivors of Oklahoma City Bombing,"
Dallas Morning News, April 19, 2005; on Daina Bradley and her family, see Marc
Peyser with Peter Annin, "Survivor: 'All I Saw Were Bright Lights,'" *Newsweek,*
June 5, 1995; particulars of victim trauma from a detailed, body part by body
part, inventory compiled by the military, titled "Body Locations," dated May 2,
1995, and obtained by Gumbel; account of OCFD rescue operations chief, see
Mike Shannon, "Rescue Operations: Doing Battle with the Building," *Fire Engi-
neering,* October 1995, pp. 64–93, Priscilla Salyers story: Daniel LeDuc, Jeffrey
Fleishman, Terence Samuel, Larry Copeland, Dan Meyers, et al,. "Just Another
Day, Then Disaster in Federal Building," *Philadelphia Inquirer,* April 30, 1995;
breakdown of fatalities: "Victims of the Oklahoma City Bombing," *Associated
Press,* June 11, 2001.
Fragility of Murrah Building:
FEMA report on the building damage: W. Gene Corley, Mete A. Sozen, Charles
H. Thornton, and Paul F. Mlakar, "The Oklahoma City Bombing: Improv-
ing Building Performance Through Multi-Hazard Mitigation," FEMA, U.S.
Government Printing Office, Washington, D.C., August 1996; a useful summary and further conclusions can be found in W. Gene Corley, "Applicability
of Seismic Design in Mitigating Progressive Collapse," CTL Group, Skokie, Il-
linois, 2004. National Research Council report: Committee on the Protection
of Federal Facilities Against Terrorism, "Protection of Federal Office Buildings
Against Terrorism," National Academy Press, Washington, D.C., 1988, line
about explosive-laden vehicle, p. 30; NRC author John Pignato and other experts
interviewed in Mike McGraw and Joe Stephens, "88 Warnings on Terrorism Left
Unheeded; Study Advised Ways to Prevent Attacks on Federal Buildings," *Kansas
City Star,* April 29, 1995; Ronald L. Howland, interview (Gumbel), January 3,
2011; Tom Hunt, interviews (Gumbel), December 16 and 17, 2010; five-hour gap
in daily security-guard coverage and other arrangements detailed in GSA Federal

Protective Service Physical Security Survey, dated February 21, 1995, obtained by Gumbel.

Bomb detonation:
Raymon Brown's initial findings are in a brief report, "Seismograms Possibly Associated with the OKC Explosion," May 9, 1995. This and more is included in rogue former FBI agent Ted Gunderson's report on the bombing, with its conclusion that the blast was the result of a super bomb. See Ted L. Gunderson and Associates, "The Gunderson Report on the Bombing of the Alfred P. Murrah Federal Building, Oklahoma City, Oklahoma. April 19, 1995," Las Vegas, November 1, 1996, amended October 26, 2000. Viewed online at http://www.tedgunderson.net, October 20, 2010; Brown told an Oklahoma County grand jury in September 1997 he now regarded the results as inconclusive and they could not, on their own, support the two-bomb theory. His boss, OGS director Charles Mankin, told the grand jury the two-bomb theory had been a mistake. See Ed Godfrey, Diana Baldwin, and Judy Kuhlman, "Grand Jury Told Seismic Readings Unclear in Bombing," *Daily Oklahoman,* September 19, 1997, and Diana Baldwin, "Expert Rejects 2-Bomb Idea, Grand Jury Told Seismic Report a Mistake," *Daily Oklahoman,* October 7, 1997; for a scientific explanation of why the seismograms are consistent with a single bomb, see Thomas L. Holzer, Joe B. Fletcher, Gary S. Fuis, Trond Ryberg, Thomas M. Brocher, and Christopher M. Dietel, "Seismograms Offer Insight into Oklahoma City Bombing," *Eos* (a publication of the American Geophysical Union), vol. 77, no. 41, October 8, 1996; Brigadier General Partin's report, "Bomb Damage Analysis of Alfred P. Murrah Federal Building, Oklahoma City, Oklahoma," is dated July 30, 1995, and was sent to Senator Trent Lott of Mississippi, then the Senate Majority Whip. For a take-down of his arguments, and a cogent explanation of the bomb blast and its effects, see Richard Sherrow, "Bombast, Bomb Blasts & Baloney," *Soldier of Fortune,* January 1996, pp. 41–43 and 72–77; others supporting Sherrow's contentions about the negative blast-pressure wave include Bill Buford, another veteran bomb expert for the ATF turned commander of the Arkansas State Police Bomb Squad, interview (Gumbel), May 11, 2010. See also, Globalsecurity.org's online article on munitions damage at http://www.globalsecurity.org/military/systems/munitions/damage.htm (accessed October 20, 2010); Dave Hollaway interview (Gumbel), May 6, 2010.

Scenes from the bowels of hell:
Franklin Alexander, account in official written statement, FBI FD-302, file no. 15498, dictated July 7, 1996; John Avera, interviewed by his police department colleagues. Report included in undated FBI document F-9442, April 20, 1995 (not in bombing case file); some details also from Mike Shannon's piece in *Fire Engineering,* op. cit.

Suspicions of Middle East connection, smart suspicions of a Waco connection:
Jim Kamen quoted in Jim Naureckas, "The Oklahoma City Bombing: The Jihad that Wasn't," *Extra!* (a publication of FAIR, or Fairness and Accuracy in Reporting), Washington, D.C., July/August 1995; warning issued to federal courthouses, see John Solomon, "Weeks Before 1995 Oklahoma Bombing, Gov-

ernment Warned of Possible Terror Bombings of Federal Buildings," *Associated Press,* June 20, 2002, and Robert Rudolph, "Lawmen Get Warning of Plot on U.S. Targets," *Newark Star-Ledger,* March 22, 1995. Also Judge Wayne Alley interview (Gumbel), August 18, 2010; Abraham Ahmad story detailed in his FBI FD-302s, file numbers 3939 (April 19, 1995, in Chicago), 3354 (April 20–21, from his FBI interrogation in northern Virginia), and 230 (April 20, itemizing the contents of his luggage recovered in Rome). Pentagon sends Arab translators: Pentagon Department of Military Support memo, obtained by authors, titled "Linguist Support for Federal Bureau of Investigation" and dated April 19, 1995, and e-mail, obtained by authors, from Lieutenant Colonel Frederick S. Gisler of Forces Command headquarters at Fort McPherson, Georgia; Ricks telling police and fire chiefs the significance of April 19, interview (Gumbel) with Assistant City Manager Joe Van Bullard, August 25, 2010. Ricks wondering if he was a target, interview (Gumbel), August 17, 2010; Danny Coulson–Rita Braver phone call, see Danny O. Coulson, with Elaine Shannon, *No Heroes: Inside the FBI's Secret Counter-Terror Force,* p. 3.

McVeigh and the missing license plate:
McVeigh's version of purchasing the Mercury, stashing it in Oklahoma City, and driving away after the bombing: see Michel and Herbeck, op. cit., pp. 206–207, 211–13, and 230–32; theories of why no license plate: Bob Ricks, the FBI special agent in charge in Oklahoma City (interview by Gumbel, August 9, 2010), thought McVeigh simply forgot to reattach it in the heat of the moment; Scott Mendeloff, a member of the government prosecution team (interview by Gumbel, July 16, 2010), thought it fell off; Weldon Kennedy, the FBI's first on-scene commander (interview by Gumbel, August 26, 2010), thought the license plate was stolen; Terry Nichols, echoing some of the crazier theories floating around the Internet, has suggested that McVeigh was programmed by a government "handler" to (a) remove the license plate and (b) make sure he was caught and take the fall for the bombing (Nichols's handwritten answers to questions posed by Salt Lake City lawyer Jesse Trentadue, dated January 27, 2010); McVeigh said (Michel and Herbeck, p. 226) he expected to be captured or killed, though he didn't say this in connection with the missing license plate. Two witnesses who saw plate dangling by a single bolt: Lea McGown, owner of the Dreamland Motel in Junction City, Kansas, where McVeigh checked in hours after purchasing the Mercury (McGown interview with MGA documentary crew, March 13, 1999, transcript obtained by authors; and Gary Lewis, the *Journal Record* employee, who saw what he believed was an Oklahoma license plate dangling by a single bolt—see notes to chapter 1); "Nice and solid, two screws right on top" quote reported by defense lawyer Jim Hankins (see notes to chapter 1) based on interview with McVeigh in May 1995. "Network of friends" letter to Jennifer, which is undated, is quoted in Michel and Herbeck, op. cit., p. 197. In her grand jury testimony on August 2, 1995, Jennifer told prosecuting attorney Vicki Behenna she thought the letter was written sometime after October 1993. (Summary of her testimony in Alliance

Services investigative memo to the Nichols federal defense team, memo written by H. C. Bodley, July 10, 1997.) Items in McVeigh's car, exhibits at his trial including nos. 447 ("abandoned do not tow" note under windshield), 448A (copy of Declaration of Independence with message on the back), 451 (quote from John Locke, hand-copied by McVeigh), 453 (photocopied excerpt from *The Turner Diaries*), and 458 (article on Lexington and Concord); Terry Nichols corroborating story about removing license plate, from Nichols's handwritten answers to author questions, March 20, 2010.

The getaway from Oklahoma City:
McVeigh's version reported by Hankins as well as Michel and Herbeck; Germaine Johnston account based on her testimony at the Terry Nichols trial (December 5, 1997). Johnston estimated she saw McVeigh 20–25 minutes after the bombing, which would not leave him enough time to drive the Mercury to the point on I-35 where he was arrested just before 10:20 A.M. The FBI never seriously considered the possibility that Johnston was mistaken about how much time had elapsed (as opposed to mistaken about absolutely everything else); the other witness who saw McVeigh in the alley was Morris John Kuper (see notes to chapter 1).

Chevie Kehoe at the Shadows Motel in Spokane:
Details in Bill Morlin, "McVeigh in Spokane Before Bombing? Innkeeper Links Kehoe, McVeigh in Months Before Oklahoma City Blast," *Spokane Spokesman Review,* January 16, 1998; Morlin, "Kehoe Implicates Brother in Bombing; Cheyne Kehoe Says He Has Knowledge of Chevie's Role in Attack on a Federal Building," *Spokane Spokesman Review,* January 21, 1998; and in Kim Murphy, "Savage Saga of Radical Right Told in Trial," *Los Angeles Times,* April 18, 1999. Kehoe at Elohim City, interview (Gumbel) with Andreas Strassmeir, June 30, 2010; talk of "delivery," see FBI FD-302 interview with Montana prison inmate John Shults, file no. 17735, dated April 2, 1997. For a more detailed report of the first interview see ATF Report of Investigation, Helena Field Office, dated April 3, 1997.

Wayne Snell's final day:
Details from death row prison guard log, as reported in Howard Pankratz's May 12, 1996, piece for the *Denver Post,* cited in chapter 1; in Associated Press's "Chronology of an Execution," published April 20, 1995; in "Snell Executed at Cummins; Last Words Lash at Governor," *Arkansas Democrat-Gazette,* April 20, 1995; and in Michael Daly, "His Hatred Survives," *New York Daily News,* April 23, 1995; Jeff Rosenzweig's account of Snell denouncing the bombing as unprofessional because it targeted children is echoed in an FBI FD-302 interview with Mary Snell, file no. 9384, August 12, 1995.

Radical anger at McVeigh/time of attack changed:
Kale Kelly, prison interview with FBI agent Tym Burkey, quoted in Dave Hall and Tym Burkey, with Katherine Ramsland, *Into the Devil's Den,* p. 78; Strassmeir quotes, interview (Gumbel), July 3, 2010; Oliphant talking about "something big," see FBI FD-302 interviews with Dyane Partridge, file no. 1215, May

10, 1995; Oliphant saying McVeigh would have been a hero if he had blown up the building at night, quoted in, e.g., Tony Perry, "Godfather of Arizona's Militiamen; Oklahoma City Bombing Puts Jack Oliphant, an Ex-Con and Survivalist, Back in Limelight," *Los Angeles Times,* May 21, 1995; Bobby Joe Farrington, FBI FD-302, file no. 13458, April 29, 1995. Terry Nichols also alluded to a series of attacks on federal courthouses, according to an FBI Synopsis of Investigation dated March 3, 2005 (when the feds were trying to establish the veracity of claims that more explosives were concealed under Nichols's old house in Herington). "Nichols advised that the aforementioned bomb components were to be used by the group to bomb other federal courthouses after the Oklahoma City bombing," the synopsis said. The word "other" implies, of course, that one had already been targeted if not actually hit. Nichols did not repeat this line in his correspondence with the authors, saying instead that he had no idea what McVeigh's target might have been; in *The Turner Diaries,* the FBI building bomb goes off at 9:15 A.M. on October 13, 1991, see Macdonald, op. cit., p. 38.

Fishy stories from the ATF:
Franey's story, from his testimony in the McVeigh trial, May 6, 1997. Also, interviews (Gumbel) March 1 and March 19, 2010; sheriff's office video shot by Sergeant Melvin Sumter, obtained by authors; Magaw interview (Gumbel), January 18, 2010; Harry Eberhardt, FBI FD-302, file no. 13012 (written by Eberhardt), February 3, 1996. Franey squirmed around considerably when challenged on his story. First, after he was shown a still picture from the sheriff's office video with his hands unbandaged, he said he "had a good chuckle," because the figure in the picture clearly was not him. Then, given the opportunity to review the video as a whole, he backed down, acknowledged the figure was him, after all, and suggested that he and a colleague from across the country jump on a plane to explain in person. Soon after that, he dropped the in-person visit idea, and said he stood by his original story. DEA agent who went up to ninth floor, see FBI interview with customs office chief Terry Don Wilson, November 16, 1995, file no. 11457; Wilson describes Dave Schickedanz going up shortly after getting out of the stalled elevator. McCauley story, see ATF news release dated May 23, 1995. Also pleading in McVeigh case, November 7, 1996, in which Joe Harztler repeats the story; Duane James and Oscar Johnson, interviewed by Tom Jarriel of ABC, November 19, 1996, transcript obtained by authors; Dave Schickedanz, interview (Gumbel), August 13, 2010. For other versions of his account, see, e.g., Pam Proctor, "A Portrait in Bravery," *Parade* magazine, October 27, 1996; the elevator story being a factor in McCauley's transfer, from interview (Gumbel) with Tommy Wittman, at the time an assistant special agent in charge in Dallas, with oversight responsibility for Oklahoma City, interview date September 27, 2010.

McVeigh arrested by Charlie Hanger:
McVeigh's version, see Michel and Herbeck, op. cit., pp. 238–43; Hanger's version taken from transcripts of testimony in the McVeigh trial, April 28, 1997, and

Terry Nichols's federal trial, November 5, 1997. Speculation on McVeigh's destination: Wichita suggested in interview (Gumbel) with Randy Yount, September 30, 2010, based on his law enforcement contacts. Fortier telling FBI McVeigh was headed to Arizona via the Kansas City airport, interview (Gumbel) with Weldon Kennedy, August 26, 2010. The possibility he was heading to Pittsburg was apparently investigated by FBI, which subpoenaed pay phone records along the most likely route from the location of McVeigh's arrest to the safe house.

10:30 bomb scare and evacuation:
Stanley Brown interview (Gumbel), September 21, 2010; also his contemporaneous notes. Second bomb bigger than the first: see John Avera's interview with the FBI, cited above. Leaving Daina Bradley: Mike Shannon's article in *Fire Engineering*, op. cit., especially pp. 69, 71; Don Browning, interviewed by MGA documentary crew, March 18, 1999. Possible causes of evacuation: Shannon interviewed by FBI, see FD-302, file no. 17238, August 22, 1996; Danny Defenbaugh interview (Gumbel), September 22, 2010. Evidence of ordinance and government weaponry in Murrah Building: assault rifles seen taken out of the rubble in a sheriff's department video shot by Sumter; see also discussion later in this chapter of TOW missile, whose presence has been confirmed; Virgil Steele, sworn statement dated June 22, 1998, obtained by authors. Such storage issues were relatively common. The Tulsa ATF office was later the subject of internal scrutiny, because of problems with its weapons inventory, as revealed by ATF supervisor Tommy Wittman, interview (Gumbel), September 27, 2010. FBI headquarters was damaged by a fire in 1987 caused by explosive materials accidentally ripping through the crime lab. The incident was investigated internally as well as by the ATF, but kept largely out of the public eye. Shane Slovacek interviewed by the FBI November 16, 1995, insert no. 13569; Randy Yount interview (Gumbel), September 30, 2010; John Magaw interview (Gumbel), January 18, 2010; John Haynie, FBI FD-302 interview, file no. 11699, October 25, 1995.

McVeigh booked at the Noble County courthouse:
Hanger's account taken from testimony in the Nichols federal trial, November 5, 1997. See also Michel and Herbeck, op. cit., p. 244. McVeigh throwing the Nichols brothers to the wolves: McVeigh also used the Decker address when checking into the Dreamland Motel in Junction City, Kansas, on April 14. Many years later, Terry Nichols expressed fury against McVeigh. "It's clear McVeigh holds some grudge or animosity of some type against me," he wrote on March 20, 2010. The use of the present tense, almost nine years after McVeigh's execution, underlines how keenly he still felt the betrayal.

FBI gets an early jump on McVeigh, which it ignores:
Interview (Gumbel) with Dennis Dutsch, June 22, 2011.

Doctors get to work rescuing Daina Bradley:
Material taken from Andy Sullivan's testimony in the McVeigh trial, June 5, 1997, and from Roy Wenzl, "In Search of an Ending; Timothy McVeigh's Deadly Act Turned Two Doctors into Reluctant Heroes," *Wichita Eagle,* May 16, 2001.

TOW missile episode:

Account from Stanley Brown's handwritten journal; FBI interviews with OHP officers Fred Horn (November 8, 1995) and John Haynie (October 25, 1995), both under insert file no. 6853; Bill Grimsley's testimony to the Oklahoma County grand jury, February 25, 1998, transcript obtained by authors; Oklahoma County Sheriff's Evidence/Ordnance Acceptance Form dated April 19, 1995, and completed by Bob Heady, the head of the sheriff's office bomb squad. That form says the missile was checked by an army explosives and ordnance disposal technician from Fort Sill; the army's own paperwork (per an e-mail, obtained by the authors, from Lieutenant Colonel Frederick S. Gisler of Forces Command headquarters, time-stamped 12:10 P.M.) shows that the 61st EOD from Fort Sill was not yet in Oklahoma City at that time. Even at 12:10 P.M., the EOD team was only on standby. The missile was shown to the county grand jury on September 15, 1998, according to an article three days later in the *Daily Oklahoman*. Bob Sanders quote taken from transcript of interview with MGA documentary crew, March 13, 1998; technical details of TOW missile, both in fully operational and inert mode, from FBI FD-302 interview with Bill Stewart of Army CID at the Anniston Army Depot, file no. 15530, June 22, 1996. Lack of paperwork on TOW missile detailed in a letter to the FBI from Bruce F. Murray, acting assistant director (operations) of Strategic Investigations Division of the U.S. Customs. The letter, dated January 13, 1997, includes this observation: "A member of my staff... personally searched all available headquarters files for any documentation relating to the inert TOW, with negative results." Murray speculates any records may have been purged. Stanley Brown quote about Bob Heady taken from interview (Gumbel), October 18, 2010. Wrong story circulated about timing of TOW missile discovery: see, e.g., Diana Baldwin, Judy Kuhlman, "Jury Shown Missile from Bomb Site Weapon Triggered Post-Explosion Bomb Scare," *Daily Oklahoman*, September 18, 1998. In this version, the missile triggered the first evacuation; the second was triggered by the discovery of a desk clock that looked like an explosive. Such a clock was on the desk of ATF agent Harry Eberhardt, but there is no evidence it was connected to either alert.

Chapter 3

Louis Freeh passes over Bob Ricks:

Ronald Kessler, *The Bureau*; I. C. Smith's review of Freeh's book *Sins of Omission* in *American Spectator*, vol. 38, issue 10 (December 1, 2005), pp. 24–29; Weldon L. Kennedy, *On-Scene Commander*; Oliver "Buck" Revell and Dwight Williams, *A G-Man's Journal*; Freeh praising field agents for doing "the real work," see Freeh, p. 200; Ricks recommended for FBI director, see Revell and Williams, pp. 448–49; Kennedy interview (Gumbel), August 26, 2010; Ricks interview (Gumbel), August 9, 2010.

Bragging rights over rear axle discovery:

McPherson version told, e.g., in Harry Levins, "The Pieces of the Puzzle; Bent Truck Axle Spotted by Alert Detective Provided Key Clue in Finding Oklahoma

Bombing Suspect," *St. Louis Post-Dispatch,* May 28, 1995; traffic cops Earl Faubion and Fred Moon variation told in Arnold Hamilton, "Puzzling Pieces Tell a Story; Officers' Efforts Yield Bomb Truck's Axles," *Dallas Morning News,* May 15, 1995; for FBI version, see Kessler, op. cit., p. 392, and also Jon Hersley, Larry Tongate, and Bob Burke, *Simple Truths,* pp. 35–39; Sumter interviewed by the FBI, FD-302, file no. 3705, May 3, 1995; Agent Jim Norman written declaration, FBI FD-302, file no. 392, April 19, 1995; Agent James F. Elliott Jr. written declarations, FBI FD-302, file nos. 12 and 1360, April 19, 1995.

Investigators lose control of the crime scene:
Joe Van Bullard interview (Gumbel), August 25, 2010; some information about perimeter also in Mike Shannon, "Rescue Operations: Doing Battle with the Building," *Fire Engineering* magazine, October 1995, p. 71; Powell, Kelso, and Gadson testimony to Department of Justice inspector general, quoted in John F. Kelly and Philip K. Wearne, *Tainting Evidence,* pp. 199–200. The interviews did not make it into the final report, titled "The FBI Laboratory: An Investigation into Laboratory Practices and Alleged Misconduct in Explosives-Related and Other Cases" (USDOJ Office of Inspector General Special Report, April 1997); John Magaw interview (Gumbel), January 18, 2010; Magaw estimates bomb at 1,000–1,200 lbs., CNN, April 19, 1995 (transcript headlined "One ATF Agent Vows Intensive Investigation into Bomb"). The same figure is later found in Forscom (U.S. Army Forces Command) logs.

Pete Langan and Richard Guthrie on the morning of the bombing:
List of ARA hardware including explosives taken from: Guthrie's FBI FD-302, dated March 4–15, 1996; from an FBI inventory of items recovered from a second safe house in Columbus, Ohio, after Langan's arrest on January 18, 1996—see Mark S. Hamm, *In Bad Company,* pp. 10–12; and from MGA documentary interview with Langan, April 7, 2000, transcript obtained by authors. ARA plans to stage multipronged attacks on the government, see Guthrie's memoir *The Taunting Bandits,* p. 74; recruitment video, *The Aryan Republican Army Presents: The Armed Struggle Underground,* obtained by authors; biographical information on Langan taken from Hamm, op. cit.; "small person you didn't wanna fuck with" quote, Hamm, p. 80; biographical information on Guthrie taken from his FBI FD-302 and from his memoir; his threat to blow up the White House taken from Secret Service memorandum, dated December 29, 1995. Evidence of McVeigh's possible involvement with ARA: Terry Nichols said in a letter to Salt Lake City lawyer Jesse Trentadue, dated October 18, 2006, that McVeigh talked "a couple of times" about robbing a bank; on the car ride from Oklahoma City back to Kansas on April 16, 1995, McVeigh alluded to big plans and Nichols asked him: "What are you going to do, rob a bank?" (from Nichols's letter to reporter John Solomon, dated September 30, 2007). Nichols's ex-wife Lana Padilla said she wondered about Nichols and McVeigh both being involved in a bank robbery after finding wigs, masks, and pantyhose, as well as $20,000 in cash, at her home and at a storage locker in Las Vegas in November 1994 (Padilla interview [Gumbel], September 25, 2010). For McVeigh telling his sister of involvement in a robbery, see Jennifer McVeigh affidavit dated May 2, 1995,

admitted into evidence at her brother's trial. Guthrie account of April 19 taken from his memoir, p. 156; Langan's account taken from MGA documentary interview, op. cit., and also from a legal declaration filed with the U.S. District Court in Salt Lake City, April 9, 2007, case no.: 2:04 CV 00772 DAK. Detail about 1979 Chevy van, see Hamm, op. cit., p. 225, and also Guthrie's FD-302 interview, March 22, 1996, pp. 25–26; details on Langan's "mysterious," see Hamm, op. cit., p. 183. McCarthy's extreme views on homosexuals and cross-dressers from a document by Mark Thomas, "Bible Cites Against Sexual Deviancy," date unknown. McCarthy, Thomas writes, "was especially disgusted by any moral departure from the Law of Moses." Thomas cites Leviticus 20:13: "If a man lieth with mankind, as he lieth with a woman, both of them have committed an abomination: they shall surely be put to death; and their blood shall be upon them." And Deuteronomy 22:5: "The woman shall not wear that which pertaineth to a man, neither shall a man put on a woman's garment: for all that do so are an abomination unto the Lord thy God." Thomas continues: "The penalty for 'abomination' is universally understood to be death. It is important to note that Identity is unique from institutional Christianity in that it is considered to be a terrible sin not to execute the penalty upon the transgressor." Langan quote about Guthrie, Hamm, op. cit., p. 22; sketch resembling Langan drawn by regular FBI sketch artist Jeanne Boylan based on the recall of David Snider, the warehouse foreman in Bricktown, who saw the Ryder truck. Sketch reproduced in Hamm, op. cit., opposite p. 119.

McCarthy and Stedeford unable to account for whereabouts:
Biographical information on McCarthy and Stedeford from Hamm, op. cit. Quote from Stedeford, see Hamm, p. 115; McCarthy's first statement to FBI, FD-302, file interview, June 17, 1996 (not in bombing case file), summarized in FD-302, file no. 15847, August 1, 1996. A follow-up statement is in FD-302, file no. 16027, September 18, 1996. The information on the Chevy Suburban comes from an FBI intra-agency memo dated August 22, 1996, which shows that the car was purchased in Fort Smith on April 17 and registered in Iowa on April 21. Quote: "The Iowa Certificate of Title was issued on 4/21/1995"; Langan's version taken from his legal declaration filed with the U.S. District Court in Salt Lake City, April 9, 2007; Guthrie's "young Mr. Wizard line" quoted by Mark Thomas in an interview with the *Allentown Morning Call* on the day of his arrest. See "Thomas Indicted in Bank Robberies," *Allentown Morning Call,* January 31, 1997; Guthrie leaves article about McVeigh at bank robbery scene, see his big FD-302 interview, March 4–15, 1996, p. 85. Detail about him being drunk on tequila, see Hamm, op. cit., p. 255; Donna Marazoff quoting Mark Thomas, see Marazoff's FBI FD-302 interview, file no. 17777, dated April 2, 1997; Thomas interview with *Washington Post* reporter Rich Leiby, January 23, 1997. Unpublished. Tape of interview kindly provided to Gumbel by Leiby.

Video surveillance cameras:
John Hippard interview (Gumbel), June 15, 2010; Tom Hunt interviews

(Gumbel), December 16 and 17, 2010; Danny Defenbaugh interview (Gumbel), December 9, 2010. Channel 4 report on surveillance tapes, exact date unknown, viewed January 4, 2011, on YouTube.com under title "Oklahoma City Bombing Federal Surveillance Tapes Coverup"; Secret Service timeline references to video tape of the detonation site at 1745 hours for April 25, 1995, and at 1930 hours for April 24, 1995. Stacy Bauerschmidt, the assistant to the special agent in charge of the Secret Service's intelligence division, testified at Terry Nichols's state trial that the government knew of no such videotape; according to the Associated Press, she said that reports in the timeline "may have been based on mere speculation and the agency does not vouch for its reliability" (John Solomon, "Secret Service Documents Cite Mystery Video in Oklahoma City Bombing," Associated Press, April 19, 2004). Confirmation of no video cameras at from GSA Federal Protective Service Physical Security Survey, dated February 21, 1995, and obtained by authors; the same report indicates that there was a video surveillance camera trained on Don Rogers's office door and another at the HUD office; Don Rogers interview (Gumbel), February 14, 2011; Regency Towers tape handover detailed in handwritten report by Oklahoma City police officer Ritch Willis (see FBI FD-302, file no. 1818, April 19, 1995) and in an undated written statement, obtained by authors, from John Hurley, the building's security chief. See also Hurley's testimony in McVeigh trial, May 13, 1997; *Journal Record* handing over tapes still in video players, see FBI FD-302 interview with Danny Payne of TMK Hogan Commercial Real Estate Services, who was in charge of the building's security; interview date April 19, 1995, file no. 4553; inventory report by FBI on video collection on April 19, insert no. E-8981, dated April 19, 1995. A different report, file no. 3105, dated April 20, 1995, states that Walt Lamar released six videotapes for transport to FBI headquarters in Washington at 9:00 A.M. on April 20. The tapes correspond to the locations given in the text. Lamar's "son of a bitch!" moment, interview (Gumbel) with FBI source speaking on condition of anonymity, January 27, 2011; FBI tries and fails to enhance *Journal Record* video footage, interviews (Gumbel) with John Hippard, June 15, 2010, and Danny Defenbaugh, December 9, 2010; gaps in post office footage detailed in a letter dated June 23, 2009, from the FBI records department to Jesse Trentadue, in response to FOIA request.

Dave Hollaway's curious memory lapse:
Hollaway's different versions, from interviews (Gumbel), May 6, May 20, May 24, July 10, and July 13, 2010, and voice-mail message left January 26, 2011. Among those sure Hollaway was not at the Waco commemoration were Jim Pate of *Soldier of Fortune,* who had hosted Hollaway at his Virginia home weeks earlier, interview (Charles), May 27, 2010, and ceremony organizer Carol Moore, interview (Charles), June 14, 2010. Video of the event available via the "Ashes of Waco" collection (the papers and documents of journalist Dick J. Reavis) at the Texas State University, San Marcos. Dick DeGuerin, interview (Gumbel, via e-mail and phone), July 13, 2010; Joe Phillips, interview (via e-mail, Gumbel),

July 18, 2010; Rick Sherrow, interview (Gumbel), January 24, 2011; Kirk Lyons, interview (Gumbel), May 27, 2010.

Andreas Strassmeir's conveniently watertight alibi:

Dave Hollaway, interview (Gumbel), July 9, 2010; Kirk Lyons, interview (Gumbel), January 26, 2011; Strassmeir alibi corroborated, e.g., in FBI FD-302 interview of Otis Phelps, file no. 14948, May 25, 1996. FBI appears to accept alibi, see FD-302 interview with Strassmeir, file no. 14897, April 30–May 1, 1996.

Strassmeir's surprising past:

Strassmeir, interviews (Gumbel), June 30–July 3, 2010; a copy of Strassmeir's open-ended multiple-entry visa obtained by Gumbel. The Justice Department would later misrepresent his entries into the United States, saying he traveled each time on single-entry tourist visas (see also chapter 9). Kirk Lyons disclosed the Petruskie story about the dead Soviet spy in an e-mail, December 1, 2010. Lyons also said Petruskie "may very well have worked for the CIA," interview (Gumbel), April 22; 2010. On Strassmeir as a possible government agent: a retired senior CIA official told Charles in 2006 that, in 1995 or 1996, he reviewed a report by the CIA inspector general in the course of his official duties and remembered seeing a mention of Strassmeir as a German government asset whose information was shared with the FBI. He gave no specifics on how this was sourced in the document or what time period it referred to. Sofameir line, story about Helmut Kohl, from Lyons interview (Gumbel), March 23, 2010. "Shameless hobo," financial arrangement enabling Strassmeir to stay after his German pay ran out, Hollaway interview (Gumbel), May 6, 2010; "Go nuclear" line confirmed by Lyons, interview (Gumbel), April 19, 2011.

FEMA makes itself unpopular:

FEMA complaints, from interviews (Gumbel) with Magaw, Bullard, and Kennedy, August 26, 2010. "Leon" story also told, slightly differently, in Danny O. Coulson, with Elaine Shannon, *No Heroes*, pp. 487–88. "Whining" line from Forscom (U.S. Army Forces Command) log for April 28, 1995, at 0915, log obtained by authors; Don Browning, interview with MGA documentary crew, March 18, 1999; Witt seeing himself as in charge, see James Lee Witt and James Morgan, *Stronger in the Broken Places*, p. 104. Kennedy accusing Witt of dragging out the rescue operation, see Witt and Morgan, pp. 112–13; line confirmed by Kennedy, interview (Gumbel), December 16, 2010. In the book, Witt characterizes the overextended rescue phase as a good thing and a personal victory; erroneous information about FEMA carrying out the bodies at the Web site of the Disaster Assistance and Rescue Team at the NASA Ames Research Center, as of December 14, 2010. http://dart2.arc.nasa.gov/Deployments/OklahomaCityBombing1995/Oklahoma.html; FEMA Web site with misleading information, as of December 14, 2010; http://www.fema.gov/emergency/usr/usrok95.shtm; Witt's failure to acknowledge Oklahoma City Fire Department, see Witt and Morgan, p. 104; Witt was given a full rundown of the accusations in this section, and chose not to comment.

The FBI reaches Eldon Elliott's body shop:
FBI FD-302 reports on interviews with Elliott (file nos. 1347 and 1348), Vicki Beemer (nos. 8570 and 1349), and Tom Kessinger (nos. 1197, 14259, 14803), April 19 and April 20, 1995; Eldon Elliott, interview with MGA documentary crew, March 9, 1995, transcript obtained by authors. Prosecutors have low opinion of body shop employees' value as witnesses, argue they talked among themselves and tainted their own reliability: interviews (Gumbel) with prosecutor Scott Mendeloff, July 16, 2010, and prosecutor Larry Mackey, October 11, 2010; Kessinger on Ray Rozycki's picture book, see Jeanne Boylan, *Portraits of Guilt,* p. 206.

Tim McVeigh at the Noble County jail:
Herbert Ferguson (mistakenly identified as a guard) quoted in Jonathan Franklin, "Timothy McVeigh, Soldier," *Playboy,* October 1995, p. 78; account of his time in the jail taken from Richard Serrano, "Clues Sought in Details from McVeigh's Arrest," *Los Angeles Times,* September 10, 1995, and Paul Queary, "Cellmate Calls McVeigh Calm at First, Then Anxious," *Associated Press,* May 19, 1995; interview with Brent Goad from David Talbot, "McVeigh Was Desperate for Freedom," *Boston Herald,* May 3, 1995. Detail about need for cosigner on bond, from Julie Delcour, "Bondsman Tells of McVeigh Call," *Tulsa World,* April 24, 1995; call to Goad captured in Noble County jail phone records subpoenaed by the FBI and obtained by the authors. The call was made at 8:23 A.M. on April 20 and lasted 2 minutes 27 seconds; for clinical details on methamphetamine withdrawal, see, e.g., C. C. Cruickshank, K. R. Dyer, "A Review of the Clinical Pharmacology of Methamphetamine," *Addiction,* July 2009, pp. 1085–99; T. F. Newton, A. D. Kalechstein, S. Duran, N. Vansluis, W. Ling, "Methampetamine Abstinence Syndrome: Preliminary Findings," *American Journal on Addictions,* May–June 2004, pp. 248–55; C. McGregor, M. Srisurapanont, J. Jittiwutikarn, S. Laobhripatr, T. Wongtan, J. M. White, "The Nature, Time Course and Severity of Methamphetamine Withdrawal," *Addiction,* September 2005, pp. 1320–29; Mark Gibson quote, interview with Ted Koppel on ABC's *Nightline,* April 21, 1995.

Mark Bouton and Garry Berges visit the Dreamland Motel:
Chronology of what Lea McGown said when, taken from FBI FD-302 interviews dated April 20–21, 1995 (single document), April 22, April 23, April 25, April 26, and April 27, 1995; file nos. 2612–2617, sequentially. The complete roster of FBI 302s, inserts, and lead sheets handed over in discovery to the defense teams in the McVeigh trial and in the two Nichols trials includes no document dated April 20 alone from either Lea or Eric McGown. McGown's account of Bouton and Berges's first visit taken from McGown interview with MGA documentary crew, March 12–13, 1999, transcript obtained by authors; Bouton's version taken from interview (Gumbel), July 24, 2010, and follow-up e-mail correspondence July 27–31, 2010, and January 14–February 12, 2011 ; Garry Berges interview (Gumbel), July 26, 2010; Joseph Bross, interview (Gumbel), December 2, 2011; through his former FBI colleagues, Bross obtained the text of the teletype he

sent from Fort Riley in the middle of the night and read it out; Michael Fleenor was considered suspicious, in part, because he faced a disciplinary proceeding over his use of a credit card, see his FBI FD-302, file no. 8005, May 1, 1995; by coincidence, Terry Nichols had bought a bedroom set from his wife Donna a few days before the bombing, see her FD-302, file no. 8004, May 1, 1995, and Nichols's answers to authors' questions, dated January 3 and January 27, 2010 (this was not yet known on April 20, however); details on the criminal division at FBI headquarters being understaffed and overwhelmed, interview (Gumbel) with I. C. Smith, who took over the night shift a day or two later, December 5, 2011. The two Dreamland guests who also saw the Ryder truck on Easter Sunday were Herta King and Renda Truong (see their testimony in McVeigh trial; both appeared on May 22, 1997). Criminal complaint against McVeigh filed in U.S. District Court in Oklahoma City, April 21, 2010.

Pat Livingston fingers McVeigh:
Pat Livingston interviews (Gumbel), August 20 and December 21, 2010; record of McVeigh's Glock purchase, ATF 4437 form and bounced check, copies obtained by Gumbel; Livingston account largely corroborated by FBI FD-302 interviews, file nos. 3946 and 3947, dated April 21, 1995; the FBI at Fort Riley not getting his information right away, per Joseph Bross e-mail correspondence with Gumbel, December 11, 2011; rapid acquisition of information on Nichols brothers, from Chancellor interview (Gumbel), see above; Sanilac County, Michigan, sheriff having information on the Nichols brothers, including Kelli Langenburg's November 1994 complaint, see Howard Pankratz and Peter G. Chronis, "Family Says U.S. Framing Nichols but Some Neighbors Saw Signs of Trouble," *Denver Post,* September 21, 1997; information, including Sheriff Virgil Strickler pegging the Nicholses as "crazies," confirmed by senior FBI source speaking on condition of anonymity; Kelli Langenburg talks to FBI, see Serrano, *One of Ours,* p. 200; her information, given without her name, is included in the criminal complaint filed against McVeigh on April 21, 2010.

Nichols shipping supplies to the Philippines, seeming flush at Fort Riley auctions, confirmed by Junction City army surplus salesman David Batsell, interview (Gumbel), August 24, 2010. Livingston talked about the overspending in an e-mail dated March 2, 2011. Nichols told the authors (handwritten answers to questions, dated February 23, 2011) that he sent a small number of military uniform items as a present for Marife's younger brother Michael, who was going through military school in the Philippines, where battle-dress uniforms were hard to find. Nichols said he spent little at the first couple of auctions he attended at Fort Riley in early 1995, because he was still getting a feel for how they worked. At the auction that raised Livingston and Batsell's eyebrows, in late March, he spent about $3,000, he said, because he saw lots of items he felt confident he could sell at shows and because it was an open auction, which he preferred to the closed type.

List of names of extreme interest posted at Oklahoma City command post, interview (Gumbel) with FBI source who did not wish to be named, August 30, 2010.

"Dust storm" postcard sent to Liberty Lobby:
Mark Lane, MGA documentary interview, June 23, 1999, transcript obtained by authors.

Nichols clears McVeigh's stuff from storage locker:
Nichols's account taken from handwritten document, "Events Leading Up to the Oklahoma City Bombing, a Condensed Narrative," dated November 9, 2006, and from his written answers to author questions, dated January 22, 2010. Some details about the electric blasting caps from handwritten document "OKC Bombing Materials and the Missing Explosives," December 1, 2007, from handwritten document "Morning of April 18, 1995," November 29, 2007, and from Michel and Herbeck, op. cit., p. 218.

Louis Freeh breathes down necks of field office SACs:
Account of Freeh's approach taken from Buck Revell's book, *A G-Man's Journal;* from Ronald Kessler's book, *The Bureau,* and from interview (Gumbel and Charles) with I. C. Smith, June 18, 2010; senior FBI manager quote, from interview on condition of anonymity, January 5, 2011. Walt Lamar initiates NCIC offline search, see Hersley, Tongate, and Burke, op. cit., pp. 53–54. Account confirmed by FBI source speaking on background.

FBI hits the jackpot with Lana Padilla:
Padilla's account laid out in her testimony at the Nichols trial, November 19, 1997; see also her book, *By Blood Betrayed;* some material from interviews, August 14 (Charles) and September 25, 2010 (Gumbel).

Carl LeBron's providential phone call to the FBI:
Bare bones of his call laid out in the criminal complaint against McVeigh filed in U.S. District Court, April 21, 2010. For more details, see Richard A. Serrano, "Friend of McVeigh Proved Key for FBI, Papers Reveal," *Los Angeles Times,* January 4, 1997. Also Serrano, *One of Ours,* p. 194.

Nichols gets rid of incriminating evidence:
Account from Nichols's written answers to author questions, January 22, 2010, and March 30, 2010. Details on disposing of the fertilizer come from his initial FBI interview, see FD-302 of Nichols, file no. 9954, interview date April 21–22, 1995; also trial testimony of Gladys Wendt, November 20, 1997. Details of 50-caliber rifle and grenade included in a memo from the FBI Kansas City office, case ID no. 11117, May 16, 2005; "dumbass" quote from Mike Batsell interview (Gumbel), August 24, 2010; nitromethane tubes and other items recovered from beneath the crawl space detailed in an FBI crime lab analysis and inventory obtained by authors, dated April 8, 2005.

Feds find McVeigh:
Account taken from Coulson, *No Heroes,* pp. 495–96, Hersley, Tongate, and Burke, op. cit., p. 54, interview (Gumbel) with Steve Chancellor (who was sitting next to Michalic), August 12, 2010, and interview (Gumbel) with FBI source who

did not want to be named, August 30, 2010. Michalic's own version, in various media interviews, is more or less consistent with the others, see, e.g., Peter Annin, Evan Thomas, and Randy Collier, "Judgment Day," *Newsweek,* March 24, 1997.

Chapter 4

FBI questions McVeigh:
Bare bones of the account taken from Serrano, *One of Ours,* pp. 3–7, Michel and Herbeck, op. cit., pp. 253–55, and Coulson and Shannon, op. cit., pp. 500–503; Mark Gibson ironed out some of the contradictions and conflicting versions, interview (Gumbel), January 10, 2011; detail of three phone calls to Royce Hobbs from Hobbs's FBI FD-302, file no. 4692, May 4, 1995; some of the Walt Lamar material and other insights provided by Hank Gibbons, interview (Gumbel), January 7, 2011; Gibbons, an FBI agent in Oklahoma City, wrote the criminal complaint against McVeigh that day, as well as the warrants to search his car and personal effects; details on news crew that got wise to events in Perry, interview (Gumbel) with former FBI agent who did not wish to be named, January 27, 2011; Jerry Cook, interview (Gumbel), February 4, 2011; "I think they think it's me" line, quoted by cell mate Cecil Brown in Paul Queary, "Cellmate Calls McVeigh Calm at First, Then Anxious," *Associated Press,* May 19, 1995.

Feds swoop on James Nichols:
Details of FBI deployment from source who was present but did not wish to be named, interview (Gumbel), January 6, 2011; details of evidence-gathering, witnesses, from the criminal complaint filed against James Nichols in the Eastern District of Michigan, April 25, 1995; James Nichols's account of the start of the raid, see James D. Nichols, as told to Robert S. Papovich, *Freedom's End,* pp. 15–20.

Agent Smith tails Terry Nichols:
See Smith's testimony in Nichols's federal trial, November 20, 1997.

Josh Nichols makes telling revelations:
Lana Padilla, *By Blood Betrayed,* pp. 41–42; Padilla interviews (Gumbel), September 25, 2010, and January 17, 2011.

Terry Nichols panics, goes to the Herington police station:
Nichols gives his own account in a handwritten document, "Events Leading Up to the Oklahoma City Bombing," dated November 9, 2006, obtained by authors; see Nichols federal trial testimony from Dale Kuhn (December 9, 1997), Barry Thacker (December 9, 1997), Marife Nichols (December 10–11, 1997), and Stephen Smith (November 20–21, 1997); details about Marife getting mad, wanting to go home to the Philippines, from Agent Smith's testimony on cross-examination (November 21, 1997) and from Nichols's handwritten answers to author questions, January 3, 2010; phone calls to James and Lana, and the call from CNN, from phone records on Nichols's home line obtained by authors.

Michael Fortier sweats:
Account from FBI FD-302 interview with Jim Rosencrans, July 5–6, 1995, file

no. 9178, and from FD-302 interview with Rosencrans's girlfriend Patty Edwards, July 1, 1995, file no. 6696. "Our boy's been busy" quote from Rosencrans interview in Richard A. Serrano and Ronald J. Ostrow, "McVeigh Viewed as 'A Driving Force' in Six-Month Plot," *Los Angeles Times,* May 4, 1995.

FBI takes McVeigh into federal custody:
Richard A. Serrano and Ronald Ostrow, "Legal Issues May Jeopardize Evidence Against McVeigh," *Los Angeles Times,* September 14, 1995; Mark Gibson interview (Gumbel), January 10, 2011; Michel and Herbeck, op. cit., pp. 255–59; Coulson and Shannon, op. cit., p. 504.

Day-care center operator recognizes McVeigh:
Danielle Hunt interview (Gumbel), February 14, 2011; Tom Hunt interview (Gumbel), December 16, 2010; FBI FD-302 interview with Danielle Hunt, file no. 466, April 29, 1995.

McVeigh not a match for John Doe One:
Eldon Elliott not asked to match McVeigh to John Doe One until June 8, from his testimony in the McVeigh trial, May 9, 1997. See also FBI FD-302, file no. 6107, dated June 8, 1995; no McVeigh fingerprints found at body shop, testimony of FBI fingerprint expert Louis Hupp at the McVeigh trial, May 15, 1997; official doubts also reflected in Secret Service timeline entry for 1440 on April 21: "SA [Special Agent] Stephenson, OKC/CP [Oklahoma City Command Post], reports that McVeigh does not physically match the composite of the two featured suspects."

Carol Howe hands the feds a monster lead, which they disregard:
Detail on swastika tattoo, other biographical details from Carol Howe's testimony in the trial of James Viefhaus in federal court in Tulsa, July 24, 1997, transcript viewed by Gumbel; Mahon appeared on *Oprah* sometime in the late 1980s, confirmed by ATF agent Tristan Moreland, who arrested him in 2009, Moreland interview (Gumbel), October 14, 2009; drug buy to test her loyalty, see Finley's testimony in pretrial hearing in federal court in Tulsa, April 24, 1997; ATF Report of Investigation on Carol Howe, May 22, 1995; also, FBI insert on Howe (named only as "Carol"), lead control no. E427, April 21, 1995; Millar's inconsequential son-in-law was Larry Duncan, who offered no information of consequence, interviewed April 22, 1995, file no. 3952; Bob Ricks interview (Gumbel), August 17, 2010; Danny Defenbaugh interview (Gumbel), May 17, 2010; Andreas Strassmeir interview (Gumbel), June 30, 2010.

Nichols sits down with the FBI:
FBI FD-302 interview with Nichols, dated April 21–22, 1995, file no. 9954; many details corroborated by Agent Stephen Smith's testimony in Nichols' federal trial, November 20–21, 1997. Application and affidavit for search warrant, signed by Scott Crabtree, April 22, 1995; Nichols's later comments on his initial interview from handwritten answers to author questions, March 20, 2010, and July 22, 2010; McVeigh thought Nichols "hosed" him, see Michel and Herbeck,

op. cit., p. 297. The timing of the material witness arrest warrant is detailed in an order issued by Judge Matsch on August 14, 1996, following a pretrial hearing on the admissibility of evidence from Nichols's nine-hour interrogation in the Herington police station; the efforts of federal public defender Dave Phillips to reach Nichols on April 21 were detailed by defense attorney Ron Woods in his opening statement in the Nichols trial, November 3, 1997.

Jennifer McVeigh tracked down in Florida:
Account taken largely from Jennifer's testimony in the McVeigh trial, May 5–6, 1997; see also Joseph B. Treaster, "The Sister's Story: For Figure in Oklahoma Inquiry, Ties of Blood and Something More," *New York Times,* August 4, 1995.

McVeigh fingered in the lineup:
Steve Chancellor interview (Gumbel), August 12, 2010; Moroz lineup outcome described in FBI FD-302, file no. 69, dated April 22, 1995.

Jimboy fiasco:
Some details on Jimboy from interview (Gumbel) with Dave Dilly, December 13, 2010. On knife scars and knife play, FBI FD-302 interview with Larry Frame, file no. 3118, May 4, 1995; Bob Ricks interview (Gumbel), August 9, 2010; N. R. Kleinfeld, "For Bombing 'Suspects,' Looks Aren't Everything," *New York Times,* April 30, 1995; investigation tracked in FBI FD-302s, file nos. 234 and 832 (April 21, 1995) and 1094 (April 22), and also in Secret Service timeline ("Jimboy has legitimate alibi"—0058, April 22—"Jimboy polygraphed through the night, eliminated as suspect—0724).

Nichols digs himself in deeper, gets arrested:
Details taken from the FBI FD-302 interview with Nichols, dated April 21–22, 1995, and from Agent Smith's testimony of November 20, 1997; the two warrants for Nichols's arrest obtained by authors. The issue arose in pretrial proceedings and is discussed in Judge Matsch's August 14, 1996, ruling, in which he broadly accepts the government's explanation that the first warrant was a mistake, but makes clear Judge Russell was not informed that Nichols was in the Herington police station and already cooperating; FBI agents look through Nichols's garage window, FBI insert, number illegible, April 24, 1995; the link between the blue plastic shards and the barrels at Nichols's home was included in the criminal complaint filed on May 9, 1995; the recycling bins, kept next to the first-floor restrooms on the south side of the building, were described to the FBI by Richard Williams, the deputy building manager, FD-302, file no. 12707, January 26, 1996.

Manic hunt for coconspirators:
Freeh picking out lineup photos, Oliver "Buck" Revell and Dwight Williams, *A G-Man's Journal*, p. 474. Story confirmed by I. C. Smith, who worked the bombing case as a senior manager at headquarters, interview (Gumbel and Charles), June 18, 2010; quote on micromanaging from Louis Freeh, *My FBI,* p. 210; Steve Chancellor interview (Gumbel), August 12, 2010.

McVeigh screws Dave Paulsen:
Charlie Hanger, testimony in Nichols trial, November 5, 1997. Details of Paulsen interrogation in FBI FD-302, file no. 727 (April 23), in which he describes his interest in AR-15 parts, his purchases, McVeigh offering blasting caps, and his explanation that he was "stringing McVeigh along"; file no. 719 (April 24, 1995), in which he admits lying about the number of phone calls he had received from McVeigh; and file no. 724, which details his polygraph test and gives his "cocksucker" line as a direct quote. The Daryl Bridges phone records entered into evidence at trial show 37 calls to Paulsen either at home or at the Paulsen's Military Supply shop; not all were completed calls. McVeigh admitting he dropped the business card as a "dirty trick," Michel and Herbeck, op. cit., p. 243; Nichols's version from answers to author questions, January 3, 2010.

The feds botch their search of Nichols's house:
Testimony of Mary Jasnowski, an evidence recovery specialist sent in from Omaha, in the McVeigh trial (May 5, 1997) and in the Nichols federal trial (November 6, 1997); consent forms signed by Terry and Marife Nichols on April 21 obtained by authors. Agent Stephen Smith erroneously testified at the Nichols federal trial (November 20, 1997) that Nichols's consent to search the house was conditional on Marife being present. The paperwork reflects no such stipulation. Nichols's home phone records, admitted into evidence and obtained by authors, show a phone call from the Herington house to James Nichols's number in Decker beginning at 8:40:45 P.M. and continuing for 19 minutes and 18 seconds; account of FBI agents' activities, from insert, number illegible, dated April 24, 1995; Marife Nichols describing how she could not return home on the night of April 21–22, see transcript of her testimony in the Nichols federal trial, December 10, 1997. She repeated the story at a pretrial hearing in state court in Oklahoma on May 9, 2003; list of items found by evidence recovery team corroborated by official inventories obtained by authors.

Nichols on discovery of ammonium nitrate receipt, answers to author questions, January 3, 2010; incredulous U.S. attorney from Danny Defenbaugh, interview (Gumbel), January 25, 2011; Bear Bryant story told by I. C. Smith, interview (Gumbel and Charles), June 18, 2010; recovery of cash, gold coins, confirmed by FBI property receipt dated April 23 and signed by agents Larry Tongate and Eugene Thomeczek. Marife alerted agents at 4:55 P.M.; the valuables were reported to be safely retrieved at 6:59 P.M; recovery of food mixer detailed in FBI FD-302, file no. 4223, dated May 8, 1995; affidavit supporting federal charges against Terry Nichols, filed May 9, 1995, with Magistrate Judge Ronald Howland of the western district of Oklahoma, case no. M-95-105-H; no lids on barrels confirmed in Jasnowski's court testimony, among other places; FBI inventory based on search through the garbage, FBI FD-302, file no. 8588, April 23, 1995. The agents who searched the garbage were C. Allen Maxwell and Everett F. Barger.

The secret history of the Daryl Bridges phone records:
Accounts that either imply or state that the reconstruction of the phone records

began with the discovery of the Daryl Bridges card at Terry Nichols's house include Coulson and Shannon, *No Heroes,* pp. 514–15, and Julie DelCour and Barbara Hoberock, "Bit by Bit, the Government Makes Its Case," *Tulsa World,* May 18, 1997. In the book *Simple Truths* (pp. 133–34), former FBI agent Jon Hersley finesses the issue when he mentions the Daryl Bridges phone calls, "evidence of which had been found in Terry Nichols's house when it was searched by the FBI. . . . The FBI *had already discovered* that the Daryl Bridges calling card was obtained from the Spotlight company in November 1993. . . ." [Italics ours. Note that Hersley ascribes the discovery to the FBI, when, in fact, this discovery was secondhand and originated with Mary Riley's investigation.]

Airbrushing Mary Riley from the record: In his testimony in the McVeigh trial (May 6, 1997), John Kane makes constant generic references to "investigators" and "they" without mentioning Riley's name. At one point he refers to "Secret Service investigators" in the plural, and is immediately interrupted by a government lawyer asking another question. One FBI FD-302 naming Riley (file no. 186, dated April 22, 1995) made it into discovery. But she was never mentioned in court. Fax copies of Mary Riley's field notes for April 20–26, 1995, titled "Information from Miami Field Office (Telephone Records)," obtained unredacted and mostly complete by the authors.

The April 14 phone call to Eldon Elliott was important to the prosecution, but it also offered an opening to the defense, because a technological glitch in the routing systems made it impossible to say conclusively that Daryl Bridges was the *Spotlight* subscriber who made this call, and because the car dealer who sold McVeigh the Mercury was interviewed eight times by the FBI, and twice more by the defense, without mentioning McVeigh leaving in the middle. At trial (May 6–8, 1997), the prosecution argued around both problems, and the defense could not get traction on its contention that the call was made by someone else.

Riley faxing her findings to Bucella and Stephenson mentioned in her notes, also substantiated by fax headers obtained by authors. Weldon Kennedy interview (Gumbel), August 26, 2010; Kennedy said in his interview that Riley had messed up the time stamps on the calls because she did not realize the West Coast Telephone records were all on Pacific time. But Riley did realize this and recorded in her notes repeated conversations with John Kane and others about both the time zone question and inaccuracies associated with the recent switch to Daylight Savings Time (mentioned in her field notes for April 22 and April 23, 1995). Danny Defenbaugh interview (Gumbel), December 9, 2010; internal investigation of Riley mentioned in John Solomon, "Secret Service Documents Cite Mystery Video in Oklahoma City Bombing," *Associated Press,* April 19, 2004, and confirmed by senior task force member cited here; John Kane interview (Gumbel), January 25, 2011.

Feds come up mostly empty at James Nichols's farm:
The most incriminating findings are detailed in the affidavit supporting James Nichols's arrest on firearms charges, May 11, 1995. Other details are in the FBI's

FD-302 interview report on Nichols, April 21, 1995, file no. 6384; see also Serrano, *One of Ours,* pp. 234–35; Nichols's perspective from Nichols and Papovic, *Freedom's End,* pp. 21, 58; law enforcement official involved in search, speaking on condition of anonymity, interview (Gumbel), January 5, 2011; Martinolich-Freeh confrontation reported by Kessler, *The Bureau,* pp. 349–50; corroborated by Revell, *A G-Man's Journal,* p. 474, by I. C. Smith, interview (Gumbel and Charles), June 18, 2010, and by confidential FBI source. Story of resignation offer/Bear Bryant phone call from confidential source.

The shortcomings of the FBI's sledgehammer approach:
Bob Ricks interview (Gumbel), August 9, 2010; Weldon Kennedy quotes information on the leaks, interview (Gumbel), August 26, 2010; James Nichols complaining that his arrest was part of a dark conspiracy to protect the "real" bombers, *Freedom's End,* op. cit., pp. 57–58.

Chapter 5

McVeigh's combat experience:
The work of Jonathan Franklin stands head and shoulders above the rest in assessing McVeigh's military career. See his pieces "Timothy McVeigh, Soldier," *Playboy,* October 1995, vol. 42, issue 10, p. 78, and "The Good Soldier," *Spin,* April 1997, p. 133; Franklin very kindly provided the raw notes from his McVeigh interview, via e-mail (Gumbel), July 29, 2010; quadrupling nightmare quote provided by Greg Henry, interview (Gumbel), February 9, 2011; James Rockwell interview (Gumbel), January 4, 2011; Dave Dilly interview (Gumbel), December 13, 2010; McVeigh's version of events from Michel and Herbeck, op. cit., pp. 66–88; medal and award citations, see McVeigh's trial exhibit nos. AA2X-AA10X; these include the Bronze Star, Army Commendation Medal, and a Certificate of Commendation from the Gulf War, plus another Army Commendation Medal and one other award for target shooting; McVeigh's marksmanship also merited a glowing write-up in the official history of the 16th Infantry, written well after his conviction and sentencing for the bombing: Steven E. Clay, *Blood and Sacrifice: The History of the 16th Infantry Regiment from the Civil War Through the Gulf War* (Cantigny First Divison Foundation, Wheaton, Illinois, 2001), p. 364.

Possible involvement in war crimes, and McVeigh's disillusionment:
The relevant sections of the Geneva Conventions are the First Convention, Articles 16 and 17 (on treatment of the dead and wounded), and the Third Convention, Article 3 (on treatment of surrendering soldiers and noncombatants). Frame's FBI FD-302, file no. 3118, May 4, 1995; Cerney's FBI FD-302, file no. 488, April 28, 1995. Frame and Regier were interviewed by Jonathan Franklin, per e-mail to Gumbel dated August 21, 2010. Frame was interviewed by Franklin on May 17, 1995, and Regier on May 22, 1995; Scott Rutter interviews (Gumbel), December 6 and December 31, 2009; James Rockwell interview (Gumbel), January 4, 2011.

Jennifer McVeigh gets the third degree:
FBI FD-302 interview of Jennifer, April 24–May 2, 1995, file no. 2298. Many other details from her testimony in the McVeigh trial, May 5–6, 1997, and from Weldon Kennedy interview (Gumbel), August 26, 2011. FBI agents showing her photographs of dead children corroborated by FBI FD-302, file no. 2024, April 29, 1995.

Brief history of the Nichols family:
Details from Lana Padilla and Ron Delpit, op. cit., pp. 36–37, and 163–68, from James Nichols and Robert Papovich, op. cit., pp. 154–57, and from Stephen Braun and Judy Pasternak, "Nichols Brothers Swept Up in Dark Maelstrom of Fury," *Los Angeles Times,* May 28, 1995; also, Padilla, interview (Gumbel), September 25, 2010, and Padilla's statements to the FBI, see her FD-302 interview reports for April 21, 1995 (file no. 9330) and April 28, 1995 (file no. 5827); Nichols's Asperger syndrome in an FBI memo of July 12, 2005, from the Oklahoma City office to the Denver office, case ID no. 11120, and confirmed both by Lana Padilla—interview (Gumbel), February 1, 2011—and by Nichols himself, written answers to author questions, February 23, 2011; "complicating matters some," from Nichols's handwritten answers to author questions, January 3, 2010.

McVeigh and Nichols in the army:
Lana Padilla interview (Gumbel), September 25, 2010; Scott Rutter interview (Gumbel), December 6, 2009; Dave Dilly interview (Gumbel), December 13, 2010; James Rockwell interview (Gumbel), January 4, 2011; McVeigh's racism and Klan membership, Michel and Herbeck, op. cit., pp. 87–88.

Jeanne Boylan corrects John Doe Two sketch, told to forget about John Doe One:
Jeanne Boylan, op. cit., pp. 201–209. Also Boylan interview by MGA documentary crew, June 1, 2000, transcript obtained by authors.

Terry Nichols maxes out his credit cards:
Nichols's written answers to author questions, January 22, 2010; Wickstrom quotes taken from Daniel Levitas, *The Terrorist Next Door,* p. 179, and from Susy Buchanan, "Return of the Pastor," Southern Poverty Law Center Intelligence Report, Winter 2004; Sanilac County court records on both the First Deposit National Bank and Chase Manhattan claims, including filings by Nichols and by the plaintiffs, exhibits, and hearing transcripts, obtained by authors.

McVeigh comes unstuck, hits the gun-show circuit:
McVeigh calling VA hospital for mental health counseling disclosed by Dr. John R. Smith, his prison psychiatrist, in an interview with NPR's Wayne Goodwin, *All Things Considered,* June 8, 2001; for McVeigh's version of the year between his discharge from the army and his departure from New York State, see Michel and Herbeck, op. cit., pp. 95–116; his letter to the *Lockport Union Sun & Journal* was published February 11, 1992; William Pierce on gun shows, quoted in Morris Dees with James Corcoran, *Gathering Storm: America's Militia Threat,* p. 79; Kristen Rand, *Gun Shows in America: Tupperware Parties for Criminals;*

McVeigh selling smoke grenades and blast simulators, Richard A. Serrano, *One of Ours*, p. 56; the best account of the Ruby Ridge fiasco is Jess Walter, *Ruby Ridge: The Truth and Tragedy of the Randy Weaver Family;* emergency meeting in Estes Park, Colorado—the Rocky Mountain Rendezvous—described at length in Dees and Corcoran, op. cit., pp. 1–2, 46–66; video of Louis Beam speech obtained by authors; Louis Beam, *Leaderless Resistance, Seditionist,* issue 12, February 1992, available at Beam's Web site www.louisbeam.com; McVeigh's grievance list detailed in Stuart A. Wright, *Patriots, Politics and the Oklahoma City Bombing,* pp. 129–38; Wright was given access to McVeigh through his defense team and interviewed him at length; McVeigh quitting security guard job on January 26, from defense memo obtained by authors; Roger Moore meeting in Fort Lauderdale and plan to share a table at upcoming Miami gun show detailed in FBI FD-302 interview with Moore on April 28, 1995, file no. 810, and also in FBI FD-302 interview with Moore's wife, Carol, on November 7, 1995, file no. 12689.

Jennifer McVeigh and the bank robbery letter:
McVeigh's letter of December 24, 1993, entered into evidence at trial; the call to the FBI crime lab is documented in a May 4 memo from the lab to Bob Ricks, Lab no. E-3427. The subject line says, "Telephone call April 26, 1995." The tests on five latent prints from a Cleveland-area robbery and one latent impression from the St. Louis area came back negative.

FBI almost misses key evidence from Geary Lake witness:
Account from Budke's testimony in the Nichols federal trial, December 11, 1997. A handwritten lead sheet about his encounter with Wahl, timed 12:45 P.M. on April 26, 1995, was (belatedly) entered into evidence at trial.

McVeigh meets Roger Moore, goes to Waco:
Fort Lauderdale meeting detailed in FBI FD-302 interviews with Roger and Carol Moore, cited above; details about the Confederate flag and the camo pants come from an FBI FD-302 interview with Karen Anderson, May 19, 1995, file no. 5435; Floyd Hays interview (Gumbel), July 14, 2010; for McVeigh's account of this period, see Michel and Herbeck, op. cit., pp. 117–20. The Waco disaster has spawned an entire literature. See for example: Dick J. Reavis, *The Ashes of Waco;* Danny O. Coulson and Elaine Shannon, *No Heroes,* pp. 429–48; Gary Noesner, *Stalling for Time,* pp. 94–132; also, Department of Justice "Report to the Deputy Attorney General on the Events at Waco, Texas," October 8, 1993. Louis Beam gave his own account of the "forbidden question" in an interview with *The Spotlight* magazine, July 12, 1993. The confrontations were covered in the local media and in Mark Potok, "Siege in Texas Attracts a Crew from the Fringes," *USA Today,* March 19, 1993. Likelihood that Beam and McVeigh met: Beam was thrown out of the news briefing on March 14 and handcuffed at the news briefing on March 17. Student journalist Michelle Rauch drove to Waco on her spring break from Southern Methodist University and later testified (on June 10, 1997) about interviewing McVeigh. She did not specify the date of her interview, but SMU's spring break that year ran from March 13 to March 21 (per

Veronica Decena of the SMU Registrar's office, e-mail sent February 10, 2011). So Beam and McVeigh were almost certainly at Waco at the same time. Jim Cavanaugh interview (Gumbel), August 2, 2010.

The FBI grills Michael Fortier:
Much of this material is from Fortier's testimony in McVeigh's trial, May 12, 1997; typewriter ribbon story from Lori Fortier's testimony in the McVeigh trial, April 29, 1997; "I'm a dead man" quote cited in U.S. Secret Service timeline for April 24, 1995, at 1930. Details of evidence the Fortiers ditched are only partly covered by their trial testimony; the Hornet rifle and galvanized tubing, which Fortier did not discuss, are detailed in an FD-302 interview report on Rosencrans, July 1, 1995, file no. 6700; and in an FD-302 on Rosencrans's girlfriend, Patty Edwards (Patricia Ann Edwards, July 1, 1995, file no. 6696). The detail about Rosencrans's half-brother being married to his mother comes from Edwards's 302, quote: "EDWARDS explained CHUCK and JIM have the same father, but different mothers. EDWARDS also advised CHUCK is JIM's priest"; Coulson's part of the story recounted in Coulson and Elaine Shannon, *No Heroes,* pp. 521–26; Rosencrans arrest story detailed in Mohave County Sheriff's Department arrest report, dated May 1, 1995, obtained by authors.

McVeigh meets Karen Anderson and Andreas Strassmeir at Tulsa gun show:
Quick trip to Kingman detailed in McVeigh defense team memo, obtained by authors; encounter with Anderson from Anderson's testimony in the Nichols trial, November 17–18, 1997. Encounter with Strassmeir, see FD-302 interview with Strassmeir, conducted by phone with two Justice Department lawyers, April 30–May 1, 1996, file no. 14897; Strassmeir interview (Gumbel), July 3, 2010; and a confidential defense memo, obtained by authors, in which McVeigh says he and Strassmeir are "brothers in arms." McVeigh variously told investigators he swapped the knife for several pairs of long johns, not the battle uniform and gloves, or that he wanted to swap the knife for the long johns but Strassmeir insisted on having the cash. Strassmeir's memory seems more reliable, since his account is more consistent and since he was the one who ended up with the items.

Offer of undercover agent to sniff out Strassmeir rebuffed:
Steve Chancellor interview (Gumbel), August 12, 2010; State Department diplomatic security memo of April 28, 1995, obtained by authors.

McVeigh visits Roger Moore's ranch, witnesses end of the Waco siege:
Account of visit to the Arkansas ranch mostly from Moore and Anderson testimony in the Nichols trial; McVeigh's account of seeing the end of the siege on television, see Michel and Herbeck, op. cit., p. 135; episode also recounted by Michael Fortier at McVeigh trial, May 12, 1997.

Roger Moore's coded letter to McVeigh:
Letter entered into evidence at the Nichols trial. For federal law enforcement considering that Moore and McVeigh were in cahoots over the robbery, see Secret Service timeline entry for April 29, 1995, at 1034: "McVeigh and Terry Nichols

may have been involved in an insurance fraud scam with a subject identified as Bob Moore AKA Roger Miller and Roger Moore. . . . An initial analysis of the letter indicates that Moore and McVeigh set up the robbery." Details of interrogation of Moore and Anderson from their FD-302s of April 28, 1995, full citation above.

McVeigh orders a significant book, discovers *Waco: The Big Lie*:
Extracts from *Homemade C-4* cited in Hersley, Tongate, and Burke, *Simple Truths: The Real Story of the Oklahoma City Bombing Investigation,* pp. 124–25; specifics of McVeigh's purchases from Paladin Press detailed by the company's Dana Rogers in the McVeigh trial, May 1, 1997; an updated version of Linda Thompson's *Waco: The Big Lie* is available online (viewed February 17, 2011, at Google Videos); promotional teaser quoted in Serrano, op. cit., p. 77.

Jennifer McVeigh comes clean:
Jennifer McVeigh affidavit, dated May 2, 1995, obtained by authors; McVeigh's mother flown in from Florida, Stephen Jones and Peter Israel, *Others Unknown,* p. 89; "Tim is fried anyways" line from her FD-302, April 24–May 2, 1995; details of FBI wanting her to testify against her brother from her testimony in McVeigh's trial, May 5, 1997; Fortier speculating on motive for Roger Moore robbery, from his testimony in McVeigh trial, May 12, 1997.

Chapter 6

McVeigh draws attention of law enforcement, FBI and ATF yawn:
Al Shearer, FBI FD-302, file no. 1974, April 28, 1995; this story was broken by Mark Flatten of the Cox News Service—see Flatten, "FBI and ATF Were Warned About McVeigh in 1993," *Seattle Post-Intelligencer,* June 2, 1995.

Coulson gets shafted, Potts gets promoted, Freeh gets distracted:
Danny Coulson interview (Gumbel), May 19, 2010; Reno announcement of Potts as deputy director contained in transcript of her news briefing, May 3, 1995, distributed by the U.S. News Service; Potts and Freeh working the Judge Vance mail-bombing case, Kessler, *The FBI,* p. 522; unreleased Department of Justice report is "Report of the Ruby Ridge Task Force to the Office of Professional Responsibility of Investigation of Allegations of Improper Governmental Conduct in the Investigation, Apprehension and Prosecution of Randall C. Weaver and Kevin L. Harris," June 10, 1994. Parts of this report were eventually released and were, as of November 2011, available at the DOJ Web site at http://www.justice .gov/opr/readingroom/rubyreportcover_39.pdf. Glenn letter covered in David Johnston, "FBI Leader at 1992 Standoff in Idaho Says Review Shielded Top Officials," *New York Times,* May 10, 1995; on Freeh's clash with Gorelick, see James Rowley, "FBI-Justice Clashes Are Nothing New," *Associated Press,* December 3, 1997; Office of Professional Responsibility investigation into Glenn allegations detailed in a Department of Justice news release, "Evidence from Investigation of 1992 Ruby Ridge Matter Only Sufficient to Charge One Official with Criminal Conduct," August 15, 1997.

Government disregards own evidence of second Ryder truck:
Rick Wahl initially identifying the pickup as gray, from lead sheet drawn up by
FBI Agent Budke on April 26, 1995; Bob Nelson testified in the Nichols trial,
November 20, 1997; Rucker and Sargent both testified in the Nichols trial on
December 4, 1997. Rucker quote from MGA documentary interview, March 6,
1999; Sargent quote from MGA documentary interview, March 25, 1999 (transcripts obtained by authors); Bob Ricks interview (Gumbel), August 9, 2010. The
government's initial interest in the second Ryder truck theory is documented, e.g.,
in attorney notes on a witness named Barbara Whittenberg, who claimed to have
served breakfast to three men who drove up to her diner in Herington in a Ryder
truck. The attorney review is dated October 22, 1996, and initialed ALM, an
apparent reference to Larry Mackey, whose initials were, in fact, LAM but were
accidentally transposed.

McVeigh creates a "network of friends":
McVeigh and Guthrie meeting: in Mark Hamm's book *In Bad Company*, p. 145,
Pete Langan is quoted as saying: "Guthrie knew McVeigh. Guthrie met him
through the gun shows"; McVeigh and Nichols stayed at a Motel 6 in Fayette-
ville on October 11–12, 1993, and the booking was in Nichols's name; copy of
McVeigh's October 12 traffic citation near Elohim City obtained by authors;
Guthrie gives an account of the planned (but never attempted) armored car heist
in the Fayetteville area in his unpublished handwritten memoir, *The Taunting
Bandits*, pp. 13–16. He says the participants were himself, Langan, and Shawn
Kenny, whom he calls Dan Kenny; Guthrie meeting Robb in 1992 included in his
FBI FD-302, March 4–15, 1996; Nichols's account from a letter to Jesse Trenta-
due, October 18, 2006, obtained by authors.

The hunt for Steve Colbern:
Colbern is first mentioned in the Secret Service timeline at 1937 on May 5:
"Steve Colburn [sic], a federal fugitive being pursued by the U.S. Marshal
Service, shared a P.O. Box with McVeigh at one time. Colbern fits description of John Doe #2." Colbern said in his first FBI interview (FD-302, file
no. 2178, May 12, 1995) that he did once have a mailbox in Kingman but not
in the last ten years. A U.S. Marshals' Report of Investigation into Colbern,
May 6, 1995, details the letter postmarked from Texarkana and confirms the
mailbox link. The report was shared with the ATF, and eventually handed
over to defense lawyers in the bombing case in 2001. McVeigh's note to
"S.C." entered into evidence at the federal trials; court documents on the
search of Colbern's pickup were unsealed in September 1995 and published,
e.g., in Michelle Boorstein, "Judge Unseals Documents on Searches Involving McVeigh, Colbern," *Associated Press*, September 14, 1995; Colbern's
neighbor Maybelle Hertig quoted in David Johnston, "Bomb Inquiry Leads
to Arrest of Biochemist," *New York Times*, May 13, 1995; details on snakes,
ex-wife, from FBI interview with Colbern's uncle, Dr. Edwin Colbern, FD-
302, file no. 3223, May 12, 1995.

The brief, disturbing life of Jason Nichols:
McVeigh sends Nichols to Pendleton, Michel and Herbeck, op. cit., p. 138; the account of McVeigh's 1993 stay in Decker and Jason's death is taken from a Nichols defense team memorandum amalgamating all of Marife Nichols's interview statements about her son, dated July 15, 1997; from Marife's FBI FD-302 interview report, file no. 4944, dated May 1, 1995; from Nichols's handwritten answers to author questions, dated January 3, 2010; and, regarding McVeigh's CPR efforts, from Michel and Herbeck, op. cit., pp. 147–50.

Evidence teams grapple with the "red pyramid":
Weldon Kennedy interview (Gumbel), December 15, 2010; a FEMA Situation Report for April 25, 1995, 1:30 P.M. EDT, reads: "On April 24, President Clinton directed the General Services Administration to rebuild the Murrah Building after the recovery effort"; people who saw sinister intent in the decision to demolish the building were largely fans of General Partin's multiple-explosive theory of the bombing (debunked in chapter 2), see, e.g., William F. Jasper, "Explosive Evidence of a Cover-Up," *New American,* August 7, 1995; Oscar Johnson, interview with a defense investigator for McVeigh, dated February 16, 1996. Defenbaugh-Eberhardt spat: interviews (Gumbel) with Defenbaugh, May 18, June 13, and September 22, 2010; interviews (Gumbel) with Eberhardt, May 26 and July 9, 2010. More than nine months after the bombing, Eberhardt wrote up an FBI FD-302 describing how he returned to his ninth-floor office sometime in early May, removed a dummy bomb device, threw it in a bag, and later disposed of it (file no. 13012, February 3, 1996). The existence and delayed timing of this 302 lend some credence to Defenbaugh's memory that Eberhardt's handling of the device was subject to FBI investigation. If there is further documentation on the matter, the FBI and ATF have not disclosed it.

Stephen Jones's inauspicious beginning as McVeigh's defense counsel:
Jones's biographical details, approach by Judge Russell, from *Others Unknown,* op. cit., pp. 11–12; Michel and Herbeck (op. cit., p. 281) have Gerry Spence turning down McVeigh's defense. But Spence said in an e-mail (to Gumbel, March 12, 2011) that, while he couldn't remember for sure, he didn't think he was ever asked. Dick DeGuerin turning it down, interview (Gumbel), July 14, 2010; Jones's first meeting with McVeigh recounted in a confidential memo by ABC producer Don Thrasher to his bosses, dated March 26, 1996, and obtained by authors; Jones's brief on halting the demolition of the Murrah Building: "Defendant's Motion to Preserve Evidence Scheduled to Be Destroyed by the Government, and Brief in Support," filed around May 10, 1995 (no date on author copy); on delay in demolition of Murrah Building, see from the *Daily Oklahoman,* Chris Casteel, "Agency Plans to Raze Building, GSA Weighs Effects of Using Explosives," May 9, 1995; Casteel, "Explosives to Demolish Building Work May Begin by This Weekend," May 10, 1995; and Nolan Clay, "Defense Experts Study Ruins, Team Disappointed to Find Crater Filled," May 21, 1995; quote from Coyle's clerk from Serrano, op. cit., p. 350.

The FBI's brief bout of insanity over Josh Nichols:
The Oklahoma City command post holding all John Doe Two leads "in abeyance," from insert E-4153, dated May 3, 1995, written by Special Agent Thomas P. Ravenelle of the San Francisco office, explaining why he was no longer pursuing a John Doe Two lead he had taken up on May 3. Josh calling Agent Calhoun after hours, see Lana Padilla and Ron Delpit, op. cit., pp. 142–43. Account of Josh being accused, op. cit., pp. 98–106, and the following FBI FD-302s: Josh Nichols, file no. 5098, May 6, 1995; Lana Padilla, file no. 5834, May 6, 1995. Nichols (handwritten answers to author questions, March 30, 2010) said he regarded the naming of Josh as John Doe Two "a form of threat and coercion." He wrote: "I took it as a sign that it would be best if I just shut my mouth and 'take the fall,' which is pretty much what I did in my federal trial." Lana and Josh in Las Vegas, handing over clothes and baseball caps, *By Blood Betrayed*, pp. 112–32; the Secret Service timeline entry for May 11 discussing the resumption of investigation into John Doe Two leads is at 1810 hours.

McVeigh spends the night with Karen Anderson:
Karen Anderson, FBI FD-302 interview, file no. 5435, May 19, 1995; Anderson "very fond" of McVeigh, from FBI FD-302 interview with Steve Colbern, file no. 5344, dated May 20, 1995; McVeigh dropping in on Lori Fortier, see testimony of Deborah Brown, Fortier's colleague at The Beach Club tanning salon, at McVeigh's trial, May 28, 1997; Jim Rosencrans, FBI FD-302, file no. 6700, July 1, 1995; Patty Edwards, FBI FD-302, file no. 6696, July 1, 1995; "Virgin McVeigh" taunt, from a self-published memoir by McVeigh's fellow federal death row inmate David Paul Hammer, with input from Jeffery Paul, *Secrets Worth Dying For: Timothy James McVeigh and the Oklahoma City Bombing* (2003).

Bill Maloney raises prospect of John Doe Three:
FBI FD-302 interview with Maloney, file no. 3576, May 10, 1995; Maloney interview (Gumbel), April 30, 2010. Terry Nichols denied being in Cassville in November 1994 (but did not say he had *never* been there) or knowing a Robert Jacques. When Marife was asked why the name Jacks or Jacques appeared in her address book, she said she was trying to write the word "yuk" or "yucky" but didn't know how to spell it and tried a number of different ways, to see what looked right. (Terry Nichols, handwritten answers to author questions, January 3, 2010; Marife Nichols, interview with defense investigator H. C. Bodley, August 17, 1995, and also FBI FD-302, file no. 14297, dated August 4–8, 1995.) The U.S. embassy official in the Philippines who interviewed Marife on this question did not find her answer wholly convincing (detailed in Teater's Robert Jacques report, see below). Bill Teater interview (Gumbel), August 11, 2010; Jeanne Boylan, op. cit., pp. 210–11 (about her interview of postal worker Debbie Nakanashi) and p. 228 (her quote about Maloney); confirmation of McVeigh's discolored tooth, from an FBI report written by Teater, "Comprehensive summary of investigation concerning Robert Jacques, possible associate of Timothy

James McVeigh and Terry Lynn Nichols," April 19, 2000, obtained by Gumbel (Teater's name redacted, but his initials in lowercase, "wet," left visible); details of Defenbaugh's biography, taken from his Web site www.dannydefenbaugh.com; he formally took over the investigation on May 11, the day after Terry Nichols's indictment on bombing charges. I. C. Smith interviews, June 18 (Gumbel and Charles) and October 4, 2010 (Gumbel). The only other senior FBI veteran willing to address the issue of Defenbaugh's leadership on the record was Bob Ricks, who contrasted Weldon Kennedy's ability to set an agenda and exercise judgment on what mattered with "other people," who "may have a limited investigative background"; "It's about different capabilities people had, and putting people in the right spots," he said; interview (Gumbel), August 9, 2010. Teater quote from interview (Gumbel), August 13, 2010; Defenbaugh characterizing his role, interviews (Gumbel), May 17, 2010, and April 4, 2011.

Colbern gets arrested, the FBI loses interest almost immediately:
Account of arrest from David Johnston, "Bomb Inquiry Leads to Arrest of Biochemist," *New York Times,* May 13, 1995; Colbern's first FBI interview detailed in FD-302, file no. 2178, May 12, 1995; Preston Haney, interviewed by the ATF, see FBI FD-302, file no. 1879, May 15, 1995; letter to Barbara Harris, from FBI interview with Harris, FD-302, file no. 1294, May 11, 1995; the Mail Room manager recognizing Colbern's picture, from Lynda Willoughby's FBI FD-302, file no. 4461, May 12, 1995 (interview conducted by the ATF). Details on the Browning video from ATF and U.S. Marshals Service files handed over in discovery to Nichols's state trial lawyers in 2001, confirmed also by Richard Hanawalt, interview (Gumbel), March 18, 2011; Edwin Colbern, FBI FD-302, file no. 3223, dated May 12, 1995; government's belief that Colbern was too weird to be involved based on subsequent documentation on Colbern (detailed in later section in this chapter) and on interview (Gumbel) with Danny Defenbaugh, May 19, 2010; Michael Tigar interview (Gumbel), March 1, 2011: Edwin Colbern's 302 described Colbern smelling like a "billy goat."

Fortier reaches out to the FBI:
FBI FD-302, file no. 4477, May 12, 1995, was written by Agent David Beiter, who received the Kit Kat wrapper from Fortier.

Stephen Jones leaks own client's guilt to the *New York Times:*
Pam Belluck, "McVeigh Is Reported to Claim Responsibility for the Bombing," *New York Times,* May 17, 1995; account of Jones's attempt to negotiate with Reno for his client's life, interview with Jones (Gumbel and Charles), September 17, 2010; leak justification in Jones and Israel, op. cit., pp. xv, 60–62. Jones never explicitly writes that he obtained authorization before talking to Belluck. The closest he comes is this line: "He gave me the authorization to proceed, and I called Pam Belluck at the *New York Times.*" Jones could have been clearer about the time sequence in this sentence considering the importance of the issue. Jones was made aware of the allegations in this section. In an initial response (an e-mail dated March 16, 2011), he wrote: "These questions and the incident I discussed

at length in the second edition of my book. I do not know I can add anything to them at this time. My memory would probably have been better ten years ago." In a second e-mail, on March 22, 2011, he raised the issue again, unprompted, and explicitly denied leaking the story before obtaining McVeigh's authorization. "I had met Pam Belluck," he wrote, "and may have talked with her briefly on the telephone, but we had no such discussion until after Mr. McVeigh and I discussed it at length and I had his authority to discuss it with her." Rob Nigh interview (Gumbel), April 5, 2011; McVeigh's version in Michel and Herbeck, op. cit., pp. 283–84.

Michael and Lori Fortier come clean . . . ish:
Account of May 17 FBI questioning taken from FD-302, file no. 3495, May 17, 1995, and from Michael Fortier's testimony in McVeigh's trial, May 12–13, 1997.

McVeigh's misadventures in Arizona:
Jim Rosencrans, FBI FD-302, July 1, 1995, file no. 6700; Michael Fortier testimony in McVeigh's trial, May 12, 1997; McCarty quoted in Serge F. Koveleski and Pierre Thomas "3rd Man's Fate Dangles in Okla. Bombing Case; Prosecutors Divided Over Strategy on Fortier," *Washington Post,* August 7, 1995; background on the Arizona Patriots, see Brent L. Smith, *Terrorism in America,* pp. 79–84, and Tony Perry, "Godfather of Arizona's Militiamen; Oklahoma City Bombing Puts Jack Oliphant, an Ex-Con and Survivalist, Back in Limelight," *Los Angeles Times,* May 21, 1995; on Oliphant and McVeigh, see Dyane Partridge's FBI FD-302 interviews, file no. 1215, dated May 10, 1995, and file no. 14486, dated March 28, 1996; also, interview (Gumbel) with the FBI agent who talked to her, Lee Fabrizio, December 11, 2009; McVeigh shooting near Oliphant's ranch, from a letter to Kingman radio journalist Dave Hawkins, postmarked April 13, 2001, provided to the authors by Hawkins; Tom Hoover interview (Gumbel), February 23, 2010, and follow-up e-mail chat, February 25, 2010.

Colbern talks to the feds, the feds drop him as a suspect:
Meeting with prosecutors detailed in Colbern FBI FD-302, file no. 5344, May 20, 1995; Moore and Anderson discuss selling .50-caliber ammunition to Colbern in their interviews of May 19, 1995, the day before Colbern's big interview; Dennis Malzac, interviewed by the ATF, FBI FD-302, file no. 3791, May 13, 1995; Malzac's 2000 revelations taken from motion filed by Terry Nichols's lawyers in state court in Oklahoma, February 9, 2004, requesting more government documents on Colbern (obtained by authors); Colbern, prisoner no. 41130-008, was released on February 24, 1999, according to Bureau of Prisons records; Richard Hanawalt interview (Gumbel), March 18, 2011; Bob Sanders interview (Charles), March 18, 2011.

Carol Howe's Elohim City investigation falls apart:
ATF Report of Investigation on Carol Howe (informant no. 53270-183), May 31, 1995; ATF Report of Investigation, May 18, 1995 (reactivating Howe); ATF Request for Advance of Funds, May 18, 1995; $250 received on May 22.

Michael Tigar goes to bat for Terry and Marife Nichols:
Tigar's filing and subsequent hearing reported in John Kifner, "Release Without Bail Is Sought for Bombing Suspect," *New York Times*, May 26, 1995, and Richard A. Serrano, "Nichols Bail Hearing Judge Faults Interrogators' Tactics," *Los Angeles Times*, June 3, 1995; Marife's visit to Nichols memorialized in FBI FD-302, file no. 5618, May 25, 1995; return of money, being told she has to pay her own way, see FBI FD-302, file nos. 3231–3, dated May 25, 26, 27, 1995 (one per day); voice mail memorialized in FBI FD-302, file no. 5748, May 31, 1995.

FBI finds a reason not to believe in John Doe Two:
Michael Hertig, FBI FD-302, file no. 5532, May 23, 1995; Todd Bunting, FBI FD-302, file nos. 5682 and 5690, May 28 and 29, 1995; Hertig acknowledged his mustache at the time of the Ryder rental in the McVeigh trial, May 23, 1997; Eldon Elliott talked about not being in the office on May 18 in the McVeigh trial, May 9, 1997; Vicki Beemer explaining how she knew Hertig, was sure two men came in on April 17, see her testimony in the McVeigh trial, May 22–23, 1997; Danny Coulson interview (Gumbel), May 19, 2010; I. C. Smith interview (Gumbel), October 4, 2010.

Fortier leads the FBI on a wild-goose chase in the desert:
Fortier FBI FD-302, file nos. 9161 and 9162, May 30, 1995; Weldon Kennedy interview (Gumbel), August 26, 2010.

FBI and prosecutors skirt holes in evidence at Eldon Elliott's body shop:
McDonald's video and timing of McVeigh's supposed walk to Eldon Elliott's body shop discussed, e.g., in Jon Hersley, Larry Tongate, and Bob Burke, *Simple Truths*, pp. 217–19. Agent Gary Witt retracing McVeigh's steps also recounted here; "light mist" line from Eldon Elliott's testimony in the McVeigh trial, May 9, 1997; Scott Mendeloff interviews (Gumbel), July 16, 2010, and October 4, 2010; McVeigh's version, Michel and Herbeck, op. cit., p. 213; Linda James interview (Gumbel), August 3, 2010, and e-mails, December 7, 2010. She saw only two indications that there might be a resemblance to McVeigh's handwriting—the "li" in "Kling" and the backward slant. But James said the slant could be misleading. Weldon L. Kennedy, *On-Scene Commander*, p. 219; Kennedy interview (Gumbel), August 26, 2010. In his FBI FD-302 interview of May 19, 1995, file no. 9256, Roger Moore described how, after spring 1994, his "only means of contact with McVeigh was when McVeigh would call, or by letter"; Karen Anderson mentioned the phone call in January or February 1994 in her testimony in the Nichols trial, November 17–18, 1997. Nichols described seeing McVeigh with a non-Bridges calling card on two occasions. He says in his handwritten document "Timeline: From April 1994 thru September 1994, Tracking McVeigh's Travels" (November 11, 2006), the card was a Fone America prepaid debit card similar to those reported to be used by the Aryan Republican Army. In answers to author questions, dated January 3, 2010, he said he didn't know what kind of card it was.

Chapter 7

Moore, McVeigh, and the Kinestik mystery:
Moore and Karen Anderson's initial stories are contained in their FBI FD-302s for April 28 and May 19, 1995. Moore did not mention meeting McVeigh at a gun show in Knob Creek, Kentucky, in 1993 in his first interview. Karen Anderson made no mention of meeting McVeigh in Kentucky, or at the Soldier of Fortune Convention in Las Vegas, in any of her FBI interviews or court appearances. Anderson said in her May 19 FBI interview that McVeigh's first visit to the Arkansas ranch, in April 1993, lasted two and a half days; Moore testified at McVeigh trial on November 18, 1997, that it lasted ten days. "Top sergeant" line from Moore's trial testimony; account of McVeigh's April 1994 visit from Moore and Anderson's FBI FD-302s of May 19, 1995, and their testimony in the Nichols trial (November 17–18, 1997).

The defense information on the Kinestik comes from a purported interview with McVeigh conducted by defense investigator Richard Reyna on December 12, 1995, write-up by Reyna obtained by authors. It was later alleged that no such interview took place (Stephen Jones, e-mail to Gumbel, March 22, 2011, and Rob Nigh, interview with Gumbel, April 5, 2011). Still, the understanding among the defense team members was that the underlying facts were accurate (Stuart Wright, interview with Gumbel, April 28, 2011). McVeigh himself also confirmed that the material was genuine (Michel and Herbeck, op. cit., p. 301). See also chapter 9.

Nichols's allegations concerning the Kinestik he said McVeigh obtained from Roger Moore are in two of his prison writings, one titled "Timeline: From April 1994 thru September 1994 Tracking McVeigh's Travels" (November 11, 2006) and the other "OKC Bombing Materials and the Missing Explosives" (December 1, 2007); more details in his answers to author questions, one batch dated April 27, 2010, and the other February 21, 2011; McVeigh's allusions to Kinestik appear on pp. 163–64 of Michel and Herbeck; Roger Moore responds to allegations in Richard A. Serrano, "Man Says He Had No Role in Oklahoma Plot," *Los Angeles Times,* May 5, 2005.

No fingerprints on nitromethane tubes or box: in a preliminary finding on May 4, 2005 (included in summary report dated June 24, 2005), the FBI crime lab reported that 16 of the 68 nitromethane tubes bore fingerprints but could not yet say if they were recoverable; almost three years later (February 21, 2008), the lab concluded that they were not—a time delay that has raised suspicions in some quarters; documents obtained by authors. Attempts to contact Moore for this book were unsuccessful. On May 4, 2010, a woman—presumably his wife, Carol, or Karen Anderson—answered the phone at his Florida residence, acknowledged receipt of a letter outlining Nichols's allegations, and said curtly: "We're not interested."

Terry Nichols teeters on the brink:
Nichols input mostly from his "Timeline" document of November 11, 2006, and

his answers to author questions, January 3, 2010, and March 20, 2010; McVeigh's version from Michel and Herbeck, op. cit., p. 158; Marion County Clerk Marquetta Eilerts, FBI FD-302, file no. 15830, August 6, 1996; Nichols's employer, Timothy Donahue, testified in the Nichols federal trial, November 5, 1997; Marife Nichols testified about her affair with McVeigh at the Nichols state trial, from Tim Talley, "Nichols's second wife says she had affair with McVeigh," Associated Press, April 8, 2004; McVeigh shooting at Nichols, told by Lana Padilla, interview (Gumbel), September 25, 2010.

Moore's quirky, murky past:
Moore biographical details from Carol Moore's FBI FD-302, file no. 12689, November 7, 1995, from Moore's interview with Roland Leeds, November 11, 1996, and from Moore's FBI FD-302 interview of May 19, 1995, file no. 9256; he described building boats for the navy in Vietnam in his first big FBI interview, FD-302, file no. 810, April 28, 1995; Bill Stoneman interviewed by defense investigator John Hough, December 16, 1996, report obtained by authors; Rodney Bowers, interviews (Gumbel), March 10 and May 6, 2010; smoke bomb incident, from Lance Powell interview with defense investigator Roland Leeds, December 10, 1996; more details from Martin "Walt" Powell interview with Leeds, November 12, 1996 (reports obtained by authors). The housekeeper was Patricia Cicatello, and details of her cash robbery are from a Garland County sheriff's report, August 11, 1986; she committed suicide in 1994 (documents obtained by authors); suicide of Moore's friend Layton Noel detailed in Garland County sheriff's report, October 20, 1986. Unverified stories about Moore: Camp Peary instructor lead from former intelligence operative, interview (Charles), April 9, 1997. Bowers had a source who suggested Moore had played a role in the U.S. government's support of the Nicaraguan contras; see also, Al Martin, *The Conspirators,* pp. 56–58; Moore's credit history investigated by Charles Sullivan for Nichols defense team, his report dated December 16, 1996, obtained by authors; Rodney Bowers and Michael Whiteley, " 'Cover' Blown, Victim Details Royal Robbery," *Arkansas Democrat-Gazette,* June 22, 1995.

Moore wriggles out of FBI, ATF investigations:
On Operation Punchout, see FBI FD-302, file no. 16800, March 13–14, 1996 (on the videotapes), and FD-302, file no. 13675, February 27, 1996, on Assistant U.S. Attorney Bruce Lubeck's decision not to prosecute Moore; defense investigator Roland Leeds's review of the surveillance tapes is dated December 31, 1996, obtained by authors; the ATF investigations of 1989 and 1993 are detailed in an FBI insert written by Special Agent Steven Crutchfield, file no. E-7052, January 11 and January 18, 1996; Birdsong interview with defense investigator John Hough, November 20, 1996; Bill Buford, interviews (Gumbel), May 11 and June 16, 2010.

McVeigh and Nichols buy ammonium nitrate, steal explosives:
Nichols narrative from the following handwritten documents: "Events Leading Up to the Oklahoma City Bombing: A Condensed Narrative," November 9, 2006; written answers to questions from investigative reporter John Solomon, Septem-

ber 30, 2007; "OKC Bombing Materials and the Missing Explosives," December 1, 2007; answers to authors' questions, March 20, 2010. Rick Schlender did not testify at trial, but his observations—minus his memory of two men making the purchase—were reported by FBI agent Christopher Budke at the McVeigh trial, May 19, 1997; Schledner's FBI FD-302 interviews of April 30, 1995 (file no. 7748), and May 2, 1995 (file no. 7772), refer to the second man as a "white male, approximately the same age [as Nichols], mid-30s or a little older, with 'clean-cut' hair" and as having "dark-colored hair, which was slightly longer than the purchaser's hair"; for McVeigh's account of quarry robbery, see Michel and Herbeck, op. cit., pp. 163–64; inventory of stolen items and sheriff's account of investigation from FBI FD-302 interview of Ed Davis, file no. 7936, April 25–26, 1995. Davis testified at a preliminary hearing in Nichols' state trial, May 7, 2003, that he notified the ATF about the robbery, but the ATF did not investigate.

Moore arrested for road rage, drops strange hints to lawyer, bail bond agent: Richard McLaughlin, FBI FD-302, file no. 12655, December 18, 1995; Dianna Sanders Burk, FBI FD-302, file no. 11941, December 8, 1995; story of the $50,000 dug up from the ranch from Bill Stoneman interview with Nichols defense investigator John Hough, December 16, 1996; detail about McLaughlin pulling a gun to run Moore out of his office from interview (Gumbel) with his brother Marty McLaughlin, April 20, 2010; Richard McLaughlin died in 1996.

McVeigh and Nichols complete their shopping spree: Nichols account from same documents as in last section, plus "Facts Regarding Roger Moore's Home Robbery," November 21, 2006, and his answers to author questions, January 22, 2010; McVeigh's version of the jug bomb, Michel and Herbeck, op. cit., p. 165; Wichita coin dealer Robert Dunlap testified in the Nichols trial, November 25, 1997; he confirmed Nichols came in on October 19, 1994, and exchanged gold coins for cash but could not recall how big the transaction was; VP Racing Fuels salesman Tim Chambers, McVeigh trial testimony, May 5, 1997; McVeigh's *Star Wars* speech, as rendered by Fortier, much quoted, example during Fortier's testimony in the Nichols federal trial, November 13, 1997.

The bizarre Roger Moore robbery from Moore's and Nichols's perspective: Moore's account is taken largely from his testimony in the Nichols trial, November 18, 1997. The detail about the serge on the ski mask is from Moore's grand jury testimony of June 1, 1995, as reported in a defense investigator's report by John Hough, February 7, 1997, obtained by authors; Terry Nichols documents on the robbery include "Facts Regarding Roger Moore's Home Robbery," November 21, 2006, and his answers to author questions, January 22, 2010, and March 20, 2010; insurance adjuster Rick Spivey interviewed by Hough, November 25, 1996; the flyer featuring the picture of the law enforcement agent in a black ski mask was entered into evidence at the Nichols trial as exhibit no. D1549; in her FBI FD-302 interview of May 19, 1995, Anderson said the only person who knew she was going to a gun show in Shreveport was the owner of a gun shop in Hot Springs; the defense team in Nichols's state trial found evidence that Guthrie possessed the shotgun and garrote wire, plus Israeli combat boots, plastic ties, and a ski mask like the ones Moore described (see defense motion in the Nichols state trial, dated April 12, 2004, and titled "Terry Lynn Nichols' Motion to Dismiss Based on the State's Failure to Comply with *Brady v. Maryland*"); Robert Miller ID found among ARA's things, task force not told, see John Solomon, "FBI Suspected McVeigh Link to Robbers," *Associated Press*, February 25, 2004.

Moore seeks help, underwhelms neighbors, police, insurance agents:
Material on the Powells from testimony in the Nichols trial (Walt on December 3, Verta and Lance on December 4, 1997) and from interviews with defense investigator Roland Leeds (Walt on November 12, Verta—misspelled Verda—on November 13, and Lance on December 10, 1996); Moore's version from his testimony in the Nichols trial, November 18, 1997, and from his FBI FD-302, dated May 19, 1995; Hough interviewed Spivey on November 25, 1996, Dies on November 12, 1996, and Priddy on November 11, 1996.

Who told McVeigh about the robbery?
Nichols walks through this argument in his document "Facts Regarding Roger Moore's Home Robbery," November 21, 2006, and his facts check out; Michael Fortier, testimony in the Nichols federal trial, November 13, 1997; the Daryl Bridges records (trial exhibit no. 554) show that at 8:09 P.M. Eastern (7:09 P.M. in Kansas), a call was placed to the Fortiers' residence from a BP gas station pay phone in Kent, Ohio, and lasted 11 minutes and 12 seconds; Fortier testified at trial that the call came in mid-morning, but either he or the reconstructed phone records are wrong; Fortier also testified that McVeigh asked him to call back from a pay phone, but the length of the call as documented in the Bridges records casts doubt on his story.

Nichols flees the country:
Nichols's narrative from document "Facts Regarding Roger Moore's Home Robbery," November 21, 2006; explanation of reason to be afraid for his life in the Philippines, details on stun guns, from Nichols's answers to author questions, April 27, 2010; more on stun guns from FBI FD-302, file no. 4261, May 2, 1995, including the Las Vegas Metropolitan Police Department report on the incident; Lana Padilla narrative from December 8, 1995, interview with defense investigator H. C. Bodley, obtained by authors, and from *By Blood Betrayed*, op. cit., p. 162.

McVeigh tries to recruit Fortier, crashes his car:
Fortier acknowledged under cross-examination in the Nichols federal trial that Lori had never told him the soup-can story, testimony on November 13, 1997; McVeigh's account of accident from his January 10, 1995, letter to Roger Moore, obtained by authors; Roger Moore interview with Nichols defense investigator Roland Leeds, November 11, 1996.

The FBI babysits Roger Moore:
Floyd Hays interview (Gumbel), July 13, 2010; Jon Hersley, Larry Tongate, and Bob Burke, *Simple Truths*, p. 173.

McVeigh and Nichols get indicted:
On Magaw, see Joyce Peterson and Nolan Clay, "ATF Chief Sees 3–4 Indictments in City Bombing; Director Says All Participants Known," *Daily Oklahoman,* August 5, 1995; Magaw interview (Gumbel), January 18, 2010; Larry Mackey interview (Gumbel), October 11, 2010.

Chapter 8

Carol Howe goes undercover at Elohim City:
Howe's assessment of Strassmeir, descriptions of Mahon and grenades, from her handwritten informant notes, dated October 9 and October 19, 1994, obtained by authors; these and subsequent findings are memorialized in Angela Finley's Reports of Investigation for the ATF, dated October, November, and December 1994 and January 1995; Millar's sermon recounted in an ATF Report of Investigation, dated January 11, 1995; Howe's report on Mahon and the 500-pound bomb, from her handwritten notes, obtained by authors; Strassmeir interview (Gumbel), June 30, 2010; Kirk Lyons interview (Gumbel), March 23, 2010; Bob Sanders's review and analysis of the Carol Howe file, performed for her criminal defense lawyer Clark Brewster, dated June 20, 1997, and obtained by authors; Dave Roberts, testimony before a county grand jury in Oklahoma City, March 23, 1998, transcript obtained by authors.

The FBI's uncomfortable history with Elohim City and the radical right:
Jack Knox, interview (Gumbel), May 10, 2010; Sarah Wallington sleeping on banknotes, story from Dave Hollaway, interview (Gumbel), May 20, 2010; a useful account of the sedition trial is in Leonard Zeskind, *Blood and Politics,* pp. 158–69; other details here taken from Bruce Campbell's essay "Louis and Sheila" (available at Beam's Web site www.louisbeam.com), from Howard Pankratz, "Blast Blamed on Revenge Attack Linked to Militant's Execution," *Denver Post,* May 12, 1996, and "A Defiant and Victorious Beam Meets a Throng of Reporters After He Is Found Innocent," *Arkansas Democrat-Gazette,* April 8, 1988; Horace Mewborn, interviews (Gumbel), May 26 and July 29, 2010; for the history of various attorney general guidelines on intelligence-gathering versus investigation, including the CISPES issue, see DOJ inspector general's report, "The Federal Bureau of Investigation's Compliance with the Attorney General's Investigative Guidelines (Redacted), Special Report," Washington, D.C., September 2005; Bob Ricks interview (Gumbel), August 9, 2010.

Strassmeir's Elohim City idyll:
Strassmeir interviews (Gumbel), June 30–July 3, 2010; the ATF issued its ban on steel-core ammunition on February 2, 1994, see, e.g., Carolyn Skorneck, "Government Bans Armor-Piercing Bullets," *Associated Press,* February 5, 1994; Kirk Lyons interviews (Gumbel), March 23, April 22, July 15, 2010, April 19, 2011; Dave Hollaway interviews (Gumbel), May 6, May 10, July 9, July 10, 2010; Bob Sisente's relationship with Louis Beam detailed in the final judgment handed down by the U.S. District Court in Houston in a suit brought by the Vietnamese

Fishermen's Association against the Ku Klux Klan, June 9, 1982; Kenny Pence's account from an interview with McVeigh defense investigators Marty Reed and Wilma Sparks, September 7, 1996, report obtained by authors.

The feds' struggles to figure out Robert Millar:

Horace Mewborn, interview (Gumbel), May 26, 2010; Bill Buford, interview (Gumbel), September 8, 2010; Buck Revell's comments from his book *A G-Man's Journal,* p. 446; early history of Millar from Somer Shook, Wesley Delano, Robert W. Balch, "Elohim City: A Participant-Observer Study of a Christian Identity Community," *Nova Religio,* vol. 2, April 1999, and from Kerry Noble, *Tabernacle of Hate,* pp. 111–12; description of Millar at the CSA siege from Coulson's book *No Heroes,* p. 305; Millar business-card wording reported in his FBI FD-302 interview, file no. 6416, dated June 21, 1995; Bethel Christian School brochure with photo of Millar doing Hitler salute, obtained by authors; Millar's child out of wedlock and other details included in a ruling by Judge D. K. Kirkland of the Hastings County family court in Belleville, Ontario, in which he awards full custody to Dan Irwin; ruling dated August 31, 1983, obtained by authors; unsuccessful police raid to reclaim Irwin's children in "Millar Expresses City's Beliefs, Connection to CSA Community," *Sequoia County Times,* July 18, 1985; Elohim City neighbors Carl Wright and Paul Powers described their feelings of intimidation in court proceedings in Adair County, Oklahoma, in the Irwin custody case; Wright (testifying on December 13, 1985) said Powers was passing information to the FBI; Powers (testifying on February 21, 1985) refused to answer a question about passing information to law enforcement. Early law enforcement interest in Elohim City: Oklahoma Department of Public safety memo, dated April 21, 1985, and ATF Report of Investigation on Elohim City, July 9, 1985; Tim Arney, interview (Gumbel), August 26, 2010; Coulson on Ricks and Miller, from his book *No Heroes,* p. 539; Bob Ricks, interview (Gumbel), August 9, 2010.

Carol Howe operation starts unraveling:

Reasons why Mahon was not pursued, Tristan Moreland, interview (Gumbel), October 14 and 15, 2009. The FBI's opinion of Mahon in the early-to-mid-1990s is laid out in a series of teletypes from the Oklahoma City division office, dated February 14, 1992; February 18, 1992; January 24, 1994; and March 29, 1994. The first two were in response to inquiries from the U.S. legal attaché in Bonn in the wake of Mahon being banned from Germany. The second two were in response to a preliminary inquiry into Mahon, opened on January 14, 1994. The March 29 teletype, which formally closed that inquiry, echoes the findings of all the previous documents. "Local and federal law enforcement sources familiar with Mahon," it read, "are in general agreement that while MAHON's rhetoric continues to be the usual, and constitutionally permitted, inflammatory 'supremacist' speech directed against Jews and minorities, his actions, at this time, are considerably less and do not rise to a criminal threshold." Clearly, those law enforcement sources did not include the ATF. Tommy Wittman, interview (Gumbel), September 27, 2010; "crap" line from interview (Gumbel) with Neal

Kirkpatrick, then an assistant U.S. attorney in Tulsa, who ended up prosecuting Carol Howe, May 24, 2010; Lester Martz quotes from his testimony before the Oklahoma County grand jury, April 23, 1998, transcript obtained by authors; "shit sandwich" line from Tim Arney, interview (Gumbel), August 26, 2010; Dave Roberts material from his testimony before the same grand jury, March 23, 1998; limited role/response from U.S. Attorney's Offices, taken from interviews (Gumbel) with Steve Lewis, then the U.S. attorney in Tulsa (May 18 and August 10, 2010) and Sheldon Sperling, then the U.S. attorney in Muskogee (August 10, 2010); Finley's correspondence with the INS, including the certificate on Strassmeir issued February 16, 1995, obtained by authors; Howe's trip to Oklahoma City, the fixed-wing aircraft flight and the two weeks of inactivity all recorded in the ATF's Report of Investigation on her for February 1995, dated February 28, 1995; Ken Stafford's "trooper safety" BOLO notice obtained by authors; Bob Ricks, interviews (Gumbel), August 9 and August 17, 2010; in his grand jury testimony, Lester Martz denied having met Ricks to discuss Elohim City, but this is contradicted both by Ricks and by the ATF's February 1995 Report of Investigation on Howe, which describes plans being made in the last week of February for Ricks and Martz to meet.

McVeigh recalibrates his plans:
Nichols's account of reconnecting with McVeigh on his return from the Philippines is from his handwritten document "McVeigh and Potts/Govt. Connection," November 23, 2007; the shadowy government operative Nichols refers to as Potts in this document appears to be similar or the same as a man he described to the FBI in April 2005 as "Top Dog #2," see FD-302 on Nichols, dated April 1, 2005, file no. 18253. Fortier's interactions with McVeigh, see his FD-302 of June 21–22, 1995, file no. 9171, and his testimony in the Nichols trial, November 13, 1997. McVeigh reaches out to Coffman, Bangerter: Bangerter and Bangerter's mother were interviewed by defense investigator Richard Reyna in February 1996 and they described meeting McVeigh at the St. George gun show a year earlier. Reyna's research is contained in a memo dated September 2–4, 1996, and titled "Michael Joseph Fortier's Involvement in the Bombing of the Alfred P. Murrah Federal Building, Oklahoma City, Oklahoma." If McVeigh made phone contact with either, it was not, at this stage, with the Daryl Bridges card. Coffman, interviewed on five separate occasions by the FBI, acknowledged receiving phone messages from a Tim Tuttle in April 1995—they were part of the Daryl Bridges phone record—but denied meeting him and denied talking about him with Bangerter. (See, e.g., his FBI FD-302, file no. 16229, of September 23–24, 1996.) However, Coffman was asked at least twice to take a polygraph test and refused (FD-302, file no. 6350, of June 12, 1995, and file no. 15876 of June 14, 1995). No FBI interview of Bangerter appears in the files handed over to the defense teams at trial. Rosencrans described McVeigh's offer in his FD-302, file no. 6700, dated July 1, 1995; Patty Edwards corroborated the story in her own FD-302 interview of the same date, file no. 6696.

The ATF closes its Elohim City operation at the worst possible moment:
Finley gave her version of Howe's association with the Tulsa skinheads in an April 24, 1997, preliminary hearing ahead of Howe's trial. Her line about not documenting every meeting with Howe comes from the same day's court proceedings. Transcript viewed by Gumbel at the National Archives repository in Fort Worth, April 4, 2011. Howe's version taken from her testimony in the trial of James Viefhaus, July 24, 1997; the emergency confidential informant removal application made by Finley on March 20, 1995, was read into the record at Viefhaus's trial during Finley's testimony, July 25, 1997; the ATF's official line on Howe—that her information was useless, and that the informant operation at Elohim City was shut down by Bob Ricks—was echoed in both particulars by the federal prosecutor, Neal Kirkpatrick, in his interview with Gumbel, see above; John Magaw, interviews (Gumbel), January 18, June 22, and October 12, 2010; among those making the case that Carol Howe warned feds in advance is William F. Jasper, "Undercover: The Howe Revelations," *New American,* September 15, 1997; Finley talked about threats "in general" and the fact that such talk was commonplace in her April 24, 1997, preliminary hearing; anecdote about DOJ spokesperson Leesa Brown told by Don Thrasher in a phone call with McVeigh's lawyer Stephen Jones, February 11, 1997; transcript of call obtained by authors. Danny Defenbaugh, interview (Gumbel), May 17, 2010; Danny Coulson, interview (Gumbel), September 27, 2010.

McVeigh's "penis party" with Richard Rogers:
Rogers was interviewed by the ATF on May 9, 1995 (later categorized as FBI FD-302, file no. 1251, dated May 10, 1995), and then by the FBI, most extensively on July 4, 1995 (FD-302, file no. 6721). The interviewing agent was Kenneth Williams, later the author of the "Phoenix Memo," which alerted the FBI two months before 9/11 to al-Qaida followers attending flight schools and planning attacks on civil aviation targets.

The ghost of McVeigh flits over Elohim City:
Joan Millar described the call from McVeigh to defense investigator Richard Reyna on October 28, 1995 (report, dated October 30, 1995, obtained by authors), and, six months later, to the FBI, FD-302, file no. 15826, May 2, 1996; the April 5 phone call is included in the Daryl Bridges records entered into evidence in the bombing trials; it was made from the Imperial Motel at 1:46 P.M. Arizona time, 3:46 in Oklahoma. The April 17 phone call to Elohim City is described in an FBI teletype from headquarters dated January 4, 1996; the same teletype also talks about April 5 as "a day that he [McVeigh] was believed to have been attempting to recruit a second conspirator to assist in the OKBOMB attack"; Richard Cohen, interview (Gumbel), June 3, 2010; Dees quoted saying McVeigh had been to Elohim City "several times" in Howard Pankratz, "Records Hint at Link with Elohim City, Blast Followed Commune Calls," *Denver Post,* May 12, 1996 (the event took place on May 3), and also in Hamm, *In Bad Company,* p. 191; Dees's appearance at Southeastern Oklahoma State Col-

lege was recorded by J. D. Cash of the *McCurtain Daily Gazette;* Mark Potok, interview (Gumbel), June 1, 2010; Bill Buford, interview (Gumbel), June 16, 2010. One possible candidate for the document Buford saw, or saw referred to, was a teletype from the FBI's Mobile, Alabama, office dated December 21, 1995, reporting on Southern Poverty Law Center intelligence concerning McVeigh and Elohim City. This document, available to the authors only in heavily redacted form, is discussed further in chapter 9. Bob Ricks, interview (Gumbel), August 17, 2010; Danny Defenbaugh, interview (Gumbel), April 4, 2011; Scott Mendeloff, interview (Gumbel), September 29, 2010. FBI agent Jim Carlile, who conducted several interviews in and around Elohim City in 1996, came out with this intriguing line in an October 18, 2010, interview with Gumbel. "Other than the fact that McVeigh had been in there and had probably tried to recruit somebody," Carlile said, "it did not appear that any of the people who remained at Elohim City were people with a positive connection to the bombing investigation. They had met McVeigh, he had been there, but of the people that remained, there was no-one with a connection." McVeigh's "pretty fucking hardcore" line reported by defense attorney Randy Coyne on December 14, 1995, and included in a defense memo obtained by authors; Tom Metzger, interview (Gumbel), December 24, 2009; McVeigh's motel records from the Imperial Motel and the Dreamland, as well as a receipt from the Arkansas City Walmart, were entered into evidence at his trial; the owner of the Imperial, Helmut Hofer, talked about the undisturbed bed in an interview with the MGA documentary crew, April 21, 1999, transcript obtained by authors; Kirk Lyons, interview (Gumbel), November 30, 2010; Millar told Richard Reyna about McVeigh possibly having visited Elohim City on December 13, 1995, memo dated December 15 and December 23–26, 1995; Millar also quoted in Jonathan Franklin, "God City," *Vibe,* November 1997; Kerry Noble quote from interview with MGA documentary team, March 22, 1999.

Chapter 9

The FBI's Night of the Long Knives:
Danny Coulson, interview (Gumbel), May 19, 2010; Revell quotes from his book, *A G-Man's Journal,* pp. 467, 469; Horace Mewborn, interview (Gumbel), May 26, 2010.

Lawyers for McVeigh and Nichols fall out:
"Sanctuary in the jungle" line from Tigar's argument before Judge Matsch for a change of venue, February 3, 1996, and quoted in Tigar's book, *Nine Principles of Litigation and Life,* pp. 73–77; Judge Alley gave an account of the damage to his offices, interview (Gumbel), August 18, 2010; Alley's September 14, 1995, refusal to recuse himself reported in John Parker, "Judge Alley Taken Off Bomb Case, 10th Circuit Cites Doubts of Impartiality," *Daily Oklahoman,* December 2, 1995; Jones's reluctance to rock the boat with Judge Alley documented in Diana

Baldwin and John Parker "Jones May Accept Lawton Venue; McVeigh's Attorney Polling Area Residents," *Daily Oklahoman*, September 27, 1995, and Lee Hancock and David Jackson, "Bomb-case Judge's Recusal Sought," *Dallas Morning News*, September 28, 1995; Michael Tigar, interviews (Gumbel), March 1 and May 7, 2011; Jones mentioned his decision to stay out of the appeal in the 1998 edition of his book *Others Unknown*, but not in the account he gave of the change of venue issue in the 2001 edition (pp. 138–39). He took issue with Tigar's claim that they had fallen out at all. ("Mike's memory fails him about Judge Alley," he wrote in an e-mail to Gumbel, March 22, 2011.) Jones on the frustrations of his assignment, from his article "Representing Timothy McVeigh," *Litigation*, vol. 28, no. 3, Spring 2002; polygraph test described in Jones and Israel, *Others Unknown*, pp. 118–25; rebuke from Judge Matsch quoted in Arnold Hamilton and Lee Hancock, "McVeigh, Nichols Appear Before New Judge in Bomb Case," *Dallas Morning News*, December 14, 1995; the hearing took place on December 12, 1995.

Strassmeir booted out of Elohim City:
Andreas Strassmeir, interviews (Gumbel), June 30 and July 1, 2010; Lyons, interview (Gumbel), July 15, 2010.

Strassmeir gets sucked into the case, prepares to flee the country:
The first news story to reference Elohim City was a *Newsweek* brief headlined "More Arrests to Come," which appeared in the May 29, 1995, print edition of the magazine; Millar's first recorded post-bombing conversation with the FBI was written up as FD-302, file no. 6146, dated June 21, 1995; Richard Reyna interviewed Grandpa Millar on October 16, October 28, and December 13, 1995. His alert about law enforcement being interested in Strassmeir was dated December 8, 1995 (all his reports obtained by authors); Kirk Lyons, interviews (Gumbel), March 23, April 22, and July 15, 2010. Evidence of media interest in Strassmeir: *New York Times* correspondent Jo Thomas filed a Freedom of Information Act request on Strassmeir with the Immigration and Naturalization Service, receipt stamp with the date December 13, 1995, obtained by authors; Dave Hollaway, interviews (Gumbel), May 24 and July 15, 2010; Andreas Strassmeir, interview (Gumbel), July 1, 2010; copies of Strassmeir's old passport, which expired June 12, 1993, and his new one, valid from October 4, 1995, obtained by authors.

Defense teams push to squeeze discovery material out of government:
Early discovery disputes summarized in a ruling by Judge Matsch, dated January 28, 1997, in which he lays the burden for proper disclosure on the prosecution, not the court; Jones's "check in the mail" remark quoted in Arnold Hamilton, "Bombing Prosecutors Criticized; McVeigh's Attorney Says U.S. Dragging Feet on Evidence," *Dallas Morning News*, November 5, 1995; details of deal on discovery described by Michael Tigar, interview (Gumbel), March 1, 2011, and confirmed, in parts, by Ron Woods, interview (Gumbel), June 1, 2011, Rob Nigh, interview (Gumbel), April 5, 2011, and Joe Hartzler, inter-

view (Gumbel), June 2, 2011. It appears the reciprocal agreement was never enshrined in a written document. If it was, it was sealed by Judge Matsch, but Matsch said (in a letter to Gumbel, May 27, 2011) that he had "no independent recollection" of such an agreement, suggesting it never went through him. The lack of a written document almost certainly helped the prosecution pick and choose the disclosures it made beyond its legal obligations under *Brady v. Maryland*. Jones describes government stonewalling on body shop witnesses, et al. in *Others Unknown*, pp. 191–93; Scott Mendeloff interview (Gumbel), July 16, 2010.

The FBI gets serious about Strassmeir, just too late:
Danny Defenbaugh, interview (Gumbel), June 13, 2010; teletype from the FBI's Mobile, Alabama, field office, dated December 21, 1995, obtained by authors. The most tantalizing line reads: "Sources have told [redacted] that [redacted redacted] Elohim City anywhere from two days before the Oklahoma City bombing to two weeks before the bombing." Since this is separate from a discussion of McVeigh's phone call to Elohim City (it comes in the next paragraph), the most plausible interpolation would be: "Sources have told [unknown] that *McVeigh visited* Elohim City . . ." Richard Cohen of the Southern Poverty Law Center, in an interview (Gumbel) on May 5, 2011, said he could not remember seeing the document before but guessed this paragraph referred not to McVeigh but Strassmeir. A senior FBI official with the investigation, however, said his best memory was that it did indeed refer to a visit by McVeigh between April 5 and April 17, although without seeing the unredacted document he could not be sure. Second teletype indicating Strassmeir was about to leave the country dated January 4, 1996, and obtained by authors; Agent John Hippard's January 11, 1996, alert to the INS obtained by authors.

Strassmeir's Great Escape:
Dave Hollaway, interviews (Gumbel), May 6, May 10, May 20, May 24, July 15, and July 18, 2010. Kirk Lyons, interview (Gumbel), May 27, 2010; Andreas Strassmeir, interviews (Gumbel), June 30 and July 2, 2010; the French resistance codes were also used in the 1984 Cold War warrior-fantasy movie *Red Dawn,* which is where Hollaway probably learned them.

The feds arrest Guthrie and Langan:
"Big *bolitas*" line from Guthrie's memoir, *The Taunting Bandits,* p. 48; collapse of ARA, ibid., pp. 204–19, 239–50, 269–71; see also his FD-302 of March 4–15, 1996. Guthrie's arrest from pp. 274–75 and from Mark S. Hamm, *In Bad Company,* pp. 266–67; account of Langan's arrest from Hamm, pp. 4–20, and from Langan's interview with the MGA documentary crew, April 7, 2000, transcript obtained by authors; FBI explosives expert William Davitch and Danny Defenbaugh quoted in Leslie Blade and Gregory Flannery, "Queen City Terror," *Cincinnati CityBeat,* September 8, 2004. On the unexamined evidence, see also John Solomon, "FBI Suspected McVeigh Link to Robbers," *Associated Press,* February 25, 2004. Defenbaugh, interview (Gumbel), January 25, 2011. He said the

Christmas wrappings were not the same, but saw plenty of other reasons to examine the caps for possible links to McVeigh.

The FBI chases, then loses interest in Strassmeir:

Defenbaugh's January 18 teletype to the legal attaché in Germany is memorialized in a later teletype from the Oklahoma City command post, dated January 29, 1996, obtained by authors; Defenbaugh, interview (Gumbel), June 13, 2010; Cash's January 1996 interview with Mahon written up in his article "Mahon: McVeigh Planned Bank Heists, Wanted to Be 'Patriot Hero,'" *McCurtain Daily Gazette,* April 1, 1997. He also described it in a sworn deposition given to the McVeigh defense team, March 26, 1996, obtained by authors, and in an FBI FD-302 interview conducted on April 14, 1997, but given a case and file number unrelated to the bombing (266A-OC-57917-82). Cash subsequently drew up a three-page letter, obtained by authors, pointing out mistakes in the FD-302. Jones passes on death threat to FBI, see FD-302, file no. 12701, dated January 27, 1996, written up by Defenbaugh; Dave Hollaway, interview (Gumbel), May 6, 2010. He was at the Bundeskriminalamt with Strassmeir. Kirk Lyons, interview (Gumbel), April 29, 2011; Strassmeir's statement dated February 1996 (exact date not specified), obtained by authors; Strassmeir's FBI FD-302, dated April 30–May 1, 1996, is file no. 14897. The prosecutors on the call were Beth Wilkinson and Aitan Goelman; the FBI agent was LouAnn Sandstrom, who had taken over the Strassmeir beat from John Hippard. Kirk Lyons was also on the call from Black Mountain; Strassmeir, interview (Gumbel), June 30, 2010; letter from Wilkinson quoted in Jones and Israel, *Others Unknown,* p. 179; the printout from the State Department was accompanied by an explanatory note from Paul Brown, the liaison to the task force from the department's diplomatic security section, dated March 18, 1996. A previous printout on December 13, 1994—generated, presumably, as a result of the ATF's investigation at Elohim City—included the "A O" status. In a pretrial hearing on March 10, 1997, prosecutor Beth Wilkinson said she had been told by the State Department that the A stood for "admitted" and the O for "overstay." There are grounds, however, to doubt this: the "A O" designation also applied to trips he took in 1988–90, when he was not an overstay. Wilkinson stated, at the same hearing, that Strassmeir came into the United States on separate single-entry visas—contradicted by the evidence of Strassmeir's own passport, obtained by the authors.

The extra leg:

Much of the previously known history of the extra leg is summarized in a prosecution court filing from February 1996, titled "Brief of the United States in Opposition to Defendant McVeigh's Motion to Allow Representatives to Attend Exhumation and Examination of Lakesha Levy"; Marshall quoted in Jones and Israel, *Others Unknown,* p. 206; Marshall gave very similar testimony at the McVeigh trial on May 22, 1997; Fred Jordan testified at the McVeigh trial, May 22, 1997; the unnamed sources cited here include one from the FBI and one forensics expert, both of whom were directly involved in the investigation; Clyde Snow, interview (Gumbel), September 15, 2011.

Carol Howe outed:

Finley informing Howe of the security breach, written up in an ATF Report of Investigation, April 1, 1996, obtained by authors; the March 20, 1995, emergency request to remove Howe as an informant was read into the record at James Viefhaus's trial in Tulsa, July 25, 1997; the May 18, 1995, request to reinstate her is in an ATF Report of Investigation of the same date, obtained by authors; further ROIs, for January 9 and January 31, 1996, first urge her removal and then accept her continuation on the ATF books; Finley's letter endorsing Howe and stating that her life was in danger, obtained by authors, is dated April 22, 1996; Howe's account is from her testimony in James Viefhaus trial, July 24, 1997.

The ARA's links to the bombing considered and then rejected:

List of items recovered from the ARA taken, in part, from Hamm, *In Bad Company*, pp. 12–13; arrest of McCarthy and Stedeford detailed ibid., pp. 269–76; Langan's story about grabbing Agent Woods's attention, from a declaration he filed in federal court in Utah on April 9, 2007; Langan discussed the government's offer of a deal in exchange for information about the Oklahoma City bombing in his interview with the MGA documentary crew, April 7, 2000; the story was corroborated by his lawyer, Kevin Durkin, in an affidavit filed at the request of the Nichols state trial defense team on April 12, 2004; Matthew Moning material from his sworn affidavit signed in Cincinnati on June 13, 2004; Guthrie's July 1 plea agreement, suicide notes, and death certificate all obtained by authors; Kelly Johnson, interview (Gumbel), April 22, 2011.

Efforts to get former FBI agent Ed Woods to talk about Guthrie, Langan, and ways in which the Oklahoma City bombing came up in his dealings with them were unsuccessful. Woods responded positively at first to an interview request (Gumbel). But he backed off in a hurry as soon as the subject of the bombing came up. "It's been a long time (15 years) so I'm not going to speculate or guess what may have been asked or answered," he wrote on April 8, 2011. On April 10, he said he would not answer questions that betrayed the author's "bias and agenda"—questions that were mostly to do with how much contact, if any, the robbery investigators had with the Oklahoma bombing investigators. When asked to comment, finally, on Moning's affidavit, he claimed not to have received the e-mail, sending it back with the words "Auto Response . . . Returned Unopened . . ." in the subject line (April 11).

Ward brother weirdness in Oregon:

Details of the Wards' arrest and detention come from the Jackson County district attorney's files, obtained by the authors; Kerry Larsen, interview (Gumbel), September 3, 2010; Pete Ward's FBI interview was on September 23, 1996, on his fifth day in custody, see FBI FD-302, file no. 16069; Ward's grandfather Richard Kirby confirmed in an interview (Gumbel, August 20, 2010) he had never been an FBI agent, although there was once an agent of the same name.

Stephen Jones travels the world, annoys his client:

Jones addressed this issue at great length in an e-mail to Gumbel, March 14, 2011;

Jones criticized for foreign travel, see David Jackson, "Oklahoma City Bombing Case Cost Justice Department $82.5 Million," Knight Ridder, November 2, 1998; Jones's writ of mandamus filed March 25, 1997; Hartzler's "wacky theories" controversy, see Jo Thomas, "Starting Date Set for Trial on Oklahoma Bombing," *New York Times,* November 16, 1996.

Prosecution team fights over evidence, separation of trials:
Larry Mackey, interviews (Gumbel), October 11 and December 3, 2011; Judge Matsch's arguments summarized in his ruling in favor of severance, October 25, 1996. Beth Wilkinson, a former military lawyer, and Scott Mendeloff, a bulldog litigator from Chicago, were generally regarded as the hawks on the team. Joseph Hartzler, also from Chicago, was somewhere in the middle. Pat Ryan, Arlene Joplin, and Vicki Behenna, who were from Oklahoma, were anxious to meet the demands of the bombing victims and their families. Mackey was seen almost universally as a gentleman, regardless of people's opinions of his positions, while Aitan Goelman, a young Justice Department attorney, was seen as a high-flier in the making, with a temperament not too far from Mackey's. Other team members had less influence.

Carol Howe is indicted on the eve of the McVeigh trial:
Details from the case file on the federal prosecution of Viefhaus and Howe; Morlin listening to the message, alerting the FBI's Ken Pernick, from Neal Kirkpatrick's opening in the Viefhaus trial, July 22, 1997, and confirmed on the stand by FBI agent Peter Rickel the same day; Angie Finley described the physical evidence in a pretrial hearing on April 24, 1997; text of the hotline message entered into evidence.

Brescia and Thomas are arrested, the ARA connection is closed down for good:
Dave Hollaway, interview (Gumbel), May 24, 2010; "Unwanted by the FBI" posters, see Hamm, *In Bad Company,* p. 295. The campaign was orchestrated by an Alabama militia leader whose online publication, the *John Doe Times,* was obsessed with Brescia for a while. The *John Doe Times* archives could still be accessed, as of April 2011, at http://www.constitution.org/okc/jdt.htm; Thomas's arrest, stories, from "Thomas Indicted in Bank Robberies," *Allentown Morning Call,* January 31, 1997, and from an interview with *Washington Post* reporter Richard Leiby; details of search of bus from later *Allentown Morning Call* article, May 3, 1997, headline unavailable; Donna Marazoff, FBI FD-302, file no. 17777, April 2, 1997, and no. 17778, April 5, 1997; Michael A. Schwartz, interview (Gumbel), June 7, 2010; Justice Department unsealing Todd Bunting material, declaring that John Doe Two does not exist, see Jo Thomas, "Suspects Sketch in Oklahoma Case Called an Error," *New York Times,* January 30, 1997.

The prosecution requestions inconvenient witnesses:
Eric McGown was challenged on his changed testimony under cross-examination in the McVeigh trial, May 8, 1997; Jeff Davis spoke to the MGA documentary crew, March 11, 1999, transcript obtained by authors; ABC News interviewed

him in April 1996. Jeanne Boylan, who worked up a sketch of the man Davis saw in room 25, described her encounter with him in *Portraits in Guilt,* p. 260. Boylan has Davis telling her that he saw a second man inside the room. But this appears to be contradicted by accounts Davis has given elsewhere. The dinner he was carrying, a serving of moo goo gai pan, was for one person only. Daina Bradley appeared at the McVeigh trial as a defense witness and was challenged on the backward-parked truck on cross-examination, May 23, 1997; Mendeloff, interviews (Gumbel), July 16 and October 4, 2010; Larry Mackey, interview (Gumbel), October 11, 2010. Interestingly, there is nothing illegal about grilling witnesses until they change their stories. Rob Nigh, the number two on the McVeigh defense team, said in an April 5, 2011, interview: "The law on eyewitness identification is bad. . . . Testimony is admissible even when the evidence suggests they are not making their identification based on actual memory but are making it based on the power of suggestion. . . . In other words, coaching of witnesses is permissible." Mendeloff said he and Hersley had asked Kessinger only open questions, not leading ones, and took issue with the notion that they had applied any undue pressure; interview (Gumbel), June 2, 2011. "We didn't have to press him on much of this, or any of this that I can remember," he said. "I don't remember pressing him." Defenbaugh, interviews (Gumbel), May 19 and September 22, 2010; Hersley's version of the Cassville evidence is in his book *Simple Truths,* pp. 249–50. One of the assertions Defenbaugh objected to was: "The FBI was able to substantiate that one day after the alleged sighting of McVeigh in Missouri, he was in Pendleton, New York, at his father's home, a fact proven by McVeigh's use of the Bridges calling card." There are, in fact, *no* Bridges phone records for November 3, 1994. Hersley turned down multiple requests to be interviewed for this book, including a specific invitation to respond to Defenbaugh's accusations.

Jones team undone by leaks, damaging revelations:
The first damaging piece was Pete Slover, "In Defense Documents, Timothy McVeigh Describes How He Bombed Oklahoma City Federal Building," *Dallas Morning News,* February 28, 1997; Jones describes the episode at length in Jones and Israel, *Others Unknown,* pp. 286–311; the *Rocky Mountain News* editorial blast was titled "Stephen Jones' Tangled Web," March 5, 1997; Pete Slover's December 1997 disciplinary hearing and its outcome from interview (Gumbel) with Slover, November 28, 2011, and from the docket of the Texas 68th District Court in Dallas County, obtained by Gumbel; Slover would not comment on the stories of how he obtained the material, citing his journalistic obligation not to discuss his sources. Jones reiterated in an e-mail to Gumbel, dated March 22, 2011, that the Reyna memos dated July and December 1995 were not legitimate defense memoranda; Rob Nigh said Reyna never spent time alone with McVeigh, interview (Gumbel), April 5, 2011; Wright quotes McVeigh on the "body count" in his book *Patriots, Politics and the Oklahoma City Bombing,* p. 6 (Wright interview with Gumbel, April 28, 2011); McVeigh standing by the

contents of the Reyna memos, see Michel and Herbeck, op. cit., p. 301; Ben Fenwick's reporting for *Playboy* culminated in a piece for the magazine, "The Road to Oklahoma City," vol. 44, no. 6, June 1997; the lawyers' dealings with Judge Matsch in this matter are summarized and, in places, cited verbatim, in Matsch's ruling, dated October 12, 2000, denying McVeigh post-conviction relief under a habeas corpus petition; final Jones quote from Jones and Jennifer Gideon, "*United States v. McVeigh*: Defending the 'Most Hated Man in America,'" *Oklahoma Law Review,* Winter 1998.

Chapter 10

Jury selection does not help McVeigh's cause:
Ryan Ross, "McVeigh's Trial Lean and Trim," *ABA Journal,* July 1997, p. 24; defense team member who called voir dire "ineffective," from an interview with Gumbel; McVeigh was described thinking of the jurors as "a staid, conservative group with whom he failed to identify in any way," see Michel and Herbeck, op. cit., p. 313 (McVeigh blamed this on Jones's jury consultants); the air force veteran who believed gun ownership should be mandatory was no. 106 and appeared on April 18 and 21, 1997; "Penalty phase fucked right here" line from Gumbel interview with Nichols defense attorney; Dick Burr, interview (Gumbel), June 13, 2011; some details of voir dire—the jury vetting process—from Jo Thomas, "McVeigh Jury Is Selected After 3 Weeks," *New York Times,* April 23, 1997; jury candidate no. 947 appeared April 1, 1997.

Justice Department inspector general blows the government's forensics out of the water:
The report by Department of Justice inspector general Michael R. Bromwich is "The FBI Laboratory: An Investigation into Laboratory Practices and Alleged Misconduct in Explosives-Related and Other Cases," published April 15, 1997; Lloyd quoted in John F. Kelly and Philip K. Wearne, *Tainting Evidence,* p. 213.

Hartzler starts the way the prosecution means to go on:
Quotes from transcript of his opening statement, April 24, 1997.

Jones hits the wrong note right away:
Quotes from transcript of his opening statement, April 24, 1997; for evidence that some people in the courtroom found Jones's opening either boring or offensive, see Paul Queary, "Families Weep as Bombing Victims Names Are Recited," Associated Press, April 24, 1997; Bill Scanlon, "Reading of Names Brings Tears," *Rocky Mountain News,* April 25, 1997; Sue Lindsay, Bill Scanlon, Karen Abbott, Lynn Bartels, "Memories Flood Courtroom," *Rocky Mountain News,* April 25, 1997; the stepfather who thought Jones was a showboat was Tom Kight, quoted in Michel and Herbeck, op. cit., p. 321; *ABA Journal* line from Ryan Ross's July 1997 piece, see above.

Prosecution keeps it emotional, defense wrongfooted:
Rob Nigh, interview (Gumbel), April 5, 2011; Jones's account of the trial is in *Others Unknown,* op. cit., pp. 315–43.

The Roger Moore question divides the government side:
Larry Mackey, interview (Gumbel), October 11, 2010; Danny Defenbaugh, interviews (Gumbel), May 19 and September 22, 2010.

Defense blasts the forensic evidence:
Fred Whitehurst and Steven Burmeister testified on May 28, 1997; the "magic crystals" line is from Chris Tritico's summation, May 29, 1997; see also Kelly and Wearne, *Tainting Evidence,* pp. 221–25.

Defense fails to get Carol Howe on the stand:
Jones's version from Jones and Israel, *Others Unknown,* pp. 334–38; Burrage expressing concern about Carol Howe interfering with the McVeigh trial, from a pretrial hearing in his court on June 11, 1997, from the official transcript; Daniel Capra, a law professor at Fordham University, thought Howe's testimony would have been "highly probative," see "Questions of Fairness in 'McVeigh' Case," *New York Law Journal,* January 8, 1999; see also Kevin Flynn, "Ruling Deals Blow to Plot Defense," *Rocky Mountain News,* May 28, 1997.

McVeigh looks engaged and open, quietly seethes:
John Ross, *Unintended Consequences*; McVeigh's account of reading *Unintended Consequences* and sitting through the trial is in Michel and Herbeck, op. cit. pp. 304–38; John R. Smith material from his interview on NPR's *All Things Considered,* "Looking into the Psyche of Timothy McVeigh," June 8, 2001; Chambers testified on May 5, 1997.

McVeigh convicted and sentenced to death:
Larry Mackey's closing statement was on May 29, 1997; Jones's closing statement followed Mackey's; the Michael Fortier line is from his testimony, under direct examination, on May 12. The verdict was delivered on June 2, Jones's summation in the penalty phase was on June 12, and the death sentence was delivered on June 13; Dick Burr, interview (Gumbel), June 13, 2011; Rob Nigh, interview (Gumbel), April 5, 2011. Jones agreed with the premise that a death sentence would make it much harder to establish the truth behind the bombing. In his penalty phase summation, on June 12, he said: "Dead men do not tell tales. I say again the government may not be the only people that want my client executed." Joe Hartzler interjected and said he found this assertion "objectionable." Matsch overruled him.

Carol Howe is acquitted, her former handlers are left to swing:
Neal Kirkpatrick, interview (Gumbel), May 24, 2010; Finley testified to the Oklahoma County grand jury on February 17, 1998, Roberts on March 23; Martz said in his grand jury testimony, on April 23, 1998, that Roberts was removed because of problems revealed by an audit of his weapons vault in Tulsa; Wittman said Roberts addressed these problems and argued that the real reason for removing him was Elohim City. Martz could not be reached for comment; Tommy Wittman, interview (Gumbel), September 27, 2010.

McVeigh blasts Jones, gets him off his appeal team:
Lou Michel, "McVeigh Rips Lawyer; Convicted Bomber Wants Jones Dismissed from Case for Allegedly Lying," *Buffalo News,* August 13, 1997. McVeigh communicated his willingness to proceed with the trial after the *Dallas Morning News*

leak in a conversation with Rob Nigh, whom he trusted. See Judge Matsch's October 12, 2000, ruling denying post-conviction habeas relief, cited in chapter 9. McVeigh statement comes from transcript of sentencing hearing, August 14, 1997; it is not clear if he realized—or cared—that Brandeis was the first Jew to be appointed to the U.S. Supreme Court. Jones's response reported in Nolan Clay, "Jones, McVeigh Not Meeting Face to Face; Judges Told Attorney Asks for Removal From Case," *Daily Oklahoman,* August 21, 1997; see also Nolan Clay, "Jones Off Bombing Case; McVeigh Gets New Lawyer," *Daily Oklahoman,* August 28, 1997.

Larry Mackey asked to replace Scott Mendeloff:
Mackey approached by Janet Reno, interview (Gumbel), December 3, 2010; details of how Mendeloff was removed, and the rest of the prosecution team's opinions of him, culled from numerous off-the-record accounts by prosecutors and investigators. Mendeloff (interview with Gumbel, June 2, 2011) would not comment on the account but also took no issue with the factual record—Litt's visit, the way his appointment to head the Nichols team was thrown into doubt, and his decision to quit rather than fight for the job.

Michael Tigar charms his way into juror no. 215's heart:
Account from voir dire transcript for September 29, 1997, and from interview (Gumbel) with Tigar, March 1, 2011.

The Nichols team triumphs in jury selection:
Matsch's apology to the juror is in the trial transcript for September 30, 1997; Michael Tigar, interview (Gumbel), March 1, 2011; one prosecutor unconnected to the Nichols trial who accused Matsch of favoring Nichols was interviewed by Gumbel. Stephen Jones also thought the judge was deliberately tipping the field in the Nichols trial—not because he was against the death penalty but because he believed other coconspirators were still out there. In *Others Unknown,* op. cit., pp. 344–55, Jones concludes: "Could it be that Richard Matsch, persuaded by evidence he refused to let our jury hear, has himself become a conspiracy theorist?"

Government's opening betrays doubts about extent of Nichols's guilt:
The opening statements were heard on November 3, 1997; Larry Mackey, interview (Gumbel), December 3, 2010.

The Nichols team's Perry Mason moments:
Louis Hupp testified on November 14, 1997; Tigar quote on Hupp testimony from the first part of his closing argument, December 15, 1997. On November 17, 1997, Tigar asked Karen Anderson: "Is it your testimony that you and Mr. Moore—or Mr. Moore—were the owners of a Ruger Mini-30 with the Serial No. 189-57425?" To which she responded: "To the best of my knowledge, yes." On November 18, Tigar produced the ATF documentation proving that the gun, in fact, belonged to Nichols. Wilkinson quote from her closing argument, December 15, 1997; Tigar quote from the second part of his closing argument, December 16, 1997. Agent Smith was cross-examined on his notes on November 21, 1997; Tigar referred to it in his December 16 summation. Theodore Udell testified for the government on November 26, 1997, and again, for the defense, on December 8; Agent Jeff Hayes testified on December 8 and said: "I

asked Mr. Mendeloff how he wanted me to report the information that I was gleaning from the conversations I had with these manufacturers. He told me to put it in a chart form, not to provide any FD-302s." Asked for a response, Mendeloff dismissed Tigar's charges that the government didn't care as a "defense lawyer argument" to make something out of "not a very big deal"; interview (Gumbel), June 2, 2011. Was it true, though, that Mendeloff had overreached and instructed an FBI agent to circumvent bureau protocols? "I can't answer one way or another," he said. "I can't remember." Judge Matsch told the jury to disregard a significant portion of the testimony on December 10; Tigar picked up the story again in his December 15 closing argument.

Budke testimony blows open the problem of the 40,000 missing lead sheets:
Tigar, interviews (Gumbel), March 1 and May 7, 2011; "time to throw up" line quoted in Michael E. Tigar, *Fighting Injustice,* p. 3; line about unprofessional conduct from Tigar, *Persuasion: The Litigator's Art,* p. xiv; Christopher Budke testified on December 11; the discovery of the lead sheet in Mackey's briefcase is not included in the trial transcript, but was confirmed by both Tigar and Mackey; Mackey, interview (Gumbel), April 28, 2011. The lead sheet issue is addressed at length in a filing in the Nichols state trial, "Defendant's Supplemental Brief Regarding Lead Sheets," dated March 26, 2001, and obtained by authors.

Nichols acquitted of first-degree murder, dodges death penalty:
Carol Howe testified on December 10, 1997; Marife Nichols testified on December 10–11. Mackey's rebuttal was on December 16. The jury then withdrew, returning their verdict on December 23. The penalty phase began after Christmas, with closing arguments on January 5, 1998. The jury announced its deadlock on the death penalty on January 7. On jury voting, see James Brooke, "Nichols's Life Was Saved by a Handful of Holdouts," *New York Times,* January 11, 1998; transcript of Deutchman's January 7 news conference viewed through Washington Transcript Service; Bob Macy quoted in James Brooke, "Nichols Could Face Death for Role in Blast," *New York Times,* December 25, 1997.

Nichols offered a deal, then sentenced:
Mackey, interview (Gumbel), October 11, 2010; Matsch quote from postconviction hearing on March 25, 1998; sentencing was on June 4. Nichols quote from handwritten prison document, "Why Am I Speaking Out Now," November 24, 2006; Kathy Wilburn left the Hersley story in a voice-mail message (to Gumbel), October 30, 2009.

McVeigh's colorful journey toward execution:
On McVeigh's friendship with Kaczynski and his sudden transfer to Terre Haute, see Michel and Herbeck, op. cit., pp. 358–73; the fine slapped on Nigh and Burr, interview (Gumbel) with Jeralyn Merritt, another of McVeigh's trial lawyers, April 15, 2011; details of Hammer's relationship with McVeigh also in a prison memoir written by Hammer and Paul, *Secrets Worth Dying For: Timothy James McVeigh and the Oklahoma City Bombing,* first written in 2003 and obtained by

the authors; the history of McVeigh's decision to waive his appeals, including his citation of the Hammer precedent, is detailed in the transcript of a December 28, 2000, hearing before Judge Matsch, in which he explained his position and successfully defended his competence to make the decision. On the late disclosure of discovery materials, see "An Investigation of the Belated Production of Documents in the Oklahoma City Bombing Case," Department of Justice, Office of the Inspector General, March 19, 2002; also the defense team's "Petition for Stay of Execution, Together with Memorandum in Support," filed May 31, 2001. On Ashcroft and some of the other reaction, see Ron Fournier, "Ashcroft Postpones McVeigh Execution," Associated Press, May 11, 2001. Ashcroft later blamed the late disclosure on the reciprocal discovery agreement and rapped prosecutors on the knuckles for ever agreeing to it. "What the law requires is plenty good in American justice," he told the *Daily Oklahoman* in an interview on October 3, 2006, to promote his memoir *Never Again.* "When the Justice Department goes above and beyond what the law requires, we get ourselves in trouble. . . . We significantly elevated the risks of disruption, which I think were unnecessary." Ashcroft is apparently alone in making this argument.

Details on the most pertinent late documents: three independent sources either directly or indirectly familiar with the contents of the sealed list compiled by McVeigh's defense team offered pointers on the documents mentioned, and these were then cross-checked against the discovery material in the authors' possession; the "smoke some Okies" line comes from an FBI FD-302 interview with John Albert Newland on January 30, 1996, file no. 15040; Dave Shafer was interviewed ten times between April 24, 1995, and April 11, 1996; the first and longest 302 on him is file no. 9848; the government's lack of faith in his credibility is memorialized in FBI FD-302, file no. 14560, dated April 11, 1996; Terry Nichols told the authors (July 22, 2010) he considered Shafer a "bozo," and the FBI concluded his account lacked credibility; Danny Defenbaugh, interview (Gumbel), May 17, 2010; Louis Freeh, *My Life,* p. 213.

McVeigh and Jones fight to the end:
McVeigh motivating Jones to update his book, see Michel and Herbeck, op. cit., p. xvii; Jones's justification, see Jones and Israel, op. cit., pp. xiii, 365–70; Tigar, interview (Gumbel), March 1, 2011; another critic of Jones's decision to break attorney-client privilege was Dick Burr, quoted in Joel Dyer, "Jonesin' for Justice: Selling Out McVeigh," *Boulder Weekly,* March 29, 2001; Jones, e-mail to Gumbel, March 22, 2011; Matsch's final decision reported in David Johnston, "Judge Refuses McVeigh's Bid for a Reprieve," *New York Times,* June 7, 2001; Nigh interview (Gumbel), April 5, 2011.

McVeigh goes very publicly to the gallows:
For Hammer's account of McVeigh's execution, as seen from Dog Unit, see his memoir *Secrets Worth Dying For,* op. cit. Also Andrew Gumbel, "McVeigh's Friend Tells of 'Bad Day' on Death Row," *The Independent* (UK), July 4, 2001; "Still breathin' " line recounted in interview (Gumbel) with Jeralyn Merritt, April

15, 2011; the execution was widely covered in the world's media, e.g., Rick Bragg, "McVeigh Dies for Oklahoma City Blast," *New York Times,* June 12, 2001; Rob Nigh's statement on McVeigh's execution, dated June 11, 2001, was carried by many news sources and is still available online, e.g., at ABCNews.com (retrieved May 12, 2011).

Afterword

The post-conviction travails of Terry Nichols:
Account of Gregory Scarpa Jr. extracting the story of the buried explosives boxes, taken from Sandra Harmon, *Mafia Son,* pp. 211–18; an affidavit by Nichols, dated November 8, 2006, obtained by authors; Nichols's handwritten answers to authors' questions, January 3, 2010, and February 21, 2011; and documents generated by the late Stephen Dresch and still, as of May 2011, posted at his Web site http://forensic-intelligence.org.

Scarpa's prison writings presenting his version of issues relating to Nichols and the Oklahoma City bombing kindly provided to Gumbel by Sandra Harmon, June 24, 2010; Rohrabacher's report, "The Oklahoma City Bombing: Was There a Foreign Connection?" was released by the Oversight and Investigations Sub-committee of the House International Relations Committee on December 26, 2006; Nichols on Rohrabacher, from Nichols letter to the Salt Lake City lawyer Jesse Trentadue, November 8, 2006, obtained by authors; Rohrabacher's inter-view of Nichols on June 27, 2005, is recounted in detail in a teletype from the FBI Denver office to headquarters dated June 28, 2005, and obtained by authors; details on the Nichols state trial from Jay Hughes, "Terry Nichols Faces State Charges," Associated Press, March 30, 1999; Tim Talley, "OKC District Attor-ney Off Nichols Case," Associated Press, October 16, 2000; "Nichols' Defense Challenges State's Key Witness; Judge Rejects Motion to Toss Murder Case," CNN, April 21, 2004; and Tim Talley, "Prison Conversion May Have Saved Nichols," Associated Press, June 13, 2004. Mark Earnest's legwork on the ARA and many other subjects is in a defense brief titled "Terry Lynn Nichols' Motion to Dismiss Based on the State's Failure to Comply With *Brady v. Maryland,*" filed April 12, 2004; Nichols's letter to John Ashcroft, dated September 3, 2004, obtained by authors; information on Josh Nichols from Lana Padilla interview (Gumbel), September 25, 2010.

De Niro–dead:
Jim Cavanaugh, interview (Gumbel), August 2, 2010; Danny Defenbaugh, in-terview (Gumbel), January 25, 2011. Defenbaugh said the only time he and his mentor Bear Bryant fought was over his decision to collect the motel records; statistics on extent of investigation supplied by Defenbaugh in an e-mail, May 21, 2010; McDonald's telephone story told by FBI agent Tim Arney, interview

(Gumbel), August 26, 2011; Defenbaugh (interview with Gumbel, May 17, 2010) confirmed he pressed for an eleventh-hour opportunity to question McVeigh; Nichols wrote about the unaccounted-for bomb components in his document "OKC Bombing Materials and the Missing Explosives," December 1, 2007; Keating quote from the foreword to Hersley, Tongate, and Burke, *Simple Truths*, p. 10; Louis Freeh, *My Life*, p. 211; Weldon Kennedy, interview (Gumbel), August 26, 2010.

SELECT BIBLIOGRAPHY

A nonexhaustive list of publications consulted and, in many cases, cited in the notes:

Abanes, Richard. *End-Time Visions: The Road to Armageddon* (New York: Four Walls Eight Windows, 1998).

Aho, James. *The Politics of Righteousness: Idaho Christian Patriotism* (Seattle: University of Washington Press, 1990).

Barkun, Michael. *Religion and the Racist Right* (Chapel Hill: University of North Carolina Press, 1994).

Bouton, Mark. *How to Spot Lies Like the FBI* (Emmett, Kansas: Cosmic Wind Press, 2010).

Boylan, Jeanne. *Portraits of Guilt: The Woman Who Profiles the Faces of America's Deadliest Criminals* (New York: Pocket Books, 2000).

Campbell, John Bruce. *The New American Man: A Call to Arms* (Carmel, California: The Press, 1983, 1988).

Clarke, Richard. *Against All Enemies: Inside America's War on Terror* (New York: Simon and Schuster, 2004).

Coates, James. *Armed and Dangerous: The Rise of the Survivalist Right* (New York: Hill and Wang, 1987).

Copeland, Thomas E. *Fool Me Twice: Intelligence Failure and Mass Casualty Terrorism* (Leiden, Netherlands: Brill, 2007).

Corcoran, James. *Bitter Harvest: Gordon Kahl and the Posse Comitatus: Murder in the Heartland* (New York: Viking, 1990, later renamed *Bitter Harvest: Gordon Kahl and the Rise of Posse Comitatus in the Heartland*).

Coulson, Danny O., with Elaine Shannon. *No Heroes: Inside the FBI's Secret Counter-Terror Force* (New York: Pocket Books, 1999).

Davis, Jayna. *The Third Terrorist: The Middle East Connection to the Oklahoma City Bombing* (Nashville, Tennessee: Thomas Nelson, 2004).

Davis, Mike. *Buda's Wagon: A Brief History of the Car Bomb* (New York: Verso, 2007).

Dees, Morris, with James Corcoran. *Gathering Storm: America's Militia Threat* (New York: HarperCollins, 1996).

Department of Justice Office of the Inspector General (Michael R. Bromwich). *The FBI Laboratory: An Investigation into Laboratory Practices and Alleged Misconduct in Explosives-Related and Other Cases* (Washington, D.C., April 15, 1997).

Department of Justice Office of the Inspector General, *The Federal Bureau of Investigation's Compliance with the Attorney General's Investigative Guidelines* (redacted), Special Report (Washington, D.C., September 2005).

Dyer, Joel. *Harvest of Rage: Why Oklahoma City Is Only the Beginning* (Boulder, Colorado: WestviewPress, 1997).

Evans-Pritchard, Ambrose. *The Secret Life of Bill Clinton: The Unreported Stories* (Washington, D.C.: Regnery, 1997).

Faludi, Susan. *Stiffed: The Betrayal of the American Man* (New York: William Morrow, 1999).

Freeh, Louis J. *My FBI: Bringing Down the Mafia, Investigating Bill Clinton, and Fighting the War on Terror* (New York: St. Martin's Press, 2005).

Gibson, James William. *Warrior Dreams: Violence and Manhood in Post-Vietnam America* (New York: Farrar, Straus and Giroux, 1994).

Hamm, Mark S. *Apocalypse in Oklahoma: Waco and Ruby Ridge Revenged* (Boston: Northeastern University Press, 1997).

———. *In Bad Company: America's Terrorist Underground* (Boston: Northeastern University Press, 2002).

———. *Terrorism as Crime: From Oklahoma City to Al-Qaeda and Beyond* (New York: New York University Press, 2007).

Hersley, Jon, Larry Tongate, and Bob Burke. *Simple Truths: The Real Story of the Oklahoma City Bombing Investigation* (Oklahoma City: Oklahoma Heritage Association, 2004).

Hoffman, David. *The Oklahoma City Bombing and the Politics of Terror* (Venice, California: Feral House, 1998).

Hoskins, Richard Kelly. *Vigilantes of Christendom: The History of the Phineas Priesthood* (Lynchburg, Virginia: The Virginia Publishing Company, 1990).

Jakes, Dale and Connie, with Clint Richmond. *False Prophets: The Firsthand Account of a Husband-Wife Team Working for the FBI and Living in Deepest Cover with the Montana Freemen* (Los Angeles: Dove Books, 1998).

Jones, Stephen, and Peter Israel. *Others Unknown: Timothy McVeigh and the Oklahoma City Bombing Conspiracy* (New York: Public Affairs, 1998, 2001).

Kaplan, Jeffrey. *Radical Religion in America: Millenarian Movements from the Far Right to the Children of Noah* (Syracuse, New York: Syracuse University Press, 1997).

Kelly, John F., and Philip K. Wearne. *Tainting Evidence: Inside the Scandals at the FBI Crime Lab* (New York: Free Press, 1998).

Kessler, Ronald. *The Bureau: The Secret History of the FBI* (New York: St. Martin's Press, 2002).

Levitas, Daniel. *The Terrorist Next Door: The Militia Movement and the Radical Right* (New York: Thomas Dunne Books, 2002).

Linenthal, Edward T. *The Unfinished Bombing: Oklahoma City in American Memory* (New York: Oxford University Press, 2001).

Lipset, Seymour Martin, and Earl Rabb, *The Politics of Unreason: Right-Wing Extremism in America* (Chicago: University of Chicago Press, 1970).

Macdonald, Andrew. *Hunter* (Hillsboro, West Virginia: National Vanguard Books, 1989).

———. *The Turner Diaries* (Hillsboro, West Virginia: National Vanguard Books, 1978).

Michel, Lou, and Dan Herbeck. *American Terrorist: Timothy McVeigh and the Oklahoma City Bombing* (New York: Regan Books, 2001).

Nichols, James D., as told to Robert S. Papovich. *Freedom's End: Conspiracy in Oklahoma* (Decker, Michigan: Freedom's End, 1997).

Noble, Kerry. *Tabernacle of Hate: Why They Bombed Oklahoma City* (Prescott, Ontario: Voyageur Publishing, 1998).

Noesner, Gary. *Stalling for Time: My Life as an FBI Hostage Negotiator* (New York: Random House, 2010).

Oklahoma Bombing Investigation Committee, *Final Report on the Bombing of the Alfred P. Murrah Federal Building, April 19, 1995* (Oklahoma City: Oklahoma Bombing Investigation Committee, 2001).

Padilla, Lana, with Ron Delpit. *By Blood Betrayed: My Life with Terry Nichols and Timothy McVeigh* (New York: HarperCollins, 1995).

Rand, Kristen. *Gun Shows in America: Tupperware Parties for Criminals* (Washington, D.C.: Violence Policy Center, 1996).

Reavis, Dick J. *The Ashes of Waco: An Investigation* (Syracuse, New York: Syracuse University Press, 1998).

Revell, Oliver "Buck," and Dwight Williams. *A G-Man's Journal: A Legendary Career Inside the FBI—From the Kennedy Assassination to the Oklahoma City Bombing* (New York: Pocket Books, 1998).

Ross, John. *Unintended Consequences* (St. Louis, Missouri: Accurate Press, 1996).

Sanders, Kathy. *After Oklahoma: A Grieving Grandmother Uncovers Shocking Truths About the Bombing . . . and Herself* (Arlington, Texas: Master Strategies Publishing, 2005).

Serrano, Richard A. *One of Ours: Timothy McVeigh and the Oklahoma City Bombing* (New York: W. W. Norton, 1998).

Seymour, Cheri, *Committee of the States: Inside the Radical Right* (Mariposa, California: Camden Place Communications, 1991).

Shook, Somer, Wesley Delano, Robert W. Balch, "Elohim City: A Participant-Observer Study of a Christian Identity Community," *Nova Religio,* vol. 2, April 1999.

Smith, Brent L. *Terrorism in America: Pipe Bombs and Pipe Dreams* (Albany, New York: SUNY Press, 1994).

Stern, Kenneth S. *Militias: A Growing Danger* (New York: American Jewish Committee, 1995).

—————. *A Force Upon the Plain: The American Militia Movement and the Politics of Hate* (New York: Simon & Schuster, 1995).

Tigar, Michael E. *Examining Witnesses,* 2nd ed. (Chicago: ABA Publishing, 2003).

—————. *Fighting Injustice* (Chicago: ABA Books, 2002).

—————.*Nine Principles of Litigation and Life* (Chicago: ABA Publishing, 2009).

—————. *Persuasion: The Litigator's Art* (Chicago: ABA Publishing, 1998).

Vidal, Gore. *Perpetual War for Perpetual Peace: How We Got to Be So Hated* (New York: Nation Books, 2002).

Walter, Jess. *Ruby Ridge: The Truth and Tragedy of the Randy Weaver Family* (New York: Regan Books, 2002; previously published in 1995 as *Every Knee Shall Bow*).

Witt, James Lee, and James Morgan. *Stronger in the Broken Places: Nine Lessons for Turning Crisis into Triumph* (New York: Henry Holt, 2002).

Wright, Stuart A. *Patriots, Politics and the Oklahoma City Bombing* (New York: Cambridge University Press, 2007).

ACKNOWLEDGMENTS

Many of those interviewed for this book challenged powerful people and institutions, including their own, to correct and enrich the historical record. Some did so knowing their own actions were far from perfect. Others were put on the spot but talked anyway. That takes guts, and our gratitude goes out accordingly. It would be impolitic to identify favorites among the 150-plus interview subjects who spoke on the record. But a handful—they know who they are—displayed a candor and intellectual honesty all too rare in a story in which many people have had an angle to push, or something to hide.

One person who needs special mention is Terry Nichols. He shares responsibility for the horrors of the bombing, but he has also been a unique resource: cooperative at every stage and often exhaustive in his attention to detail. He took a risk in consenting to release the full archive of privileged documents held by his defense lawyers, and he wrote tens of thousands of words in response to our questions, however pointed. He was obliged to do none of these things. While we have reserved the right to judge his words and actions against the broader factual record, we are grateful for his willingness to speak out, to confess his crimes and other personal failings, and to add texture and depth to our story.

For on-the-record interview contributions (some of whom are not in the text, often because they were able to knock down false leads and misconceptions), many thanks (in alphabetical order) to: Julia Allen, Wayne Alley, David Allred, Gregory Argyros, Karyn

Armstrong, Tim Arney, Paul Baker, David Batsell, Garry Berges, Mark Bouton, Rodney Bowers, Jeanne Boylan, Joseph Bross, Stanley Brown, Bill Buford, Joe Van Bullard, Dick Burr, Bruce Campbell, Vincent Cannistraro, Jim Carlile, Jim Cavanaugh, Steve Chancellor, Richard Cohen, Jerry Cook, Danny Coulson, Jannie Coverdale, Bill and Sandy Crigler, Claude Criss, Danny Defenbaugh, Dick DeGuerin, Jim Denny, Dave Dilly, Dennis Dutsch, Harry Eberhardt, Lee Fabrizio, Ladell Farley, Luke Franey, Alexis Franklin, Mary Lou Fultz, Hank Gibbons, Mark Gibson, Aitan Goelman, Marie Louise Hagen, Judy Hamilton Morse, David Paul Hammer, Richard Hanawalt, Joe Hartzler, John Haynie, Floyd Hays, Greg Henry, John Hippard, Dave Hollaway, Tom Hoover, Ronald Howland, Greg Hug, Danielle Hunt, Tom Hunt, Linda James, Suzanne James, Adolph Januszkiewicz, Kelly Johnson, Mike Johnston, Dean Jones, Stephen Jones, John Kane, Weldon Kennedy, Kyle Kilgore, Richard Kirby, Neal Kirkpatrick, Gary Knight, Jack Knox, Frank Koch, Eric Kruss, Corey Lamb, Kerry Larsen, Diane Leonard, Steve Lewis, Pat Livingston, Kirk Lyons, Larry Mackey, John Magaw, Bill Maloney, Chris Matlock, Linda Matlock, Michael McGovern, Marty McLaughlin, Scott Mendeloff, Jeralyn Merritt, Tom Metzger, Horace Mewborn, Lou Michel, Dick Miller, Carol Moore, Tristan Moreland, Reid Mullins, Terry Nichols, Rob Nigh, Melva Noakes, Kerry Noble, Gary Noesner, Richard O'Carroll, Jim Otte, Lana Padilla, Jim Pate, Joe Phillips, Mike Reynolds, Bob Ricks, James Rockwell, Don Rogers, Dana Rohrabacher, Tom Ross, Scott Rutter, Bob Sanders, Kathy Sanders, Greg Scarpa Jr., David Schickedanz, Michael Schwartz, Jack Schworm, Cheri Seymour, Rick Sherrow, Pete Slover, I. C. Smith, Clyde Snow, Gerry Spence, Sheldon Sperling, Karl Stankovic, Rick Stephens, Ken Stern, Andi Strassmeir, Bill Teater, Michael Tigar, James Tillison, Pharis Williams, Ritch Willis, Tommy Wittman, Ed Woods, Ron Woods, Carl Worden, Stuart Wright, Janice Yeary, and Randy Yount.

Thank-you also to those who did not speak for attribution but provided invaluable firsthand information. Some needed to remain anonymous to protect themselves or others. Two outstanding individuals chose not to put their names forward because they didn't want to be accused of grandstanding. While we would have preferred to print their names, their lack of ego is admirable.

An enterprise of this nature rests on the shoulders of those who have mined and explored this material in the past. We want to acknowledge the sterling work done by many law enforcement agents, even in the context of a flawed investigation, and also by the defense, especially the Nichols team, whose research and analysis have gone largely unpublicized until now. Some people provided valuable unpublished documents: Tom Hunt and his archive of materials from the Federal Protective Service in Oklahoma City; Stanley Brown and his handwritten journal of the day of the bombing; Kirk Lyons and the copies he provided of Andreas Strassmeir's passports and U.S. visa. The late J. D. Cash, an investigator and journalist from rural Oklahoma, was himself an indefatigable collector of documents we are lucky to have inherited. Most useful were Mary Riley's field notes (see chapter 4), Richard Guthrie's irresistibly quotable handwritten prison memoir, and the transcripts of interviews conducted in 1999–2000 (many by Cash himself) for a never-released documentary on the bombing.

For the discovery materials, thank-you not only to Nichols but to Brian Hermanson, his chief lawyer in the Oklahoma state trial; Richard Demarest, who volunteered to convert and send the files; and Jesse Trentadue, a lawyer from Salt Lake City, who first forged a relationship with Nichols and made access to him possible. Trentadue's persistent Freedom of Information Act requests and lawsuits against the government—all filed in the name of justice for his brother who died in federal custody in Oklahoma in 1995—have provided a valuable public service.

Many journalists, academics, lawyers, and investigators have been generous in sharing materials and offering support. John Solomon, who has done his own groundbreaking reporting on this subject, was the project's unofficial godfather. Mark Hamm of Indiana State University has been a selfless contributor to our research for a decade. Don Devereux and Bob Arthur tracked down many hard-to-find interview subjects and acted as unofficial Arizona fixers. Jonathan Franklin opened doors and offered the raw notes of his face-to-face interview with McVeigh. Sandra Harmon put Andrew Gumbel in touch with Gregory Scarpa Jr. and shared Scarpa's correspondence on Terry Nichols. Mary Mapes, in Dallas, and Dave Hawkins, in Kingman, offered material and much-appreciated hospitality. Rich Leiby of the *Washington Post* shared his taped interview with Mark Thomas and wins the prize for most gloriously laugh-out-loud question put to a neo-Nazi. Mark Earnest, one of Nichols's state trial lawyers, provided court filings and much valuable analysis. Thanks also to David Shuster and his former colleagues at KATV, Randy Dixon and Rusty Mizell, to Jerry Bohnen of KTOK in Oklahoma City, to Jack Cashill and Mike Tharp.

A number of people provided direct research assistance: Eli Smukler (who outdid himself), Cody Reneau, Ginny Charles, and Beth Bartel. Thanks also to those who provided logistical help, or facilitated access, or talked through issues, or delivered pieces of information, or hardened up facts. In alphabetical order: Skip Baker, MaryAnne Beatty, Pam Bell, John Berger, Leslie Blade, Sherry Boyce, David Brog, Sheryll Brown, Rico Carisch, Glynda Chu, Steven Clay, Jimmy Coker, Don Cox, Beverly David, Veronica Decena, Margot Dunne, Mickey Edwards, Dan Froomkin, Miki Goral, Phil Hall, Dave Hart, Gregg Hastings, Walt Haussner, Josh Hunsucker, Manny Johnson, Chuck Karfonta, Dean Kuipers, Angie Lanier, Allan Lengel, Harry Lett, Claudine LoMonaco, Judge Richard P. Matsch, Robin Mayper, Kevin Moloney, Matt Moning, Jay Mumford, Wendy Painting, Suzie Paulson, Sheree Powell, Adam Rappaport, Ron Replogle, Joey Senat, Tara Setmayer, Kathleen Staunton,

Helen Stiefmiller, David Sobonya, Dan Thomasson, Carole Turner, Luke Vislay, Anne Weismann, Jan White, Fred Whitehurst, Pamela Williams, Evan Wright, and Marge York. Our apologies to anyone we have forgotten.

ANDREW GUMBEL WOULD LIKE TO THANK HENRY FERRIS, AN AS-siduous, exceptionally fine editor who understood just how to tell this huge and gripping story; Trina Hunn, whose editorial eye was as keen as her legal prowess; the rest of the William Morrow team, whose excitement was infectious; the ever-gracious Gail Ross and the Ross Yoon agency; Dana Newman and Miles Feldman, who went above and beyond; Charles Noble and Edward Olson; Larry George, generous to a fault; Max and Raffaella, who followed the story, asked great questions, and put up with months of me staring into the middle distance; Sammy, who arrived just in time to put the rest in perspective; and, most of all, my wife, Naomi Seligman, the ideal partner in this and all things. Your love, intelligence, many contributions, and wicked humor held everything else together.

ROGER CHARLES WOULD LIKE TO THANK STEPHEN JONES, FOR UN-stinting support and friendship; the late Glenn Wilburn; Kathy Wilburn Sanders; Ken Blood, Clark Brewster, Pat Briley, Bill Cowan, John Culbertson, David Fechheimer, Mark Hampton, Ambassador Robert Hennemeyer, Mike Hubbard, Charles Key, Kris Kolesnik, V. Z. Lawton, Gil Macklin, Rick Ojeda, Dale Phillips, Bill Rhegness, Bob Sheridan, Michael Turner, Fred Whitehurst, and Mike Vanderboegh. Tom McCally, Lawrence E. Carr Jr., and Michael Minnis gave indispensable legal counsel. Bruce Willingham of the *McCurtain Daily Gazette* deserves special mention. Also: Robert K. Brown, Rita Cosby, Ambrose Evans-Pritchard, Jeff Fager, James Giles, Karen Gullo, Patty Hassler, David Hoffman, John F. Kelly, Tom Jarriel,

Bill Jasper, Scott Malone, Gary Matsumoto, Mike McCarville, Don McLean, Mike McNulty, Victor Newfeld, Ivan O'Mahoney, Dan Rather, Jim Ridgeway, Ryan Ross, Bob Ruth, Diane Sawyer, John Siceloff, Dwight Swift, Judy Thomas, Donald K. Thrasher, and Gordon Whitkin.

For my family, it's very simple. Without the unqualified love and support of my wife, Mary Lee, and of our daughters, Katie, Ginny, and Ellen, I would not have been able to sustain my work on this story. They tolerated many absences, phone calls, and dinner guests, and convinced me to go forward when the easier path would have been to back off. To the loved ones of those who are not alive to see the publication of this book: would that we could share the fruits of our labors with them.

INDEX